WESTERN CIVILIZATION

Sources, Images, and Interpretations

WESTERN CIVILIZATION

Sources, Images, and Interpretations

FOURTH EDITION
VOLUME II: SINCE 1660

edited by **Dennis Sherman**

JOHN JAY COLLEGE OF CRIMINAL JUSTICE, CITY UNIVERSITY OF NEW YORK

McGRAW-HILL, INC.
New York   St. Louis   San Francisco   Auckland   Bogotá   Caracas
Lisbon   London   Madrid   Mexico City   Milan   Montreal   New Delhi
San Juan   Singapore   Sydney   Tokyo   Toronto

WESTERN CIVILIZATION
Sources, Images, and Interpretations
Volume II: Since 1660

This book is printed on acid-free paper.

3 4 5 6 7 8 9 0 DOC DOC 9 0 9 8 7

ISBN 0-07-056949-5

This book was set in New Caledonia by Ruttle, Shaw & Wetherill, Inc.
The editors were Pamela Gordon and Larry Goldberg;
the production supervisor was Paula Keller.
The cover was designed by Carla Bauer.
R. R. Donnelley & Sons Company was printer and binder.

Cover painting: Industrial Landscape by L. S. Lowry, 1955.
　　　　　　Courtesy of Mrs. Carol Ann Danes,
　　　　　　Tate Gallery, London / Art Resources, NY.

Library of Congress Cataloging-in-Publication Data

Western civilization: sources, images, and interpretations / edited
　by Dennis Sherman. — 4th ed.
　　　p.　　　cm.
　　Includes bibliographical references.
　　Contents: v. 1. To 1700 — v. 2. Since 1660 — v. 3. From the
　Renaissance to the present.
　　　ISBN 0-07-056948-7 (v. 1)—ISBN 0-07-056949-5 (v. 2)—ISBN 0-07-056950-9 (v. 3)
　　　1. Civilization, Western—History—Sources.　　2. Civilization,
　Western—History.　　I. Sherman, Dennis.
　CB245.W4835　　　　1995
　909'.09821—dc20　　　　　　　　　　　　　　　　　　　　94-16726

ABOUT THE EDITOR

Dennis Sherman is Professor of History at John Jay College of Criminal Justice, the City University of New York. He received his B.A. (1962) and J.D. (1965) degrees from the University of California at Berkeley and his Ph.D. (1970) from the University of Michigan. He was Visiting Professor at the University of Paris (1978–1979; 1985). He received the Ford Foundation Prize Fellowship (1968–1969, 1969–1970), a fellowship from the Council for Research on Economic History (1971–1972), and fellowships from the National Endowment for the Humanities (1973–1976). His publications include *A Short History of Western Civilization*, Eighth Edition (co-author); *A Study Guide for the Western Experience* (1995); *World Civilizations: Sources, Images, and Interpretations* (co-author); a series of introductions in the Garland Library of War and Peace; several articles and reviews on nineteenth-century French economic and social history in American and European journals; and short stories in literary reviews.

To Pat, Joe, Darryl, Vera, and Raymond

In time choice, change, and obligation merge;
How quietly we listen to ourselves.

CONTENTS

ix

Chapter Six: The Age of Napoleon   111

Chapter Seven: Reaction, Reform, Revolution, and Romanticism: 1815–1848   125

**PART III   THE TWENTIETH CENTURY:
1914 TO THE PRESENT**

Chapter Eleven: War and Revolution: 1914–1920

PRIMARY SOURCES

VISUAL SOURCES

SECONDARY SOURCES

Chapter Twelve: Democracy, Depression, and Instability: The 1920s and 1930s

PRIMARY SOURCES

PREFACE

In the fourth edition of *Western Civilization: Sources, Images, and Interpretations,* some important changes have been made. Three new sections designed as guides to using primary, visual, and secondary sources have been added to the first chapter of each volume. Many new secondary sources reflecting historical scholarship over the past fifteen years have been added, replacing older sources. The final chapter has been extensively revised to reflect changing developments and perceptions of the past two decades. Otherwise the structure, approach, and length of this book remain as in the first three editions.

This book provides a broad introduction to the sources historians use, the kind of interpretations historians make, and the evolution of Western civilization over the past six thousand years. A large selection of documents, photographs, and maps is presented along with introductions, commentaries, and questions designed to place each selection in a meaningful context and facilitate an understanding of its historical significance. The selections and accompanying notes should also provide insights into how historians work and some of the problems they face.

A brief look at the task facing historians of Western civilization will supply a background to what will be covered in this book. To discover what people thought and did and to organize this into a chronological record of the human past, historians must search for evidence—for the sources of history. Most sources are written materials, ranging from government records to gravestone inscriptions, memoirs, and poetry. Other sources include paintings, photographs, sculpture, buildings, maps, pottery, and oral traditions. In searching for sources, historians usually have something in mind—some tentative goals or conclusions that guide their search. Thus, in the process of working with sources, historians must decide which ones to emphasize. What historians ultimately write is a synthesis of the questions posed, the sources used, and their own ideas.

Historians of Western civilization consider their subject to be what is today Europe, along with those offshoots of Europe that have become established in various parts of the world. As they look back into the past, they focus on the origins of today's Western civilization in the Mediterranean basin, a cultural region that includes parts of North Africa and the Near East as well as Europe itself.

STRUCTURE OF THE BOOK

The basic organization of this book is chronological, beginning with the origins of Western civilization in the ancient Near East and gradually moving up to the present. From time to time this chronological approach is modified and certain important developments such as the Renaissance or totalitarianism are pulled out of the chapter covering their period of occurrence and are discussed separately. All the chapters, however, are organized the same way. Each chapter is broken into sections consisting of the following features:

Each chapter opens with a **chapter introduction,** in which the period of history and the general topics to be dealt with in the chapter are described. The introduction provides a brief sketch of some of the most important developments, but no effort is made to cover the period. Instead, the purpose is to introduce the topics, issues, and questions that the sources in the chapter focus on, and to place these sources in the historical context of Western civilization.

The introduction is followed by a **time line,** showing the relevant dates, people, events, and developments of the period, to provide a historical context for the selections in the chapter. In addition, a time line at the beginning of each of the six parts in the book puts the developments covered in each chapter into a broader perspective.

The chapter time line is followed by the **primary sources.** These are documents written by individuals involved in the matter under investigation. Historians consider these documents their main building blocks for learning about and interpreting the past. They are pieces of evidence that show what people thought, how they acted, and what they accomplished. At the same time historians must criticize these sources both externally—to attempt to uncover forgeries and errors—and internally—to find the authors' motives, inconsistencies within the documents, and different meanings of words and phrases.

Each document is preceded by a **headnote.** The headnote provides some information on the nature of the source, places it in a specific historical context, and indicates its particular focus.

The headnotes end with suggestions of **points to consider.** These points are not simply facts to be searched for in the selection. Rather, they are designed to stimulate analytical thought about the selections and to indicate some of the uses of each source.

The primary sources are followed by visual sources, including maps, and then by **secondary sources.**

Secondary sources are documents written by scholars about the time in question. Usually, they are interpretations of what occurred based on examination of numerous primary documents and other sources. They reflect choices the authors have made and their own particular understandings of what has happened. Often there are important differences of opinion among scholars about how to understand significant historical developments. Secondary sources should therefore be read with these questions in mind: What sort of evidence does the author use? Does the author's argument make sense? What political or ideological preferences are revealed in the author's interpretation? How might one argue against the interpretation presented by the author? At times the distinction between primary and secondary documents becomes blurred, as when the author is a contemporary of the events he or she is interpreting. If a document by that author is read as an interpretation of what occurred, it would be a secondary source. As evidence for the assumptions and attitudes of the author's times, however, the document would be a primary source.

Like the primary documents, all the secondary documents are preceded by headnotes and suggestions for points to consider.

Visual sources are paintings, drawings, sculpture, ceramics, photographs, buildings, monuments, coins, and so forth, that can provide valuable historical insights or information. Although they often include characteristics of secondary documents, they are usually most valuable when used in the same way as primary documents. In this book their purpose is not merely to supplement the documents or provide examples of the great pieces of art throughout history. It is to show how these visual materials can be used as sources of history and to provide insights difficult to gain solely through written documents. To this end, each visual source is accompanied by a relatively extensive interpretive description. Care should be taken in viewing these sources and using these descriptions. By their very nature, visual sources usually have a less clear meaning than written documents. Scholars differ greatly over how sources such as paintings, ceramics, and coins should be interpreted. Therefore, the descriptions accompanying the visual sources are open to debate. They are designed to show how it is possible for historians to use visual materials as sources of history—as unwritten evidence for what people thought and did in the past.

Maps often combine elements of primary documents, secondary documents, and visual sources. However, here they are usually used to help establish relationships, such as the connections between geographic factors and political developments, thereby enabling us to interpret what occurred differently than we could have if we had relied on written sources alone. As is the case with visual sources, each map is accompanied by an interpretive description. These descriptions indicate some of the ways maps might be used by historians.

Each chapter ends with **chapter questions.** These are designed to draw major themes of the chapter together in a challenging way. Answers to these questions require some analytical thought and the use of several of the selections in the chapter.

Finally, in the first chapter of each volume there are three special sections: **Using Primary Sources, Using Visual Sources,** and **Using Secondary Sources.** They are designed as guides to specific ways these three different kinds of sources can be used and analyzed.

Since a book of this size can only sample what is available and outline what has occurred, this book is truly an introduction to Western civilization and its sources. Indeed, it is my hope that the materials presented here will reveal the range of sources that can be used to deepen our understanding of Western civilization and serve as a jumping-off point for further exploration into history and the historian's discipline.

McGraw-Hill and the editor would like to thank the following reviewers for their many helpful comments and suggestions: Gary Ferngren, Oregon State University; Paul B. Goodwin, University of Connecticut; Carolyn Happer, Meredith College; William E. Kinsella, Jr., Northern Virginia Community College; Paul F. McClung, Santa Barbara City College; Kathryn Norberg, University of California, Los Angeles; John F. Robertson, Central Michigan University; and Robert Zaller, Drexel University.

WESTERN CIVILIZATION

Sources, Images, and Interpretations

Schematic of Evolution of Western Civilization

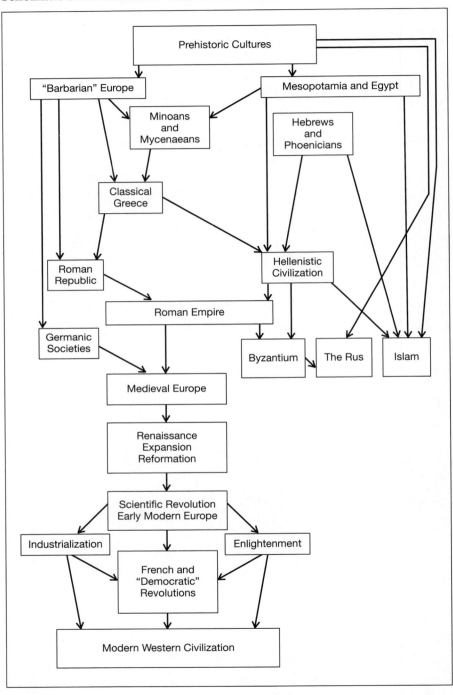

THE EVOLUTION OF WESTERN CIVILIZATION

This chart is a schematic illustration of the development of Western civilization up to modern times. Caution should be exercised when reading such a chart. The connections made are more a matter of judgment than fact. Moreover, what is missing—the how and why of the connections—is of great importance. Nevertheless, the chart can make it easier to see some of the broadest connections between societies and civilizations, connections that are often lost when a single period or society is examined in detail.

Consider:
Possible reasons for the various connections within the chart; what might be added to this chart to make it more useful.

I

THE EARLY MODERN PERIOD

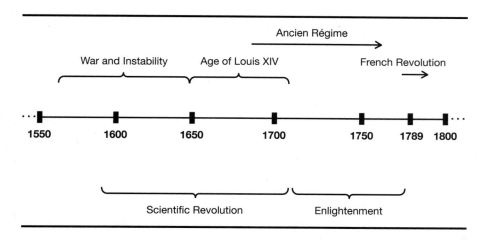

CHAPTER ONE

Aristocracy and Absolutism in the Seventeenth Century

The second half of the seventeenth century was a period of relative political stability in Europe. Although wars still occurred, they lacked the intensity of the preceding period. In the ascendant states, such as France, Prussia, Austria, Russia, and England, central governments were gaining authority. The primary power, and for many states the model of political authority, was France. There, Louis XIV, supported by a strong standing army, a policy of mercantilism, and a growing bureaucracy, wielded absolute power. There were similar situations in Prussia, Austria, and Russia. A different pattern occurred in England, where the central government remained strong while the monarchy itself weakened. There, after the return to power of the Stuart kings between 1660 and 1688, a revolution furthered the authority of Parliament.

During this period, important social, political, and economic changes occurred unevenly and generally benefited those who were already prominent and well to do. Aristocrats lost some of their independence to kings in countries like France and Prussia, but they continued to staff most of the important government offices, to maintain their elevated prestige, and to influence cultural styles and tastes. For most people, the structure of society, the way of life, and the relevant institutions changed little throughout this period.

This chapter concentrates on two broad topics: the growth of central government and Early Modern society. The selections address a number of questions. For the first topic, what was the nature of monarchical absolutism in France? How did it differ from Prussian monarchical absolutism? How did the pattern of monarchical absolutism compare with the growth of parliamentary power in England? What institutions and policies were developed to facilitate the growth of central governments? For the second topic, what was the nature of the family in Early Modern Europe? What were typical attitudes toward childhood? What were the traditional values and patterns of life for commoners during this period?

This dual focus should provide some broad insights into Europe during the seventeenth century and help establish a background for eighteenth-century developments.

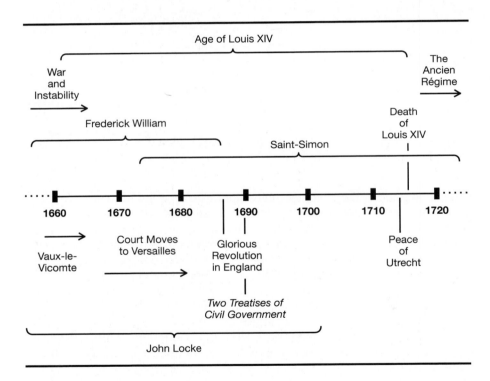

PRIMARY SOURCES

Using Primary Sources: Austria Over All If She Only Will: Mercantilism

Primary sources are briefly defined and discussed in the Preface. What follows is a more specific guide to the use of primary sources, focusing on our first primary source, *Austria Over All If She Only Will,* which immediately follows as an example.

1.   When reading a written primary source such as the following excerpt from *Austria Over All If She Only Will,* try to think of every line as evidence. Assume that you are a historian who knows very little about seventeenth-century Europe and that this document falls into your hands. Your job is to use this document as evidence to support some conclusions about the Renaissance.

Actually, before you read this source you already know something about the seventeenth century and mercantilism from the chapter introduction, the time line, and the headnote preceding this source. You can use this information to better place the source in a historical context, to gain a sense of how the evidence in the source can be used.

2.   Think of questions as you read a primary source. This can keep you alert to how words, lines, and sections of the source can be used as evidence. A general question to keep in mind might be, "What does this tell me about this civilization, about how people behaved, how they thought, what they believed?" Try reading each line as a piece of evidence to answer part of this general question. More specific questions can be derived from the headnote and the "consider" points just before the beginning of a source.

Here the headnote and the "consider" points indicate that the source might be particularly useful for providing evidence about the nature of mercantilism, its purposes, and policies that flowed from it.

3.   There are several ways the material in this source might be used as evidence. Read the first paragraph. It might be argued that this paragraph is evidence for the conclusion that at the core of mercantilism was a belief that national power ("the might and eminence of a country") depends on gaining a favorable balance of trade and especially bullion ("surplus of gold, silver, and all other things necessary") so as to minimize dependence on others ("with as little *dependence* as possible upon foreign countries").

Read the second paragraph. At the end of the first paragraph the author told the reader that he would list nine rules to achieve the ends of a mercantilist policy. This is the first, and it is evidence that mercantilism favored finding domestic sources for agricultural products ("every useful form of *plant*"), gold, and silver. The emphasis is on discovering bullion ("above all, no trouble or expense should be spared to discover gold and silver").

Read the third paragraph. The author recommends that commodities be manufactured domestically ("worked up within the country").

Read the fourth paragraph. The author recommends supporting population growth ("as large as the country can support") and greater productivity ("from idleness to remunerative *professions* . . . instructed and encouraged") to encourage domestic economic production.

Read the fifth paragraph. The author again reveals concern about gold and silver, that as much of it be retained ("under no circumstances to be taken out") and kept in circulation ("must always remain in *circulation*") so as to ensure national wealth ("it will be impossible . . . ever to sink into poverty").

Read the rest of the paragraphs. How can each of these be used as evidence for what the policies of mercantilism were and why they were recommended?

4.   After working on the various parts of the source, pull back and consider the source as a whole. Among other things, these economic recommendations provide evidence for what mercantilism was (a set of policies such as maximizing domestic production, acquiring bullion, and minimizing imports) and what the goals of mercantilist economic policies were (to increase the power and status of a country and to minimize dependence on foreign countries).

Finally, use the headnote to keep in mind who the author (Philipp W. von Hornick) was (an Austrian lawyer and government official) and how this document might have been received (as an influential statement). Consider whether this gives the document greater weight as evidence.

Austria Over All If She Only Will: Mercantilism
Philipp W. von Hornick

Mercantilism, a loose set of economic ideas and corresponding government policies, was a common component of political absolutism during the seventeenth century. Typical mercantilist goals were the acquisition of bullion, a positive balance of trade, and economic self-sufficiency. An unusually clear and influential statement of mercantilist policies was published in 1684 by Philipp Wilhelm von Hornick. A lawyer and later a government official, Hornick set down what he considered to be the nine principal rules for a proper economic policy. These are excerpted here.

> **Consider:** *The political and military purposes served by encouraging mercantilist policies; the foreign policy decisions such economic policies would support; the political and economic circumstances that would make it easiest for a country to adhere to and benefit from mercantilist policies.*

NINE PRINCIPAL RULES OF NATIONAL ECONOMY

If the might and eminence of a country consist in its surplus of gold, silver, and all other things necessary or convenient for its *subsistence*, derived, so far as

SOURCE: Philipp W. von Hornick, "Austria Over All If She Only Will," in Arthur Eli Monroe, ed., *Early Economic Thought*. Reprinted by permission of Harvard University Press (Cambridge, Mass., 1927), pp. 223–225. Copyright © 1924 by The President and Fellows of Harvard College.

possible, from its own resources, without *dependence* upon other countries, and in the proper fostering, use, and application of these, then it follows that a general national *economy (Landes-Oeconomie)* should consider how such a surplus, fostering, and enjoyment can be brought about, without *dependence* upon others, or where this is not feasible in every respect, with as little *dependence* as possible upon foreign countries, and sparing use of the country's own cash. For this purpose the following nine rules are especially serviceable.

First, to inspect the country's soil with the greatest care, and not to leave the agricultural possibilities or a single corner or clod of earth unconsidered. Every useful form of *plant* under the sun should be experimented with, to see whether it is adapted to the country, for the distance or nearness of the sun is not all that counts. Above all, no trouble or expense should be spared to discover gold and silver.

Second, all commodities found in a country, which cannot be used in their natural state, should be worked up within the country; since the payment for *manufacturing* generally exceeds the value of the raw material by two, three, ten, twenty, and even a hundred fold, and the neglect of this is an abomination to prudent managers.

Third, for carrying out the above two rules, there will be need of people, both for producing and cultivating the raw materials and for working them up. Therefore, attention should be given to the population, that it may be as large as the country can support, this being a well-ordered state's most important concern, but, unfortunately, one that is often neglected. And the people should be turned by all possible means from idleness to remunerative *professions;* instructed and encouraged in all kinds of *inventions,* arts, and trades; and, if necessary, instructors should be brought in from foreign countries for this.

Fourth, gold and silver once in the country, whether from its own mines or obtained by *industry* from foreign countries, are under no circumstances to be taken out for any purpose, so far as possible, or allowed to be buried in chests or coffers, but must always remain in *circulation;* nor should much be permitted in uses where they are at once *destroyed* and cannot be utilized again. For under these conditions, it will be impossible for a country that has once acquired a considerable supply of cash, especially one that possesses gold and silver mines, ever to sink into poverty; indeed, it is impossible that it should not continually increase in wealth and property. Therefore,

Fifth, the inhabitants of the country should make every effort to get along with their domestic products, to confine their luxury to these alone, and to do without foreign products as far as possible (except where great need leaves no alternative, or if not need, wide-spread, unavoidable abuse, of which Indian spices are an example). And so on.

Sixth, in case the said purchases were indispensable because of necessity or *irremediable* abuse, they should be obtained from these foreigners at first hand, so far as possible, and not for gold or silver, but in exchange for other domestic wares.

Seventh, such foreign commodities should in this case be imported in unfinished form, and worked up within the country, thus earning the wages of *manufacture* there.

Eighth, opportunities should be sought night and day for selling the country's superfluous goods to these foreigners in manufactured form, so far as this is necessary, and for gold and silver; and to this end, *consumption*, so to speak, must be sought in the farthest ends of the earth, and developed in every possible way.

Ninth, except for important considerations, no importation should be allowed under any circumstances of commodities of which there is sufficient supply of suitable quality at home; and in this matter neither sympathy nor compassion should be shown foreigners, be they friends, kinsfolk, *allies*, or enemies. For all friendship ceases, when it involves my own weakness and ruin. And this holds good, even if the domestic commodities are of poorer quality, or even higher priced. For it would be better to pay for an article two dollars which remain in the country than only one which goes out, however strange this may seem to the ill-informed.

A Secret Letter: Monarchical Authority in Prussia
Frederick William, The Great Elector

Seventeenth-century monarchs attained unprecedented authority within their realms, often through the skillful use of policies designed to enhance their power. The most dramatic consolidation of power was made by the head of the Hohenzollerns, Frederick William (1640–1688), known as the "great elector" of Brandenburg-Prussia. He instituted new taxes, developed a trained bureaucracy staffed by members of the nobility, modernized his army, and asserted his own authority over competing claims from the nobility and representative institutions. In 1667 he wrote a secret letter of advice to his son, who was in line to inherit the throne. An excerpt of this letter appears here.

> **Consider:** *The greatest threats to monarchical authority according to Frederick William; the policies Frederick William thought were most important for maintaining power; which of Frederick William's recommendations echo the attitudes expressed in mercantilist doctrines.*

It is necessary that you conduct yourself as a good father to your people, that you love your subjects regardless of their religious convictions, and that you try to promote their welfare at all times. Work to stimulate trade everywhere, and keep in mind the population increase of the Mark of Brandenburg. Take advantage of the advice of the clergy and nobility as much as you can; listen to them and be gracious to them all, as befits one of your position; recognize ability where you

SOURCE: Louis L. Snyder, ed., *Documents of German History*. Reprinted by permission of Rutgers University Press (New Brunswick, N.J., 1958), pp. 94–95. Copyright © 1958 by Rutgers, The State University.

find it, so that you will increase the love and affection of your subjects toward you. But, it is essential that you always be moderate in your attitudes, in order not to endanger your position and lose respect. With those of your own station in life, be careful never to give way in matters of precedence and in all to which you are entitled; on the contrary, hold fast to the eminence of your superior position. Remember that one can lose one's superior position if one allows too great pomposity and too great a show upon the part of members of the court.

Be keenly interested in the administration of justice throughout your land. See to it that justice is maintained for the poor as well as for the rich without discrimination of any kind. See to it that lawsuits are carried out without delay, without procrastination, for in doing this, you will solidify your own position. . . .

Seek to maintain friendly relations with the princes and the nobility of the Empire. Correspond with them frequently and maintain your friendship with them. Be certain not to give them cause for ill-will; try not to arouse emotions of jealousy or enmity, but be sure that you are always in a strong position to maintain your weight in disputes that may arise. . . .

It is wise to have alliances, if necessary, but it is better to rely on your own strength. You are in a weak position if you do not have the means and do not possess the confidence of the people. These are the things, God be praised, which have made me powerful since the time I began to have them. I only regret that, in the beginning of my reign, I forsook these policies and followed the advice of others against my will.

Mémoires: The Aristocracy Undermined in France

Saint-Simon

Louis XIV of France was the most powerful ruler of his time. He had inherited the throne as a child in 1643. He took personal command by 1661, ruling France until his death in 1715. Contemporary rulers viewed him as a model ruler. One of the ways in which he reinforced his position was by conducting a magnificent court life at his palace of Versailles. There, nobles hoping for favors or appointments competed for his attention and increasingly became dependent upon royal whim. One of those nobles, the Duke of Saint-Simon (1675–1755), felt slighted and grew to resent the king. Saint-Simon chronicled life at Versailles in his Mémoires. *In the following excerpt, he shows how Louis XIV used this court life to his own ends.*

> **Consider:** *How the king's activities undermined the position of the nobility; the options available to a noble who wanted to maintain or increase his own power; how the king's activities compare with the great elector's recommendations to his son.*

SOURCE: Orest Ranum and Patricia Ranum, eds. and trans., *The Century of Louis XIV*. Reprinted by permission of Harper & Row (New York, 1972), pp. 81, 83, 87–88.

Frequent fetes, private walks at Versailles, and excursions were means which the King seized upon in order to single out or to mortify [individuals] by naming the persons who should be there each time, and in order to keep each person assiduous and attentive to pleasing him. He sensed that he lacked by far enough favors to distribute in order to create a continuous effect. Therefore he substituted imaginary favors for real ones, through jealousy—little preferences which were shown daily, and one might say at each moment—[and] through his artfulness. The hopes to which these little preferences and these honors gave birth, and the deference which resulted from them—no one was more ingenious than he in unceasingly inventing these sorts of things. Marly, eventually, was of great use to him in this respect; and Trianon, where everyone, as a matter of fact, could go pay court to him, but where ladies had the honor of eating with him and where they were chosen at each meal; the candlestick which he had held for him each evening at bedtime by a courtier whom he wished to honor, and always from among the most worthy of those present, whom he named aloud upon coming out from saying his prayers.

Louis XIV carefully trained himself to be well informed about what was happening everywhere, in public places, in private homes, in public encounters, in the secrecy of families or of [amorous] liaisons. Spies and tell tales were countless. They existed in all forms: some who were unaware that their denunciations went as far as [the King], others who knew it; some who wrote him directly by having their letters delivered by routes which he had established for them, and those letters were seen only by him, and always before all other things; and lastly, some others who sometimes spoke to him secretly in his cabinets, by the back passageways. These secret communications broke the necks of an infinity of persons of all social positions, without their ever having been able to discover the cause, often very unjustly, and the King, once warned, never reconsidered, or so rarely that nothing was more [determined]. . . .

In everything he loved splendor, magnificence, profusion. He turned this taste into a maxim for political reasons, and instilled it into his court on all matters. One could please him by throwing oneself into fine food, clothes, retinue, buildings, gambling. These were occasions which enabled him to talk to people. The essence of it was that by this he attempted and succeeded in exhausting everyone by making luxury a virtue, and for certain persons a necessity, and thus he gradually reduced everyone to depending entirely upon his generosity in order to subsist. In this he also found satisfaction for his pride through a court which was superb in all respects, and through a greater confusion which increasingly destroyed natural distinctions. This is an evil which, once introduced, became the internal cancer which is devouring all individuals—because from the court it promptly spread to Paris and into the provinces and the armies, where persons, whatever their position, are considered important only in proportion to the table they lay and their magnificence ever since this unfortunate innovation—which is devouring all individuals, which forces those who are in a position to steal not to restrain themselves from doing so for the most part, in their need to keep up with their expenditures; [a cancer] which is nourished by the confusion of social positions, pride, and even decency, and which by a mad desire to grow keeps constantly increasing, whose consequences are infinite and lead to nothing less than ruin and general upheaval.

Second Treatise of Civil Government: Legislative Power
John Locke

In England royal absolutism had been under attack throughout the seventeenth century and finally was defeated by the Glorious Revolution of 1688–1689. At that point there was a definitive shift in power to Parliament, which was controlled by the upper classes. John Locke (1632–1704), in his Two Treatises of Civil Government *(1690), justified the revolution and the new political constitution of England and expounded political ideas that became influential during the eighteenth and nineteenth centuries. This work and other writings established Locke as a first-rate empirical philosopher and political theorist. In the following selection from his* Second Treatise of Civil Government, *Locke analyzes legislative power.*

Consider: *The purposes for entering into society; the extent of and limitations on legislative power; how Locke justifies his argument; how these ideas are contrary to monarchical absolutism.*

134. The great end of men's entering into society being the enjoyment of their properties in peace and safety, and the great instrument and means of that being the laws established in that society, the first and fundamental positive law of all commonwealths is the establishing of the legislative power, as the first and fundamental natural law which is to govern even the legislative. Itself is the preservation of the society and (as far as will consist with the public good) of every person in it. This legislative is not only the supreme power of the commonwealth, but sacred and unalterable in the hands where the community have once placed it. Nor can any edict of anybody else, in what form soever conceived, or by what power soever backed, have the force and obligation of a law which has not its sanction from that legislative which the public has chosen and appointed; for without this the law could not have that which is absolutely necessary to its being a law, the consent of the society, over whom nobody can have a power to make laws but by their own consent and by authority received from them; and therefore all the obedience, which by the most solemn ties any one can be obliged to pay, ultimately terminates in this supreme power, and is directed by those laws which it enacts. Nor can any oaths to any foreign power whatsoever, or any domestic

SOURCE: John Locke, *Two Treatises of Civil Government* (London: J. M. Dent, Everyman, 1924), pp. 183–184, 189–190.

subordinate power, discharge any member of the society from his obedience to the legislative, acting pursuant to their trust, nor oblige him to any obedience contrary to the laws so enacted or farther than they do allow, it being ridiculous to imagine one can be tied ultimately to obey any power in the society which is not the supreme.

❈

142. These are the bounds which the trust that is put in them by the society and the law of God and Nature have set to the legislative power of every commonwealth, in all forms of government. First: They are to govern by promulgated established laws, not to be varied in particular cases, but to have one rule for rich and poor, for the favourite at Court, and the countryman at plough. Secondly: These laws also ought to be designed for no other end ultimately but the good of the people. Thirdly: They must not raise taxes on the property of the people without the consent of the people given by themselves or their deputies. And this properly concerns only such governments where the legislative is always in being, or at least where the people have not reserved any part of the legislative to deputies, to be from time to time chosen by themselves. Fourthly: Legislative neither must nor can transfer the power of making laws to anybody else, or place it anywhere but where the people have.

VISUAL SOURCES

Using Visual Sources: The Early Modern Château

Visual sources are briefly defined and discussed in the Preface. What follows is a more specific guide to the use of visual sources, focusing on our first visual source, *The Early Modern Château*, which immediately follows as an example.

   1.   Try to look at visual sources as if they were written, primary documents. As with primary documents, assume that you are a historian who knows very little about the Renaissance and discovers this visual source, a photo of an early modern château, Vaux-le-Vicomte in France. Your goal is to try to "read" it as evidence to support some conclusions about early modern times.

   Without some guidance, "reading" a visual source as historical evidence is more difficult than using a written source. The reproduction makes the details harder to see, and most people are not used to looking at a photo in this analytical way. Therefore, the headnote contains information about the château and about what appears in the visual source; the headnote also includes an analysis of the evidence that might be drawn from the photo. Here, as with most visual sources, it is useful to go back and forth between the photo and the written description and analysis that accompany the photo.

2. As with primary documents, think of questions as you look at the visual source and as you read the written guide to it. The general question to keep in mind is, "What does this tell me about this civilization, about how people behaved, how they thought, or what they believed?" Here this general question might be rephrased to, "What does this tell me about the culture and society of seventeenth- and eighteenth-century Europe?" Other questions might be suggested by the headnote and in the "consider" points, such as why such châteaux were built in this way.

3. Here the headnote alerts us to the fact that this château was not insignificant, for it was ordered by a prominent figure (France's superintendent of finance), designed by a famous architect (Le Vau), painter (Lebrun), and landscape gardener (Le Nôtre), and served as a model for other châteaux (Versailles). The headnote also suggests that the viewer notice the qualities (geometric orderliness and balance) and the nature (not for military defense like medieval castles) of the château and its grounds.

The headnote further shows some of the ways the information derived from this photo of Vaux-le-Vicomte might be used as historical evidence about early modern times. Some qualities (orderliness and balance) reflect the Classical style, which was popular throughout the arts during this period. Other qualities (conquest and manipulation of nature by human reason) evidence the growing scientific spirit of those times. The size, opulence, and ownership of the château can be used as evidence that early modern society was dominated by an aristocratic elite.

4. Now pull back and consider the source as a whole. What might it mean that this society, in which the vast majority of people lived at near-subsistence levels, supported the construction of such châteaux? Why are these châteaux so different from medieval castles? In what ways might a similar sort of building project be carried out today and for what purposes?

The Early Modern Château

The following picture of the château, grounds, and park of Vaux-le-Vicomte in France reveals both the wealth of France and certain trends of the seventeenth century. The château was built between 1657 and 1660 on the orders of France's superintendent of finance, Fouquet, and according to the plans of the architect Le Vau, the painter Lebrun, and the landscape gardener Le Nôtre. With its geometric orderliness and balance, it exemplifies the Classical style. In its conquest and manipulation of nature according to the rational plans of humans, it reflects the growing scientific spirit of the age. It also reflects a fundamentally stable society that was still dominated politically, socially, and economically by a small elite. It and buildings like it do not call out for military defense as did medieval castles. It later served as a model for Versailles, which itself became the model of monarchical splendor in seventeenth- and eighteenth-century Europe.

Consider: *Why such buildings and parks might have been built and how Saint-Simon might have viewed such projects.*

Photo 1-1

Alain Perceval

Maternal Care
Pieter de Hooch

This scene of domestic life is painted by the seventeenth-century Dutch artist Pieter de Hooch. Entitled Maternal Care, *it shows a girl kneeling while her mother examines and delouses her head. The scene takes place in Holland, the most urban and commercial European country. The moderate wealth of the rooms, revealed particularly by the paintings and the quality of the drapes, and the emphasis on cleanliness, privacy, and relative austerity, indicate that this is a middle-class home.*

Consider: *What the painter intended to communicate to the viewer of this painting.*

Photo 1-2

Fotocommissie Rijksmuseum Amsterdam

SECONDARY SOURCES

Using Secondary Sources: Absolutism: Myth and Reality

Secondary sources are briefly defined and discussed in the Preface. What follows is a more specific guide to the use of secondary sources, focusing on our first secondary source, *Absolutism: Myth and Reality,* which immediately follows as an example.

   1. Try to read a secondary source like *Absolutism: Myth and Reality* by G. Durand not as historical evidence (as you would read a primary source), but as a set of conclusions—an interpretation of the evidence from primary sources—by a scholar (usually a historian). Your job is to try to understand what the writer's interpretation is, to evaluate whether any arguments or evidence the writer presents seems to support it adequately, and to decide in what ways you agree or disagree with that interpretation.

   2. Try to think of questions when reading a secondary source. This can keep you alert to why the author selects and presents only certain information and what conclusions the author is trying to convey to the reader. Perhaps the two most important questions to keep in mind are, "What question is this author trying to answer?" and "What does all of what the author has written add up to?" For each secondary source, some guidance for these two questions and related questions is provided in the headnote to the source and in the "consider" points.

   Here the headnote to this secondary source tells us that the author, G. Durand, is going to analyze absolutism, particularly the extent to which political absolutism was a myth and a reality. The "consider" points and the headnote alert us to the fact that many historians are in disagreement over whether the term "absolutism" is useful and that Durand views absolutism as a "tendency."

   3. Try reading and summarizing in a few words what the author is trying to say or argue in each paragraph. What conclusions is he making?

   One could summarize the first paragraph by saying that Durand is trying to convince us that absolutism was a tendency, not a political system. To convince us, he argues that monarchs tried to maximize their power ("the sovereign sought to free himself . . . the monarch tried to rule through . . . he also tried to recover control of. . . .") and those efforts ("tendencies") created two institutions everywhere ("common to every state").

   In the second paragraph, the author tells us what the first of those two institutions was ("a small, inner or secret council").

   In the third paragraph, the author tells us what the second of those two institutions was ("a system of unifying and centralising judicial institutions"). In the rest of the second and third paragraphs, Durand tries to convince us that these two institutions were everywhere by citing some examples (France, England, Austria, Russia, Spain).

   In the fourth paragraph Durand claims that what he has argued supports ("From this we may infer") his conclusion that there was a tendency ("a general climate") toward absolutism, not an existing political system of absolutism ("offered the monarch no more than the opportunity to deliberate on. . . .").

Read the final paragraph. What conclusion or interpretation is Durand making here? What argument does he go on to make to support that conclusion?

4.   Pull back and consider the secondary source as a whole. Try to formulate the author's arguments and conclusions in a nutshell.

Here you might say that Durand concludes that absolutism did exist as a tendency, for monarchs successfully created institutions to increase their own power, but absolutism did not exist as an actual political system, for monarchs neither thought of themselves as absolute nor tried for absolute power.

Finally, do you agree with the author? Does the final line ("In practice absolutism seems much more the result of circumstances and personalities") imply that absolutism in fact existed, thereby weakening Durand's case?

Absolutism: Myth and Reality
G. Durand

During the seventeenth century, several monarchs attained such unprecedented power and authority that historians have used the term "absolutism" to describe these political systems. Other historians have argued that the term is misleading, that neither the ambitions of the monarchs nor the results constituted political absolutism. In the following selection G. Durand analyzes the myth and the reality of absolutism.

> **Consider:** *Why Durand prefers to view absolutism as a tendency; how Durand evaluates the goals and attitudes of the monarchs; whether the primary sources by Frederick William and Saint-Simon support Durand's analysis.*

Viewed as a tendency rather than as a political system, absolutism is an undeniable reality. In every state the sovereign sought to free himself from pressure and control. The means were everywhere the same; the monarch tried to rule through councillors whom he chose rather than nobles who claimed such positions as their right. He also tried to recover control of the administration of justice which had been taken over by the feudal nobility and the church. These tendencies produced two institutions common to every state.

First a small, inner or secret council, a cabinet ('Conseil des Affaires'), distinct from the traditional councils which had grown from the division of the functions of the old *Curia Regis*. There is great similarity between, for instance, the *Consejo de Estado* in Castile, the inner circle of the privy council in England, the Austrian Council of State of 1748 and the Imperial council set up by Catherine the Great in 1769.

SOURCE: G. Durand, "What Is Absolutism?" in *Louis XIV and Absolutism*, ed. Ragnhild Hatton (London: The Macmillan Press; Columbus: Ohio State University Press, 1976), pp. 23–24.

Second, a system of unifying and centralising judicial institutions. In France the drafting of customary law in the sixteenth century and the publication of the Codes and Great Ordinances in the seventeenth, formed the basis for royal intervention in the judicial process. The procedures of *évocation* to a higher court, or judgement by special commissioners named by the king, were specifically French; but an institution like the *conseil des parties* had its counterpart in the Royal Council of Castile, the English Star Chamber, or the Austrian *Hofrat*.

From this we may infer the existence of a general climate of absolutism, more or less pervasive, which offered the monarch no more than the opportunity to deliberate on matters of state without being affected by intrigue and pressure, and to ensure that the judicial process followed his wishes and directives.

As an actual political system, absolutism is a myth. The monarchs themselves never regarded themselves as absolute, except in the case of the autocrats of Russia, where the lack of fundamental laws, of established customs and corporate orders within the state allowed the growth of a dictatorial form of government. In France, however, even Louis XIV never planned to abolish the Parlement, but merely curbed its pretensions and in December 1655 limited its right of remonstrance; nor did he try to abolish the estates. Monarchs did not try to create a system of institutions which would destroy any possibility of resistance through inertia. They merely sought to restrict the activities of persons who might cause trouble and to set up a new administrative structure parallel to the old; a handful of commissioners directed, urged on and controlled the system inherited from a time when counsel, remonstrance and shared power were the rule. Sovereigns also continued to delegate their administrative powers through the sale of offices, or to farm them out to financial potentates who became virtual states within the state. The kings of Spain suffered the tyranny of their own councils. In practice absolutism seems much more the result of circumstances and personalities than of a deliberate intention to revolutionise the whole structure of the state.

The English Revolution, 1688–1689

George Macaulay Trevelyan

In England two blows to monarchical authority proved to be turning points. The first was the civil war and the execution of Charles I in the 1640s. But although this was a victory for Parliament, the Cromwellian period that followed and the return from exile of Charles II in 1660 cast doubt on the permanence of Parliament's victory. The second was the "Glorious Revolution" of 1688, which removed James II from power without the tur-

---

SOURCE: George Macaulay Trevelyan, *The English Revolution, 1688–1689.* Reprinted by permission of Oxford University Press (Oxford, England, 1938), pp. 164–166.

moil of the first revolution. In the following selection Cambridge historian George Macaulay Trevelyan compares the two revolutions and analyzes the significance of the second one. Following the Whig tradition, Trevelyan views these trends in British history as constructive and progressive. More than most historians, he sees this revolution as an admirable triumph for Parliament.

Consider: *Why the second revolution was a more clear-cut victory for Parliament than the first; factors that contributed to the victory of Parliament.*

The fundamental question at issue in 1688 had been this—Is the law above the King, or is the King above the law? The interest of Parliament was identified with that of the law, because, undoubtedly, Parliament could alter the law. It followed that, if law stood above the King's will, yet remained alterable by Parliament, Parliament would be the supreme power in the State.

James II attempted to make the law alterable wholesale by the King. This, if it had been permitted, must have made the King supreme over Parliament, and, in fact, a despot. The events of the winter of 1688–9 gave the victory to the opposite idea, which Chief Justice Coke and Selden had enunciated early in the century, that the King was the chief servant of the law, but not its master; the executant of the law, not its source; the laws should only be alterable by Parliament—Kings, Lords and Commons together. It is this that makes the Revolution the decisive event in the history of the English Constitution. It was decisive because it was never undone, as most of the work of the Cromwellian Revolution had been undone.

It is true that the first Civil War had been fought partly on this same issue:— the Common Law in league with Parliament had, on the field of Naseby, triumphed over the King in the struggle for the supreme place in the Constitution. But the victory of Law and Parliament had, on that occasion, been won only because Puritanism, the strongest religious passion of the hour, had supplied the fighting force. And religious passion very soon confused the Constitutional issue. Puritanism burst the legal bounds and, coupled with militarism, overthrew law and Parliament as well as King. Hence the necessity of the restoration in 1660 of King, law and Parliament together, without any clear definition of their ultimate mutual relations.

Now, in this second crisis of 1688, law and Parliament had on their side not only the Puritan passion, which had greatly declined, but the whole force of Protestant-Anglicanism, which was then at its height, and the rising influence of Latitudinarian scepticism—all arrayed against the weak Roman Catholic interest to which James had attached the political fortunes of the royal cause. The ultimate victor of the seventeenth-century struggle was not Pym or Cromwell, with their Puritan ideals, but Coke and Selden with their secular idea of the supremacy of law. In 1689 the Puritans had to be content with a bare toleration. But law triumphed, and therefore the law-making Parliament triumphed finally over the King.

Centuries of Childhood
Philippe Ariès

Through analysis of paintings such as Maternal Care *by Pieter de Hooch as well as other kinds of evidence, historians have changed our assumptions about attitudes toward childhood in Early Modern times. The most important of these historians is Philippe Ariès. The following is a selection from his* Centuries of Childhood.

> **Consider:** *How this reading relates to Hooch's painting; the differences between the seventeenth-century family, the medieval family, and the modern family according to Ariès.*

Between the end of the Middle Ages and the seventeenth century, the child had won a place beside his parents to which he could not lay claim at a time when it was customary to entrust him to strangers. This return of the children to the home was a great event: it gave the seventeenth-century family its principal characteristic, which distinguished it from the medieval family. The child became an indispensable element of everyday life, and his parents worried about his education, his career, his future. He was not yet the pivot of the whole system, but he had become a much more important character. Yet this seventeenth-century family was not the modern family: it was distinguished from the latter by the enormous mass of sociability which it retained. Where the family existed, that is to say in the big houses, it was a centre of social relations, the capital of a little complex and graduated society under the command of the paterfamilias.

The modern family, on the contrary, cuts itself off from the world and opposes to society the isolated group of parents and children. All the energy of the group is expended on helping the children to rise in the world, individually and without any collective ambition: the children rather than the family.

SOURCE: Philippe Ariès, *Centuries of Childhood*, trans. Robert Baldick. Reprinted by permission of Alfred A. Knopf, Inc. (New York, 1962), pp. 403–404. Copyright © 1962 by Alfred A. Knopf, Inc.

The World We Have Lost:
The Early Modern Family

Peter Laslett

The family is a tremendously important institution in any society. Changes in its structure and functions occur very slowly and gradually. With the passage of centuries since Early Modern times, we can see some sharp differences between the family of that period and the family of today. In the following selection Peter Laslett, a social historian from Cambridge who has written extensively on the Early Modern period, points out these differences.

> **Consider:** *The economic and social functions of the family revealed in this selection; what this document adds to the image of the family provided in the painting by Hooch and the document by Ariès; how the structure of this family differs from that of a typical twentieth-century family.*

In the year 1619 the bakers of London applied to the authorities for an increase in the price of bread. They sent in support of their claim a complete description of a bakery and an account of its weekly costs. There were thirteen or fourteen people in such an establishment: the baker and his wife, four paid employees who were called journeymen, two apprentices, two maidservants and the three or four children of the master baker himself. . . .

The only word used at that time to describe such a group of people was "family." The man at the head of the group, the entrepreneur, the employer, or the manager, was then known as the master or head of the family. He was father to some of its members and in place of father to the rest. There was no sharp distinction between his domestic and his economic functions. His wife was both his partner and his subordinate, a partner because she ran the family, took charge of the food and managed the women-servants, a subordinate because she was woman and wife, mother and in place of mother to the rest.

The paid servants of both sexes had their specified and familiar position in the family, as much part of it as the children but not quite in the same position. At that time the family was not one society only but three societies fused together: the society of man and wife, of parents and children and of master and servant. But when they were young, and servants were, for the most part, young, unmarried people, they were very close to children in their status and their function. . . .

Apprentices, therefore, were workers who were also children, extra sons or extra daughters (for girls could be apprenticed too), clothed and educated as well as fed, obliged to obedience and forbidden to marry, unpaid and absolutely dependent until the age of twenty-one. If apprentices were workers in the position

---

of sons and daughters, the sons and daughters of the house were workers too. John Locke laid it down in 1697 that the children of the poor must work for some part of the day when they reached the age of three. The sons and daughters of a London baker were not free to go to school for many years of their young lives, or even to play as they wished when they came back home. Soon they would find themselves doing what they could in *bolting*, that is sieving flour, or in helping the maidservant with her panniers of loaves on the way to the market stall, or in playing their small parts in preparing the never-ending succession of meals for the whole household.

We may see at once, therefore, that the world we have lost, as I have chosen to call it, was no paradise or golden age of equality, tolerance or loving kindness. It is so important that I should not be misunderstood on this point that I will say at once that the coming of industry cannot be shown to have brought economic oppression and exploitation along with it. It was there already. The patriarchal arrangements which we have begun to explore were not new in the England of Shakespeare and Elizabeth. They were as old as the Greeks, as old as European history, and not confined to Europe. And it may well be that they abused and enslaved people quite as remorselessly as the economic arrangements which had replaced them in the England of Blake and Victoria. When people could expect to live for only thirty years in all, how must a man have felt when he realized that so much of his adult life, perhaps all, must go in working for his keep and very little more in someone else's family?

Chapter Questions

1. What conditions facilitated the development of monarchical absolutism in the seventeenth century? What policies were used by kings to this end?
2. Why might mercantilist doctrines be particularly appealing to seventeenth-century monarchs?
3. How does family life reflect broader social, economic, and political aspects of the seventeenth century?

CHAPTER TWO

The Scientific Revolution

One of the most important intellectual revolutions in Western civilization occurred in the seventeenth century. Building on some sixteenth-century breakthroughs and a more deeply rooted interest in the workings of the natural world, a small elite of thinkers and scientists—Descartes, Galileo, Newton, Kepler, Bacon, and Boyle—established the foundations for the modern sciences of astronomy, mathematics, physics, and chemistry. Although at first their work was known to only a few, their ideas spread widely during the eighteenth century.

In the process of developing the modern sciences, these thinkers challenged the established conception of the universe as well as previous assumptions about knowledge. This ultimately successful challenge, now known as the Scientific Revolution, had a number of key elements. First, the view of the universe as being stable, fixed, and finite, with the earth at its center, gave way to a view of the universe as moving and almost infinite, with the earth merely one of millions of bodies, all subject to the laws of nature. Second, earlier methods for ascertaining the truth, which primarily involved referring to traditional authorities such as Aristotle, Ptolemy, and the Church, were replaced by methods that emphasized scepticism, rationalism, and rigorous reasoning based on observed facts and mathematical laws. Third, although these thinkers remained concerned with their own deeply held religious beliefs, the general scientific orientation shifted from theological questions to secular questions that focused on how things worked.

The primary documents in this chapter emphasize two broad questions that faced these seventeenth-century scientists. First, how can one ascertain the truth? The answers of Descartes, Galileo, and Newton are examined. Second, what is the proper line between science and scriptural authority? Galileo, who came most directly into conflict with Church authorities, provides us with clues.

The secondary documents concentrate on the nature and causes of the Scientific Revolution. In what ways was seventeenth-century science different from the science of earlier centuries? What explains these differences? What were the motives of seventeenth-century scientists?

Most of these intellectual developments were known to only a few throughout Europe. In the eighteenth century these scientific ideas and methods became popularized as part of the intellectual ferment of the Enlightenment.

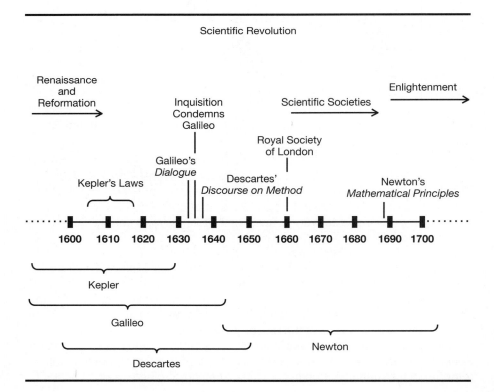

PRIMARY SOURCES

The Discourse on Method
René Descartes

Seventeenth-century science needed new philosophical and methodological standards for truth to replace those traditionally used to support scientific assumptions. These were forcefully provided by René Descartes (1596–1650) in his Discourse on Method *(1637). Born and educated in France, but spending his most productive years in Holland, Descartes gained fame as a mathematician, physicist, and metaphysical philosopher. The following excerpt from his* Discourse *contains the best-known statement of his approach to discovering truth.*

> **Consider:** *The ways in which Descartes' approach constitutes a break with traditional ways of ascertaining the truth; the weaknesses of this approach and how a modern scientist might criticize this method; how this approach reflects Descartes' background as a mathematician.*

In place of the multitude of precepts of which logic is composed, I believed I should find the four following rules quite sufficient, provided I should firmly and steadfastly resolve not to fail of observing them in a single instance.

The first rule was never to receive anything as a truth which I did not clearly know to be such; that is, to avoid haste and prejudice, and not to comprehend anything more in my judgments than that which should present itself so clearly and so distinctly to my mind that I should have no occasion to entertain a doubt of it.

The second rule was to divide every difficulty which I should examine into as many parts as possible, or as might be required for resolving it.

The third rule was to conduct my thoughts in an orderly manner, beginning with objects the most simple and the easiest to understand, in order to ascend as it were by steps to the knowledge of the most composite, assuming some order to exist even in things which did not appear to be naturally connected.

The last rule was to make enumerations so complete, and reviews so comprehensive, that I should be certain of omitting nothing.

Those long chains of reasoning, quite simple and easy, which geometers are wont to employ in the accomplishment of their most difficult demonstrations, led me to think that everything which might fall under the cognizance of the human mind might be connected together in a similar manner, and that, provided only one should take care not to receive anything as true which was not so, and if one

SOURCE: René Descartes, *The Discourse on Method,* in *The Philosophy of Descartes,* ed. and trans. Henry A. P. Torrey (New York: Henry Holt, 1982), pp. 46–48.

were always careful to preserve the order necessary for deducing one truth from another, there would be none so remote at which he might not at last arrive, nor so concealed which he might not discover. And I had no great difficulty in finding those with which to make a beginning, for I knew already that these must be the simplest and easiest to apprehend; and considering that, among all those who had up to this time made discoveries in the sciences, it was the mathematicians alone who had been able to arrive at demonstrations—that is to say, at proofs certain and evident—I did not doubt that I should begin with the same truths which they investigated.

Letter to Christina of Tuscany: Science and Scripture
Galileo Galilei

The most renowned scientist at the beginning of the seventeenth century was the Italian astronomer, mathematician, and physicist Galileo Galilei (1564–1642). His discoveries about gravity, velocity, and the movement of astronomical bodies were grounded in a scientific method that ran contrary to the accepted standards for truth and authority. In the following excerpt from a letter to the Grand Duchess Christina of Tuscany (1615), Galileo defends his ideas and delineates his view of the correct line between science and scriptural authority.

> **Consider:** *According to Galileo's view, the kinds of topics or questions that are appropriately scientific and those that are appropriately theological; how Galileo's views compare with those of Descartes; why Galileo's views are so crucial to the Scientific Revolution.*

I think that in discussions of physical problems we ought to begin not from the authority of scriptural passages, but from sense-experiences and necessary demonstrations; for the holy Bible and the phenomena of nature proceed alike from the divine Word, the former as the dictate of the Holy Ghost and the latter as the observant executrix of God's commands. It is necessary for the Bible, in order to be accommodated to the understanding of every man, to speak many things which appear to differ from the absolute truth so far as the bare meaning of the words is concerned. But Nature, on the other hand, is inexorable and immutable; she never transgresses the laws imposed upon her, or cares a whit whether her abstruse reasons and methods of operation are understandable to men. For that reason it

SOURCE: From Galileo Galilei, *Discoveries and Opinions of Galileo*, Stillman Drake, ed. and trans. Reprinted by permission of Doubleday & Company, Inc. (New York, 1957), pp. 182–183. Copyright © 1957 by Stillman Drake.

appears that nothing physical which sense-experience sets before our eyes, or which necessary demonstrations prove to us, ought to be called in question (much less condemned) upon the testimony of biblical passages which may have some different meaning beneath their words. For the Bible is not chained in every expression to conditions as strict as those which govern all physical effects; nor is God any less excellently revealed in Nature's actions than in the sacred statements of the Bible. . . .

From this I do not mean to infer that we need not have an extraordinary esteem for the passages of holy Scripture. On the contrary, having arrived at any certainties in physics, we ought to utilize these as the most appropriate aids in the true exposition of the Bible and in the investigation of those meanings which are necessarily contained therein, for these must be concordant with demonstrated truths. I should judge that the authority of the Bible was designed to persuade men of those articles and propositions which, surpassing all human reasoning, could not be made credible by science, or by any other means than through the very mouth of the Holy Spirit.

Yet even in those propositions which are not matters of faith, this authority ought to be preferred over that of all human writings which are supported only by bare assertions or probable arguments, and not set forth in a demonstrative way. This I hold to be necessary and proper to the same extent that divine wisdom surpasses all human judgment and conjecture.

But I do not feel obliged to believe that that same God who has endowed us with senses, reason, and intellect has intended to forgo their use and by some other means to give us knowledge which we can attain by them.

The Papal Inquisition of 1633: Galileo Condemned

Not surprisingly, Galileo found his views under attack from a variety of corners, including important groups within the Church. Ultimately his defense of Copernicanism, which held that the earth was not the center of the universe, was formally condemned by the Church. When he argumentatively summarized these ideas again in his Dialogue Concerning the Two Chief World Systems *(1632), he was brought before the Papal Inquisition, forced to recant his views, and confined to a villa on the outskirts of Florence. The following are some of the main charges against Galileo during his trial for heresy before the Inquisition in 1633.*

> **Consider:** *Why Galileo's views were so threatening to the Church; some of the long-range consequences of such a stance by the Church toward these views.*

Source: Georgio de Santillana, *The Crime of Galileo*. Reprinted by permission of The University of Chicago Press (Chicago, 1955), p. 310. Copyright © 1955.

We say, pronounce, sentence, and declare that you, the said Galileo, by reason of the matters adduced in trial, and by you confessed as above, have rendered yourself in the judgment of this Holy Office vehemently suspected of heresy, namely, of having believed and held the doctrine—which is false and contrary to the sacred and divine Scriptures—that the Sun is the center of the world and does not move from east to west and that the Earth moves and is not the center of the world; and that an opinion may be held and defended as probable after it has been declared and defined to be contrary to the Holy Scripture; and that consequently you have incurred all the censures and penalties imposed and promulgated in the sacred canons and other constitutions, general and particular, against such delinquents. From which we are content that you be absolved, provided that, first, with a sincere heart and unfeigned faith, you abjure, curse, and detest before us the aforesaid errors and heresies and every other error and heresy contrary to the Catholic and Apostolic Roman Church in the form to be prescribed by us for you.

Mathematical Principles of Natural Philosophy
Sir Isaac Newton

The greatest scientific synthesis of the seventeenth century was made by Isaac Newton (1642–1727), who was born in England and attained a post as professor of mathematics at Cambridge University. Newton made his most important discoveries early in life. By the beginning of the eighteenth century he was the most admired scientific figure in Europe. He made fundamental discoveries concerning gravity, light, and differential calculus. Most important, he synthesized various scientific findings and methods into a description of the universe as working according to measurable, predictable mechanical laws. Newton's most famous work, Mathematical Principles of Natural Philosophy *(1687), contains his theory of universal gravitation. In the following selection from that work, Newton describes his four rules for arriving at knowledge.*

Consider: *Why Newton's rules might be particularly useful for the experimental sciences; ways these rules differ from those of Descartes.*

RULE I

We are to admit no more causes of natural things than such as are both true and sufficient to explain their appearances.

To this purpose the philosophers say that Nature does nothing in vain, and more is in vain when less will serve; for Nature is pleased with simplicity, and affects not the pomp of superfluous causes.

SOURCE: Sir Isaac Newton, *Mathematical Principles of Natural Philosophy*, trans. Andrew Motte, rev. Florian Cajori (Berkeley, Calif.: University of California Press, 1947), pp. 398, 400. Reprinted by permission of the University of California Press.

RULE II

Therefore to the same natural effects we must, as far as possible, assign the same causes.

As to respiration in a man and in a beast; the descent of stones in *Europe* and in *America;* the light of our culinary fire and of the sun; the reflection of light in the earth, and in the planets.

RULE III

The qualities of bodies, which admit neither intensification nor remission of degrees, and which are found to belong to all bodies within the reach of our experiments, are to be esteemed the universal qualities of all bodies whatsoever.

For since the qualities of bodies are only known to us by experiments, we are to hold for universal all such as universally agree with experiments; and such as are not liable to diminution can never be quite taken away.

RULE IV

In experimental philosophy we are to look upon propositions inferred by general induction from phenomena as accurately or very nearly true, notwithstanding any contrary hypotheses that may be imagined, till such time as other phenomena occur, by which they may either be made more accurate, or liable to exceptions.

This rule we must follow, that the argument of induction may not be evaded by hypotheses.

VISUAL SOURCES

A Vision of the New Science

One of the most important figures of the Scientific Revolution was the astronomer and mathematician Johannes Kepler (1571–1630). On the following page from the front of one of his works, first printed in Nuremberg in 1627, the "edifice" of astronomy is presented allegorically. The older but still respectable pillars of astronomy of Hipparchus and Ptolemy give way to the new, sturdy pillars of Kepler's immediate predecessors, Copernicus and Tycho Brahe. In the lower left panel Kepler is pictured in his study; in the center panel is a map of the island where Brahe's observatory was located; in the right-hand panel is a picture of two people working on a printing press. Throughout are various instruments used in astronomy.

The picture reveals much about the Scientific Revolution. The instruments emphasize

Photo 2-1

how important measurement and observation were to the new science. The depiction of the old and new pillars suggests that the new scientists were replacing if not necessarily challenging the old, accepted scientific authorities by building on the work of their immediate predecessors—here Brahe on Copernicus, and Kepler on Brahe and Copernicus. The importance of communication among scientists is indicated by tribute to the printing press.

Consider: *How this picture illustrates the ways in which seventeenth-century scientists were breaking with earlier scientific assumptions.*

SECONDARY SOURCES

Why Was Science Backward in the Middle Ages?
Michael Postan

The scientific advances of the seventeenth century are commonly considered revolutionary because of their contrast with the previous state of science. One way to gain insight into the origins of the seventeenth-century developments is to look at earlier periods to see whether something was missing then that explains this contrast. In the following selection Michael Postan takes this approach, focusing specifically on the lack of scientific incentives in the Middle Ages.

Consider: *Why scientific incentives were lacking in the Middle Ages; the typically medieval traits that discouraged the men of the Middle Ages from scientific exploration; how the concerns and problems faced by Galileo relate to this argument.*

It is generally agreed that the Middle Ages preserved for the use of later times the science of the ancients. Therein lies both the scientific achievement and the scientific failure of the medieval civilization. . . . What the Middle Ages took over they did not very much enrich. Indeed so small was their own contribution that historians of science are apt to regard the Middle Ages as something of a pause. . . .

Thus some advance on planes both purely intellectual and technical there was; yet taken together and placed against the vast panorama of medieval life, or indeed

SOURCE: Michael Postan, "Why Was Science Backward in the Middle Ages?" in *A Short History of Science: Origins and Results of the Scientific Revolution* (London: Routledge and Kegan Paul), pp. 10–17. Reprinted by permission of Routledge and Kegan Paul, Ltd.

against the achievements of Greek and Hellenistic science in the fourth century B.C., or with the scientific activity of the seventeenth century, all these achievements are bound to appear very poor. Why then this poverty?

To this question many answers can be and have been given. But what most of them boil down to is the absence in medieval life of what I should be inclined to call scientific incentives. Students of science sometimes differ about the true inspiration of scientific progress. Some seek and find it in man's intellectual curiosity, in his desire to understand the workings of nature. Others believe that scientific knowledge grew and still grows out of man's attempts to improve his tools and his methods of production; that, in short, scientific truth is a by-product of technical progress. I do not want here to take sides in this particular controversy; what I want to suggest is that the Middle Ages were doubly unfortunate in that both the inspirations, the intellectual as well as the practical, failed more or less.

The easiest to account for is the intellectual. The Middle Ages were the age of faith, and to that extent they were unfavourable to scientific speculation. It is not that scientists as such were proscribed. For on the whole the persecution of men for their scientific ideas was very rare: rare because men with dangerous ideas, or indeed with any scientific ideas at all, were themselves very rare; and it is indeed surprising that there were any at all. This does not mean that there were no intellectual giants. All it means is that in an age which was one of faith, men of intellect and spirit found the calls of faith itself—its elucidation, its controversies, and its conquests—a task sufficient to absorb them. To put it simply, they had no time for occupations like science.

In fact they had neither the time nor the inclination. For even if there had been enough men to engage in activities as mundane as science, there would still be very little reason for them to do so. In times when medieval religious dogma stood whole and unshaken the intellectual objects and the methods of science were, to say the least, superfluous. The purpose of scientific enquiry is to build up piecemeal a unified theory of the universe, of its origin and of its working. But in the Middle Ages was that process really necessary? Did not medieval man already possess in God, in the story of Creation and in the doctrine of Omnipotent Will, a complete explanation of how the world came about and of how, by what means and to what purpose, it was being conducted? Why build up in laborious and painstaking mosaic a design, which was already there from the outset, clear and visible to all?

So much for intellectual incentive. The practical incentive was almost equally feeble. Greater understanding of nature could not come from technical improvements, chiefly because technical improvements were so few. Medieval occupations continued for centuries without appreciable change of method. After the great period of initial development, i.e., after the late eleventh century, the routine of medieval farming in the greater part of Europe became as fixed as the landscape itself. In the history of the smithies, the weaving shops, or the potteries, there were occasional periods of innovation, but taking the Middle Ages as a whole technical improvement was very rare and very slow. For this medieval economic policy was largely to blame. In the course of centuries economic activities got surrounded with a vast structure of bye-laws and regulations. . . . For bye-laws were as a rule based on the technical methods in existence when they were framed; and once framed they were to stand in the way of all subsequent change.

What is more, so deeply ingrained was the spirit of protection that in every local trade the technical methods were treated as a secret. . . . The men of the Middle Ages were unable to do more than they did because they were lacking in scientific incentive. What they achieved in advancing the practical arts of humanity or in preserving and transmitting ancient learning, they did in so far and as long as they were not typically medieval.

Early Modern Europe: Motives for the Scientific Revolution
Sir George Clark

By the seventeenth century, certain broad historical developments had set the stage for individuals to make the discoveries we associate with the Scientific Revolution. In addition, these individuals were motivated in ways that medieval people were not and used the new and growing body of techniques, materials, and knowledge to make their discoveries. In the following selection, British historian Sir George Clark, a recognized authority on the seventeenth century, examines some of the motives that led people to engage in scientific work.

> **Consider:** *The distinctions Clark makes among different people engaged in scientific work; why, more than thirteenth- or fourteenth-century people, these seventeenth-century people had a "disinterested desire to know."*

There were an infinite number of motives which led men to engage in scientific work and to clear the scientific point of view from encumbrances; but we may group together some of the most important under general headings, always remembering that in actual life each of them was compounded with the others. There were economic motives. The Portuguese explorers wanted their new instrument for navigation; the German mine-owners asked questions about metallurgy and about machines for lifting and carrying heavy loads; Italian engineers improved their canals and locks and harbours by applying the principles of hydrostatics; English trading companies employed experts who used new methods of drawing charts. Not far removed from the economic motives were those of the physicians and surgeons, who revolutionized anatomy and physiology, and did much more good than harm with their new medicines and new operations, though some of them now seem absurd. Like the doctors, the soldiers called science to

SOURCE: Sir George Clark, *Early Modern Europe*. Reprinted by permission of The Oxford University Press (Oxford, England, 1957), pp. 164–165.

their aid in designing and aiming artillery or in planning fortifications. But there were other motives far removed from the economic sphere. Jewellers learnt much about precious and semi-precious stones, but so did magicians. Musicians learnt the mathematics of harmony; painters and architects studied light and colour, substances and proportions, not only as craftsmen but as artists. For a number of reasons religion impelled men to scientific study. The most definite and old-established was the desire to reach absolute correctness in calculating the dates for the annual fixed and movable festivals of the Church: it was a pope who presided over the astronomical researchers by which the calendar was reformed in the sixteenth century. Deeper and stronger was the desire to study the wonders of science, and the order which it unravelled in the universe, as manifestations of the Creator's will. This was closer than any of the other motives to the central impulse which actuated them all, the disinterested desire to know.

The Scientific Role: A Sociocultural Interpretation of the Scientific Revolution
Joseph Ben-David

During the seventeenth century, new institutions such as the Royal Society were formed that helped create a sense of community and permanence among scientists. The achievements of scientists were increasingly recognized, and scientists gained both respect and acceptance into high social circles. These sociological aspects of the Scientific Revolution are stressed in the following selection by Israeli sociologist Joseph Ben-David. Ben-David argues that step by step scientists gained legitimacy and permanence to the point where science became a "self-perpetuating domain of culture."

> **Consider:** *How science was facilitated by nonscientific segments of society; how Ben-David's argument could be used to explain the previous lack of scientific achievement.*

Traditionally, natural science was subordinated to theology and philosophy. A first step towards the modern efflorescence occurred when it began to become more differentiated from theology and philosophy with respect to its subject-matter and procedures. Even when this point was reached, science continued to be a peripheral and secondary interest, but once its continuity was assured by its patient singularity and the steadiness of the concern which it attracted, it ceased to be subject to intermittent deterioration and there was even a probability of some slow but regular accumulation of scientific knowledge. The next step occurred

---

SOURCE: Joseph Ben-David, "The Scientific Role: The Conditions of Its Establishment in Europe," *Minerva*, vol. IV, no. 1 (Autumn 1965), pp. 16–17. Reprinted by permission of Edward Shils.

when this peripheral subject, which had had a low status, relative to other intellectual fields, came to be regarded by groups, with class, religious and political interests opposed to the established order, as intellectually more meaningful to them than the existing theological, philosophical and literary culture. For these groups, the sciences became a central part of their culture. Under these circumstances, men interested in science were impelled to redefine their roles as philosophers in such a way that science became increasingly central instead of peripheral to their conception of what they were doing. With the enhancement of the wealth, power and status of the classes which adopted an outlook sympathetic to science and in opposition to the inherited outlook, the status of the new type of philosopher was elevated. With the advancement of the status of scientific activity, the numbers of intellectuals of the highest quality moving into the field increased. The final steps occurred in the seventeenth century when the political success of the classes adopting the scientific outlook, combined with the intellectual success of the new philosophers, led to a more elaborate organisation of science and the establishment of scientific journals. In the course of these developments, men who did scientific work came to regard themselves and to be regarded by others as different from philosophers. They came to regard themselves as carrying on a significantly distinctive category of activity, disjunctively separated from the intellectual activity of philosophers and theologians. Increasing in numbers and having more occasion to meet and discuss with each other, they developed their own culture, their own norms and traditions in which their scientific work was embedded. The motivation and curiosity sustained by the stabilised stimulus inherent in such intensified and persistent scientific activity made for a greater continuity in scientific development. With a larger number of persons convinced of the value of science and devoting themselves actively and fully to its cultivation, science became, in a sense, a self-perpetuating domain of culture, and more independent than before of the variations in its environment.

A further contributory factor was the relative openness and decentralisation of the social system of European intellectual life. The Continent, including England, constituted a cultural whole, as a result of the unity of the church and its adoption of Roman traditions; persons and writings travelled across political borders with relative ease. Ideas evolved in one place would be readily appreciated in another. At the same time the various political units were sufficiently different from each other to permit beginnings, which were constricted in their places of origin (because they clashed with important vested interests), to be developed elsewhere, where the same vested interests were for some reason weaker.

No Scientific Revolution for Women

Bonnie S. Anderson and
Judith P. Zinsser

The Scientific Revolution was generally carried out by men. A few women participated directly in the Scientific Revolution, but they were the exception rather than the rule. The Scientific Revolution was based on principles such as observing, measuring, experimenting, and coming to reasoned conclusions. Were these principles applied by men to change assumptions about women, particularly about female physiology? Bonnie S. Anderson and Judith P. Zinsser address this question in their interpretive survey of women in European history, A History of Their Own.

> **Consider:** *According to Anderson and Zinsser, why there was no Scientific Revolution for women; how perceptions of female physiology relate to broader assumptions about women and men.*

In the sixteenth and seventeenth centuries Europe's learned men questioned, altered, and dismissed some of the most hallowed precepts of Europe's inherited wisdom. The intellectual upheaval of the Scientific Revolution caused them to examine and describe anew the nature of the universe and its forces, the nature of the human body and its functions. Men used telescopes and rejected the traditional insistence on the smooth surface of the moon. Galileo, Leibnitz, and Newton studied and charted the movement of the planets, discovered gravity and the true relationship between the earth and the sun. Fallopio dissected the human body, Harvey discovered the circulation of the blood, and Leeuwenhoek found spermatozoa with his microscope.

For women, however, there was no Scientific Revolution. When men studied female anatomy, when they spoke of female physiology, of women's reproductive organs, of the female role in procreation, they ceased to be scientific. They suspended reason and did not accept the evidence of their senses. Tradition, prejudice, and imagination, not scientific observation, governed their conclusions about women. The writings of the classical authors like Aristotle and Galen continued to carry the same authority as they had when first written, long after they had been discarded in other areas. Men spoke in the name of the new "science" but mouthed words and phrases from the old misogyny. In the name of "science" they gave a supposed physiological basis to the traditional views of women's nature, function, and role. Science affirmed what men had always known, what custom, law, and religion had postulated and justified. With the authority of their "objective," "rational" inquiry they restated ancient premises and arrived at the same traditional conclusions: the innate superiority of the male and the justifiable subordination of the female.

Chapter Questions

1. What were the main ways in which the science of the seventeenth century constituted a break from the past? What were some of the main problems facing seventeenth-century scientists in making this break? How did they handle these problems?

2. How would you explain the occurrence of the Scientific Revolution in the seventeenth century rather than in the sixteenth or eighteenth century?

CHAPTER THREE

Politics and Society in the Ancien Régime

By the time of the death of Louis XIV in 1715, France no longer threatened to overwhelm the rest of Europe. Indeed, during most of the eighteenth century a rough balance of power developed amid the shifting diplomatic alliances and wars. There were two major sets of rivalries among states between 1715 and 1789. In Central Europe, the older Hapsburg Empire was pitted against the newer, assertive Prussia. Although Prussia acquired the status of a major power as a result of this competition, the Hapsburg Empire managed to hold on to most of its lands and to expand at the cost of weaker states like Poland and the Ottoman Empire. Outside of Europe, England and France struggled for supremacy over colonial territories in the Great War for Empire.

During this period preceding the French Revolution, referred to as the "Ancien Régime," most of the same political and social trends that had characterized the second half of the seventeenth century continued, namely, aristocratic dominance, strong monarchies, expanding central governments, and traditional ways of life. Important changes that were initiated—such as agricultural, commercial, and industrial developments that strengthened the middle classes and led to urban growth—were limited in scope and area.

The sources in this chapter center on four aspects of the Ancien Régime between 1715 and 1789. First, the nature and position of the still-dominant aristocracy are examined. What were its responsibilities? What was the position of women within the aristocracy and outside of the aristocracy? Is it true that the aristocracy was frivolous? How did the aristocracy react to pressures from the monarchy on the one side and the middle classes on the other? What were the attitudes of the aristocracy toward the peasantry? Second, the development of the eighteenth-century state is analyzed. What role did Prussia's monarchs play in making her a major power? How did wars contribute to and reflect the growing importance of the state? Third, the importance of commerce and the middle class in England is explored. What were the connections among commerce, the middle classes, and the English aristocracy? What was the relationship between the development of commerce and industry and England's colonial concerns and growing nationalism? What were some of the effects of the commerce in slaves engaged in by the English and others? Fourth, the assumptions most people held during the Ancien Régime are examined.

The sources in this chapter stress the relative political stability that characterized much of the period between 1715 and 1789. Stability was not the rule in intellectual matters, as will be seen in the next chapter.

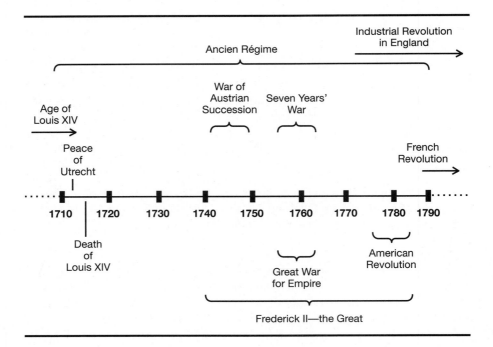

PRIMARY SOURCES

Political Testament
Frederick the Great

From a distance it may seem that eighteenth-century monarchs were much like those of the seventeenth century, similar in powers, position, and prestige. On closer examination, however, some differences are evident. Frederick II (the Great) of Prussia (1712–1786) was one of the most admired eighteenth-century monarchs. He ascended the throne in 1740 and ruled actively until his death in 1786. Frederick II continued the Prussian tradition of relying on a strong army to maintain and increase his holdings and prestige. At the same time he reorganized the army and the bureaucracy and introduced new ideas into both the theory and the practice of government. In the following excerpts from his Political Testament *(1752), he sets out his conception of politics and the proper role of the sovereign.*

> **Consider:** *How this conception of the monarch differs from that expressed by seventeenth-century monarchs; why Frederick emphasized the need to protect and support the nobility; who the crown's greatest political rivals for power were; the advantages and disadvantages to the monarch of religious toleration.*

Politics is the science of always using the most convenient means in accord with one's own interests. In order to act in conformity with one's interests one must know what these interests are, and in order to gain this knowledge one must study their history and application. . . . One must attempt, above all, to know the special genius of the people which one wants to govern in order to know if one must treat them leniently or severely, if they are inclined to revolt . . . to intrigue. . . .

[The Prussian nobility] has sacrificed its life and goods for the service of the state, its loyalty and merit have earned it the protection of all its rulers, and it is one of the duties [of the ruler] to aid those [noble] families which have become impoverished in order to keep them in possession of their lands: for they are to be regarded as the pedestals and the pillars of the state. In such a state no factions or rebellions need be feared . . . it is one goal of the policy of this state to preserve the nobility.

A well conducted government must have an underlying concept so well integrated that it could be likened to a system of philosophy. All actions taken must be well reasoned, and all financial, political and military matters must flow towards one goal: which is the strengthening of the state and the furthering of its power. However, such a system can flow but from a single brain, and this must be that

SOURCE: Frederick II, *Political Testament*, in *Europe in Review*, eds. George L. Mosse et al. (Chicago: Rand McNally, 1957), pp. 110–112. Reprinted by permission of George L. Mosse.

of the sovereign. Laziness, hedonism and imbecility, these are the causes which restrain princes in working at the noble task of bringing happiness to their subjects . . . a sovereign is not elevated to his high position, supreme power has not been confined to him in order that he may live in lazy luxury, enriching himself by the labor of the people, being happy while everyone else suffers. The sovereign is the first servant of the state. He is well paid in order that he may sustain the dignity of his office, but one demands that he work efficiently for the good of the state, and that he, at the very least, pay personal attention to the most important problems. . . .

You can see, without doubt, how important it is that the King of Prussia govern personally. Just as it would have been impossible for Newton to arrive at his system of attractions if he had worked in harness with Leibnitz and Descartes, so a system of politics cannot be arrived at and continued if it has not sprung from a single brain. . . . All parts of the government are inexorably linked with each other. Finance, politics and military affairs are inseparable; it does not suffice that one will be well administered; they must all be . . . a Prince who governs personally, who has formed his [own] political system, will not be handicapped when occasions arise where he has to act swiftly: for he can guide all matters towards the end which he has set for himself. . . .

Catholics, Lutherans, Reformed, Jews and other Christian sects live in this state, and live together in peace: if the sovereign, actuated by a mistaken zeal, declares himself for one religion or another, parties will spring up, heated disputes ensue, little by little persecutions will commence and, in the end, the religion persecuted will leave the fatherland and millions of subjects will enrich our neighbors by their skill and industry.

It is of no concern in politics whether the ruler has a religion or whether he has none. All religions, if one examines them, are founded on superstitious systems, more or less absurd. It is impossible for a man of good sense, who dissects their contents, not to see their error; but these prejudices, these errors and mysteries were made for men, and one must know enough to respect the public and not to outrage its faith, whatever religion be involved.

The Complete English Tradesman
Daniel Defoe

During the eighteenth century England was growing in strength and prosperity, particularly in the areas of commerce and manufacturing. A primary beneficiary of these economic developments was the rising commercial middle class. This class was becoming more assertive as the English were becoming more nationalistic. Daniel Defoe

---

SOURCE: Daniel Defoe, *The Complete English Tradesman*, vols. 17–18 of *The Novels and Miscellaneous Works of Daniel Defoe* (London: Thomas Tegg, 1840–1841), chap. 25.

(1659?–1731) speaks about these trends in the following selection from The Complete English Tradesman *(1726). Although best known for* Robinson Crusoe, *Defoe wrote many works and followed a commercial career for some time.*

> **Consider:** *The support Defoe offers for his view that commerce rightly dominates the country economically; how the economic policies that Defoe would recommend compare with policies typical of mercantilism; the connections between commerce and social class in England; the apparent advantages of having colonies and the colonial policies that Defoe's views imply.*

I . . . advance these three points in honour of our country—1. That we are the greatest trading country in the world, because we have the greatest exportation of the growth and product of our land, and of the manufacture and labour of our people; and the greatest importation and consumption of the growth, product, and manufactures of other countries from abroad, of any nation in the world.

2. That our climate is the best and most agreeable to live in, because a man can be more out of doors in England than in other countries.

3. That our men are the stoutest and best, because, strip them naked from the waist upwards, and give them no weapons at all but their hands and heels, and turn them into a room or stage, and lock them in with the like number of other men of any nation, man for man, and they shall beat the best men you shall find in the world.

And so many of our noble and wealthy families, as we have shown, are raised by and derived from trade, so it is true, and indeed it cannot well be otherwise, that many of the younger branches of our gentry, and even of the nobility itself, have descended again into the spring from whence they flowed, and have become tradesmen; and thence it is that, as I said above, our tradesmen in England are not, as it generally is in other countries, always of the meanest of our people. Nor is trade itself in England, as it generally is in other countries, the meanest thing that men can turn their hand to; but, on the contrary, trade is the readiest way for men to raise their fortunes and families; and therefore it is a field for men of figure and of good families to enter upon. . . .

As to the wealth of the nation, that undoubtedly lies chiefly among the trading part of the people; and though there are a great many families raised within few years, in the late war, by great employments and by great actions abroad, to the honour of the English gentry, yet how many more families among the tradesmen have been raised to immense estates, even during the same time, by the attending circumstances of the war; such as the clothing, the paying, the victualling and furnishing, &c., both army and navy. And by whom have the prodigious taxes been paid, the loans supplied, and money advanced upon all occasions? By whom are the banks and companies carried on, and on whom are the customs and excises levied? Have not the trade and tradesmen borne the burden of the war? And do they not still pay four millions a year interest for the public debts? On whom are the funds levied, and by whom the public credit supported? Is not trade the inexhausted fund of all funds, and upon which all the rest depend?

Again; in how superior a port or figure (as we now call it) do our tradesmen live, to what the middling gentry either do or can support! An ordinary tradesman now, not in the city only, but in the country, shall spend more money by the year, than a gentleman of four or five hundred pounds a year can do, and shall increase and lay up every year too; whereas the gentleman shall at the best stand stock still just where he began, nay, perhaps, decline: and as for the lower gentry, from a hundred pounds a year to three hundred, or thereabouts, though they are often as proud and high in their appearance as the other; as to them, I say, a shoemaker in London shall keep a better house, spend more money, clothe his family better, and yet grow rich too. It is evident where the difference lies; an estate's a pond, but trade's a spring: the first, if it keeps full, and the water wholesome, by the ordinary supplies and drains from the neighbouring grounds, it is well, and it is all that is expected; but the other is an inexhausted current, which not only fills the pond, and keeps it full, but is continually running over, and fills all the lower ponds and places about it.

This being the case in England, and our trade being so vastly great, it is no wonder that the tradesmen in England fill the lists of our nobility and gentry; no wonder that the gentlemen of the best families marry tradesmen's daughters, and put their younger sons apprentices to tradesmen; and how often do these younger sons come to buy the elder sons' estates, and restore the family, when the elder and head of the house, proving rakish and extravagant, has wasted his patrimony, and is obliged to make out the blessing of Israel's family, where the younger son bought the birthright, and the elder was doomed to serve him!

Trade is so far here from being inconsistent with a gentleman, that, in short, trade in England makes gentlemen, and has peopled this nation with gentlemen; for, after a generation or two, the tradesman's children, or at least their grandchildren, come to be as good gentlemen, statesmen, parliamentarian, privy-counsellors, judges, bishops, and noblemen, as those of the highest birth and the most ancient families; as we have shown. . . .

All this confirms what I have said before, viz., that trade in England neither is or ought to be levelled with what it is in other countries; or the tradesmen depreciated as they are abroad, and as some of our gentry would pretend to do in England; but that as many of our best families rose from trade, so many branches of the best families in England, under the nobility, have stooped so low as to be put apprentices to tradesmen in London, and to set up and follow those trades when they have come out of their times, and have thought it no dishonour to their blood. . . .

The greatness of the British nation is not owing to war and conquests, to enlarging its dominions by the sword, or subjecting the people of other countries to our power; but it is all owing to trade, to the increase of our commerce at home, and the extending it abroad.

It is owing to trade, that new discoveries have been made in lands unknown, and new settlements and plantations made, new colonies planted, and new governments formed, in the uninhabited islands, and the uncultivated continent of America; and those plantings and settlements have again enlarged and increased the trade, and thereby the wealth and power of the nation by whom they were discovered and planted; we have not increased our power, or the number of our subjects, by subduing the nations which possess those countries, and incorporating them into our own; but have entirely planted our colonies, and peopled the countries with our own subjects, natives of this island; and, excepting the negroes, which we transport from Africa to America, as slaves to work in the sugar and tobacco plantations, all our colonies, as well in the islands, as on the continent of America, are entirely peopled from Great Britain and Ireland, and chiefly the former; the natives having either removed further up into the country, or, by their own folly and treachery raising war against us, been destroyed and cut off. . . .

The Slave Trade
Anonymous

Part of the commercial prosperity enjoyed by several Western nations was built on the slave trade, which flourished in the seventeenth and eighteenth centuries. Slaves were generally shipped in British vessels, but the French and others engaged in this trade as well. Most slaves were taken across the Atlantic to Europe's colonial holdings, which in turn shipped goods such as sugar, metals, and wood products to the home country. Although there was little widespread opposition to slavery in Europe during the seventeenth and early eighteenth centuries, by the middle of the eighteenth century antislavery sentiments were growing. The following is an account of what was involved in the slave trade, written in 1771 by an anonymous Frenchman who argued for its abolition.

Consider: *The attitudes that permitted and supported the slave trade; the effects of this experience on the blacks; the legacy of this trade for the colonies.*

As soon as the ships have lowered their anchors off the coast of Guinea, the price at which the captains have decided to buy the captives is announced to the Negroes who buy prisoners from various princes and sell them to the Europeans. Presents are sent to the sovereign who rules over that particular part of the coast, and permission to trade is given. Immediately the slaves are brought by inhuman brokers like so many victims dragged to a sacrifice. White men who covet that portion of the human race receive them in a little house they have erected on the shore, where they have entrenched themselves with two pieces of cannon and twenty guards. As soon as the bargain is concluded, the Negro is put in chains and led aboard the vessel, where he meets his fellow sufferers. Here sinister reflections come to his mind; everything shocks and frightens him and his uncertain destiny gives rise to the greatest anxiety. At first he is convinced that he is to serve as a repast to the white men, and the wine which the sailors drink confirms him in this cruel thought, for he imagines that this liquid is the blood of his fellows.

The vessel sets sail for the Antilles, and the Negroes are chained in a hold of

SOURCE: Leon Apt and Robert E. Herzstein, eds., *The Evolution of Western Society*, vol. II (Hinsdale, Ill.: The Dryden Press, 1978), pp. 279–280.

the ship, a kind of lugubrious prison where the light of day does not penetrate, but into which air is introduced by means of a pump. Twice a day some disgusting food is distributed to them. Their consuming sorrow and the sad state to which they are reduced would make them commit suicide if they were not deprived of all the means for an attempt upon their lives. Without any kind of clothing it would be difficult to conceal from the watchful eyes of the sailors in charge of any instrument apt to alleviate their despair. The fear of a revolt, such as sometimes happens on the voyage from Guinea, is the basis of a common concern and produces as many guards as there are men in the crew. The slightest noise or a secret conversation among two Negroes is punished with utmost severity. All in all, the voyage is made in a continuous state of alarm on the part of the white men, who fear a revolt, and in a cruel state of uncertainty on the part of the Negroes, who do not know the fate awaiting them.

When the vessel arrives at a port in the Antilles, they are taken to a warehouse where they are displayed, like any merchandise, to the eyes of buyers. The plantation owner pays according to the age, strength and health of the Negro he is buying. He has him taken to his plantation, and there he is delivered to an overseer who then and there becomes his tormentor. In order to domesticate him, the Negro is granted a few days of rest in his new place, but soon he is given a hoe and a sickle and made to join a work gang. Then he ceases to wonder about his fate; he understands that only labor is demanded of him. But he does not know yet how excessive this labor will be. As a matter of fact, his work begins at dawn and does not end before nightfall; it is interrupted for only two hours at dinnertime. The food a full-grown Negro is given each week consists of two pounds of salt beef or cod and two pots of tapioca meal, amounting to about two pints of Paris. A Negro of twelve or thirteen years or under is given only one pot of meal and one pound of beef or cod. In place of food some planters give their Negroes the liberty of working for themselves every Saturday; others are even less generous and grant them this liberty only on Sundays and holidays. Therefore, since the nourishment of the Negroes is insufficient, their tendency to cheat must be attributed to the necessity of finding the food they lack.

Letter to Lady R., 1716: Women and the Aristocracy
Lady Mary Wortley Montagu

During the eighteenth century women continued to remain limited in the economic and political roles they could play, but it was possible for aristocratic women to take up influential social and cultural roles. In particular, many women used letter writing as an art, and from these letters much insight about the position and attitudes of women can be

Source: Mary Wortley Montagu, *Works*, vol. II (London: Richard Phillips, 1803), pp. 57–59.

gained. Lady Mary Wortley Montagu (1689–1762) was a well-known British literary fig-
ure, writing essays and poetry in addition to her volumes of letters. The following is a
selection from a letter written in 1716 to Lady R.

> **Consider:** *The assumptions about marriage among the aristocracy; connections*
> *among marriage, love, and economic interests; the position of aristocratic women*
> *reflected by this letter.*

No woman dares appear coquette enough to encourage two lovers at a time. And I have not seen any such prudes as to pretend fidelity to their husbands, who are certainly the best natured set of people in the world, and look upon their wives' gallants as favourably as men do upon their deputies, that take the troublesome part of their business off their hands. They have not however the less to do on that account; for they are generally deputies in another place themselves; in one word, 'tis the established custom for every lady to have two husbands, one that bears the name, and another that performs the duties. And these engagements are so well known, that it would be a downright affront, and publicly resented, if you invited a woman of quality to dinner, without, at the same time, inviting her two attendants of lover and husband, between whom she sits in state with great gravity. The submarriages generally last twenty years together, and the lady often commands the poor lover's estate, even to the utter ruin of his family.

These connections, indeed, are as seldom begun by any real passion as other matches; for a man makes but an ill figure that is not in some commerce of this nature; and a woman looks out for a lover as soon as she's married, as part of her equipage, without which she could not be genteel; and the first article of the treaty is establishing the pension, which remains to the lady, in case the gallant should prove inconstant. This chargeable point of honour I look upon as the real foundation of so many wonderful instances of constancy. I really know some women of the first quality, whose pensions are as well known as their annual rents, and yet nobody esteems them the less; on the contrary, their discretion would be called in question, if they should be suspected to be mistresses for nothing. A great part of their emulation consists in trying who shall get most. . . .

Women of the Third Estate

The vast majority of eighteenth-century Europeans were not members of the aristocracy.
Over 90 percent were peasants, artisans, domestics, and laborers—often referred to in
France as members of the Third Estate. While both men and women of the Third Estate
shared much, women's positions and grievances often differed from those of men. Articu-
late records of these women's grievances are difficult to find, but the flood of formal

---

SOURCE: Excerpts from *Not in God's Image* by Julia O'Faolain and Lauro Martines. Copyright © 1973 by Julia O'Faolain and Lauro Martines. Reprinted by permission of Harper & Row, Publishers, Inc.

petitions preceding the French Revolution of 1789 provides us with some rich sources. The following is a "Petition of the Women of the Third Estate to the King," dated several months prior to the outbreak of the French Revolution.

> **Consider:** *What options seem available to women; the problems identified and so-lutions proposed; ways in which men's interests and women's interests might clash.*

1 January 1789. Almost all women of the Third Estate are born poor. Their education is either neglected or misconceived, for it consists in sending them to learn from teachers who do not themselves know the first word of the language they are supposed to be teaching. . . . At the age of fifteen or sixteen, girls can earn five or six sous a day. If nature has not granted them good looks, they get married, without a dowry, to unfortunate artisans and drag out a grueling existence in the depths of the provinces, producing children whom they are unable to bring up. If, on the other hand, they are born pretty, being without culture, principles, or any notion of morality, they fall prey to the first seducer, make one slip, come to Paris to conceal it, go totally to the bad here, and end up dying as victims of debauchery.

Today, when the difficulty of earning a living forces thousands of women to offer themselves to the highest bidder and men prefer buying them for a spell to winning them for good, any woman drawn to virtue, eager to educate herself, and with natural taste . . . is faced with the choice either of casting herself into a cloister which will accept a modest dowry or of going into domestic service. . . .

If old age overtakes unmarried women, they spend it in tears and as objects of contempt for their nearest relatives.

To counter such misfortunes, Sire, we ask that men be excluded from practicing those crafts that are women's prerogative, such as dressmaking, embroidery, mil-linery, etc. Let them leave us the needle and the spindle and we pledge our word never to handle the compass or the set-square.

We ask, Sire . . . to be instructed and given jobs, not that we may usurp men's authority but so that we may have a means of livelihood, and so that the weaker among us who are dazzled by luxury and led astray by example should not be forced to join the ranks of the wretched who encumber the streets and whose lewd audacity disgraces both our sex and the men who frequent them.

VISUAL SOURCES

Happy Accidents of the Swing
Jean-Honoré Fragonard

The aristocracy remained dominant culturally during the Ancien Régime, commissioning most of the art of the period. It is not surprising, then, that the art reflected aristocratic values and tastes. Happy Accidents of the Swing *by Jean-Honoré Fragonard exemplifies a type of painting quite popular among France's eighteenth-century aristocracy.*

Fragonard was commissioned by Baron de Saint-Julien in 1767 to paint a picture of his mistress on a swing being pushed by a bishop who did not know that the woman was the baron's mistress, with the baron himself watching from a strategic place of hiding. In the picture the woman on the swing seems well aware of what is happening, flinging off her shoe toward a statue of the god of discretion in such a way as to cause her gown to billow out revealingly.

This painting reflects a certain religious irreverence on the part of the eighteenth-century aristocracy, for the joke is on the unknowing bishop. The significance of this irreverence is magnified by the fact that Saint-Julien had numerous dealings with the clergy, since he was at this time a government official responsible for overseeing clerical wealth.

The lush setting of the painting and the tenor of the scene suggest the love of romantic luxury and concern for sensual indulgence by this most privileged but soon to be declining part of society.

> **Consider:** *The evidence in this picture of the attitudes of life style of the eighteenth-century French aristocracy.*

Photo 3-1

Act of Humanity
Jean Defraine

In Act of Humanity *(circa 1783), painter Jean Defraine shows that the old tradition of aristocratic responsibility for social welfare is still upheld in the eighteenth century. Here, an aristocrat is visiting a family stricken by both illness and poverty. The realistic depiction of poverty is accompanied by the comforting suggestion that its effects can be alleviated through charitable gestures. Such humanitarian acts on the part of the aristocracy were considered one of the few appropriate cures for social problems of the poor.*

Consider: *How this picture compares with* Happy Accidents of the Swing.

Photo 3-2

Bibliothèque Nationale, Paris

The Battle of Fontenoy
C. C. P. Lawson

War, though still common in the eighteenth century, was more controlled and orderly and less vicious than during the first half of the seventeenth century. This is suggested in this painting by C. C. P. Lawson of a typical eighteenth-century land battle, the Battle of Fontenoy. Aristocratic traditions are maintained by the commanders, who calmly salute each other before the battle begins. The troops are uniformed and orderly, apparently under the firm control of officers. The characteristics of eighteenth-century battles depicted here reflect the realities of military tactics and economics. As argued by the modern historian R. J. White in Europe in the Eighteenth Century *(New York: St. Martin's Press, 1965),*

> *"a supposedly wholesome mixture of aristocrats and scum was the principal substance of the armed forces everywhere in the eighteenth century. Warfare was predominantly defensive, dogged by caution and conducted according to strict rules of procedure. The almost baroque movements of armed forces in the stately game of siege warfare, the rigid adherence to the rules of the game as laid down in* Fighting

Photo 3-3

National Army Museum, Department of Records

Instructions [*a standard military manual*], *which often appear so ludicrous to modern observers, were not invented to charm later generations, but were the offspring of the peculiar necessities of a world of limited material resources and rationally conceived purposes.*"

Consider: *How the arrangement of the troops in this picture reflects the social structure of the eighteenth century.*

SECONDARY SOURCES

The Ancien Régime: Ideals and Realities
John Roberts

It is difficult to look back at past societies with other than our own assumptions. However, people in the Ancien Régime—eighteenth-century Europe—had their own beliefs, values, and perceptions about the world and their place in it. In the following selection John Roberts describes what most eighteenth-century Europeans would take for granted, emphasizing their mental conservatism.

Consider: *The ways in which their assumptions differ from our own; the ways in which they are the same; why their view of innovation and the past is so important.*

What would be taken for granted by most continental Europeans in the eighteenth century and, to some extent, by Englishmen and English settlers abroad, would be assumptions which can be sketched briefly in such propositions as these: God made the world and gave it a moral and social structure; His revelation in Jesus Christ imposes a duty upon society to protect the Church, Christian truth and moral principles in a positive way by promoting sound behaviour and belief and harrying bad; Christianity teaches that the existing structure of society is in principle good and should be upheld; this structure is organized hierarchically and for the most part its hierarchies are hereditary, their apex usually being found in a monarch; privileges and duties are distributed in a manner which can be justified

SOURCE: From John Roberts, *Revolution and Improvement: The Western World, 1775–1847,* pp. 34–35. Copyright © 1976 John Roberts. Reprinted by permission of the Regents of the University of California Press, and the University of California Press.

by reference to this hierarchy. It is also true (our list of assumptions could continue) that while the organization of society around hereditary units was a fundamental datum of society under the *ancien régime*, it took for granted respect for other groups in which men came together for religious, professional, economic or social purposes; corporations with these ends were thought the proper regulators of much of daily life—the practice of trade or the enjoyment of legal rights, for example—and the interests of individuals belonging to them came emphatically second to those of these legal persons. . . .

It was also then assumed that much more of personal behaviour should be regulated by law and traditional practice than today. . . .

Social restraint reflected the pervasive anti-individualism of the *ancien régime*. Moreover, moral and ideological truth were thought indivisible and this left little room in theory for the vagaries of the individual. . . .

Across all these assumptions ran an overriding mental conservatism. One of the deepest differences between our own age and the *ancien régime* is the pervading conviction of those times that it was innovation which needed to be justified, not the past. A huge inertia generated by usage, tradition, prescription and the brutal fact of simple ignorance, lay heavily upon the institutions of the eighteenth century. As there had been for centuries, there was a self-evident justification for the ways of our fathers, for the forms and laws they had evolved and set down. One way in which this expressed itself was in an intense legalism, a fascination with old documents, judgments, lineage and inheritance. The higher classes were preoccupied with questions of blood, ancestry and family honour. Yet none of this preoccupation with the past was true historical-mindedness. Men were obsessed with the past as guidance, as precedent, even as spectacle, but not for its own sake. Few men had much sense that they were not looking at the same world as their ancestors. . . .

The Resurgent Aristocracy
Leonard Krieger

Historians have at times exaggerated the importance of the rise of the middle class and the decline of the aristocracy in the eighteenth century. Recently, historians have begun to emphasize the middle of the eighteenth century as a period during which the aristocracy was actually resurgent, making efforts to regain its position and increase its influence— often with considerable success. This view is illustrated in the following selection by Leonard Krieger of the University of Chicago.

SOURCE: Reprinted from *Kings and Philosophers, 1689–1789*, by Leonard Krieger, with the permission of W. W. Norton & Company, Inc. Copyright © 1970 by W. W. Norton & Company, Inc.

Consider: *The evidence Krieger offers for a resurgence of the aristocracy; the ways in which the aristocracy adapted to eighteenth-century political needs.*

In the eighteenth century, surprisingly, aristocracies—or at least important parts of them—were resurgent. Appreciating the principle of what would later become a proverbial prescription for men to join what they could not beat, nobles in the several countries of Europe picked themselves up and began to appropriate commanding positions in the governmental structures of the new states and even in the network of commercial relations. The Whig oligarchy that ruled Britain without serious challenge between the accession of the Hanoverian dynasty in 1714 and George III's assertion of royal influence after 1760 represented a landowning aristocracy that was sponsoring a capitalized and scientific agriculture in response to demands of the market and that had economic ties with merchants and bankers of the City. The French peers, refueled by Louis XIV's calculated infusion of subsidies, made a serious bid to refashion the monarchy in their own image after the death of the Sun King in 1715, and when this attempt failed, a more economically progressive and modern-minded judicial and administrative aristocracy (*noblesse de robe* and *noblesse d'office*) rose to continue the counteroffensive on behalf of the privileged. In Russia various sections of the military and landed nobility dictated the succession to the throne—in general they preferred tsarinas in the expectation that they would behave consistently as members of the "weaker sex"—and dominated the social policy of the government from the death of Peter the Great in 1725 through the accession of Catherine the Great in 1762. The long period from 1718 to 1772 that the Swedes euphemistically called their "era of liberty" was actually an age of aristocratic sovereignty, exercised constitutionally in a nominal monarchy through the nobles' oligarchic control over both the *Riksdag*, or parliament, and the bureaucracy. The Dutch gave the same high-flown label to the period from 1702 to 1747, when the small but influential class of Regents, an oligarchy comprised of urban patricians, resumed its sway after the death of William III and kept the office of *stadholder* vacant. The seven provinces that made up the Dutch "Republic" were, in this respect, expanded versions of the independent city-states in Europe. Concentrated mainly in Switzerland and Germany, they too were stabilized during the first half of the eighteenth century under the rule of exclusive patrician oligarchies. . . .

The aristocracies' new lease on life for the eighteenth century was thus predicated upon the modernization of their premises, and they thereby shifted the arena of social conflict from outside to inside the structure of the state. Where they had formerly defended their privileged rights to landownership, manorial lordship, judicial immunities, and tax exemptions by denying the jurisdiction of the central governments, they now defended these privileges by occupying and controlling the governmental agencies which exercised the jurisdiction. This aristocratic penetration of the state ran counter to the standards of general law, equal citizenship, and uniform administration which had served and continued to serve bureaucrats as guides in extending the scope of central government. But the hierarchical tendency was no mere atavism. Despite the obvious and reciprocal hostility between it and the leveling tendency with which it shared the state, the coexistence of the two tendencies, however mismatched in logic, was a faithful response to a fundamental social demand of the age. European society required, for the military security of its inhabitants, for the direction and subsidization of its economy, and for the prevention of religious turbulence and popular disorder, the imposition of unified control over a larger area and more people than the contemporary instruments of government could manage. Hence the employment of the traditional social and corporate hierarchies by the government as extensions of the governing arm into the mass of inhabitants. All people were subject, but some were more subject than others.

Lords and Peasants
Jerome Blum

The aristocracy made up a small percentage of Europe's population. Some 80 to 90 percent of the people were still peasants. While peasants lived in a variety of different circumstances, most lived at not much more than a subsistence level. They were usually thought of as at the bottom of society. In the following selection Jerome Blum analyzes attitudes held toward the peasants by seigniors (lords) and by peasants themselves.

> **Consider:** *How lords viewed peasants in relation to themselves; how the lords' attitudes reflected actual social conditions; possible consequences of the negative attitudes held about peasants.*

With the ownership of land went power and authority over the peasants who lived on the land. There were a multitude of variations in the nature of that authority and in the nature of the peasants' subservience to their seigniors, in the compass of the seigniors' supervision and control, and in the obligations that the peasants had to pay their lords. The peasants themselves were known by many different names, and so, too, were the obligations they owed the seigniors. But, whatever the differences, the status of the peasant everywhere in the servile lands was associated with unfreedom and constraint. In the hierarchical ladder of the traditional order he stood on the bottom rung. He was "the stepchild of the age, the broad, patient back who bore the weight of the entire social pyramid . . . the clumsy lout who was deprived and mocked by court, noble and city." . . .

The subservience of the peasant and his dependence upon his lord were mirrored in the attitudes and opinions of the seigniors of east and west alike. They

---

SOURCE: From Blum, Jerome, *The End of the Old Order in Rural Europe*, pp. 29–31, 44–49. Copyright 1978 by Princeton University Press. Reprinted by permission of Princeton University Press.

believed that the natural order of things had divided humankind into masters and servants, those who commanded and those who obeyed. They believed themselves to be naturally superior beings and looked upon those who they believed were destined to serve them as their natural inferiors. At best their attitude toward the peasantry was the condescension of paternalism. More often it was disdain and contempt. Contemporary expressions of opinion repeatedly stressed the ignorance, irresponsibility, laziness, and general worthlessness of the peasantry, and in the eastern lands the free use of the whip was recommended as the only way to get things done. The peasant was considered some lesser and sub-human form of life; "a hybrid between animal and human" was the way a Bavarian official put it in 1737. An eyewitness of a rural rising in Provence in 1752 described the peasant as "an evil animal, cunning, a ferocious half-civilized beast; he has neither heart nor honesty. . . ." The Moldavian Basil Balsch reported that the peasants of his land were "strangers to any discipline, order, economy or cleanliness . . .; a thoroughly lazy, mendacious . . . people who are accustomed to do the little work that they do only under invectives or blows." A counselor of the duke of Mecklenburg in an official statement in 1750 described the peasant there as a "head of cattle" and declared that he must be treated accordingly. . . .

The conviction of their own superiority harbored by the seigniors was often compounded by ethnic and religious differences between lord and peasant. In many parts of central and eastern Europe the masters belonged to a conquering people who had established their domination over the native population. German seigniors ruled over Slavic peasants in Bohemia, Galicia, East Prussia and Silesia, and over Letts and Estonians in the Baltic lands; Polish lords were the masters of Ukrainian, Lithuanian, and White Russian peasants; Great Russians owned manors peopled by Ukrainians and Lithuanians and Poles; Magyars lorded it over Slovaks and Romanians and Slovenes—to list only some of the macroethnic differences. Few peoples of the rest of the world can match Europeans in their awareness of and, generally, contempt for or at least disdain for other ethnic and religious groups. . . . The dominant group, though greatly outnumbered, successfully maintained its cultural identity precisely because it considered the peasants over whom it ruled as lesser breeds of mankind, even pariahs. . . .

Schooling for most peasants was, at best, pitifully inadequate and usually entirely absent, even where laws declared elementary education compulsory. . . . [B]y far the greatest part of Europe's peasantry lived out their lives in darkest ignorance.

The peasants themselves, oppressed, condemned, and kept in ignorance by their social betters, accepted the stamp of inferiority pressed upon them. "I am only a serf" the peasant would reply when asked to identify himself. They seemed without pride or self-respect, dirty, lazy, crafty, and always suspicious of their masters and of the world that lay outside their village. Even friendly observers were put off by the way they looked and by their behavior. One commentator complained in the 1760's that "one would have more pity for them if their wild and brutish appearance did not seem to justify their hard lot."

Chapter Questions

1. In what ways did competing groups and historical conditions put pressure on aristocrats who wanted to maintain their position and influence?
2. What were the assets and liabilities of the eighteenth-century aristocracy in the face of pressures to diminish its position and influence?
3. How do eighteenth-century assumptions reflect the nature of politics and society during the Ancien Régime?

CHAPTER FOUR

The Enlightenment

As a period of intellectual history in Western civilization, the eighteenth century is known quite appropriately as the Enlightenment. At that time a group of thinkers, called the *philosophes*, developed and popularized related sets of ideas that formed a basis for modern thought. Their methods emphasized scepticism, empirical reasoning, and satire. They spread their ideas through works ranging from pamphlets to the great *Encyclopedia* and numerous meetings in aristocratic "salons." Although centered in France, this intellectual movement took place throughout Europe.

Most of the philosophes believed that Western civilization was on the verge of enlightenment, that reasoning and education could quickly dispel the darkness of the past that had kept people in a state of immaturity. The main objects of their criticism were institutions, such as governments and the Church, and irrational customs that perpetuated old ways of thinking and thus hindered progress. While critical and combative, the philosophes were not political or social revolutionaries. Their ideas were revolutionary in many ways, but in practice these thinkers hoped for rather painless change—often through reform from above by enlightened monarchs. Enlightenment thinkers usually admired England, where liberal ideas and practices were most developed.

The sources in this chapter concern three issues. First, what was the nature of Enlightenment thought? What was the professed spirit of the Enlightenment? What patterns of morality were embodied in Enlightenment ideas? In what ways was authority rejected and nature elevated to great importance? Second, how should we characterize the philosophes? Who were they? What were their common psychological traits, their religious beliefs, and their interactions? Finally, how did Enlightenment thought affect eighteenth-century politics before the French Revolution? Was there such a phenomenon as "enlightened despotism," and if so, what did it mean?

Together, the sources should reveal an intellectual movement still tied to the traditional society of the Ancien Régime but with strikingly modern characteristics. Toward the end of the eighteenth century, many of the ideas of the Enlightenment played an important role in the French Revolution—the subject of the next chapter.

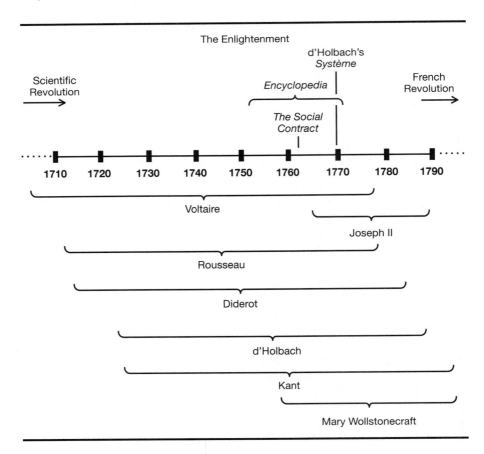

PRIMARY SOURCES

What Is Enlightenment?
Immanuel Kant

One of the most pervasive themes among Enlightenment thinkers was a self-conscious sense of a spirit of enlightenment. This is illustrated in the following excerpt from a short essay by Immanuel Kant (1724–1804) of Königsberg in East Prussia. Kant, one of the world's most profound philosophers, is particularly known for his analysis of the human mind and how it relates to nature, as set forth in his Critique of Pure Reason *(1781). In the following essay, written in 1784, Kant defines the spirit of the Enlightenment and describes some of its implications.*

> **Consider:** *What Kant means by "freedom" and why he feels freedom is so central to the Enlightenment; how people can become enlightened and the appropriate environment to facilitate this enlightenment; what Kant would consider "mature"; how Kant relates enlightenment and politics.*

Enlightenment is man's leaving his self-caused immaturity. Immaturity is the incapacity to use one's intelligence without the guidance of another. Such immaturity is self-caused if it is not caused by lack of intelligence, but by lack of determination and courage to use one's intelligence without being guided by another. *Sapere Aude!* Have the courage to use your own intelligence! is therefore the motto of the enlightenment.

Through laziness and cowardice a large part of mankind, even after nature has freed them from alien guidance, gladly remain immature. It is because of laziness and cowardice that it is so easy for others to usurp the role of guardians. It is so comfortable to be a minor! If I have a book which provides meaning for me, a pastor who has conscience for me, a doctor who will judge my diet for me and so on, then I do not need to exert myself. I do not have any need to think; if I can pay, others will take over the tedious job for me. The guardians who have kindly undertaken the supervision will see to it that by far the largest part of mankind, including the entire "beautiful sex," should consider the step into maturity, not only as difficult but as very dangerous. . . .

But it is more nearly possible for a public to enlighten itself: this is even inescapable if only the public is given its freedom. . . .

All that is required for this enlightenment is *freedom;* and particularly the least harmful of all that may be called freedom, namely, the freedom for man to make *public use* of his reason in all matters. . . .

SOURCE: Immanuel Kant, "What Is Enlightenment?" in *The Philosophy of Kant*, Carl J. Friedrich, ed. Reprinted by permission of Random House, Inc. (New York, 1949), pp. 132–134, 138–139. Copyright © 1949 by Random House, Inc.

The question may now be put: Do we live at present in an enlightened age? The answer is: No, but in an age of enlightenment. Much still prevents men from being placed in a position or even being placed into position to use their own minds securely and well in matters of religion. But we do have very definite indications that this field of endeavor is being opened up for men to work freely and reduce gradually the hindrances preventing a general enlightenment and an escape from self-caused immaturity. In this sense, this age is the age of enlightenment and the age of Frederick (The Great). . . .

I have emphasized the main point of enlightenment, that is of man's release from his self-caused immaturity, primarily *in matters of religion*. I have done this because our rulers have no interest in playing the guardian of their subjects in matters of arts and sciences. Furthermore immaturity in matters of religion is not only most noxious but also most dishonorable. But the point of view of a head of state who favors freedom in the arts and sciences goes even farther; for he understands that there is no danger in legislation permitting his subjects to make *public* use of their own reason and to submit *publicly* their thoughts regarding a better framing of such laws together with a frank criticism of existing *legislation*. We have a shining example of this; no prince excels him whom we admire. Only he who is himself enlightened does not fear spectres when he at the same time has a well-disciplined army at his disposal as a guarantee of public peace. Only he can say what (the ruler of a) free state dare not say: *Argue as much as you want and about whatever you want but obey!*

The System of Nature
Baron d'Holbach

Most Enlightenment thinkers rejected traditional sources of authority such as the Church or custom. Instead, they argued that people should rely on reason, experience, and nature as their guides. Baron d'Holbach (1723–1789) exemplifies this in his varied writings. A German aristocrat and scientist who assumed French citizenship, d'Holbach is best known for his attacks on organized religion and his contributions to Diderot's Encyclopedia. *In the following selection from his* System of Nature *(1770), d'Holbach focuses on the meaning of enlightenment and what should be done to obtain this enlightenment.*

> **Consider:** *Why enlightenment is so important; whether "nature" has a meaning similar to God for d'Holbach; the views about the nature of enlightenment that Kant and d'Holbach share.*

The source of man's unhappiness is his ignorance of Nature. The pertinacity with which he clings to blind opinions imbibed in his infancy, which interweave them-

SOURCE: Baron d'Holbach, *The System of Nature*, trans. H. D. Robinson (Boston: J. P. Mendum, 1853), pp. viii–ix, 12–13, 15.

selves with his existence, the consequent prejudice that warps his mind, that prevents its expansion, that renders him the slave of fiction, appears to doom him to continual errour. He resembles a child destitute of experience, full of idle notions: a dangerous leaven mixes itself with all his knowledge: it is of necessity obscure, it is vacillating and false:—He takes the tone of his ideas on the authority of others, who are themselves in errour, or else have an interest in deceiving him. To remove this Cimmerian darkness, these barriers to the improvement of his condition; to disentangle him from the clouds of errour that envelop him, that obscure the path he ought to tread; to guide him out of this Cretan labyrinth, requires the clue of Ariadne, with all the love she could bestow on Theseus. It exacts more than common exertion; it needs a most determined, a most undaunted courage—it is never effected but by a persevering resolution to act, to think for himself; to examine with rigour and impartiality the opinions he has adopted. . . .

The most important of our duties, then, is to seek means by which we may destroy delusions that can never do more than mislead us. The remedies for these evils must be sought for in Nature herself; it is only in the abundance of her resources, that we can rationally expect to find antidotes to the mischiefs brought upon us by an ill-directed, by an overpowering enthusiasm. It is time these remedies were sought; it is time to look the evil boldly in the face, to examine its foundations, to scrutinize its super-structure: reason, with its faithful guide experience, must attack in their entrenchments those prejudices to which the human race has but too long been the victim. For this purpose reason must be restored to its proper rank,—it must be rescued from the evil company with which it is associated. . . .

Truth speaks not to these perverse beings:—her voice can only be heard by generous minds accustomed to reflection, whose sensibilities make them lament the numberless calamities showered on the earth by political and religious tyranny—whose enlightened minds contemplate with horrour the immensity, the ponderosity of that series of misfortunes with which errour has in all ages overwhelmed mankind.

The *civilized man*, is he whom experience and social life have enabled to draw from nature the means of his own happiness; because he has learned to oppose resistance to those impulses he receives from exterior beings, when experience has taught him they would be injurious to his welfare.

The *enlightened man*, is man in his maturity, in his perfection; who is capable of pursuing his own happiness; because he has learned to examine, to think for himself, and not to take that for truth upon the authority of others, which experience has taught him examination will frequently prove erroneous. . . .

It necessarily results, that man in his researches ought always to fall back on experience, and natural philosophy: These are what he should consult in his religion—in his morals—in his legislation—in his political government—in the arts—in the sciences—in his pleasures—in his misfortunes. Experience teaches that Nature acts by simple, uniform, and invariable laws. It is by his senses man is bound to this universal Nature; it is by his senses he must penetrate her secrets; it is from his senses he must draw experience of her laws. Whenever, therefore, he either fails to acquire experience or quits its path, he stumbles into an abyss, his imagination leads him astray.

Prospectus for the Encyclopedia of Arts and Sciences
Denis Diderot

More than any other work, the Encyclopedia of Arts and Sciences, *edited by Denis Diderot (1713–1784) and Jean-le-Rond d'Alembert (1717–1783), epitomizes the Enlightenment. Written between 1745 and 1780, it presented to the public the sum of knowledge considered important by Enlightenment thinkers. The critical Enlightenment spirit underlying the* Encyclopedia *led traditional authorities to condemn it and to suppress it more than once. The following is an excerpt from the* Prospectus *that appeared in 1750, announcing the forthcoming* Encyclopedia. *The* Prospectus *was written by Diderot, a philosopher, novelist, and playwright who had already been in trouble with the authorities for his writings. The* Prospectus *apparently aroused widespread expectations; even before the first volume of the* Encyclopedia *appeared, more than a thousand orders for it had been received.*

> **Consider:** *What a reader could hope to gain by purchasing the* Encyclopedia *and how these hopes themselves reflect the spirit of the Enlightenment; how this selection from the* Prospectus *reflects the same ideas expressed by Kant and d'Holbach; how the Enlightenment as described here related to the scientific revolution of the seventeenth century.*

It cannot be denied that, since the revival of letters among us, we owe partly to dictionaries the general enlightenment that has spread in society and the germ of science that is gradually preparing men's minds for more profound knowledge. How valuable would it not be, then, to have a book of this kind that one could consult on all subjects and that would serve as much to guide those who have the courage to work at the instruction of others as to enlighten those who only instruct themselves!

This is one advantage we thought of, but it is not the only one. In condensing to dictionary form all that concerns the arts and sciences, it remained necessary to make people aware of the assistance they lend each other; to make use of this assistance to render principles more certain and their consequences clearer; to indicate the distant and close relationships of the beings that make up nature,

---

SOURCE: "The Encyclopedia Announced" from *Major Crises in Western Civilization, Volume II, 1745 to the Nuclear Age* by Richard W. Lyman and Lewis W. Spitz, copyright © 1965 by Harcourt Brace & Company and renewed 1993 by Richard W. Lyman and Lewis W. Spitz, reprinted by permission of the publisher.

which have occupied men; to show, by showing the interlacing both of roots and of branches, the impossibility of understanding thoroughly some parts of the whole without exploring many others; to produce a general picture of the efforts of the human spirit in all areas and in all centuries; to present these matters with clarity; to give to each the proper scope, and to prove, if possible, our epigraph by our success:. . . .

The majority of these works appeared during the last century and were not completely scorned. It was found that if they did not show much talent, they at least bore the marks of labor and of knowledge. But what would these encyclopedias mean to us? What progress have we not made since then in the arts and sciences? How many truths discovered today, which were not foreseen then? True philosophy was in its cradle; the geometry of infinity did not yet exist; experimental physics was just appearing; there was no dialectic at all; the laws of sound criticism were entirely unknown. Descartes, Boyle, Huyghens, Newton, Leibnitz, the Bernoullis, Locke, Bayle, Pascal, Corneille, Racine, Bourdaloue, Bossuet, etc., either had not yet been born or had not yet written. The spirit of research and competition did not motivate the scholars: another spirit, less fecund perhaps, but rarer, that of precision and method, had not yet conquered the various divisions of literature; and the academies, whose efforts have advanced the arts and sciences to such an extent, were not yet established. . . . At the end of this project you will find the tree of human knowledge, indicating the connection of ideas, which has directed us in this vast operation.

The Philosophe

Enlightenment thinkers often referred to themselves as "philosophes," which is technically the French word for philosophers. The term had a special meaning bound up with the spirit of the Enlightenment. This is dealt with directly in the following selection, "The Philosopher," from the Encyclopedia *It has traditionally been assumed that Diderot is the author of "The Philosopher," but it may have been written by another person, perhaps Du Marsais. In any case, it is an authoritative treatment of the topic according to Enlightenment precepts.*

> **Consider:** *The characteristics of the philosopher; how this compares to Kant's definition of enlightenment and d'Holbach's definition of a civilized or enlightened man; how a twentieth-century philosopher might differ with this definition of a philosopher.*

Other men make up their minds to act without thinking, nor are they conscious of the causes which move them, not even knowing that such exist. The philosopher,

Source: Merrick Whitcomb, ed., "French Philosophers of the Eighteenth Century," in *Translations and Reprints from the Original Sources of European History*, vol. VI, no. 1, ed. Department of History of the University of Pennsylvania (Philadelphia: University of Pennsylvania Press, 1898), pp. 21–23.

on the contrary, distinguishes the causes to what extent he may, often anticipates them, and knowingly surrenders himself to them. In this manner he avoids objects that may cause him sensations that are not conducive to his well being or his rational existence, and seeks those which may excite in him affections agreeable with the state in which he finds himself. Reason is in the estimation of the philosopher what grace is to the Christian. Grace determines the Christian's action; reason the philosopher's.

Other men are carried away by their passions, so that the acts which they produce do not proceed from reflection. These are the men who move in darkness; while the philosopher, even in his passions, moves only after reflection. He marches at night, but a torch goes on ahead.

The philosopher forms his principles upon an infinity of individual observations. The people adopt the principle without a thought of the observations which have produced it, believing that the maxim exists, so to speak, of itself; but the philosopher takes the maxim at its source, he examines its origin, he knows its real value, and only makes use of it, if it seems to him satisfactory.

Truth is not for the philosopher a mistress who vitiates his imagination, and whom he believes to find everywhere. He contents himself with being able to discover it wherever he may chance to find it. He does not confound it with its semblance; but takes for true that which is true, for false that which is false, for doubtful that which is doubtful, and for probable that which is only probable. He does more—and this is the great perfection of philosophy; that when he has no real grounds for passing judgment, he knows how to remain undetermined.

The world is full of persons of understanding, even of much understanding, who always pass judgment. They are guessing always, because it is guessing to pass judgment without knowing when one has proper grounds for judgment. They misjudge of the capacity of the human mind; they believe it is possible to know everything, and so they are ashamed not to be prepared to pass judgment, and they imagine that understanding consists in passing judgment. The philosopher believes that it consists in judging well: he is better pleased with himself when he has suspended the faculty of determining, than if he had determined before having acquired proper grounds for his decision.

°

The philosophic spirit is then a spirit of observation and of exactness, which refers everything to its true principles; but it is not the understanding alone which the philosopher cultivates; he carries further his attention and his labors.

Man is not a monster, made to live only at the bottom of the sea or in the depths of the forest; the very necessities of his life render intercourse with others necessary; and in whatsoever state we find him, his needs and his well-being lead him to live in society. To that reason demands of him that he should know, that he should study and that he should labor to acquire social qualities.

Our philosopher does not believe himself an exile in the world; he does not believe himself in the enemy's country; he wishes to enjoy, like a wise economist, the goods that nature offers him; he wishes to find his pleasure with others; and in order to find it, it is necessary to assist in producing it; so he seeks to harmonize with those with whom chance or his choice has determined he shall live; and he finds at the same time that which suits him: he is an honest man who wishes to please and render himself useful.

*

The philosopher is then an honest man, actuated in everything by reason, one who joins to the spirit of reflection and of accuracy the manners and qualities of society.

Philosophical Dictionary: The English Model
Voltaire

François Marie Arouet, who later adopted the name Voltaire (1694–1778), was certainly the most famous of the philosophes. Writing almost every type of literature, from drama and satire to history and essays, he exhibited most of the main elements of the Enlightenment. One of these was the philosophes' admiration for and idealization of England's political system. Voltaire gained familiarity with England during a three-year visit, from 1726 to 1729, and played an important role in popularizing the ideas of English scientists and the principles of the English political system. The following is an excerpt from his Philosophical Dictionary, *first published in 1764.*

> **Consider:** *What Voltaire admires about the English constitution; the implied criticism of the French political system; whether Voltaire idealizes the English system.*

The English constitution has, in fact, arrived at that point of excellence, in consequence of which all men are restored to those natural rights, which, in nearly all monarchies, they are deprived of. These rights are, entire liberty of person and property; freedom of the press; the right of being tried in all criminal cases by a jury of independent men—the right of being tried only according to the strict letter of the law; and the right of every man to profess, unmolested, what religion he chooses, while he renounces offices, which the members of the Anglican or established church alone can hold. These are denominated privileges. And, in truth, invaluable privileges they are in comparison with the usages of most other nations of the world! To be secure on lying down that you shall rise in possession of the same property with which you retired to rest; that you shall not be torn from the arms of your wife, and from your children, in the dead of night, to be thrown into a dungeon, or buried in exile in a desert; that, when rising from the bed of sleep, you will have the power of publishing all your thoughts; and that, if

---

SOURCE: Voltaire, *Philosophical Dictionary*, in Voltaire, *Works*, trans. W. F. Fleming (New York: E. R. Dumont, 1901), vol. 5, pp. 293–294.

you are accused of having either acted, spoken, or written wrongly, you can be tried only according to law. These privileges attach to every one who sets his foot on English ground. A foreigner enjoys perfect liberty to dispose of his property and person; and, if accused of any offence, he can demand that half the jury shall be composed of foreigners.

I will venture to assert, that, were the human race solemnly assembled for the purpose of making laws, such are the laws they would make for their security.

A Vindication of the Rights of Woman
Mary Wollstonecraft

While the Enlightenment was dominated by men, there were possibilities for active involvement by women. Several women played particularly important roles as patrons and intellectual contributors to the gatherings of philosophes and members of the upper-middle-class and aristocratic elite held in the salons of Paris and elsewhere. It was, however, far more difficult for a woman to publish serious essays in the Enlightenment tradition. Indeed, Enlightenment thinkers did little to change basic attitudes about the inferiority of women. One person who managed to do both was Mary Wollstonecraft (1759–1797), a British author who in 1792 published A Vindication of the Rights of Woman. *The book was a sharply reasoned attack against the oppression of women and an argument for educational change. In the following excerpt Wollstonecraft addresses the author of a proposed new constitution for France that, in her opinion, does not adequately deal with the rights of women.*

> **Consider:** *Why education is so central to her argument; the ways in which this argument reflects the methods and ideals of the Enlightenment.*

Contending for the rights of woman, my main argument is built on this simple principle, that if she be not prepared by education to become the companion of man, she will stop the progress of knowledge and virtue; for truth must be common to all, or it will be inefficacious with respect to its influence on general practice. And how can woman be expected to co-operate unless she knows why she ought to be virtuous? unless freedom strengthens her reason till she comprehends her duty, and sees in what manner it is connected with her real good. If children are to be educated to understand the true principle of patriotism, their mother must be a patriot; and the love of mankind, from which an orderly train of virtues spring, can only be produced by considering the moral and civil interest of mankind; but the education and situation of woman at present shuts her out from such investigations.

SOURCE: Mary Wollstonecraft, *The Rights of Woman* (London: J. M. Dent and Sons, Ltd., 1929), pp. 10–11.

In this work I have produced many arguments, which to me were conclusive, to prove that the prevailing notion respecting a sexual character was subversive of mortality, and I have contended, that to render the human body and mind more perfect, chastity must more universally prevail, and that chastity will never be respected in the male world till the person of a woman is not, as it were, idolised, when little virtue or sense embellish it with the grand traces of mental beauty, or the interesting simplicity of affection.

Consider, sir, dispassionately these observations, for a glimpse of this truth seemed to open before you when you observed, "that to see one-half of the human race excluded by the other from all participation of government was a political phenomenon, that, according to abstract principles, it was impossible to explain." If so, on what does your constitution rest? If the abstract rights of man will bear discussion and explanation, those of woman, by a parity of reasoning, will not shrink from the same test; though a different opinion prevails in this country, built on the very arguments which you use to justify the oppression of woman—prescription.

Consider—I address you as a legislator—whether, when men contend for their freedom, and to be allowed to judge for themselves respecting their own happiness, it be not inconsistent and unjust to subjugate women, even though you firmly believe that you are acting in the manner best calculated to promote their happiness? Who made man the exclusive judge, if woman partake with him of the gift of reason?

The Age of Reason: Deism
Thomas Paine

Many Enlightenment thinkers were strongly opposed to traditional religious institutions and ideas. Yet only a few went so far as to profess atheism. More typical was some form of deism, a belief in a God who created a rational universe with natural laws but who no longer intervened in the course of events. A good example of this belief is found in the following excerpt from Thomas Paine's Age of Reason *(1794). Paine (1737–1809) was an unusually international person. Born in England, he became an American patriot and later a member of the French Convention (1792–1793). His most famous works are* Common Sense *and* The Rights of Man, *in both of which he justifies revolution. In* The Age of Reason *Paine places himself within the tradition of Enlightenment thought and summarizes his religious views.*

> **Consider:** *Why Paine is so opposed to traditional religious institutions; how this opposition is consistent with other Enlightenment thought; how a sincere, sophisticated member of the Catholic Church might have responded to this.*

SOURCE: Moncure Daniel Conway, ed., *The Writings of Thomas Paine*, vol. IV (New York: G. P. Putnam's Sons, 1896), pp. 21–23.

As several of my colleagues, and others of my fellow-citizens of France, have given me the example of making their voluntary and individual profession of faith, I also will make mine; and I do this with all that sincerity and frankness with which the mind of man communicates with itself.

I believe in one God, and no more; and I hope for happiness beyond this life.

I believe the equality of man, and I believe that religious duties consist in doing justice, loving mercy, and endeavouring to make our fellow-creatures happy.

But, lest it should be supposed that I believe many other things in addition to these, I shall, in the progress of this work, declare the things I do not believe, and my reasons for not believing them.

I do not believe in the creed professed by the Jewish church, by the Roman church, by the Greek church, by the Turkish church, by the Protestant church, nor by any church that I know of. My own mind is my own church.

All national institutions of churches, whether Jewish, Christian, or Turkish, appear to me no other than human inventions set up to terrify and enslave mankind, and monopolize power and profit.

I do not mean by this declaration to condemn those who believe otherwise; they have the same right to their belief as I have to mine. But it is necessary to the happiness of man, that he be mentally faithful to himself. Infidelity does not consist in believing, or in disbelieving; it consists in professing to believe what he does not believe.

It is impossible to calculate the moral mischief, if I may so express it, that mental lying has produced in society. When a man has so far corrupted and prostituted the chastity of his mind, as to subscribe his professional belief to things he does not believe, he has prepared himself for the commission of every other crime. He takes up the trade of a priest for the sake of gain, and, in order to qualify himself for that trade, he begins with a perjury. Can we conceive anything more destructive to morality than this?

Soon after I had published the pamphlet *Common Sense*, in America, I saw the exceeding probability that a revolution in the system of government would be followed by a revolution in the system of religion. The adulterous connection of church and state, wherever it had taken place, whether Jewish, Christian, or Turkish, had so effectually prohibited, by pains and penalties, every discussion upon established creeds, and upon first principles of religion, that until the system of government should be changed, those subjects could not be brought fairly and openly before the world; but that whenever this should be done, a revolution in the system of religion would follow. Human inventions and priest-craft would be detected; and man would return to the pure, unmixed, and unadulterated belief of one God, and no more.

The Social Contract
Jean Jacques Rousseau

More than anyone else, Jean Jacques Rousseau (1712–1778) tested the outer limits of Enlightenment thought and went on to criticize its very foundations. Born in Geneva, he spent much of his life in France (mainly in Paris), where he became one of the philosophes who contributed to the Encyclopedia. *Yet he also undermined Enlightenment thought by holding that social institutions had corrupted people and that human beings in the state of nature were purer, freer, and happier than they were in modern civilization. This line of thought provided a foundation for the growth of Romanticism in the late eighteenth and early nineteenth centuries. Rousseau's most important political work was* The Social Contract *(1762), in which he argued for popular sovereignty. In the following selection from that work, Rousseau focuses on what he considers the fundamental argument of the book—the passage from the state of nature to the civil state by means of the social contract.*

> **Consider:** *Rousseau's solution to the main problem of* The Social Contract; *the advantages and disadvantages of the social contract; what characteristics of Enlightenment thought are reflected in this selection.*

"The problem is to find a form of association which will defend and protect with the whole common force the person and goods of each associate, and in which each, while uniting himself with all, may still obey himself alone, and remain as free as before." This is the fundamental problem of which *The Social Contract* provides the solution.

The clauses of this contract are so determined by the nature of the act that the slightest modification would make them vain and ineffective; so that, although they have perhaps never been formally set forth, they are everywhere the same and everywhere tacitly admitted and recognised, until, on the violation of the social compact, each regains his original rights and resumes his natural liberty, while losing the conventional liberty in favour of which he renounced it.

These clauses, properly understood, may be reduced to one—the total alienation of each associate, together with all his rights, to the whole community; for, in the first place, as each gives himself absolutely, the conditions are the same for all; and, this being so, no one has any interest in making them burdensome to others.

Moreover, the alienation being without reserve, the union is as perfect as it can be, and no associate has anything more to demand: for, if the individuals retained certain rights, as there would be no common superior to decide between them and the public, each, being on one point his own judge, would ask to be so on all; the state of nature would thus continue, and the association would necessarily become inoperative or tyrannical.

SOURCE: Jean Jacques Rousseau, *The Social Contract and Discourses* (London: J. M. Dent, Everyman Library, 1913), pp. 14–15, 18–19.

Finally, each man, in giving himself to all, gives himself to nobody; and as there is no associate over whom he does not acquire the same right as he yields others over himself, he gains on equivalent for everything he loses, and an increase of force for the preservation of what he has.

If then we discard from the social compact what is not of its essence, we shall find that it reduces itself to the following terms—

Each of us puts his person and all his power in common under the supreme direction of the general will, and, in our corporate capacity, we receive each member as an indivisible part of the whole.

✿

The passage from the state of nature to the civil state produces a very remarkable change in man, by substituting justice for instinct in his conduct, and giving his actions the morality they had formerly lacked. Then only, when the voice of duty takes the place of physical impulses and right of appetite, does man, who so far had considered only himself, find that he is forced to act on different principles, and to consult his reason before listening to his inclinations. Although, in this state, he deprives himself of some advantages which he got from nature, he gains in return others so great, his faculties are so stimulated and developed, his ideas so extended, his feelings so ennobled, and his whole soul so uplifted, that, did not the abuses of this new condition often degrade him below that which he left, he would be bound to bless continually the happy moment which took him from it for ever, and, instead of a stupid and unimaginative animal, made him an intelligent being and a man.

Let us draw up the whole account in terms easily commensurable. What man loses by the social contract is his natural liberty and an unlimited right to everything he tries to get and succeeds in getting; what he gains is civil liberty and the proprietorship of all he possesses. If we are to avoid mistake in weighing one against the other, we must clearly distinguish natural liberty, which is bounded only by the strength of the individual, from civil liberty, which is limited by the general will; and possession, which is merely the effect of force or the right of the first occupier, from property, which can be founded only on a positive title.

We might, over and above all this, add, to what man acquires in the civil state, moral liberty, which alone makes him truly master of himself; for the mere impulse of appetite is slavery, while obedience to a law which we prescribe to ourselves is liberty. But I have already said too much on this head, and the philosophical meaning of the word liberty does not now concern us.

VISUAL SOURCES

Experiment with an Air Pump
Joseph Wright

Few paintings provide a better image of the Enlightenment than Experiment with an Air Pump *(1768) by the British artist Joseph Wright. The experiment takes place in the center of the picture; its apparent success is evidenced by the dead bird inside a closed glass bowl from which the air has been pumped out. The informally dressed experimenter is carefully observing his work. Around him are members of his family and some well-dressed friends.*

The form and content of this picture symbolize the Enlightenment. A small source of light is sufficient to enlighten humanity and reveal the laws of nature. Science is not just for specialists but something amateurs can understand and practice to obtain practical results. That it is a British painting is particularly significant, for the English led in developing useful machines and were identified as having a more pragmatic approach to sci-

Photo 4-1

© The Tate Gallery, London

*ence and ideas than other peoples. The painting also reveals customary images of the
sexes: the experimenter boldly forging on while to his left a friend or associate calmly
explains what is happening to a woman and her daughter, whose sensibilities are as appropriately fragile as the dying bird—the main object of their concern.*

> **Consider:** *Any common themes in this painting and the documents by Kant,
> d'Holbach, and Diderot.*

Propaganda and the Enlightened Monarch
Joseph II of Austria

*Emperor Joseph II of Austria (1765–1790) is generally thought to have been one of the
most enlightened eighteenth-century kings and indeed considered himself to be an enlightened monarch. Some of what this meant is indicated by this picture Joseph II had painted
of himself. It shows him plowing a field with a farmer (to his left) and members of his
court (to his right). To make sure he and his office were recognizable to viewers, Joseph
remained appropriately dressed, including wearing his powdered wig. This scene also*

Photo 4-2

Courtesy, Austrian Press & Information Service

Source: "Letters of Joseph II," in *The Pamphleteer*, vol. XIX (London, 1882), pp. 282, 288–290.

affirms the growing interest in agricultural improvements during the eighteenth century, particularly among aristocratic innovators. Joseph II tells of some of his hopes in a number of letters excerpted here.

Consider: *What there was about this scene and these letters that could be considered enlightened; any inconsistencies with these statements and the reality of being a monarch; how Kant might have viewed Joseph II.*

Mr. Vice-Chancellor—The present system of taxation in my dominions, and the inequality of the taxes which are imposed on the nation, form a subject too important to escape my attention. I have discovered that the principles on which it is founded are unsound, and have become injurious to the industry of the peasant; that there is neither equality, nor equity, between the hereditary provinces with each other, nor between individual proprietors, and therefore it can no longer continue.

With this view I give you the necessary orders to introduce a new system of taxation, by which the contribution, requisite for the wants of the state, may be effected without augmenting the present taxes, and the industry of the peasant, at the same time, be freed from all impediments.

❀

Since my accession to the throne, I have ever been anxious to conquer the prejudices against my station, and have taken pains to gain the confidence of my people; I have several times since given proof, that the welfare of my subjects is my passion; that to satisfy it, I shun neither labor, nor trouble, nor even vexations, and reflect well on the means which are likely to promote my views; and yet in my reforms, I everywhere find opposition from people, of whom I least expect it.

❀

Sir,—Till now the Protestant religion has been opposed in my states; its adherents have been treated like foreigners; civil rights, possession of estates, titles, and appointments, all were refused them.

I determined from the very commencement of my reign to adorn my diadem with the love of my people, to act in the administration of affairs according to just, impartial, and liberal principles; consequently, I granted toleration, and removed the yoke which had oppressed the protestants for centuries.

Fanaticism shall in future be known in my states only by the contempt I have for it; nobody shall any longer be exposed to hardships on account of his creed; no man shall be compelled in future to profess the religion of the state, if it be contrary to his persuasion, and if he have other ideas of the right way of insuring blessedness.

In future my Empire shall not be the scene of abominable intolerance. Fortunately no sacrifices like those of Calas and Sirven have ever disgraced any reign in this country.

If, in former times, the will of the monarch furnished opportunities for injustice, if the limits of executive power were exceeded, and private hatred acted her part, I can only pity those monarchs who were nothing but kings.

Tolerance is an effect of that beneficient increase of knowledge which now enlightens Europe, and which is owing to philosophy and the efforts of great men; it is a convincing proof of the improvement of the human mind, which has boldly reopened a road through the dominions of superstition, which was trodden centuries ago by Zoroaster and Confucius, and which, fortunately for mankind, has now become the highway of monarchs. Adieu!

SECONDARY SOURCES

The Age of Enlightenment
Lester G. Crocker

The Enlightenment owes its substance to the thought of a relatively small group of eighteenth-century philosophes who came from many countries but were centered in France. Although they often argued among themselves, there was a set of approaches and propositions upon which most of them agreed. In the following selection Lester Crocker analyzes what unified the philosophes.

> **Consider:** *How the primary sources support or contradict Crocker's interpretations; why the philosophes were so concerned with Christianity and the Church; the elements of this outlook that make the most sense to you for today's world.*

What we call the Enlightenment gradually took shape in individual minds, over several generations, before it became conscious of itself as a movement during the late 1740's. The principal galvanizing forces were Voltaire's ceaseless efforts in propagandizing and in whipping up "party" spirit, and the prolonged battle over the *Encyclopédie*, which served to unite many of the *philosophes*, as we call the writers who were engaged in furthering the goals of the Enlightenment. The *philosophes* were more often than not at odds among themselves on the answers they proposed to various questions or problems. Their solidarity lay in their awareness of a common foe—the *status quo*, and those who supported it, particularly Christianity and the Church. It lay also in their agreement on what the questions and problems were. The *philosophes* held certain ideas and aims in common.

SOURCE: Excerpted from *The Age of Enlightenment*, pp. 2–3, by Lester G. Crocker. Copyright © 1969 by Lester G. Crocker. Reprinted by permission of HarperCollins Publishers, Inc.

Among these were religious tolerance (belief in toleration of all ideas as well as personal tolerance was not universal among the *philosophes*); the conviction that human life can be improved through the improvement of society, since men are (more or less) shaped by laws and government; the idea that the enlightened group should influence those who govern, both directly and through public opinion. Their stance rested on a base of secularism and humanism. Regardless of their varying religious beliefs, all the *philosophes* held that the proper business (if there was any) of organized churches was the salvation of souls. Science, government, economic policy, even (many thought) moral values and personal morality had to be freed from the dead hand of Christian authority. The Enlightenment was for unfettered critical reason, for social experience to indicate what course men should take in meeting the challenges involved in ameliorating human affairs. God, if he existed, had no influence on these—Bayle had demonstrated that, before the end of the seventeenth century. To the *philosophes*, churches were what we would now call "power groups" and, like all such groups, interested primarily in themselves. Revealed religions were fantasies or downright frauds. Christianity, especially, was hostile to the demands of human nature and pretended (the critics claimed) to direct men away from their self-interest in this life to a mythical paradise in a nonexistent life beyond. Reaction against the Christian world view and religious control of thought had been the very origin of the freethinking (*libertin*) movement in the seventeenth century. The *philosophes* were united by the conviction, above all else, that man must control his own destiny for the sole purpose of a better life on earth and that he must do everything possible to enlarge that control.

The Heavenly City of the Eighteenth-Century Philosophers
Carl L. Becker

Another point of interpretive division among historians of the Enlightenment centers on how modern and secular the philosophes were. Nineteenth- and early-twentieth-century historians argued that the philosophes were more modern than medieval and indeed drew more from the Classical pagan world than from the medieval world. This view still predominates among historians of the period. A famous challenge to this view was made more than sixty years ago by Cornell historian Carl Becker. His book, The Heavenly City of the Eighteenth-Century Philosophers *(1932), became the most influential book on the subject, although today it is no longer as popular as it once was. In the following selection from this work, Becker presents the substance of his thesis.*

SOURCE: Carl L. Becker, *The Heavenly City of the Eighteenth-Century Philosophers*. Reprinted by permission of Yale University Press (New Haven, Conn., 1932), pp. 29–31, 102–103.

Consider: *The ways in which the philosophes were more medieval than modern; the support Becker offers for his argument that there was much Christian philosophy in the philosophes' writings; how Kant would react to Becker's interpretation.*

We are accustomed to think of the eighteenth century as essentially modern in its temper. Certainly, the *Philosophes* themselves made a great point of having renounced the superstition and hocus-pocus of medieval Christian thought, and we have usually been willing to take them at their word. Surely, we say, the eighteenth century was preëminently the age of reason, surely the *Philosophes* were a skeptical lot, atheists in effect if not by profession, addicted to science and the scientific method, always out to crush the infamous, valiant defenders of liberty, equality, fraternity, freedom of speech, and what you will. All very true. And yet I think the *Philosophes* were nearer the Middle Ages, less emancipated from the preconceptions of medieval Christian thought, than they quite realized or we have commonly supposed. . . .

But, if we examine the foundations of their faith, we find that at every turn the *Philosophes* betray their debt to medieval thought without being aware of it. They denounced Christian philosophy, but rather too much, after the manner of those who are but half emancipated from the "superstitions" they scorn. They had put off the fear of God, but maintained a respectful attitude toward the Deity. They ridiculed the idea that the universe had been created in six days, but still believed it to be a beautifully articulated machine designed by the Supreme Being according to a rational plan as an abiding place for mankind. The Garden of Eden was for them a myth, no doubt, but they looked enviously back to the golden age of Roman virtue, or across the waters to the unspoiled innocence of an Arcadian civilization that flourished in Pennsylvania. They renounced the authority of church and Bible, but exhibited a naïve faith in the authority of nature and reason. They scorned metaphysics, but were proud to be called philosophers. They dismantled heaven, somewhat prematurely it seems, since they retained their faith in the immortality of the soul. They courageously discussed atheism, but not before the servants. They defended toleration valiantly, but could with difficulty tolerate priests. They denied that miracles ever happened, but believed in the perfectibility of the human race. We feel that these Philosophers were at once too credulous and too skeptical. They were the victims of common sense. In spite of their rationalism and their humane sympathies, in spite of their aversion to hocus-pocus and enthusiasm and dim perspectives, in spite of their skepticism, their engaging cynicism, their brave youthful blasphemies and talk of hanging the last king in the entrails of the last priest—in spite of all of it, there is more of the Christian philosophy in the writings of the *Philosophes* than has yet been dreamt of in our histories.

Women in the Salons

Bonnie S. Anderson and
Judith P. Zinsser

As with the Renaissance and Scientific Revolution, the central figures of the Enlightenment were men. However, some women did directly participate as writers, and perhaps even more importantly, they participated as salonières—*organizers of gatherings in the salons of homes where Enlightenment figures mingled with women and men of the social and cultural elite. Did the men of the Enlightenment try to change traditional views of women in the same way they tried to change traditional views about men and human nature? In the following selection Bonnie S. Anderson and Judith P. Zinsser address this question.*

> **Consider:** *Why, according to Anderson and Zinsser, there was no Enlightenment for women; ways in which the Enlightenment, in the long run, might have bene-fited women.*

. . . Parisian women established the institution of the salon by the last quarter of the seventeenth century. Aspiring hostesses competed to attract the talented, the witty, and the powerful to their homes. Outside the powerful French court and frequently in opposition to it, these new social circles offered women a new possibility: that of being a salonière, who by her graciousness and skill enabled conversation to flourish, artists to find patrons, and aristocrats to be amused. As a salonière, a woman brought the circles of power into her home. In the environment she created, she could help or hinder not only artistic and literary reputations, but political policies as well. The financial remedies for France's economy were debated in the salons; the king's choices of ministers were strongly influenced by the backing of powerful salonières. Salonières were privy to court secrets; salons were frequented by statesmen and ambassadors as well as intellectuals and artists. Salonières could make or break careers and often provided havens for new political philosophies and the new political opposition to the monarchy. . . .

In the salon, a woman could meet and marry a man of superior social rank or wealth. In the salon, a woman of enterprise could make her way by attracting the famous. The salon became the base of influential women who swayed kings, governments, political opinion, and literary and artistic taste. . . .

Rational conversation, sociability between women and men, delight in the pleasures of this world are the hallmarks of Enlightenment culture. The men who mingled with the Bluestockings and frequented the salons were the men who produced the Enlightenment. It is a tragedy for women that these men, who were aided, sponsored, and lionized by the salonières, produced—with very few exceptions—art and writing which either ignored women completely or upheld the most

---

Source: Excerpts from *A History of Their Own*, vol. II, by Bonnie Anderson and Judith Zinsser. Copyright © 1988 by Harper & Row, Publishers, Inc. Reprinted by permission of Harper & Row, Publishers, Inc.

traditional views of womanhood. Just as there was no Renaissance or Scientific Revolution for women, in the sense that the goals and ideals of those movements were perceived as applicable only to men, so there was no Enlightenment for women. Enlightenment thinkers questioned all the traditional limits on men—and indeed challenged the validity of tradition itself. They championed the rights of commoners, the rights of citizens, the rights of slaves, Jews, Indians, and children, but not those of women. Instead, often at great cost to their own logic and rationality, they continued to reaffirm the most ancient inherited traditions about women: that they were inferior to men in the crucial faculties of reason and ethics and so should be subordinated to men. In philosophy and in art, men of the Enlightenment upheld the traditional ideal of woman: silent, obedient, subservient, modest, and chaste. The salonière—witty, independent, powerful, well-read, and sometimes libertine—was condemned and mocked. A few Enlightenment thinkers did question and even reject subordinating traditions about women. But those who argued for a larger role for women—like the Englishwoman Mary Wollstonecraft in her *Vindication of the Rights of Woman* (1792), the French Marquis de Condorcet in his *Admission of Women to Civic Rights* (1790), the German Theodor von Hippel in his *On the Civic Improvement of Women* (1792), the Spaniard Josefa Amar y Borbón in her *Discourse in Defense of Women's Talent and Their Capacity for Government and Other Positions Held by Men* (1786)—prompted outrage and then were forgotten. Instead, most philosophers and writers reiterated the most limiting traditions of European culture regarding women, often in works which condemned traditional behavior for men.

The Problem of Enlightened Absolutism
H. M. Scott

Historians have long debated exactly how much the Enlightenment influenced monarchs of the time. Traditionally, there has been considerable acceptance of the view that monarchs such as Joseph II of Austria and Frederick II of Prussia were enlightened. In recent decades this view was seriously narrowed and questioned to the point where many historians felt that enlightened despotism and enlightened absolutism were no longer terms that could usefully be applied to these eighteenth-century monarchs. More recently, other historians have come to the conclusion that the term is useful. In the following selection H. M. Scott surveys this controversy and concludes that enlightened absolutism was real.

Consider: *The characteristics of enlightened absolutism; why Joseph II (see the visual sources in this chapter) and Frederick II (see the primary sources in the*

SOURCE: H. M. Scott, "The Problem of Enlightened Absolutism," in *Enlightened Absolutism: Reform and Reformers in Late Eighteenth-Century Europe,* ed. H. M. Scott. © 1990 H. M. Scott; published in the United States of America by the University of Michigan Press.

preceding chapter) might be considered enlightened monarchs; how enlightened ab-
solutism differs from seventeenth-century absolutism (see sources in Chapter One).

Few historical concepts have had their obituaries written more frequently than
enlightened absolutism, yet so obstinately refuse to die. In its classical form, the
theory of enlightened absolutism asserted that during the second half of the
eighteenth century the domestic policies of most European states were influenced
and even dictated by the ideas of the Enlightenment and were therefore sharply
distinguished from what had gone before. Government became a systematic and
rational attempt to apply the best recent knowledge to the task of ruling, while
the main aim of internal policy came to be the improvement of educational
opportunities, social conditions and economic life. . . .

Together, rulers and their influential advisers carried through a wide-ranging
series of reforms, the principal inspiration for which was the political philosophy
of the Enlightenment. Administrations and legal and fiscal systems were modern-
ised; commercial and economic development was encouraged; efforts were made
to improve agriculture and even to abolish the institution of serfdom; state control
over the Catholic Church was extended and a determined attempt was made to
channel some of its wealth into increased and improved pastoral activity; teaching
in universities was brought up to date; and the provision of secondary and primary
education was vastly increased. These reforms, and the amount of success
achieved, were remarkable in the context of the later eighteenth century, and the
sense of social responsibility which lay behind many of these measures was also
novel and striking. Though the precise policies adopted varied from country to
country, a common explanation was found in the movement of ideas known as
the European Enlightenment, which was at its peak exactly when the policies of
enlightened absolutism were being pursued: the middle decades of the eighteenth
century until the outbreak of the French Revolution in 1789.

During the past two generations, the historical reputation of enlightened absolutism has undergone remarkable vicissitudes, above all in Anglo-American
historical writing about later eighteenth-century Europe. It first rose to prominence during the 1930s, and for a generation thereafter was widely accepted
among historians. By the 1960s, however, the tide was beginning to turn and the
sceptics, who saw only the conventional aims of state-building in these policies
and regarded the enlightened professions which accompanied them as mere win-
dow-dressing, were gaining the ascendant. The critics of enlightened absolutism
argued that few monarchs, and certainly none of the major rulers, could afford to
adhere blindly to an enlightened blueprint and ignore, or even neglect, the demands of self-defence. The competitive states-system within which the great
powers operated required large and powerful armies and administrative and fiscal
systems to support them. These priorities pre-empted much of the scope for
enlightened reform. Above all, critics of the notion of enlightened absolutism
argued that the success of these initiatives was often incomplete and could, at
times, be very limited indeed. . . .

During the 1970s, the widespread assumption that enlightened absolutism was a fiction came to be challenged by a growing number of monographic studies of particular countries which make clear that the reforms of this period were influenced by ideas and were not simply another stage in the growth of the absolutist state. This trend has increased during the 1980s. . . .

[I]t has become clear that enlightened absolutism is not an idea in the mind of historians. The remarkable extent and the considerable success of the reforming initiatives is now established beyond question.

Chapter Questions

1. What core of ideas and attitudes most clearly connects Enlightenment thinkers as revealed in these sources? How do these ideas relate to eighteenth-century society and institutions?

2. What policies would an eighteenth-century ruler have to pursue to fit to the greatest degree the ideas and assumptions of Enlightenment thinkers? What hindrances were faced by monarchs who wanted to be more enlightened?

3. What ideas and attitudes of Enlightenment thinkers do you think remain valid for the problems facing today's world? What Enlightenment ideas and attitudes no longer seem valid or appropriate?

4. In what ways do the sources support the argument that together, the Scientific Revolution and the Enlightenment constitute a single intellectual revolution of great long-term significance?

II

THE NINETEENTH CENTURY

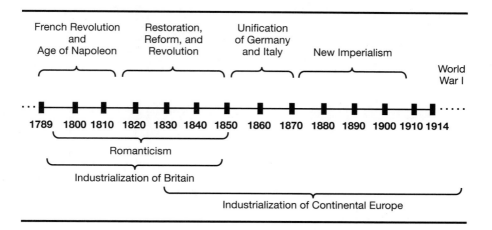

| French Revolution and Age of Napoleon | Restoration, Reform, and Revolution | Unification of Germany and Italy | New Imperialism | World War I |

1789 1800 1810 1820 1830 1840 1850 1860 1870 1880 1890 1900 1910 1914

Romanticism

Industrialization of Britain

Industrialization of Continental Europe

CHAPTER FIVE

The French Revolution

In 1789 the French Revolution ended the relative political and social stability of the Ancien Régime. This, and the earlier American Revolution, led to political and social changes that swept through Western civilization in the nineteenth and twentieth centuries.

Although the causes of the French Revolution are deep and controversial, most agree it was precipitated by financial problems that led Louis XVI to call a meeting of an old representative institution, the Estates General, in 1789. A struggle for power soon developed between a resurgent aristocracy and a rising middle class, both demanding support from the king. In an environment where peasants were turning against the aristocracy in the countryside and crowds were resorting to violence in Paris, the king managed to alienate both sides. Revolutionary legislation soon followed. By 1792 France was a constitutional monarchy, feudalism was abolished, liberal principles echoing Enlightenment thought were formally recognized, Church lands were confiscated, and government administration was reorganized. The country was at war internally with counterrevolutionary forces and externally with much of the rest of Europe.

A second revolution in 1792 set France on a more radical course. Louis XVI was executed, and the government was declared a republic. Real power rested in the hands of the small Committee of Public Safety, which attacked internal dissent through the Reign of Terror and external wars through national mobilization. The period ended with a return to a more moderate course in 1794 and 1795, known as Thermidorian Reaction. With power in the hands of the well-to-do middle class, an uneasy balance was maintained between forces clamoring for more radical policies and those wishing to return the monarchy until 1799, when Napoleon Bonaparte rose to power by means of a *coup d'état*.

Historians are fascinated by revolutions, for change is unusually rapid and dramatic. They are particularly interested in the causes of revolutions. In this chapter several primary documents address questions related to the causes of the French Revolution. What were some early signs of revolutionary discontent? What complaints were voiced by the middle class and by the commoners—the Third Estate? How did leaders of this Third Estate see themselves? Related secondary documents explore some of the interpretive debates over the revolution: Was this mainly a social revolution? What was the influence of politics on the French Revolution? Other sources examine the course and effects of the French Revolution. What happened is of particular importance, since the French Revolution was seen as a model for other

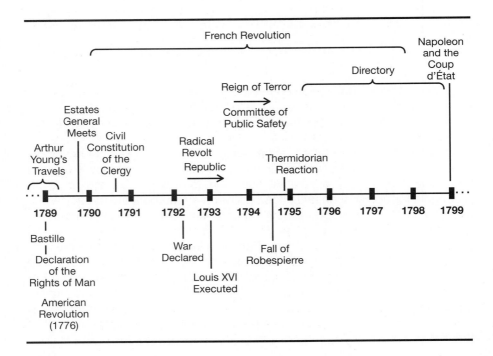

revolutions and hoped-for revolutions. What were the main changes enacted during the revolution? How can we explain the most radical phase—the Reign of Terror? What role did women play in revolutionary events? What part did nationalism play in revolutionary developments?

In short, the selections should provide broad insights into the nature and significance of the French Revolution, which more than any other event marks a dividing line between the Early Modern and the Modern eras of Western civilization.

PRIMARY SOURCES

Travels in France: Signs of Revolution
Arthur Young

In one sense, the French Revolution came as a great surprise. One of the last places people might have expected a revolution to occur was in a country so advanced and with such a stable monarchy as France. Yet to some sensitive observers of the time, the signs of revolution were at hand during the late 1780s. One of these observers was Arthur Young (1741–1820), a British farmer and diarist, best known for his writings on agricultural subjects. Between 1787 and 1789 he traveled extensively throughout France, keeping a diary of his experiences. In the following selection from that diary, Young notes deep dissatisfactions among the French.

> **Consider:** *The problems and dissatisfactions that gave the French a sense of impending revolution; the specific problems that seemed most likely to lead to a revolutionary crisis and the steps that might have been taken to avoid such a crisis; how Young felt about these problems and dissatisfactions.*

PARIS, OCTOBER 17, 1787

One opinion pervaded the whole company, that they are on the eve of some great revolution in the government: that every thing points to it: the confusion in the finances great; with a *deficit* impossible to provide for without the states-general of the kingdom, yet no ideas formed of what would be the consequence of their

SOURCE: Arthur Young, *Arthur Young's Travels in France During the Years 1787, 1788, 1789,* 4th ed., ed. Miss Betham-Edwards (London: Bell, 1892), pp. 97–98, 124, 134.

meeting: no minister existing, or to be looked to in or out of power, with such decisive talents as to promise any other remedy than palliative ones: a prince on the throne, with excellent dispositions, but without the resources of a mind that could govern in such a moment without ministers: a court buried in pleasure and dissipation; and adding to the distress, instead of endeavouring to be placed in a more independent situation: a great ferment amongst all ranks of men, who are eager for some change, without knowing what to look to, or to hope for: and a strong leaven of liberty, increasing every hour since the American revolution; altogether form a combination of circumstances that promise e'er long to ferment into motion, if some master hand, of very superior talents, and inflexible courage, is not found at the helm to guide events, instead of being driven by them. It is very remarkable, that such conversation never occurs, but a bankruptcy is a topic: the curious question on which is, *would a bankruptcy occasion a civil war, and a total overthrow of the government?* These answers that I have received to this question, appear to be just: such a measure, conducted by a man of abilities, vigour, and firmness, would certainly not occasion either one or the other. But the same measure, attempted by a man of a different character, might possibly do both. All agree, that the states of the kingdom cannot assemble without more liberty being the consequence; but I meet with so few men that have any just ideas of freedom, that I question much the species of this new liberty that is to arise. They know not how to value the privileges of THE PEOPLE: as to the nobility and the clergy, if a revolution added any thing to their scale, I think it would do more mischief than good. . . .

RENNES, SEPTEMBER 2, 1788

The discontents of the people have been double, first on account of the high price of bread, and secondly for the banishment of the parliament. The former cause is natural enough, but why the people should love their parliament was what I could not understand, since the members, as well as of the states, are all noble, and the distinction between the *noblesse* and *roturiers* no where stronger, more offensive, or more abominable than in Bretagne. They assured me, however, that the populace have been blown up to violence by every art of deception, and even by money distributed for that purpose. The commotions rose to such a height before the camp was established, that the troops here were utterly unable to keep the peace. . . .

NANTES, SEPTEMBER 22, 1788

Nantes is as *enflammé* in the cause of liberty, as any town in France can be; the conversations I witnessed here, prove how great a change is effected in the minds of the French, nor do I believe it will be possible for the present government to last half a century longer, unless the clearest and most decided talents are at the helm. The American revolution has laid the foundation of another in France, if government does not take care of itself.

The Cahiers: Discontents
of the Third Estate

Pressured by discontent and financial problems, Louis XVI called for a meeting of the Estates General in 1789. This representative institution, which had not met for 175 years, reflected the traditional formal divisions in French society: the First Estate, the clergy; the Second Estate, the nobility; and the Third Estate, all the rest from banker and lawyer to peasant. In anticipation of the meeting of the Estates General, the king requested and received cahiers, *lists of grievances drawn up by local groups of each of the three Estates. These* cahiers *have provided historians with an unusually rich source of materials revealing what was bothering people just before the outbreak of the revolution in 1789. The following is an excerpt from a* cahier *from the Third Estate in Carcassonne.*

Consider: *How these grievances of the Third Estate compare to the grievances noted by Young; why these grievances might be revolutionary; the ways in which these grievances are peculiar to the Third Estate and not shared by the First and Second Estates.*

8. Among these rights the following should be especially noted: the nation should hereafter be subject only to such laws and taxes as it shall itself freely ratify.

9. The meetings of the Estates General of the kingdom should be fixed for definite periods, and the subsidies judged necessary for the support of the state and the public service should be noted for no longer a period than to the close of the year in which the next meeting of the Estates General is to occur.

10. In order to assure to the third estate the influence to which it is entitled in view of the number of its members, the amount of its contributions to the public treasury, and the manifold interests which it has to defend or promote in the national assemblies, its votes in the assembly should be taken and counted by head.

11. No order, corporation, or individual citizen may lay claim to any pecuniary exemptions. . . . All taxes should be assessed on the same system throughout the nation.

12. The due exacted from commoners holding fiefs should be abolished, and also the general or particular regulations which exclude members of the third estate from certain positions, offices, and ranks which have hitherto been bestowed on nobles either for life or hereditarily. A law should be passed declaring members of the third estate qualified to fill all such offices for which they are judged to be personally fitted.

13. Since individual liberty is intimately associated with national liberty, his

---

SOURCE: "Cahier of the Grievances, Complaints, and Protests of the Electoral District of Carcassonne. . . ." From James Harvey Robinson, ed., *Readings in European History*, vol. II (Boston: Ginn, 1904), pp. 399–400.

Majesty is hereby petitioned not to permit that it be hereafter interfered with by arbitrary orders for imprisonment. . . .

14. Freedom should be granted also to the press, which should however be subjected, by means of strict regulations, to the principles of religion, morality, and public decency. . . .

What Is the Third Estate?
Emmanuel Joseph Sieyès

Before the Estates General met, issues arose among the Estates, particularly over whether the combined First and Second Estates should be able to hold the preponderance of power when the Estates General met. One of the most wide-ranging attacks on the privileged orders and assertion of Third Estate rights came from Emmanuel Joseph Sieyès (1748–1836). A clergyman strongly influenced by Enlightenment ideas, Sieyès was eventually elected as a representative of the Third Estate and played an active role in events throughout the revolutionary and Napoleonic periods. The following is a selection from his pamphlet, What Is the Third Estate?, *which was published in January 1789 and gained quick popularity.*

> **Consider:** *The basis for the attack by Sieyès on the nobility; why members of the bourgeoisie might find this pamphlet very appealing; how the tone and content of this pamphlet compare with the* cahier.

It suffices here to have made it clear that the pretended utility of a privileged order for the public service is nothing more than a chimera; that with it all that which is burdensome in this service is performed by the Third Estate; that without it the superior places would be infinitely better filled; that they naturally ought to be the lot and the recompense of ability and recognized services, and that if privileged persons have come to usurp all the lucrative and honorable posts, it is a hateful injustice to the rank and file of citizens and at the same time a treason to the public weal.

Who then shall dare to say that the Third Estate has not within itself all that is necessary for the formation of a complete nation? It is the strong and robust man who has one arm still shackled. If the privileged order should be abolished, the nation would be nothing less, but something more. Therefore, what is the Third Estate? Everything; but an everything shackled and oppressed. What would it be without the privileged order? Everything, but an everything free and flourishing. Nothing can succeed without it, everything would be infinitely better without the others. . . .

Source: From Merrick Whitcomb, ed., "French Philosophers of the Eighteenth Century," in *Translations and Reprints from the Original Sources of European History*, vol. VI, no. 1, ed. Department of History of the University of Pennsylvania (Philadelphia: University of Pennsylvania Press, 1898), pp. 34–35.

What is a nation? A body of associates, living under a common law, and represented by the same legislature, etc.

Is it not evident that the noble order has privileges and expenditures which it dares to call its rights, but which are apart from the rights of the great body of citizens? It departs there from the common order, from the common law. So its civil rights make of it an isolated people in the midst of the great nation. This is truly *imperium in imperio.*

In regard to its political rights, these also it exercises apart. It has its special representatives, which are not charged with securing the interests of the people. The body of its deputies sit apart; and when it is assembled in the same hall with the deputies of simple citizens, it is none the less true that its representation is essentially distinct and separate; it is a stranger to the nation, in the first place, by its origin, since its commission is not derived from the people; then by its object, which consists of defending not the general, but the particular interest.

The Third Estate embraces then all that which belongs to the nation; and all that which is not the Third Estate, cannot be regarded as being of the nation. What is the Third Estate? It is the whole.

Revolutionary Legislation: Abolition of the Feudal System

During the summer of 1789, France was swept with a variety of revolutionary activities. The Third Estate had successfully formed the National Assembly. On July 14 a mob had stormed the Bastille, an act that symbolized a violent tearing down of the Ancien Régime and the beginning of the popular revolution. In the countryside the peasantry rose against the nobility. Faced with these pressures, elements of the nobility in the National Assembly moved on August 4 and 5 to abolish their own feudal rights and privileges. In sum, these laws constituted a formal repudiation of the feudal system and many of the institutions of the Ancien Régime. The following selection comes from that legislation.

Consider: *The extent to which these measures satisfied the grievances of the Third Estate as expressed in the* cahier *and the pamphlet by Sieyès; why members of the nobility proposed and supported these measures themselves; whether these measures should be interpreted as a repudiation of the monarchy as an institution or specifically of Louis XVI as the king.*

ARTICLE I. The National Assembly hereby completely abolishes the feudal system. It decrees that, among the existing rights and dues, . . . all those originating in or

---

SOURCE: From James Harvey Robinson, ed., "The French Revolution, 1789–1791," in *Translations and Reprints from the Original Sources of European History*, vol. I, no. 5, ed. Department of History of the University of Pennsylvania (Philadelphia: University of Pennsylvania Press, 1898), pp. 2–5.

representing real or personal serfdom or personal servitude, shall be abolished without indemnification.

*

IV. All manorial courts are hereby suppressed without indemnification. . . .

V. Tithes of every description, as well as the dues which have been substituted for them . . . are abolished, on condition, however, that some other method be devised to provide for the expenses of divine worship, the support of the officiating clergy, for the assistance of the poor, for repairs and rebuilding of churches and parsonages, and for the maintenance of all institutions, seminaries, schools, academies, asylums, and organizations to which the present funds are devoted.

*

VII. The sale of judicial and municipal offices shall be suppressed forthwith. Justice shall be dispensed *gratis*.

*

IX. Pecuniary privileges, personal or real, in the payment of taxes are abolished forever. Taxes shall be collected from all the citizens, and from all property, in the same manner and in the same form. . . .

X. . . . All the peculiar privileges, pecuniary or otherwise, of the provinces, principalities, districts, cantons, cities and communes, are once for all abolished and are absorbed into the law common to all Frenchmen.

XI. All citizens, without distinction of birth, are eligible to any office or dignity, whether ecclesiastical, civil or military; and no profession shall imply any derogation.

*

XVII. The National Assembly solemnly proclaims the King, Louis XVI, the *Restorer of French Liberty*.

XVIII. The National Assembly shall present itself in a body before the King, in order to submit to him the decrees which have just been passed, to tender to him the tokens of its most respectful gratitude. . . .

XIX. The National Assembly shall consider, immediately after the constitution, the drawing up of the laws necessary for the development of the principles which it has laid down in the present decree.

The Declaration of the Rights of Man and Citizen

No document better summarizes the ideals underlying the French Revolution than The Declaration of the Rights of Man and Citizen. *After an extended discussion, this document was passed by the National Assembly on August 27, 1789; later a revised version of it was incorporated into the Constitution of 1791. Its provisions are a combination of general statements about human rights and specific statements about what the government should and should not do. This document corresponds to the American* Declaration of Independence. *It is also viewed more broadly as containing the general principles for democratic revolutions in the eighteenth and nineteenth centuries.*

> **Consider:** *How this document reflects ideals of the Enlightenment; at which social groups this document was aimed; who would suffer most from or be most infuriated by its provisions; the ways in which this document is inconsistent with monarchical government; how a monarch might retain meaningful powers while still conforming to this document.*

The representatives of the French people, organized as a National Assembly, believing that the ignorance, neglect or contempt of the rights of man are the sole cause of public calamities and of the corruption of governments, have determined to set forth in a solemn declaration the natural, inalienable and sacred rights of man, in order that this declaration, being constantly before all the members of the social body, shall remind them continually of their rights and duties; in order that the acts of the legislative power, as well as those of the executive power, may be compared at any moment with the ends of all political institutions and may thus be more respected; and, lastly, in order that the grievances of the citizens, based hereafter upon simple and incontestable principles, shall tend to the maintenance of the constitution and redound to the happiness of all. Therefore the National Assembly recognizes and proclaims, in the presence and under the auspices of the Supreme Being, the following rights of man and of the citizen:—

ARTICLE 1. Men are born and remain free and equal in rights. Social distinctions may only be founded upon the general good.

2. The aim of all political association is the preservation of the natural and imprescriptible rights of man. These rights are liberty, property, security and resistance to oppression.

3. The principle of all sovereignty resides essentially in the nation. No body nor

SOURCE: James Harvey Robinson, ed., "The French Revolution, 1789–1791," in *Translations and Reprints from the Original Sources of European History*, vol. I, no. 5, ed. Department of History of the University of Pennsylvania (Philadelphia: University of Pennsylvania Press, 1898), pp. 6–8.

individual may exercise any authority which does not proceed directly from the nation.

4. Liberty consists in the freedom to do everything which injures no one else; hence the exercise of the natural rights of each man has no limits except those which assure to the other members of the society the enjoyment of the same rights. These limits can only be determined by law.

5. Law can only prohibit such actions as are hurtful to society. Nothing may be prevented which is not forbidden by law, and no one may be forced to do anything not provided for by law.

6. Law is the expression of the general will. Every citizen has a right to participate personally or through his representative in its formation. It must be the same for all, whether it protects or punishes. All citizens, being equal in the eyes of the law, are equally eligible to all dignities and to all public positions and occupations, according to their abilities, and without distinction except that of their virtues and talents.

7. No person shall be accused, arrested or imprisoned except in the cases and according to the forms prescribed by law. Any one soliciting, transmitting, executing or causing to be executed any arbitrary order shall be punished. But any citizen summoned or arrested in virtue of the law shall submit without delay, as resistance constitutes an offence.

8. The law shall provide for such punishments only as are strictly and obviously necessary, and no one shall suffer punishment except it be legally inflicted in virtue of a law passed and promulgated before the commission of the offence.

9. As all persons are held innocent until they shall have been declared guilty, if arrest shall be deemed indispensable, all harshness not essential to the securing of the prisoner's person shall be severely repressed by law.

10. No one shall be disquieted on account of his opinions, including his religious views, provided their manifestation does not disturb the public order established by law.

11. The free communication of ideas and opinions is one of the most precious of the rights of man. Every citizen may, accordingly, speak, write and print with freedom, but shall be responsible for such abuses of this freedom as shall be defined by law.

12. The security of the rights of man and of the citizen requires public military force. These forces are, therefore, established for the good of all and not for the personal advantage of those to whom they shall be entrusted.

13. A common contribution is essential for the maintenance of the public forces and for the cost of administration. This should be equitably distributed among all the citizens in proportion to their means.

14. All the citizens have a right to decide, either personally or by their representatives, as to the necessity of the public contribution; to grant this freely; to know to what uses it is put; and to fix the proportion, the mode of assessment, and of collection, and the duration of the taxes.

15. Society has the right to require of every public agent an account of his administration.

16. A society in which the observance of the law is not assured, nor the separation of powers defined, has no constitution at all.

17. Since property is an inviolable and sacred right, no one shall be deprived thereof except where public necessity, legally determined, shall clearly demand it, and then only on condition that the owner shall have been previously and equitably indemnified.

The Declaration of Independence

The American Revolution preceded the French Revolution by a few years. Yet its priority in time does not give it priority in historical importance. At that time America was at the fringes of Western civilization while France was at its heart. Nevertheless, the American Revolution influenced the French Revolution in a variety of ways. One similarity between the two is their two great declarations: the American Declaration of Independence *(1776) and the French* Declaration of the Rights of Man and Citizen *(1789). Although it is uncertain whether the French were directly influenced by the American document, both are products of common ideas of the late eighteenth century and show evidence of a strong relationship between these ideas and revolutionary activities in Western civilization. The* Declaration of Independence *was written primarily by Thomas Jefferson. The following selection comes from the beginning of this document.*

Consider: *The usefulness of this standard for evaluating the legitimacy of a revolution; similarities between the French and American declarations; how these two documents differ in purpose and substance.*

When in the Course of human events, it becomes necessary for one people to dissolve the political bonds which have connected them with another, and to assume among the powers of the earth, the separate and equal station to which the Laws of Nature and of Nature's God entitle them, a decent respect to the opinions of mankind requires that they should declare the causes which impel them to the separation.—We hold these truths to be self-evident, that all men are created equal, that they are endowed by their Creator with certain unalienable Rights, that among these are Life, Liberty and the pursuit of Happiness.—That to secure these rights, Governments are instituted among Men, deriving their just powers from the consent of the governed,—That whenever any Form of Government becomes destructive of these ends, it is the Right of the People to alter or to abolish it, and to institute new Government, laying its foundation on such principles and organizing its powers in such form, as to them shall seem most likely to effect their Safety and Happiness. Prudence, indeed, will dictate that

SOURCE: *The Declaration of Independence, 1776* (Washington, D.C.: U.S. Department of State, 1911), pp. 3–8.

Governments long established should not be changed for light and transient causes; and accordingly all experience hath shewn, that mankind are more disposed to suffer, while evils are sufferable, than to right themselves by abolishing the forms to which they are accustomed. But when a long train of abuses and usurpations, pursuing invariably the same Object evinces a design to reduce them under absolute Despotism, it is their right, it is their duty, to throw off such Government, and to provide new Guards for their future security.—Such has been the patient sufferance of these Colonies; and such is now the necessity which constrains them to alter their former Systems of Government.

Speech to the National Convention— February 5, 1794: The Terror Justified

Maximilien Robespierre

Between 1793 and 1794, France experienced the most radical phase of the revolution, known as the Reign of Terror. During this period France was essentially ruled by the twelve-member Committee of Public Safety elected by the National Convention every month. The outstanding member of this committee was Maximilien Robespierre (1758—1794), a provincial lawyer who rose within the Jacobin Club and gained a reputation for incorruptibility and superb oratory. Historians have argued over Robespierre, some singling him out as a bloodthirsty individual with the major responsibility for the executions during the Reign of Terror, others seeing him as a sincere, idealistic, effective revolutionary leader called to the fore by events of the time. In the following speech to the National Convention on February 5, 1794, Robespierre defines the revolution and justifies extreme actions, including terror, in its defense.

> **Consider:** *What Robespierre means when he argues that terror flows from virtue; how the use of terror relates to the essence of the revolution; how this speech might be interpreted as an Enlightenment attack on the Ancien Régime carried to its logical conclusion.*

It is time to mark clearly the aim of the Revolution and the end toward which we wish to move; it is time to take stock of ourselves, of the obstacles which we still face, and of the means which we ought to adopt to attain our objectives. . . .

What is the goal for which we strive? A peaceful enjoyment of liberty and equality, the rule of that eternal justice whose laws are engraved, not upon marble or stone, but in the hearts of all men.

SOURCE: Raymond P. Stearns, ed., *Pageant of Europe*. Reprinted by permission of Harcourt Brace Jovanovich, Inc. (New York, 1947), pp. 404–405.

We wish an order of things where all low and cruel passions are enchained by the laws, all beneficent and generous feelings aroused; where ambition is the desire to merit glory and to serve one's fatherland; where distinctions are born only of equality itself; where the citizen is subject to the magistrate, the magistrate to the people, the people to justice; where the nation safeguards the welfare of each individual, and each individual proudly enjoys the prosperity and glory of his fatherland; where all spirits are enlarged by the constant exchange of republican sentiments and by the need of earning the respect of a great people; where the arts are the adornment of liberty, which ennobles them; and where commerce is the source of public wealth, not simply of monstrous opulence for a few families.

In our country we wish to substitute morality for egotism, probity for honor, principles for conventions, duties for etiquette, the empire of reason for the tyranny of customs, contempt for vice for contempt for misfortune, pride for insolence, the love of honor for the love of money . . . that is to say, all the virtues and miracles of the Republic for all the vices and snobbishness of the monarchy.

We wish in a word to fulfill the requirements of nature, to accomplish the destiny of mankind, to make good the promises of philosophy . . . that France, hitherto illustrious among slave states, may eclipse the glory of all free peoples that have existed, become the model of all nations. . . . That is our ambition; that is our aim.

What kind of government can realize these marvels? Only a democratic government. . . . But to found and to consolidate among us this democracy, to realize the peaceable rule of constitutional laws, it is necessary to conclude the war of liberty against tyranny and to pass successfully through the storms of revolution. Such is the aim of the revolutionary system which you have set up. . . .

Now what is the fundamental principle of democratic, or popular government— that is to say, the essential mainspring upon which it depends and which makes it function? It is virtue: I mean public virtue . . . that virtue which is nothing else but love of fatherland and its laws. . . .

The splendor of the goal of the French Revolution is simultaneously the source of our strength and of our weakness: our strength, because it gives us an ascendancy of truth over falsehood, and of public rights over private interests; our weakness, because it rallies against us all vicious men, all those who in their hearts seek to despoil the people. . . . It is necessary to stifle the domestic and foreign enemies of the Republic or perish with them. Now in these circumstances, the first maxim of our politics ought to be to lead the people by means of reason and the enemies of the people by terror.

If the basis of popular government in time of peace is virtue, the basis of popular government in time of revolution is both virtue and terror: virtue without which terror is murderous, terror without which virtue is powerless. Terror is nothing else than swift, severe, indomitable justice; it flows, then, from virtue.

A Soldier's Letters to His Mother: Revolutionary Nationalism

François-Xavier Joliclerc

Despite tremendous internal difficulties, including counterrevolutionary movements in a number of provinces, French armies held back foreign forces after war broke out in 1792, but by 1794 the French forces had made gains even beyond the 1789 borders. Part of the reason for this success was the nationalistic enthusiasm that developed along with the revolution. This nationalism is demonstrated by the following letters from François-Xavier Joliclerc, a conscript in the French army, to his mother.

> **Consider:** *The divisions within French society revealed in these letters; why such sentiments among soldiers are so important and how political leaders or military strategists might capitalize on them; whether the nationalism revealed in these letters is inherent in the nature of the French Revolution or in any particular phase of that revolution.*

13 December, 1793

My dear mother,

You continue to point out to me, in all your letters, that we must get out of the army, cost what it may. Here are the difficulties and the obstacles that I can see.

First of all, it is difficult to find replacements despite the enormous sums that are expended for this purpose. Secondly, we have just had a call-up of men eighteen to twenty-five; and the call-up of those from twenty-five to thirty-five is being prepared. As soon as we got home, we would have to get ready to go back, regretting the money we had spent. Thirdly, when *la patrie* calls us to her defense, we ought to fly there as if running to a good meal. Our life, our wealth, and our talents do not belong to us. It is to the nation, *la patrie*, that all that belongs.

I know well that you and all the others in our village do not share these sentiments. They are not aroused by the cries of an outraged fatherland, and all that they do results from being compelled to. But I have been brought up in conscience and thought, and have always been republican in spirit, although obliged to live in a monarchy. These principles of love for *la patrie, la liberté, la république*, are not only engraved in my heart, but are deeply etched and will remain there as long as it will please the Supreme Being to sustain in me the breath of life.

SOURCE: From Ludwig F. Schaefer, Daniel P. Resnick, and George F. Netterville, eds., *The Shaping of Western Civilization*, vol. II, trans. Daniel P. Resnick (New York: Holt, Rinehart and Winston, Inc., 1970), p. 216. Reprinted by permission of the editors.

Even if it cost me three quarters of my possessions to have you share these sentiments with me, I would gladly part with them and consider it a very small sacrifice. Oh, if only one day you could know the price of liberty and lose your senseless attachment to material things.

30 May, 1794

What about my lot? I am at my post, where I ought to be, and every good man who knows what's what ought to fly to the aid of his country in danger. If I should perish there, you ought to rejoice. Can one make a finer sacrifice than to die for one's country? Can one die for a more just, glorious, and fairer cause? No! Would you rather see me die on a mattress of straw in my bed at Froidefontaine [his home village] working with wood or stone?

No, dear mother. Think that I am at my post and you will be consoled. If your conscience reproaches you in some way, sell even the last of your petticoats for *la patrie*. She is our only rudder, and it is she who guides us and gives us happiness. . . .

Your son, Joliclerc

VISUAL SOURCES

Allegory of the Revolution
Jeaurat de Bertray

Jeaurat de Bertray's Allegory of the Revolution *is literally a jumble of historical and revolutionary symbols. At the top is a portrait of Jean Jacques Rousseau, at the time considered by many the spiritual and intellectual father of the French Revolution, even though he never advocated revolution and died eleven years before it began. Below him are the new flags of the French Republic, the one on the left with the nationalistic words "love of country." Further to the left is a triangular monument to Equality, below it two maidens representing Goodness and Good Faith, and in the center a bundle of rods and arms topped by a red liberty cap, all symbolizing a fair, forceful republican government. Just below is paper money, the* assignats, *that helped finance the revolution and pay off debts, and in the center right grows a liberty tree. To the right are two unfinished pillars, the first dedicated to the regeneration of morals and* The Declaration of the Rights of Man and Citizen, *the second to the French Revolution. Just below them and in the background are symbols of forceful determination to uphold and defend the revolution: a guillotine, a cannon, and a soldier. In the right foreground is a peasant wearing a liberty cap and sowing a field. This painting pulls together many symbols and elements of the revolu-*

Photo 5-1

Courtesy, Musée Carnavalet/Photographie Bulloz

tionary ideology. It was painted in 1794, the time of the most radical phase of the revolution.

> **Consider:** *Connections between this picture,* The Declaration of the Rights of Man and Citizen, *and the Enlightenment; the ways in which the Ancien Régime is rejected symbolically in this picture.*

Internal Disturbances and the Reign of Terror

Understanding of the Reign of Terror has often been distorted by an image of random and purposeless brutality. One way to gain clearer insights into the Terror is through the use of maps and statistics, which reveal where the Terror occurred, how intensive it was, and who its victims were. The following two maps compare the amount of civil disturbance facing government officials and the number of executions occurring in the various departments of France during the period of the Terror. The two pie charts (pp. 102–103) compare the estimated percentages of France's population belonging to the various classes in 1789 and during the Terror from March 1793 to August 1794.

> **Consider:** *How these maps and charts support an argument that the Reign of Terror was not random or purposeless; the hypotheses that might be drawn from these maps and charts about the causes or effects of the Terror.*

Map 5-1   Internal Disturbances

Map 5-2   The Incidence of the Terror

Chart 5-1   Classes in France

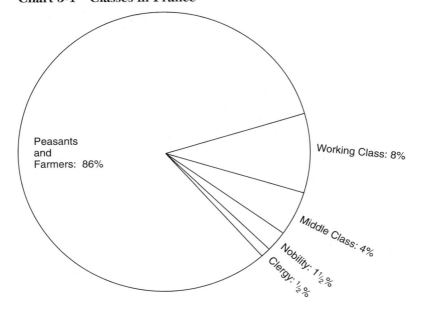

Chart 5-2   Executions During the Reign of Terror

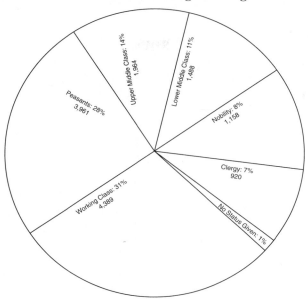

Upper Middle Class: 14%
1,964

Lower Middle Class: 11%
1,488

Peasants: 28%
3,961

Nobility: 8%
1,158

Clergy: 7%
920

Working Class: 31%
4,389

No Status Given: 1%

SECONDARY SOURCES

The Coming
of the
French Revolution
Georges Lefebvre

Probably no event in modern history has been interpreted at greater length and with greater passion than the French Revolution. The historiographic tradition related to this event is so extensive that numerous books and articles have been written on this historiography itself. A central controversy involves the cause or causes of the revolution and is dealt with in the following selection from The Coming of the French Revolution *by*

SOURCE: From Lefebvre, George, *The Coming of the French Revolution*, pp. 1–3. Copyright 1947 by Princeton University Press. Reprinted by permission of Princeton University Press.

*Georges Lefebvre. Lefebvre held the prestigious chair of French revolutionary history at
the Sorbonne until his death in 1959. His work on the French Revolution continues to be
highly respected.*

> **Consider:** *The most important cause of the French Revolution, according to
> Lefebvre; how this interpretation relates the revolution in France to areas outside
> of France; how social, economic, and political factors are linked in this interpreta-
> tion of the French Revolution; how this view is supported by the primary docu-
> ments.*

The ultimate cause of the French Revolution of 1789 goes deep into the history
of France and of the western world. At the end of the eighteenth century the
social structure of France was aristocratic. It showed the traces of having originated
at a time when land was almost the only form of wealth, and when the possessors
of land were the masters of those who needed it to work and to live. It is true
that in the course of age-old struggles (of which the Fronde, the last revolt of the
aristocracy, was as recent as the seventeenth century) the king had been able
gradually to deprive the lords of their political power and subject nobles and clergy
to his authority. But he had left them the first place in the social hierarchy. Still
restless at being merely his "subjects," they remained privileged persons.

Meanwhile the growth of commerce and industry had created, step by step, a
new form of wealth, mobile or commercial wealth, and a new class, called in
France the bourgeoisie, which since the fourteenth century had taken its place as
the Third Estate in the General Estates of the kingdom. This class had grown
much stronger with the maritime discoveries of the fifteenth and sixteenth centuries and the ensuing exploitation of new worlds, and also because it proved
highly useful to the monarchical state in supplying it with money and competent
officials. In the eighteenth century commerce, industry and finance occupied an
increasingly important place in the national economy. It was the bourgeoisie that
rescued the royal treasury in moments of crisis. From its ranks were recruited
most members of the liberal professions and most public employees. It had developed a new ideology which the "philosophers" and "economists" of the time
had simply put into definite form. The role of the nobility had correspondingly
declined; and the clergy, as the ideal which it proclaimed lost prestige, found its
authority growing weaker. These groups preserved the highest rank in the legal
structure of the country, but in reality economic power, personal abilities and
confidence in the future had passed largely to the bourgeoisie. Such a discrepancy
never lasts forever. The Revolution of 1789 restored the harmony between fact
and law. This transformation spread in the nineteenth century throughout the
west and then to the whole globe, and in this sense the ideas of 1789 toured the
world.

The Revolution of the Notables
Donald M. G. Sutherland

Georges Lefebvre's interpretation for the causes of the French Revolution became part of what has been called the "classical view" of the origins of the revolution. In recent years this view has been strongly criticized by increasing numbers of historians, most of whom reject Lefebvre's social-economic view in favor of a more political analysis. In the following selection Donald M. G. Sutherland reviews this controversy.

> **Consider:** *The basis for the attack on the classical view; why "exclusivism" is so important for these interpretations; how a representative of the classical view might respond.*

There was a time when historians could be fairly confident in describing the origins of the French Revolution. The operative concept was 'aristocratic reaction'. It meant several things at once. Politically, it referred to the undermining of the absolutism of Louis XIV which was thought to have subverted the independence and privileges of the aristocracy. The parlements, the regional sovereign and appeal courts of which that of Paris was by far the most important, were the driving forces behind the noble offensive. They were able to transform their right of registering laws and edicts into a veto on progressive royal legislation. The Crown was consequently much weaker. This had implications in the social sphere as well. In the course of the eighteenth century, the aristocracy ended up monopolizing the highest offices in government, the military, the Church and judiciary. This in turn had its effects on the bourgeoisie. No longer able to advance to the top of the major social and political institutions of the day, the bourgeoisie became increasingly alienated from the state and from respectable society. Frustrated from achieving its highest ambitions, its loyalties strained, ever open to suggestive criticisms of the system, it was well placed to take advantage of the political crisis of 1788–9 to overthrow the old order altogether. One of the many crises of the Old Regime was a crisis of social mobility.

The argument was irresistibly attractive, partly because of its internal elegance and partly because it explained so much. It made sense of the reign of Louis XIV, the eighteenth century and the Revolution too. The struggle between revolution and counterrevolution could be reduced to two actors, the bourgeoisie and the aristocracy, who had first come to blows in the closing years of the reign of Louis XIV. The aristocracy lost, of course, and specialists of the nineteenth century could move on to the next round, the struggle between the bourgeoisie and the working class.

Unfortunately, research and reflective criticism over the past twenty years have rendered the classical view of the origins of the Revolution utterly untenable. In

---

SOURCE: From Donald Sutherland, *France,* 1789–1815, pp. 15–18, © 1986 Oxford University Press. Reprinted by permission of HarperCollins Publishers, Ltd, and Oxford University Press.

the first place, it assumes rather than demonstrates the aristocracy's progressive monopoly of high posts. It assumes, too, that the society of the seventeenth century was more open than its successor but relies on incomplete evidence and a limited range of contemporary complaints. The Duc de Saint-Simon's famous observation that Louis XIV raised up the 'vile bourgeoisie' turns out to be untrue in the case of the episcopate, partially true but grossly misleading of the ministry and unknown in the case of the officer corps of the army. . . .

Closer examination of some of the major signs of noble exclusivism shows that restrictions were often aimed at excluding the rich parvenu nobles, not a rising bourgeoisie. . . . The Old Regime aristocracy was thus comparatively young and was in a constant process of renewal.

The doors of the Second Estate were well oiled to men of talent but above all to those with money. Society was therefore capable of absorbing the most thrusting, entrepreneurial and ambitious men of the plutocracy. . . .

The effect of the revisionist critique of the classical interpretation has been to reassert the importance of the political origins of the Revolution. If the nobility had always been a dominant class, if whatever trends there were towards exclusivism are problematic to interpret, if opportunities for advancement were far greater than was ever suspected, and if nobles and bourgeois shared similar economic functions and interests, the notion that the Revolution originated in a struggle between two distinct classes has to be abandoned. Politics remains. Both groups could agree to unite to overthrow absolutism in favour of a liberal constitution but, according to which revisionist historian one follows, they fell out either over means or because of a failure of political leadership or the form the political crisis took, or even over something as amorphous as 'style'.

Loaves and Liberty: Women in the French Revolution
Ruth Graham

Historians have long recognized that women played an important role in certain aspects of the French Revolution. But only in the last twenty years have extensive examinations been made of the significance of the French Revolution for women's history. The following selection by Ruth Graham is a good example of this work.

> **Consider:** *Any connections between sex and class lines in the French Revolution; the ways in which women became a "revolutionary force unprecedented in history" during the revolution; what Graham means by women's victories and defeats.*

SOURCE: Ruth Graham, "Loaves and Liberty: Women in the French Revolution," in *Becoming Visible: Women in European History*, ed. Renate Bridenthal and Claudia Koonz (Boston: Houghton Mifflin, 1977), pp. 251–253.

It would be wrong to assume that because women had come into the Revolution in 1789 asking for bread and liberty and had come out in 1795 with starvation and restriction of their movements, they had gained nothing. They won laws protecting their rights in marriage, property, and education. True, women were denied political rights in the French Revolution (as were the majority of men when the Convention scrapped the democratic constitution of 1793) but nowhere else at the time did women share political rights with men.

Although women were a cohesive group during the Revolution, they responded mainly to the needs of their class and were never an autonomous force. The ideology of the revolutionary authorities who distrusted women's political movements derived seemingly from Rousseau, but actually from the facts of their lives: France's small-scale, home-based economy needed middle- and working-class women to contribute their special skills and labor to their families. Women were not yet a large, independent group in the working class.

In the early days of the French Revolution, women from the middle classes (as can be seen from cahiers written by them) welcomed the restoration of their natural rights as wives and mothers to participate in society as men's "natural companions." Women of the urban poor—wage earners, artisans of women's crafts, owners of small enterprises, such as the market women—agitated for bread rather than for women's rights. There is, however, evidence that "respectable" middle-class women joined them. Although these movements crossed class lines, which were perhaps not rigidly fixed, they did not cross sex lines. When men participated, as they did in the October Days of 1789, they came as armed escorts or separate detachments.

As the Revolution entered its more radical phase, as economic crisis followed war and civil strife, the polarization between the rich and the poor sharpened the older stuggle between aristocrat and patriot. During the last days of the National Convention, the women who surged into the hall crying "Bread and the Constitution of 1793!" truly represented the poor, whom the upper classes and their women now feared. The bread riots belonged to the women of the poor, who incited their men to insurrection, but the insurrection belonged to both of them, the sans-culottes and their women.

Yet, the Revolution had called upon women to make great sacrifices and they did; in consequence, women became a revolutionary force unprecedented in history. The men in power feared women who challenged the Revolution's failure to guarantee bread for the poor. So feared were the women of the French Revolution that they became legendary—they became Mme. Defarge later to those who feared revolution itself.

A new elite of the upper middle class, men of wealth and talent, rose to power in the four years of the Directory following the dissolution in 1795 of the National Convention. Their women had no political rights but emerged as influential ladies of the salon, such as the brilliant writer Mme. de Staël, and Mme. Tallien, former wife of an aristocrat and now derisively called "Our Lady of Thermidor," as a symbol of the reaction. One of these ladies, Josephine de Beauharnais, the widow of a general, became the mistress of one of the Directors before she married the young Napoleon Bonaparte, who soon afterward became general of the armies in Italy.

Outside of Paris, away from the glamour of these women, middle-class morality prevailed. Napoleon subscribed to this morality. When he became emperor in 1804, he wrote laws into his code to strengthen the authority of the husband and father of the family as a safeguard for private property. Women lost whatever rights they had gained in the Revolution, for now they had to obey their husbands unconditionally. Napoleon left women the right to divorce (for Napoleon to use against Josephine when she failed to provide him an heir), but this right was taken from them after 1815 by the restoration of the Bourbon monarchy.

What could not be taken from women was their memory of victories during the French Revolution: their march to Versailles in the October Days, their petitions to the legislature, their club meetings, their processions, their insurrections. Their defeats served as lessons for next time. "We are simple women," a woman was reported to have said at a club meeting in the days of the uprising of the Paris Commune in May 1871, nearly a century later, "but not made of weaker stuff than our grandmothers of '93. Let us not cause their shades to blush for us, but be up and doing, as they would be were they living now."

An Evaluation of the French Revolution
William Doyle

Although most would say that rapid and vast changes occurred during the French Revolution, it is difficult to evaluate the extent to which these changes were more apparent than real. Many historians have concluded that while the revolution stood for much, most of the promises made by the revolution were not carried out. Others argue that much that has been attributed to the revolution would probably have come about anyway. In the following selection William Doyle attempts to strike a balance between what was and was not accomplished by the revolution.

> **Consider:** *How Doyle determines what changes would in all probability have come about in any case; what Doyle attributes directly to the revolution; how Doyle's argument might be used by those opposing revolutions in general.*

The shadow of the Revolution, therefore, fell across the whole of the nineteenth century and beyond. Until 1917 few would have disputed that it was the greatest revolution in the history of the world; and even after that its claims to primacy remain strong. It was the first modern revolution, the archetypal one. After it, nothing in the European world remained the same, and we are all heirs to its

---

SOURCE: From William Doyle, *The Oxford History of the French Revolution*, pp. 423–425. Copyright 1989. Reprinted by permission of Oxford University Press.

influence. And yet, it can be argued, much that was attributed to it would in all probability have come about in any case. Before 1789 there were plenty of signs that the structure of French society was evolving towards domination by a single élite in which property counted for more than birth. The century-long expansion of the bourgeoisie which underlay this trend already looked irreversible; and greater participation by men of property in government, as constant experiments with provincial assemblies showed, seemed bound to come. Meanwhile many of the reforms the Revolution brought in were already being tried or thought about by the absolute monarchy—law codification, fiscal rationalization, diminution of venality, free trade, religious toleration. With all these changes under way or in contemplation, the power of government looked set for steady growth, too—which ironically was one of the complaints of the despotism-obsessed men of 1789. In the Church, the monastic ideal was already shrivelling and the status of parish priests commanding more and more public sympathy. Economically, the colonial trade had already peaked, and failure to compete industrially with Great Britain was increasingly manifest. In other structural areas, meanwhile, the great upheaval appears to have made no difference at all. Conservative investment habits still characterized the early nineteenth century, agricultural inertia and unentrepreneurial business likewise. And in international affairs, it is hard to believe that Great Britain would not have dominated the world's seas and trade throughout the nineteenth century, that Austro-Prussian rivalry would not have run much the course it did, or that Latin America would not have asserted its independence in some form or other, if the French Revolution had never happened. In all these fields, the effect was to accelerate or retard certain trends, but not to change their general drift.

Against all this, it is equally hard to believe that the specifically anti-aristocratic, anti-feudal revolutionary ideology of the Rights of Man would have emerged as it did without the jumble of accident, miscalculation, and misunderstanding which coalesced into a revolution in specifically French circumstances. It is equally hard to believe that anything as extraordinary as dechristianization would have occurred without the monumental misjudgement which produced the Revolution's quarrel with the Catholic Church. Without that quarrel, the dramatic revival in the authority of the papacy also seems inconceivable. Representative government may well have been on the horizon, but how long would the ideal of popular democracy have taken to establish itself without the example of the sansculotte movement? It certainly transformed and widened out of all recognition the cause of parliamentary reform in England—although the blood-stained figure of the sansculotte probably galvanized conservative resistance on the other side. Above all, the revolutionaries' decision to go to war, which all historians agree revolutionized the Revolution, destroyed an established pattern of warfare in a way no old regime government would otherwise have promoted. Arming the people was the last thing they would have dreamed of. The emergencies of that war in turn produced the scenes which have indelibly marked our memory of the Revolution: the Terror. Massacres were nothing new, and the worst ones of the 1790s occurred outside France. But there was something horribly new and unimaginable in the prospect of a government systematically executing its opponents by the cartload for months on end, and by a device which, however humane in concept, made the streets run with blood. And this occurred in what had passed for the most civilized country in Europe, whose writers had taught the eighteenth century to pride itself on its increasing mildness, good sense, and humanity. This great drama transformed the whole meaning of political change, and the contemporary world would be inconceivable if it had not happened.

In other words it transformed men's outlook.

Chapter Questions

1. What seems to have motivated many of the revolutionaries, as revealed by the demands made prior to the French Revolution and the actions taken during the revolution?

2. What factors help explain why this revolution occurred in France, one of the most prosperous and powerful nations of Europe? What does this explanation add to the significance of the revolution?

3. With the advantage of hindsight, what might the monarchy have done to retain control and minimize revolutionary changes?

4. In what ways should the French Revolution be considered a middle-class revolution or a revolution of the notables?

CHAPTER SIX

The Age of Napoleon

In 1799 members of the ruling Directory conspired with the well-known military leader Napoleon Bonaparte (1769–1821) to take over the French government by means of a *coup d'état*. It was successful, and Napoleon quickly asserted his own dominance over others. By 1802 he had full power, and by 1804 he was the self-proclaimed Emperor Napoleon I.

The period from 1799 to 1815 is generally known as the Age of Napoleon. Rising with opportunities presented by the French Revolution, Napoleon gained power not only in France, but directly and indirectly throughout much of continental Europe. Within France he crushed threats from both radicals and royalists who wanted to extend or reverse the French Revolution. Through administrative reforms, codification of laws, and settlement with the Church, he institutionalized some of the changes brought about by the revolution and took the heart out of others. Backed by the ideological force of the revolution and strong nationalism, his armies extended French rule, institutions, and influence throughout Europe. In 1814 Napoleon's forces, weakened by overextension and a disastrous Russian campaign, were defeated by a coalition of European powers. After Napoleon's defeat, the major powers, meeting at Vienna, attempted to establish a new stability that would minimize the revolutionary and Napoleonic experiences.

The sources in this chapter focus on the principal interpretive debate connected with Napoleon: How should Napoleon and his policies be understood? Is Napoleon best viewed as a moderate defender of the French Revolution or as an enlightened despot in the eighteenth-century tradition? To provide insight into these issues, the selections will examine Napoleon's rise to power and his ideas, external policies, and internal institutions.

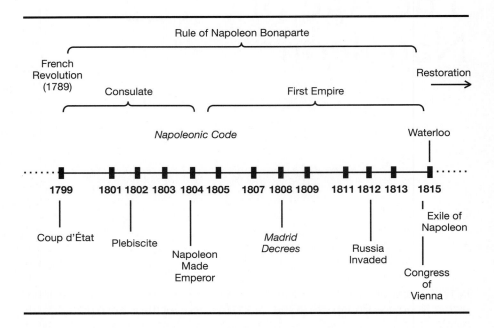

PRIMARY SOURCES

Memoirs: Napoleon's Appeal
Madame de Remusat

Napoleon was neither the candidate of those longing to turn France to a more revolutionary course nor of those who wanted to return France to the legitimacy of the Ancien Régime. He came to power promising to uphold both revolutionary principles and order. Scholars have analyzed the question of why he was able to rise to power. Some see him as a military and political genius; others argue that he was an opportunist who took advantage of circumstances as they arose. One of the earliest analyses of Napoleon's rise to power was written by Madame de Remusat (1780–1821). As a lady in waiting to Empress Josephine and wife of a Napoleonic official, she observed Napoleon firsthand and described him in her Memoirs.

Consider: *Why, according to Remusat, Napoleon was so appealing to the French; the means Napoleon used to secure his power.*

I can understand how it was that men worn out by the turmoil of the Revolution, and afraid of that liberty which had long been associated with death, looked for repose under the dominion of an able ruler on whom fortune was seemingly revolved to smile. I can conceive that they regarded his elevation as a degree of destiny and fondly believed that in the irrevocable they should find peace. I may confidently assert that those persons believed quite sincerely that Bonaparte, whether as consul or emperor, would exert his authority to oppose the intrigue of faction and would save us from the perils of anarchy.

None dared to utter the word "republic," so deeply had the Terror stained that name; and the government of the Directory had perished in the contempt with which its chiefs were regarded. The return of the Bourbons could only be brought about by the aid of a revolution; and the slightest disturbance terrified the French people, in whom enthusiasm of every kind seemed dead. Besides, the men in whom they had trusted had one after the other deceived them; and as, this time, they were yielding to force, they were at least certain that they were not deceiving themselves.

The belief, or rather the error, that only despotism could at that epoch maintain order in France was very widespread. It became the mainstay of Bonaparte; and it is due to him to say that he also believed it. The factions played into his hands by imprudent attempts which he turned to his own advantage. He had some grounds for his belief that he was necessary; France believed it, too; and he even

SOURCE: From James Harvey Robinson, ed., *Readings in European History*, vol. II (Boston: Ginn, 1904), pp. 491–492.

succeeded in persuading foreign sovereigns that he constituted a barrier against republican influences, which, but for him, might spread widely. At the moment when Bonaparte placed the imperial crown upon his head there was not a king in Europe who did not believe that he wore his own crown more securely because of that event. Had the new emperor granted a liberal constitution, the peace of nations and of kings might really have been forever secured.

Memoirs: Napoleon's Secret Police

Joseph Fouché

Although historians have found various aspects of Napoleonic rule admirable, most condemn Napoleon's use of the secret police. Joseph Fouché, Duke of Otranto (1763–1820), headed this institution for most of the period between 1802 and 1810. Fouché combined the attributes of a powerful politician, a police officer, and an opportunist. In the following selection from his Memoirs, *Fouché boasts of his accomplishments.*

Consider: *The credibility of this document; whether it was reasonable of Napoleon to have Fouché carry out these activities.*

With regard to the interior, an important spring was wanted, that of the general police, which might have rallied the past round the present, and guaranteed the security of the empire. Napoleon himself perceived the void, and, by an imperial decree of the 10th July, re-established me at the head of the police; at the same time investing me with stronger functions than those which I had possessed, before the absurd fusion of the police with the department of justice. . . .

It will not be doubted that I had salaried spies in all ranks and orders; I had some of both sexes, hired at the rate of a thousand or two thousand francs per month, according to their importance and their services. I received their reports directly in writing, having a conventional mark. Every three months, I communicated my list to the emperor, in order that there might be no double employment; and also in order that the nature of the service, occasionally permanent, often temporary, might be rewarded either by places or remunerations.

As to the government's police abroad, it had two essential objects, namely, to watch friendly powers, and counteract hostile governments. In both cases, it was composed of individuals purchased or pensioned, and commissioned to reside near each government, or in each principal town, independent of numerous secret agents sent into all countries, either by the minister of foreign affairs, or by the emperor himself.

I also had my foreign spies. It was in my cabinet, also, that the foreign gazettes,

SOURCE: Joseph Fouché, *Memoirs* (London: Gibbings and Co., 1894), pp. 188–191.

prohibited to the perusal of the French people, were collected, abstracts of which were made for my own use. By that means, I held in my hands the most important strings of foreign politics; and I discharged, in conjunction with the chief of the government, a task capable of controlling or balancing that of the minister charged with foreign relations.

I was thus far from limiting my duties to *espionnage*. All the state prisons were under my control, as well as the *gendarmerie*. The delivery of the *visa* of passports belonged to me. To me was assigned the duty of watching amnestied individuals and foreigners. I established general commissariats in the principal towns of the kingdom, which extended the net-work of the police over the whole of France, and especially our frontiers.

My police acquired so high a renown, that the world went so far as to pretend that I had, among my secret agents, three nobles of the *ancien régime*, distinguished by princely titles, and who daily communicated to me the result of their observations.

I confess that such an establishment was expensive; it swallowed up several millions, the funds of which were secretly provided from taxes laid upon gambling and prostitution, and from the granting of passports. Notwithstanding all that has been said against gambling, reflecting and firm minds must allow, that in the actual state of society, the legal converting of vice into profit is a necessary evil. . . .

It became necessary to organize the gambling-houses upon a much larger scale, for the produce of them was not solely destined to reward my moving phalanxes of spies. I nominated as superintendent-general of the gambling-houses in France, Perrein the elder, who already farmed them, and who, after the coronation, extended his privilege over all of the chief towns of the empire, upon condition of paying fourteen millions yearly, independent of three thousand francs daily to the minister of the police, which, however, did not remain entirely in his hands.

Napoleon's Imperial Decree at Madrid—December 4, 1808

When Napoleon succeeded militarily outside of French soil, more was required of the conquered people than subservience to French rule. Typically some of the reforms and institutions of the French Revolution were applied to the conquered areas. This is shown in the following decree issued from Napoleon's imperial camp at Madrid on December 4, 1808.

> **Consider:** *The benefits Napoleon might have been hoping for by issuing this decree; to whom this decree would be most threatening; the ways in which these measures were consistent with the acts or spirit of the French Revolution.*

SOURCE: From James Harvey Robinson, ed., *Readings in European History*, vol. II (Boston: Ginn, 1904), p. 512.

To date from the publication of the present decree, feudal rights are abolished in Spain.

All personal obligations, all exclusive fishing rights and other rights of similar nature on the coast or on rivers and streams, all feudal monopolies (*banalités*) of ovens, mills, and inns are suppressed. It shall be free to every one who shall conform to the laws to develop his industry without restraint.

The tribunal of the Inquisiton is abolished, as inconsistent with the civil sovereignty and authority.

The property of the Inquisition shall be sequestered and fall to the Spanish state, to serve as security for the bonded debt.

Considering that the members of the various monastic orders have increased to an undue degree and that, although a certain number of them are useful in assisting the ministers of the altar in the administration of the sacraments, the existence of too great a number interferes with the prosperity of the state, we have decreed and do decree as follows:

The number of convents now in existence in Spain shall be reduced to a third of their present number. This reduction shall be accomplished by uniting the members of several convents of the same order into one.

From the publication of the present decree, no one shall be admitted to the novitiate or permitted to take the monastic vow until the number of the religious of both sexes has been reduced to one third of that now in existence. . . .

All regular ecclesiastics who desire to renounce the monastic life and live as secular ecclesiastics are at liberty to leave their monasteries. . . .

In view of the fact that the institution which stands most in the way of the internal prosperity of Spain is that of the customs lines separating the provinces, we have decreed and do decree what follows:

To date from January 1 next, the barriers existing between the provinces shall be suppressed. The custom houses shall be removed to the frontiers and there established.

Napoleon's Diary

Napoleon's accomplishments and place in history are explained in part by the type of individual he was. The principal sources of information on his personality are his diaries, memoirs, and letters, particularly the portions in which he reflects on himself. The following selection comes from diary entries made between 1798 and 1817.

> **Consider:** *Napoleon's opinions about what made him successful; Napoleon's analysis of his power and his personality; how Napoleon wants to be remembered.*

SOURCE: R. M. Johnston, ed., *The Corsican: A Diary of Napoleon's Life in His Own Words* (Boston: Houghton Mifflin Co., 1910), pp. 74, 140, 166, 492, 496.

Paris, January 1, 1798

Paris has a short memory. If I remain longer doing nothing, I am lost. In this great Babylon one reputation quickly succeeds another. After I have been seen three times at the theatre, I shall not be looked at again; I shall therefore not go very frequently.

Paris, January 29, 1798

I will not remain here; there is nothing to be done. They will listen to nothing. I realize that if I stay my reputation will soon be gone. All things fade here, and my reputation is almost forgotten; this little Europe affords too slight a scope; I must go to the Orient; all great reputations have been won there. If the success of an expedition to England should prove doubtful, as I fear, the army of England will become the army of the East, and I shall go to Egypt.

The Orient awaits a man!

Milan, June 17, 1800

I have just reached Milan, somewhat fatigued.

Some Hungarian grenadiers and German prisoners passing by, who had already been prisoners in the campaigns of 1796 and 1797, recognized the First Consul. Many began to shout, with apparent enthusiasm: "Vive Bonaparte!"

What a thing is imagination! Here are men who don't know me, who have never seen me, but who only knew of me, and they are moved by my presence, they would do anything for me! And this same incident arises in all centuries and in all countries! Such is fanaticism! Yes, imagination rules the world. The defect of our modern institutions is that they do not speak to the imagination. By that alone can man be governed; without it he is but a brute.

December 30, 1802

My power proceeds from my reputation, and my reputation from the victories I have won. My power would fall if I were not to support it with more glory and move victories. Conquest has made me what I am; only conquest can maintain me.

Friendship is only a word; I love nobody; no, not even my brothers. Perhaps Joseph a little; even then it's a matter of habit, it's because he is my elder.— Duroc? Ah, yes, I love him; but why? His character attracts me: he is cool, dry, severe; and Duroc never sheds tears. As for me, you don't suppose I care; I know perfectly well I have no real friends. As long as I remain what I am, I shall have as many as I need so far as the appearance goes. Let the women whimper, that's their business, but for me, give me no sentiment. A man must be firm, have a stout heart, or else leave on one side war and government.

Saint Helena, March 3, 1817

In spite of all the libels, I have no fear whatever about my fame. Posterity will do me justice. The truth will be known; and the good I have done will be compared with the faults I have committed. I am not uneasy as to the result. Had I succeeded, I would have died with the reputation of the greatest man that ever existed. As it is, although I have failed, I shall be considered as an extraordinary man: my elevation was unparalleled, because unaccompanied by crime. I have fought fifty pitched battles, almost all of which I have won. I have framed and carried into effect a code of laws that will bear my name to the most distant posterity. I raised myself from nothing to be the most powerful monarch in the world. Europe was at my feet. I have always been of opinion that the sovereignty lay in the people. In fact, the imperial government was a kind of republic. Called to the head of it by the voice of the nation, my maxim was, *la carrière est ouverte aux talent* without distinction of birth or fortune, and this system of equality is the reason that your oligarchy hates me so much.

Saint Helena, August 28, 1817

Jesus was hanged, like so many fanatics who posed as a prophet, a messiah; there were several every year. What is certain is that at that epoch opinion was setting towards a single God, and those who first preached the doctrine were well received: circumstances made for it. It is just like in my case, sprung from the lower ranks of society I became an emperor, because circumstances, opinion, were with me.

VISUAL SOURCES

Napoleon Crossing the Alps
Jacques Louis David

Jacques Louis David was a leading painter of the late eighteenth and early nineteenth centuries and one of the first great painters to consciously devote his talents to the art of propaganda. A republican during the French Revolution, he painted a number of pictures supportive of the revolution and what it stood for. David argued that "the arts should . . . contribute forcefully to the education of the public" and that art "should have grandeur and a moral"; if a painting is properly presented, the "marks of heroism and civic virtue offered the eyes of the people will electrify its soul, and plant the seeds of glory and devotion to the fatherland."

When Napoleon rose to power, David became a Bonapartist. In 1800 he was asked by Napoleon to paint a picture of him leading his army across the Alps. The result, Napoleon Crossing the Alps, *shows Napoleon in a heroic pose on a white charger following the* glorious footsteps of Hannibal and Charlemagne (whose names are carved in the rocks below) across the Alps. Napoleon is pointing upward, probably both to heaven and to the top of the mountains, while a wind blows at his back—a traditional symbol of victory. Under the horse's belly are troops and cannon moving up the trail. In reality, Napoleon wisely rode a sure-footed mule. He also posed only briefly for David, informing him that "it is the character and what animates the physiognomy that needs to be painted. No one inquires if the portraits of great men are likenesses. It is enough that their genius lives in them."

> **Consider:** The way this painting and the circumstances surrounding its execution by David illustrate connections between politics and art of the period.

Photo 6-1

Musée Versailles/Giraudon

SECONDARY SOURCES

France Under Napoleon: Napoleon as Enlightened Despot
Louis Bergeron

As with most charismatic figures, it has been difficult to evaluate Napoleon objectively from a historical perspective. Even before his death, a number of myths were developing about him. Since then much of the debate among scholars has dealt with whether Napoleon should be considered a defender or a destroyer of the revolution, whether his rise to power reversed the revolutionary tide or consolidated it. In the following selection the French historian Louis Bergeron focuses on the consequences for France of Napoleon's rule and argues that he should be viewed more as an eighteenth-century enlightened despot than as anything else.

> **Consider:** *Why Bergeron calls Napoleon the last of the enlightened despots and a prophet of the modern state; what, according to Bergeron, was beyond Napoleon's control; whether the primary and visual sources support Bergeron's interpretation.*

There is thus no doubt about the interpretation to be given to the historic role of Napoleon Bonaparte. For the rest of the world, indeed, he remained the fearsome propagator of the Revolution, or the admirable instrument of reason governing the world, of progress of the spirit in its long "discourse with time" (Hegel). But for France? . . . Bonaparte belongs to the Revolution, surely, in matters that seemed irreversible at the time—civil equality, the destruction of feudalism, the ruin of the privileged position of the Catholic Church. As for the rest, the enjoyment of liberties, the form of political institutions, there had been since 1789 so much instability, so many contradictions between grand principles and the practice of governments, so much persistent uncertainty on the outcome of the war and the unity of the nation, that the field lay open for a strong man who, on condition of preserving the essential conquests of the Revolution, would do something new in the matter of government and refuse to be embarrassed by scruples. By anchoring France securely to the shores that the Constituent Assembly had been unwilling to leave, Bonaparte accomplished somewhat late in the day that "revolution from above" of which the old monarchy had been incapable. The political trade-off was a certain number of amputations of the immediate Revolutionary inheritance, a few backward movements, and disconcerting borrowings from the Old Régime. In a sense, the dynamism of Bonaparte and his rigorous administra-

SOURCE: From Bergeron, Louis, *France Under Napoleon.* Copyright 1981 by the Princeton University Press.

tion revived the experiment of enlightened despotism, somewhat belatedly, since in the setting of Western Europe it was already a bit out of date. . . .

It was his political genius, as it is generally agreed to call it, to combine his own clear and strongly held personal ideas and convictions, reinforced by his great individual prestige, with a sure sense of the necessary and the possible in revolutionary France—after ten years of revolution. "My policy is to govern men as the great number wish to be governed. That, I think, is the way to recognize the sovereignty of the people." While implacably suppressing the most actively opposed minorities, he overcame the apathy and the wait-and-see attitude of the majority of the French. In matters of social hierarchy and the administrative system he forced upon the French, who from citizens were soon to become subjects again, a coherent construction which he intended to be permanent, and which reflected his taste for uniformity, symmetry and efficiency, the signs of a rational organization in which a single mind transmitted impulses to the most distant members. What we see as rigid or even oppressive in the survivals of the Napoleonic system were at the time the source of its strength, making of it a model to be envied, and one of unequaled modernity.

Napoleon as Preserver of the Revolution
George Rudé

In recent years historians have become more reluctant to categorize Napoleon under any one label. Instead, they tend to interpret more judiciously his words and deeds, taking care to note that both were inconsistent and even contradictory at various times. This tendency among historians is exemplified in the following selection by the well-known British social historian George Rudé. Rudé, who has emphasized looking at history from the bottom up, sees Napoleon as sympathetic to and supportive of the revolution.

> **Consider:** *How Bergeron might react to Rudé's interpretation; the ways in which this interpretation is supported or contradicted by the primary documents.*

Napoleon himself believed that his work was a kind of crowning of the Revolution, and he was remarkably honest about his friendship with Robespierre's brother. He defended Robespierre from the charge of being bloodthirsty; he respected him as a man of probity. Napoleon would never have imagined that his own career could have flourished as it did without the surgery performed on French society by the Revolution. He was born in Corsica of poor, proud, petty-noble parents, and before the Revolution he could not possibly have risen above

SOURCE: Norman F. Cantor, *Perspectives on the European Past,* vol. II. Reprinted by permission of Macmillan (New York, 1971), pp. 59–60. Copyright © 1971 by Macmillan Publishing Co., Inc.

the rank of captain in the French army. Also, he had read Rousseau and sympathized with much of the Jacobin philosophy.

Napoleon had two different aspects. He believed in the overthrow of the old aristocracy of privilege; on the other hand, he believed in strong government—and he learned both of these beliefs from the Revolution. He was both an authoritarian and an egalitarian. Yet, admittedly little of this seems to fit the man who created a new aristocracy, who prided himself on being the son-in-law of Francis of Austria, referred to his late "brother" Louis XVI, and aspired to found a new imperial dynasty.

However, if we judge Napoleon on what he actually did and not only on those things that are usually remembered (despotism and foreign conquest), we must concede that his armies "liberalized" the constitutions of many European countries. They overthrew the aristocratic system in Italy and Germany, and even, to some extent, in Poland and Spain. A great many European liberals rallied to Napoleon's banners, particularly where French administration was at its best (as under Napoleon's brother Jerome in Westphalia). Napoleon's armies did bring many of the ideals of the Revolution to Europe: the basic ideas of the overthrow of aristocratic privilege, of a constitution, of the *Code Napoléon* (which was a codification of the laws of the French Revolution). In this sense Napoleon was a revolutionary. He turned his back on revolution to the extent that he was authoritarian and contemptuous of "the little man," but certain important accomplishments of the Revolution—peasant ownership of land free from feudal obligations, expropriation of the possessions of the Church and of the émigré nobility—were retained and even extended beyond France's borders. Napoleon was indeed a military despot, but he did not destroy the work of the Revolution; in a sense, in a wider European context, he rounded off its work.

Women and the Napoleonic Code
Bonnie G. Smith

However they evaluate Napoleon and his rule, most historians point to the set of rationally organized laws—the Napoleonic Code—as one of Napoleon's most important and lasting legacies. The Code embodied many principles of the Enlightenment and the French Revolution, and the Code was modified and adopted outside of France in Europe and the Western Hemisphere. While it has been generally considered a progressive legal system, historians now point out that it may have represented a step back for women. In the following selection from her comprehensive survey, Changing Lives: Women in European History Since 1700, *Bonnie G. Smith analyzes the significance of the Napoleonic Code for women.*

SOURCE: From Bonnie G. Smith, *Changing Lives: Women in European History Since 1700,* pp. 120–122. Copyright 1989 by D.C. Heath and Co. Reprinted by permission of the publisher.

Consider: *Ways the Code made women legally and economically dependent on men; what concept of woman's proper role the Code supported; what concept of man's proper role the Code supported.*

First, women acquired the nationality of their husbands upon marriage. This made a woman's relationship to the state an indirect one because it was dependent on her husband's. Second, a woman had to reside where her husband desired. Women could not participate in lawsuits or serve as witnesses in court or as witnesses to civil acts such as births, deaths, and marriages. Such a reduction in woman's civil status enhanced that of the individual male. Moreover, the Code reduced, if not eliminated, male accountability for sexual acts and thrust it squarely on women. For example, men were no longer susceptible to paternity suits or legally responsible for the support of illegitimate children. Women were weakened economically if they bore illegitimate children, whereas men were not so affected if they fathered them. Finally, female adultery was punished by imprisonment and fines unless the husband relented and took his wife back. Men, however, suffered no such sanctions unless they brought their sexual partner into the home. The sexual behavior of women was open to scrutiny and prescribed by law, whereas that of men, almost without exception, had no criminal aspect attached to it. Thus male sexuality was accepted with few limitations, but women's was only acceptable if it remained within strict domestic boundaries. The Napoleonic Code institutionalized the republican responsibility of women to generate virtue—a term that began to acquire sexual overtones to its civic definition.

The Napoleonic Code also defined the space women would occupy in the new regime as marital, maternal, and domestic—all public matters would be determined by men. This circumscription was made more effective by the way the property law undercut the possibilities for women's economic independence and existence in a world beyond the home. In general, a woman had no control over property. Even if she was married under a contract that ensured a separate accounting of her dowry, her husband still had administrative control of funds. This administrative power of the husband and father replaced arbitrary patriarchal rule and was more in tune with modern ideas of government. Instead of serving the king's whim, governmental officials served the best interests of the nation just as the father increased the well-being of the family. This kind of economic control of women held in all classes. Women's wages went to their husbands, and market women and others engaged in business could not do so without permission from their husbands. Once a woman gained permission she did acquire some kind of legal status, in that a business woman could be sued. On the other hand, she had no control of her profits—these always passed to her husband, and court records demonstrate the continuing enforcement of this kind of control. Moreover, the husband's right to a business woman's property meant that the property passed to his descendants rather than hers. All of these provisions meant that, in the strictest sense, women could not act freely or independently.

The Napoleonic Code influenced many legal systems in Europe and the New World and set the terms for the treatment of women on a widespread basis. Establishing male power by transferring autonomy and economic goods from women to men, the Code organized gender roles for more than a century. "From the way the Code treats women, you can tell it was written by men," so older women reacted to the new decree. Women's publications protested the sudden repression after a decade of more equitable laws. Even in the 1820s, books explaining the Code to women always recognized their anger. The justification for the Code's provisions involved reminders about men's chivalrous character and women's weakness. Arguments were based on nature both to invoke the equality of all men and to reinforce the consequences of women's supposed physical inferiority. Looking at nature, one writer saw in terms of gender man's "greater strength, his propensity to be active and assertive in comparison to woman's weakness, lack of vigor and natural modesty." At the time the Code was written, the codifiers were looking at nature in two ways. In theorizing about men alone, nature was redolent of abstract rights. As far as women were concerned, however, nature became empirical in that women had less physical stature than men. Although short men were equal to tall men, women were simply smaller than men and thus were unequal.

According to jurists, therefore, women needed protection, and this protection was to be found within the domicile. The law, they maintained, still offered women protection from individual male brutality, in the rare cases when that might occur. Legislators thus used the law officially to carve out a private space for women in which they had no rights. At the same time, law codes were supposed to protect women from the abuses allowed in the first place. The small number of abuses that might result were not seen as significant drawbacks by the jurists. They saw the Code as "insuring the safety of patrimonies and restoring order in families." It mattered little to them that the old regime carried over for women in the form of an "estate"—a term that indicated an unchangeable lifetime situation into which people were born and would always remain. Estates had been abolished for men in favor of mobility, but it continued for women.

By the time the Napoleonic Code went into effect, little remained of liberal revolutionary programs for women except the provisions for equal inheritance by sisters and brothers. The Code cleared the way for the rule of property and for individual triumph. It ushered in an age of mobility, marked by the rise of the energetic and heroic. The Code gave women little room for that kind of acquisitiveness or for heroism. Instead, women's realm was to encompass virtue, reproduction, and family.

Chapter Questions

1. Considering the materials in this chapter, how would you explain Napoleon's rise to power and his effective exercise of it?
2. In what ways did Napoleon preserve and support the principles of the French Revolution? In what ways did he undermine these principles?

CHAPTER SEVEN

Reaction, Reform, Revolution, and Romanticism: 1815–1848

The European powers met at the Congress of Vienna (1814–1815) to decide how to proceed now that Napoleon had been defeated. Conservative sentiments, exemplified by the views of Prince Metternich of Austria, predominated at this congress. Although the final settlement was not punitive or humiliating to France, it did represent an effort by conservative leaders to reject changes instituted during the revolutionary and Napoleonic periods, to restore traditional groups and governments to power, and to resist liberalism and nationalism. As a result of this and other developments, the aristocracy regained some of its prominence, monarchs such as Louis XVIII (brother of Louis XVI) returned to power, and armies intervened (as in Spain and Italy) to crush threats to the status quo.

Nevertheless, movements for national liberation and liberal reform surfaced during the 1820s, 1830s, and 1840s. In the 1820s and 1830s, Greece and Belgium gained independence and less successful nationalistic movements arose in Italy and Poland. Liberalism, encompassing demands for greater freedom, constitutional government, and political rights, was particularly strong in Western Europe. In England a series of legislative acts in the 1830s and 1840s clearly recognized liberal demands. In France a revolution in 1830 brought to power groups more open to liberal ideas.

A climax came in 1848, when revolutions erupted across Europe. Although each revolution was different, in general the middle and working classes demanded changes in the name of nationalism or liberalism. At first, established governments weakened or fell, but the revolutionaries found it difficult to remain unified once power was in their hands. Soon groups standing for authoritarian rule took advantage of this disunity and regained power.

The conservatism and liberalism that characterized so many of the political developments of this period were reflected in certain artistic and literary styles. Romanticism was the most important of these, reflecting, in different ways, both conservatism and liberalism. From its beginning in the late eighteenth century, it spread until it became the dominant cultural movement of the first half of the nineteenth century. Romanticism rejected the formalism of the previously dominant Classical style, refused to be limited by Enlightenment rationalism or the stark realism of everyday life, and emphasized emotion and freedom.

The documents in this chapter focus on (1) conservatism (What were some of the main characteristics of conservatism? What did it stand against? What policies fit with conservative attitudes? In what ways did the Congress of Vienna reflect the conservatism of the period?), (2) liberalism and movements for reform (What did liberalism mean in the first half of the nineteenth century? What reforms did liberals demand? What was the nature of reform movements, as exemplified by Chartism in England?), (3) the revolutions of 1848 (In what ways did the revolutions of 1848 bring to a head some of the main trends of the period? Who might be considered the "winners" and "losers"

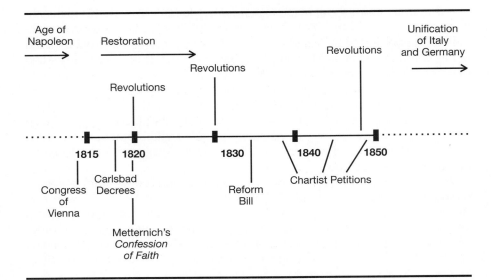

in these revolutions? Why did a revolution not occur in England at the same time?), and (4) the nature of Romanticism, particularly as it is revealed in literature and art (What were some of the ties between Romanticism and conservatism? How was Romanticism related to liberal and even revolutionary ideals?).

What emerges from these selections is a picture of Europeans trying to deal politically and culturally with the legacy of the French Revolution and the Enlightenment. The economic and social developments of the period will be covered in the next chapter.

PRIMARY SOURCES

Secret Memorandum to Tsar Alexander I, 1820: Conservative Principles
Prince Klemens von Metternich

The outstanding leader of the conservative tide that rose with the fall of Napoleon was Prince Klemens von Metternich (1773–1859). From his post as Austrian Minister of Foreign Affairs, Metternich hosted the Congress of Vienna and played a dominating role within Austria and among the conservative states of Europe between 1815 and 1848. Both in principle and in practice, he represented a conservatism that rejected the changes wrought by the French Revolution and stood against liberalism and nationalism. The following is an excerpt from a secret memorandum that Metternich sent to Tsar Alexander I of Russia in 1820, explaining his political principles. While not a sophisticated statement of political theory, it does reflect key elements of conservative attitudes and ideas.

> **Consider:** *What threats Metternich perceives; how Metternich connects "presumption" with the middle class; how this document reflects the experience of the revolutionary and Napoleonic periods; the kinds of policies that would logically flow from these attitudes.*

'L'Europe,' a celebrated writer has recently said, *'fait aujourd'hui pitié à l'homme d'esprit et horreur à l'homme vertueux.'*[1]

SOURCE: Prince Richard Metternich, ed., *Memoirs of Prince Metternich, 1815–1829*, vol. III, trans. Mrs. Alexander Napier (New York: Charles Scribner's Sons, 1881), pp. 454–455, 458–460, 468–469.

[1]Europe . . . is pitied by men of spirit and abhorred by men of virtue.

It would be difficult to comprise in a few words a more exact picture of the situation at the time we are writing these lines!

Kings have to calculate the chances of their very existence in the immediate future; passions are let loose, and league together to overthrow everything which society respects as the basis of its existence; religion, public morality, laws, customs, rights, and duties, all are attacked, confounded, overthrown, or called in question. The great mass of the people are tranquil spectators of these attacks and revolutions, and of the absolute want of all means of defense. A few are carried off by the torrent, but the wishes of the immense majority are to maintain a repose which exists no longer, and of which even the first elements seem to be lost. . . .

Having now thrown a rapid glance over the first causes of the present state of society, it is necessary to point out in a more particular manner the evil which threatens to deprive it, at one blow, of the real blessings, the fruits of genuine civilisation, and to disturb it in the midst of its enjoyments. This evil may be described in one word—presumption; the natural effect of the rapid progression of the human mind towards the perfecting of so many things. This it is which at the present day leads so many individuals astray, for it has become an almost universal sentiment.

Religion, morality, legislation, economy, politics, administration, all have become common and accessible to everyone. Knowledge seems to come by inspiration; experience has no value for the presumptuous man; faith is nothing to him; he substitutes for it a pretended individual conviction, and to arrive at this conviction dispenses with all inquiry and with all study; for these means appear too trivial to a mind which believes itself strong enough to embrace at one glance all questions and all facts. Laws have no value for him, because he has not contributed to make them, and it would be beneath a man of his parts to recognise the limits traced by rude and ignorant generations. Power resides in himself; why should he submit himself to that which was only useful for the man deprived of light and knowledge? That which, according to him, was required in an age of weakness cannot be suitable in an age of reason and vigour amounting to universal perfection, which the German innovators designate by the idea, absurd in itself, of the Emancipation of the People! Morality itself he does not attack openly, for without it he could not be sure for a single instant of his own existence; but he interprets its essence after his own fashion, and allows every other person to do so likewise, provided that other person neither kills nor robs him.

In thus tracing the character of the presumptuous man, we believe we have traced that of the society of the day, composed of like elements, if the denomination of society is applicable to an order of things which only tends in principle towards individualising all the elements of which society is composed. Presumption makes every man the guide of his own belief, the arbiter of laws according to which he is pleased to govern himself, or to allow some one else to govern him and his neighbours; it makes him, in short, the sole judge of his own faith, his own actions, and the principles according to which he guides them. . . .

The Governments, having lost their balance, are frightened, intimidated, and thrown into confusion by the cries of the intermediary class of society, which, placed between the Kings and their subjects, breaks the sceptre of the monarch, and usurps the cry of the people—the class so often disowned by the people, and nevertheless too much listened to, caressed and feared by those who could with one word reduce it again to nothingness.

We see this intermediary class abandon itself with a blind fury and animosity which proves much more its own fears than any confidence in the success of its enterprises, to all the means which seem proper to assuage its thirst for power, applying itself to the task of persuading Kings that their rights are confined to sitting upon a throne, while those of the people are to govern, and to attack all that centuries have bequeathed as holy and worthy of man's respect—denying, in fact, the value of the past, and declaring themselves the masters of the future. We see this class take all sorts of disguises, uniting and subdividing as occasion offers, helping each other in the hour of danger, and the next day depriving each other of all their conquests. It takes possession of the press, and employs it to promote impiety, disobedience to the laws of religion and the State, and goes so far as to preach murder as a duty for those who desire what is good.

The Carlsbad Decrees, 1819:
Conservative Repression

One way political leaders tried to assert conservatism against any perceived threats such as liberalism or nationalism was through international cooperation and action, a policy known as the Concert of Europe. Another way was through taking internal measures against the same threats, such as occurred in Germany in 1819 with the issuance of the Carlsbad Decrees. These decrees were pushed through the Diet of the German Confederation by Austria and Prussia, but particularly by Prince Metternich, in reaction to nationalist student movements against the principles of the Congress of Vienna. The following excerpts from those decrees concern the universities, the press, and all "revolutionary plots."

> **Consider:** *The purposes of these decrees and the means used to effect these purposes; whether these decrees are consistent with attitudes expressed by Metternich in the "confession of faith" he makes in his secret memorandum to Tsar Alexander I; the consequences of the effective enforcement of these decrees.*

PROVISIONAL DECREE RELATING TO THE UNIVERSITIES,
UNANIMOUSLY ADOPTED SEPTEMBER 20, 1819

§2. The confederated governments mutually pledge themselves to remove from the universities or other public educational institutions all teachers who, by obvious

---

SOURCE: From James Harvey Robinson, ed., "The Reaction after 1815 and European Policy of Metternich," in *Translations and Reprints from the Original Sources of European History*, vol. I, no. 3, ed. Department of History of the University of Pennsylvania (Philadelphia: University of Pennsylvania Press, 1898), pp. 16–20.

deviation from their duty or by exceeding the limits of their functions, or by the abuse of their legitimate influence over the youthful minds, or by propagating harmful doctrines hostile to public order or subversive of existing governmental institutions, shall have unmistakably proved their unfitness for the important office intrusted to them. . . .

§3. Those laws which have for a long period been directed against secret and unauthorized societies in the universities, shall be strictly enforced. These laws apply especially to that association established some years since under the name Universal Students' Union (*Allgemeine Burschenschaft*), since the very conception of the society implies the utterly unallowable plan of permanent fellowship and constant communication between the various universities. The duty of especial watchfulness in this matter should be impressed upon the special agents of the government.

✧

PRESS LAWS FOR FIVE YEARS

§1. So long as this decree shall remain in force no publication which appears in the form of daily issues or as a serial not exceeding twenty sheets of printed matter shall go to press in any state of the Union without the previous knowledge and approval of the state officials.

✧

§6. . . . The Diet shall have the right, moreover, to suppress on its own authority, without being petitioned, such writings included in Section 1, in whatever German state they may appear, as in the opinion of a commission appointed by it, are inimical to the honor of the Union, the safety of individual states or the maintenance of peace and quiet in Germany. There shall be no appeal from such decisions and the governments involved are bound to see that they are put into execution.

✧

ESTABLISHMENT OF AN INVESTIGATING COMMITTEE AT MAINZ

ARTICLE I. Within a fortnight, reckoned from the passage of this decree, there shall convene, under the auspices of the Confederation, in the city and federal fortress of Mainz, an Extraordinary Commission of Investigation to consist of seven members including the chairman.

ARTICLE II. The object of the Commission shall be a joint investigation, as thorough and extensive as possible, of the facts relating to the origin and manifold ramifications of the revolutionary plots and demagogical associations directed against the existing Constitutional and internal peace both of the Union and of the individual states: of the existence of which plots more or less clear evidence is to be had already, or may be produced in the course of the investigation.

English Liberalism
Jeremy Bentham

The roots of liberalism are deep and varied, stretching back to the writings of John Locke in the seventeenth century and further. By the time liberalism started to flourish during the nineteenth century, it had a particularly strong English tradition. Perhaps the most influential of the early-nineteenth-century English liberals was Jeremy Bentham (1748–1832). He is best known as the author of the theory of utilitarianism and for advocating reform of many English institutions. The ideas and efforts of Bentham and his followers, who include James Mill and John Stuart Mill, formed one of the mainstreams of English liberalism and liberal reform in the nineteenth century. The first of the following two selections comes from Bentham's An Introduction to the Principles of Morals and Legislation *(1789) and focuses on the principle of utility. The second is from his* Manual of Political Economy *(1798) and indicates his views toward governmental economic policy.*

> **Consider:** *What exactly Bentham means by the principle of utility; what, according to the principle of utility, the proper role of government in general is; his explanation for the proper role of the government in economic affairs.*

I. Nature has placed mankind under the governance of two sovereign masters, *pain* and *pleasure*. It is for them alone to point out what we ought to do, as well as to determine what we shall do. On the one hand the standard of right and wrong, on the other chains of causes and effects, are fastened to their throne. They govern us in all we do, in all we say, in all we think: every effort we can make to throw off our subjection, will serve to demonstrate and confirm it. In words a man may pretend to abjure their empire: but in reality he will remain subject to it all the while. The *principle of utility* recognizes this subjection, and assumes it for the foundation of that system, the object of which is to rear the fabric of felicity by the hands of reason and of law. Systems which attempt to question it, deal in sounds instead of sense, in caprice instead of reason, in darkness instead of light.

But enough of metaphor and declamation: it is not by such means that moral science is to be improved.

II. The principle of utility is the foundation of the present work: it will be proper therefore at the outset to give an explicit and determinate account of what is meant by it. By the principle of utility is meant that principle which approves or disapproves of every action whatsoever, according to the tendency which it appears to have to augment or diminish the happiness of the party whose interest is in question: or, what is the same thing in other words, to promote or to oppose that

SOURCES: Jeremy Bentham, *An Introduction to the Principles of Morals and Legislation* (Oxford: Clarendon Press, 1876), pp. 1–3; John Bowring, ed., *Bentham's Works*, vol. III (Edinburgh: William Tait, 1843), pp. 33–35.

happiness. I say of every action whatsoever; and therefore not only of every action of a private individual, but of every measure of government.

III. By utility is meant that property in any object, whereby it tends to produce benefit, advantage, pleasure, good, or happiness (all this in the present case comes to the same thing) or (what comes again to the same thing) to prevent the happening of mischief, pain, evil, or unhappiness to the party whose interest is considered: if that party be the community in general, then the happiness of the community: if a particular individual, then the happiness of that individual.

IV. The interest of the community is one of the most general expressions that can occur in the phraseology of morals: no wonder that the meaning of it is often lost. When it has a meaning, it is this. The community is a fictitious *body*, composed of the individual persons who are considered as constituting as it were its *members*. The interest of the community then is, what?—the sum of the interests of the several members who compose it.

V. It is in vain to talk of the interest of the community, without understanding what is the interest of the individual. A thing is said to promote the interest, or to be *for* the interest, of an individual, when it tends to add to the sum total of his pleasures: or, what comes to the same thing, to diminish the sum total of his pains.

VI. An action then may be said to be conformable to the principle of utility, or, for shortness sake, to utility (meaning with respect to the community at large) when the tendency it has to augment the happiness of the community is greater than any it has to diminish it.

VII. A measure of government (which is but a particular kind of action, performed by a particular person or persons) may be said to be conformable to or dictated by the principle of utility, when in like manner the tendency which it has to augment the happiness of the community is greater than any which it has to diminish it. . . .

✦

The practical questions, therefore, are how far the end in view is best promoted by individuals acting for themselves? and in what cases these ends may be promoted by the hands of government?

With the view of causing an increase to take place in the mass of national wealth, or with a view to increase of the means either of subsistence or enjoyment, without some special reason, the general rule is, that nothing ought to be done or attempted by government. The motto, or watchword of government, on these occasions, ought to be—*Be quiet*.

For this quietism there are two main reasons:

1. Generally speaking, any interference for this purpose on the part of government is needless. The wealth of the whole community is composed of the wealth of the several individuals belonging to it taken together. But to increase his particular portion is, generally speaking, among the constant objects of each individual's exertions and care. Generally speaking, there is no one who knows what is for your interest so well as yourself—no one who is disposed with so much ardour and constancy to pursue it.

2. Generally speaking, it is moreover likely to be pernicious, viz. by being unconducive, or even obstructive, with reference to the attainment of the end in view. Each individual bestowing more time and attention upon the means of preserving and increasing his portion of wealth, than is or can be bestowed by government, is likely to take a more effectual course than what, in his instance and on his behalf, would be taken by government.

It is, moreover, universally and constantly pernicious in another way, by the restraint or constraint imposed on the free agency of the individual. . . .

. . . With few exceptions, and those not very considerable ones, the attainment of the maximum of enjoyment will be most effectually secured by leaving each individual to pursue his own maximum of enjoyment, in proportion as he is in possession of the means. Inclination in this respect will not be wanting on the part of any one. Power, the species of power applicable to this case—viz. wealth, pecuniary power—could not be given by the hand of government to one, without being taken from another; so that by such interference there would not be any gain of power upon the whole.

The gain to be produced in this article by the interposition of government, respects principally the head of knowledge. There are cases in which, for the benefit of the public at large, it may be in the power of government to cause this or that portion of knowledge to be produced and diffused, which, without the demand for it produced by government, would either not have been produced, or would not have been diffused.

We have seen above the grounds on which the general rule in this behalf—*Be quiet*—rests. Whatever measures, therefore, cannot be justified as exceptions to that rule, may be considered as *non agenda* on the part of government. The art, therefore, is reduced within a small compass: *security* and *freedom* are all that industry requires. The request which agriculture, manufactures and commerce present to governments, is modest and reasonable as that which Diogenes made to Alexander: *"Stand out of my sunshine."* We have no need of favour—we require only a secure and open path.

Liberalism: Progress and Optimism
The Economist, 1851

Liberals usually believed in progress and were optimistic about their own times and the future. By mid-century, liberalism was most widespread in England, Europe's dominant economic power. English liberals living in the mid-nineteenth century were therefore particularly confident and proud, as indicated by the following excerpts from two 1851 arti-

SOURCE: *The Economist* (London), vol. IX, January 4, 1851, p. 5; January 18, 1851, p. 57.

cles published in The Economist. *This journal appealed to England's prosperous middle class.*

> **Consider:** *What liberals considered the great improvements of the first half of the nineteenth century; who benefited most from these changes; how conservatives or socialists might respond.*

Economists are supposed to be, by nature and occupation, cold, arithmetical, and unenthusiastic. We shall not, we hope, do discredit to this chapter when we say that we consider it a happiness and a privilege to have had our lot cast in the first fifty years of this century. . . .

It has witnessed a leap forward in all the elements of material well-being such as neither scientific vision nor poetic fancy ever pictured. It is not too much to say that, in wealth, in the arts of life, in the discoveries of science and their application to the comfort, the health, the safety, and the capabilities of man, in public and private morality, in the diffusion if not in the advancement of knowledge, in the sense of social charity and justice, in religious freedom, and in political wisdom,—the period of the last fifty years has carried us forward faster and further than any other half-century in modern times . . . in many of the particulars we have enumerated, it has witnessed a more rapid and astonishing progress than *all* the centuries which have preceded it. In several vital points the difference between the 18th and the 19th century, is greater than between the first and the 18th, as far as civilised Europe is concerned.

✻

When we refer to a few only of the extraordinary improvements of the half century just elapsed—such as the 35 years' peace, so far as morals are concerned; such as the philanthropic and just conviction that the welfare of the multitude, not of one or two classes, is the proper object of social solicitude; the humane direction which the mind has received towards the abolition of slavery; the amelioration of all penal systems, and the doubts that have been generated of their utility; the advances in religious toleration, and in forbearing one with another: and such as the application of steam to locomotives on water and land, and the consequent vast extension of communication all over the world, so far as physics are concerned;—such as the invention and general introduction of gas; the use of railroads and electric telegraphs; the extended application of machinery to all the arts of life, almost putting an end to very severe injurious bodily toil, except in agriculture, in which, though the labourers are speedily doubled up with rheumatism, and become, from poverty and excessive labour in all kinds of weather, prematurely old, great improvements have nevertheless been made:—when we refer to a few events of this kind, we become convinced that the half century just elapsed is more full of wonders than any other on record.

The First Chartist Petition: Demands for Change in England

Movements for reform occurred throughout Europe between 1815 and 1848 despite the efforts of conservatives to quash them. Eventually almost all countries in Europe experienced the revolutions conservatives feared so much. One exception was England, but even there political movements threatened to turn into violent revolts against the failure of the government to change. The most important of these was the Chartist movement, made up primarily of members of the working class who wanted reforms for themselves. The following is an excerpt from the first charter presented to the House of Commons in 1838. Subsequent charters were presented in 1842 and 1848. In each case the potential existed for a mass movement to turn into a violent revolt, and in each case Parliament rejected the Chartist demands. Only later in the century were most of these demands met.

Consider: *The nature of the Chartists' demands; by what means the Chartists hoped to achieve their ends; how Metternich might analyze these demands.*

Required, as we are universally, to support and obey the laws, nature and reason entitle us to demand that in the making of the laws the universal voice shall be implicitly listened to. We perform the duties of freemen; we must have the privileges of freemen. Therefore, we demand universal suffrage. The suffrage, to be exempt from the corruption of the wealthy and the violence of the powerful, must be secret. The assertion of our right necessarily involves the power of our uncontrolled exercise. We ask for the reality of a good, not for its semblance, therefore we demand the ballot. The connection between the representatives and the people, to be beneficial, must be intimate. The legislative and constituent powers, for correction and for instruction, ought to be brought into frequent contact. Errors which are comparatively light, when susceptible of a speedy popular remedy, may produce the most disastrous effects when permitted to grow inveterate through years of compulsory endurance. To public safety, as well as public confidence, frequent elections are essential. Therefore, we demand annual parliaments. With power to choose, and freedom in choosing, the range of our choice must be unrestricted. We are compelled, by the existing laws, to take for our representatives men who are incapable of appreciating our difficulties, or have little sympathy with them; merchants who have retired from trade and no longer feel its harrassings; proprietors of land who are alike ignorant of its evils and its cure; lawyers by whom the notoriety of the senate is courted only as a means of obtaining notice in the courts. The labours of a representative who is sedulous in the discharge of his duty are numerous and burdensome. It is neither just, nor reasonable, nor safe, that they should continue to be gratuitously rendered. We

SOURCE: From R. G. Gammage, *History of the Chartist Movement*, 2d ed. (Newcastle-on-Tyne, England: Browne and Browne, 1894), pp. 88–90.

demand that in the future election of members of your honourable house, the approbation of the constituency shall be the sole qualification, and that to every representative so chosen, shall be assigned out of the public taxes, a fair and adequate remunerative for the time which he is called upon to devote to the public service. The management of his mighty kingdom has hitherto been a subject for contending factions to try their selfish experiments upon. We have felt the consequences in our sorrowful experience. Short glimmerings of uncertain enjoyment, swallowed up by long and dark seasons of suffering. If the self-government of the people should not remove their distresses, it will, at least, remove their repinings. Universal suffrage will, and it alone can, bring true and lasting peace to the nation; we firmly believe that it will also bring prosperity. May it therefore please your honourable house, to take this our petition into your most serious consideration, and to use your utmost endeavours, by all constitutional means, to have a law passed, granting to every male of lawful age, sane mind, and unconvicted of crime, the right of voting for members of parliament, and directing all future elections of members of parliament to be in the way of secret ballot, and ordaining that the duration of parliament, so chosen, shall in no case exceed one year, and abolishing all property qualifications in the members, and providing for their due remuneration while in attendance on their parliamentary duties.

"And your petitioners shall ever pray."

An Eyewitness Account of the Revolutions of 1848 in Germany
Annual Register, 1848

In 1848 revolutions broke out throughout Europe. The February Revolution in France seemed to act as a spark for revolutions elsewhere, particularly in the German states. Indeed, within a few days of the outbreak in France, the established governments of the German states were faced with demands for change, demonstrations, and revolutions. The following is an account by an eyewitness of some of the events in Germany during March 1848, as reported in the London Annual Register.

Consider: *Whether this indicates any pattern to the revolutionary activities; the nature of the demands for change; how the established governments reacted.*

In order to give a clear and distinct narrative of the complicated events which have taken place during the present year in Germany, we have had to consider carefully the question of arrangement; for, independently of the revolutionary movements in the separate kingdoms, there has been a long-sustained attempt

---

SOURCE: Louis L. Snyder, ed., *Documents of German History* (New Brunswick, N.J.: Rutgers University Press, 1958), pp. 174–175.

to construct a new German nationality on the basis of a Confederation of all the states, with one great Parliament or Diet, and a Central Executive at Frankfort.
. . .

It was in the southwestern states of Germany that the effects of the French Revolution began first to manifest themselves. On the 29th of February the Grand Duke of Baden received a deputation from his subjects who demanded liberty of the press, the establishment of a national guard, and trial by jury. They succeeded in their object, and M. Welcker, who had distinguished himself as a Liberal leader, was appointed one of the ministers.

On the 3d of March, the Rhenish provinces, headed by Cologne, followed the same example. On the 4th similar demonstrations took place at Wiesbaden and Frankfort, and on the 5th at Düsseldorf. At Cologne, on the 3d of March, the populace asembled in crowds before the Stadthaus, or town hall, where the town council were sitting, and demanded the concession of certain rights, which were inscribed on slips of paper and handed about amongst the mob. They were as follows: (1) Universal suffrage; all legislation and government to proceed from the people. (2) Liberty of the press and freedom of speech. (3) Abolition of the standing army and the armament of the people, who are to elect their own officers. (4) Full rights of public meeting. (5) Protection to labor, and a guarantee for the supply of all necessaries. (6) State education for all children.

The military were, however, called out, and the streets were cleared without much difficulty.

At Wiesbaden, in Nassau, a large concourse of people met opposite the palace on the 4th, and demanded a general arming of the people under their own elective leaders; entire liberty of the press; a German Parliament; right of public meeting; public and oral trial by jury; the control of the duchy domain; convocation of the second chamber to frame a new electoral law on the basis of population, and to remove all restrictions on religious liberty. The Duke was absent at Berlin, but the Duchess, from the balcony of the palace, assured the people that their demands would be fully conceded by the Duke, her stepson. Subsequently appeared a proclamation in which the Duchess *guaranteed* the concession of these demands; and on the same day, in the afternoon, the Duke returned, and, immediately addressing the people, he ratified all the concessions made by the Duchess and his ministers.

The Genius of Christianity
René de Châteaubriand

The Romantic movement of the late eighteenth century and first half of the nineteenth century was in part a rebellion against new trends such as rationalism, urbanization, and secularism. Many historians have noted specific connections between Romanticism and

SOURCE: Viscount de Châteaubriand, *The Genius of Christianity*, trans. Charles I. White (Baltimore, Md.: John Murphy, 1856), pp. 385–387.

conservatism, particularly in the longing for a less complex life, the respect for traditional religion, and the sense of unity between rural life and human institutions. This is illustrated in the following selection from The Genius of Christianity *by René de Châteaubriand (1768–1848), a conservative French politician and writer. Published in 1802, it gained considerable popularity and helped Châteaubriand achieve a leading position among French conservatives. Here Châteaubriand describes the Gothic churches of the Middle Ages.*

> **Consider:** *Why this description might appeal to members of the aristocracy and the Catholic Church; by implication, the aspects of Châteaubriand's own times that he was attacking.*

You could not enter a Gothic church without feeling a kind of awe and a vague sentiment of the Divinity. You were all at once carried back to those times when a fraternity of cenobites, after having meditated in the woods of their monasteries, met to prostrate themselves before the altar and to chant the praises of the Lord, amid the tranquillity and the silence of night. Ancient France seemed to revive altogether; you beheld all those singular costumes, all that nation so different from what it is at present; you were reminded of its revolutions, its productions, and its arts. The more remote were these times the more magical they appeared, the more they inspired ideas which always end with a reflection on the nothingness of man and the rapidity of life. . . .

The forests of Gaul were, in their turn, introduced into the temples of our ancestors, and those celebrated woods of oaks thus maintained their sacred character. Those ceilings sculptured into foliage of different kinds, those buttresses which prop the walls and terminate abruptly like the broken trunks of trees, the coolness of the vaults, the darkness of the sanctuary, the dim twilight of the aisles, the secret passages, the low doorways,—in a word, every thing in a Gothic church reminds you of the labyrinths of a wood; every thing excites a feeling of religious awe, of mystery, and of the Divinity.

The two lofty towers erected at the entrance of the edifice overtop the elms and yew-trees of the churchyard, and produce the most picturesque effect on the azure of heaven. Sometimes their twin heads are illumined by the first rays of dawn; at others they appear crowned with a capital of clouds or magnified in a foggy atmosphere. The birds themselves seem to make a mistake in regard to them, and to take them for the trees of the forest; they hover over their summits, and perch upon their pinnacles. But, lo! confused noises suddenly issue from the top of these towers and scare away the affrighted birds. The Christian architect, not content with building forests, has been desirous to retain their murmurs; and, by means of the organ and of bells, he has attached to the Gothic temple the very winds and thunders that roar in the recesses of the woods. Past ages, conjured up by these religious sounds, raise their venerable voices from the bosom of the stones, and are heard in every corner of the ancient Sibyl; loud-tongued bells swing over your head, while the vaults of death under your feet are profoundly silent.

The Tables Turned: The Glories of Nature
William Wordsworth

Romantic themes were reflected in poetry as much as in other cultural forms. The British poet William Wordsworth (1770–1850) focused early on romantic themes in his work. He emphasized the connection between the individual and the glories of nature. Wordsworth gained much recognition in his own lifetime and was eventually appointed Poet Laureate of England. The following poem, "The Tables Turned," was first published in 1798.

Consider: *How this poem might be viewed as a rejection of the Enlightenment; the ways in which this poem relates to themes stressed by Châteaubriand.*

Up! up! my Friend, and quit your books;
Or surely you'll grow double:

Up! up! my Friend, and clear your looks;
Why all this toil and trouble?

The sun, above the mountain's head,
A freshening lustre mellow
Through all the long green fields has spread,
His first sweet evening yellow.

Books! 'tis a dull and endless strife:
Come, hear the woodland linnet,
How sweet his music! on my life,
There's more of wisdom in it.

And hark! how blithe the throstle sings!
He, too, is no mean preacher:
Come forth into the light of things,
Let Nature be your Teacher.

She has a world of ready wealth,
Our minds and hearts to bless—
Spontaneous wisdom breathed by health,
Truth breathed by cheerfulness.

One impulse from a vernal wood
May teach you more of man,
Of moral evil and of good,
Than all the sages can.

SOURCE: Edward Dowden, ed., *The Poetical Works of William Wordsworth*, vol. IV (London: George Bell and Sons, 1893), pp. 198–199.

Sweet is the lore which Nature brings;
Our meddling intellect
Mis-shapes the beauteous forms of things:—
We murder to dissect.

Enough of Science and of Art;
Close up those barren leaves;
Come forth, and bring with you a heart
That watches and receives.

VISUAL SOURCES

Abbey Graveyard in the Snow
Caspar David Friedrich

Abbey Graveyard in the Snow *(1819) was painted by the well-known North German artist Caspar David Friedrich. In the center are the ruins of a Gothic choir of a monastic church surrounded by a snow-covered graveyard and leafless winter forest. To the left a procession of monks follows a coffin into the ruins.*

This painting exemplifies many elements typical of Romanticism, particularly German Romanticism. The scene, while visually accurate, goes beyond realism: The light is too perfectly placed, the church remains are too majestic, the surrounding forest is too symmetrical a frame, and the funeral procession is out of place (funerals did not take place in ruins). By implication, this painting rejects the limits of Enlightenment rationalism and the reality of nineteenth-century urban life. Instead, a Romantic version of the Middle Ages, the spirituality of nature, and the glories of Christianity are evoked. The Romantic longing to be overwhelmed by eternal nature is suggested, particularly by the rendering of small human figures in a large landscape. Romanticism typically exalted the emotional over the rational, even if it was a melancholy sensitivity that was being displayed.

Consider: *The ways in which the Romanticism of this painting is consistent with that of Wordsworth's poetry and Châteaubriand's description of a Gothic cathedral.*

Photo 7-1

Bildarchiv Preussischer Kulturbesitz

Liberty Leading the People: Romanticism and Liberalism
Eugène Delacroix

A number of historical themes of the first half of the nineteenth century are combined in Liberty Leading the People *(1830) by the French painter Eugène Delacroix. The painting shows an important event of the revolution of 1830 in Paris—revolutionaries fighting off government troops at a bridge in the center of the city. The revolutionaries are led by a feminine figure symbolizing liberty and carrying a Republican flag in one hand, a gun in the other. She is followed by people of all classes and ages.*

In both style and content this painting reveals some of the connections between liberalism and Romanticism. The scene represents the high moral purposes of the revolution: the people struggling for the ideals of liberalism and nationalism. Despite the turmoil of the event, the people's faces convey a calm, firm assurance of the rightness and the outcome of their liberal cause. At the same time, the style of the painting is in the Romantic

Photo 7-2

Musée du Louvre/Photographie Giraudon

tradition, above all in its emphasis on heroism and the attainment of ideal goals—here liberal goals—beyond the normal expectations of life.

> **Consider:** *The ways in which this painting represents what Metternich and the Congress of Vienna struggled against.*

SECONDARY SOURCES

The Congress of Vienna
Hajo Holborn

Hindsight allows historians to evaluate diplomatic events with a sharply critical eye. Often great settlements between nations have been criticized for not taking into account the historical forces that would soon undo the stability that the peace treaties were supposed to establish. Although this critical view applies to the Congress of Vienna, there are historians who see it as relatively successful, particularly in comparison with the settlement after World War I. One of these historians is Hajo Holborn of Yale University. In the following selection Holborn evaluates the Congress of Vienna from the point of view of what was realistic for the parties at that time.

> **Consider:** *Why Holborn feels that the Congress of Vienna produced a constructive peace treaty; how other historians might criticize this view.*

The Vienna settlement created a European political system whose foundations lasted for a full century. For a hundred years there occurred no wars of worldwide scope like those of the twenty-odd years after 1792. Europe experienced frightful wars, particularly between 1854 and 1878, but none of them was a war in which all the European states or even all the great European powers participated. The European wars of the nineteenth century produced shifts of power, but they were shifts within the European political system and did not upset that system as such.

The peace settlement of Vienna has more often been condemned than praised. The accusation most frequently levelled against the Congress of Vienna has been that it lacked foresight in appraising the forces of modern nationalism and liberalism. Foresight is, indeed, one of the main qualities that distinguishes the statesman from the mere political professional. But even a statesman can only build

---

Source: Hajo Holborn, *The Political Collapse of Europe*. Reprinted by permission of Alfred A. Knopf, Inc. (New York, 1965), pp. 27–28. Copyright © 1965 by Alfred A. Knopf, Inc.

with the bricks at hand and cannot hope to construct the second floor before he has modelled the first by which to shelter his own generation. His foresight of future developments can often express itself only by cautious attempts at keeping the way open for an evolution of the new forces.

It is questionable how successful the Congress of Vienna was in this respect. None of the Congress representatives was a statesman or political thinker of the first historic rank. All of them were strong partisans of conservatism or outright reaction, and they found the rectitude of their convictions confirmed by the victory of the old powers over the revolutionary usurper. Still, they did not make a reactionary peace. They recognized that France could not live without a constitutional charter, and they knew, too, that the Holy Roman Empire was beyond resurrection. The new German Confederation represented a great improvement of the political conditions of Germany if one remembers that in Germany as well as in Italy the national movements were not strong enough to serve as pillars of a new order. In eastern Europe, furthermore, the modern ideas of nationality had hardly found more than a small academic and literary audience. A peace treaty cannot create new historical forces; it can only place the existing ones in a relationship most conducive to the maintenance of mutual confidence and least likely to lead to future conflict. The rest must be left to the ever continuing and never finished daily work of the statesmen.

In this light the Vienna settlement was a constructive peace treaty.

Western Liberalism
E. K. Bramsted and K. J. Melhuish

Although liberalism varied throughout Europe in accordance with the circumstances facing each country, there were broad similarities among the various liberal ideas and demands during the first half of the nineteenth century. In the following selection E. K. Bramsted and K. J. Melhuish summarize the common elements of liberal doctrine and attitudes in Europe.

> **Consider:** *How these doctrines and attitudes differ from conservatism; why liberalism would be more appealing to the middle class than to the aristocracy or the working class.*

In spite of the variations in the three main strands of liberalism, the features which classic liberals from Locke to John Stuart Mill had in common should not be overlooked. Rooted largely in the outlook of Enlightenment there was a constant emphasis on man's fundamental rationality and reasonableness. Privileges of the ruling strata based on mere tradition and custom were questioned and often rejected. Everywhere we encounter a strong urge to expand the rights of the

SOURCE: From E. K. Bramsted and K. J. Melhuish, eds., *Western Liberalism: A History in Documents from Locke to Croce,* pp. 35–36. Copyright © 1978 Longman Publishing Group, UK. Reprinted by permission.

individual and to reduce the powers of the State and of the government. However widely their arguments differed, liberal thinkers of the period . . . argued mainly in favour of the rights and the social usefulness of the individual citizen and stressed the need for parliamentary control of the powers of the government and of the accountability of its civil servants. Throughout, liberalism presumed a pluralism of existing political and religious opinions; everywhere it tended to make a plea for the rights of minorities, rights which should be protected. Civil disabilities on account of religious or political dissent were to be abolished, provided the dissenters kept their activities within the rule of the law. The right to own property and the obligation of the government to safeguard it were essential features of the liberal ideology. It was not accidental that most liberals insisted on property qualifications to be attached to the right to vote. . . .

While by no means all liberals shared Guizot's famous slogan 'Enrichissez vous!',[1] people without property were not much respected by most of them, but were regarded as the concern of charity, if not of socialists and anarchists. Instead liberals busied themselves with the belief in a rational political order, based on a constitution and promoted by a government with limited powers. Ministers were to be responsible to Parliament.

The belief in progress, in an advancing civilization, was another characteristic of most liberal thought. . . . The continuous improvement of mankind, helped by the advance of science and the new self-confidence of the diligent middle classes, was never seriously doubted.

The Revolutions of 1848
John Weiss

The revolutions of 1848 have been at the center of historical debate for a long time. To some, 1848 represents the end of the system set up by the Congress of Vienna; to others, it represents the great battle between the forces of liberalism and conservatism; and to still others, it represents the point at which liberalism, nationalism, socialism, and Romanticism met. Perhaps the most persistent historiographical tradition views 1848 as a point at which history made a "wrong" turn. Aspects of this historical debate are reflected in the following interpretation of 1848 by John Weiss. Here he de-emphasizes the role of liberalism, stressing instead the role played by artisans and peasants in the revolutions.

Consider: *According to Weiss, the social and economic causes of the revolutions; how Weiss supports his conclusion that it is misleading to label these revolutions liberal.*

The revolutions of 1848 were the last in Europe, excluding those caused by defeat in war. Their suppression also marked the last triumph of the semi-feudal varieties

---

SOURCE: From John Weiss, *Conservatism in Europe*, p. 56. Reprinted by permission of Thames & Hudson, Ltd.

[1]Make yourself wealthy.

of conservatism discussed previously. It is misleading to label these revolutions liberal, as is usually done. The revolutions were started and maintained by artisans and peasants who were either fighting to maintain some elements of the traditional order, or whose status had been dislocated by the intrusion of liberal commercial capitalism. It is true that liberals assumed leadership once the outbreaks had started, but they wanted reform, not revolution. Moreover, the liberals did not represent the middle class as a whole, but only the politically aware professional groups—lawyers, civil servants, educators and students. There was no mass following for liberal reforms in Europe, and the middle classes in general had no clearly perceived class enemy blocking their social mobility as in 1789. Consequently they were much more wary of the potential for social upheaval from below.

The liberal leaders of the revolutions were isolated from their own class and, as it turned out, had little to offer the artisans and peasants in revolt that could not as easily have been granted by conservatives. Only in Hungary and Italy, where nationalism incited mass risings against the Austrians, were the revolutions truly violent and sweeping. Elsewhere, we find only urban revolts accompanied by sporadic peasant uprisings. Excluding France, frightened conservative élites were never overthrown; they merely made paper concessions and withdrew temporarily until the weakness of the revolutionaries was evident, whereupon they returned in force. East of France traditionalists could still dominate the forms of social upheaval characteristic of pre-industrial society. In 1848 the industrial proletariat played almost no role whatsoever, and the outbreaks had familiar traditional causes: 1846 and 1847 were the years of the most terrible crop failures of nineteenth-century Europe, from which stemmed famine, inflation, shrinking markets and unemployment.

The Age of Paradox: 1848—
The English Exception
John W. Dodds

Although threatened by movements such as Chartism, England avoided the revolutions that struck almost every other European nation in 1848. Why? In the following selection from The Age of Paradox, *John W. Dodds addresses this question.*

> **Consider:** *Whether the content of the Chartist Petition of 1838 supports Dodds' interpretation; how this interpretation differs from that of Weiss; other differences between England and continental European nations at the time.*

What saved England from the whirlpool of revolution that engulfed the Continent in 1848? Here was a country in which six sevenths of the adult male population

SOURCE: John W. Dodds, *The Age of Paradox* (New York: Rinehart, 1952), pp. 331–332.

could not vote and where the representation in the Commons was so unfairly distributed that the great congested center of Manchester, with twice the population of Buckinghamshire, returned only two members as against the latter's eleven. Hunger and possible starvation looked just as ghastly to the Liverpool Irishman or the Glasgow operative as it did to the French workman. "It is quite new," wrote Greville, "to hear any Englishman coolly recommend assassination." How did England escape catastrophe?

In the first place, the Chartist leadership was divided within its own house. Such "moral force" men as Lovett would have nothing to do with the seditious threats of those who urged violent opposition to the Government. The leadership of the "physical force" group was itself vacillating: witness Feargus O'Connor's performance on Kennington Common. There was, too, a new and growing class of superior artisans—notably those essential to the great engineering developments in factories and railways—who wooed respectability, trusted in the developing organization of trade unionism to secure their rights, and threw their social weight with the middle classes. And, unlike the French, the English middle classes were one with the aristocracy in defense of the established order; the householders who patrolled the streets on April 10th as special constables were more important as symbols of a national *esprit* than they knew. Moreover, England had an aristocracy of which even the more stiff-necked members had the sense to bow constitutionally before the inevitable, and many of whom exerted themselves actively to temper the winds of distress. The energetic philanthropic and liberal efforts of such men as Lord Ashley, Sir William Molesworth, Lord Morpeth, and Lord Dudley Stuart (friend of Poland and champion of Kossuth) told heavily. The repeal of the Corn Laws, too, had come just in time; and there had never been any question about the freedom of the British press. The result of all this was that even the underprivileged Englishman felt that he was living under a constitutional government, that he could appeal to a sympathetic Queen and her "most honourable ministers" for relief. Hence an almost pathetic faith in monster petitions. Street barricades were simply not an Englishman's way of life. He might march endlessly with angry banners, but under such a friendly monarchy he would never tear up his own trees in Hyde Park to block Constitution Hill.

Chapter Questions

1. In a debate between liberals and conservatives of the early nineteenth century over how the French Revolution should be evaluated, what points would each side make?

2. In what ways might conservatives find Romanticism to their liking? What aspects of Romanticism might appeal to liberals?

3. Analyze nineteenth-century conservatism, liberalism, and Romanticism as alternative ways in which Europeans attempted to deal with the changes in Western civilization that had been occurring since the second half of the eighteenth century.

CHAPTER EIGHT

Industrialization and Social Change

The Industrial Revolution, which transformed economic life in the West, began in England in the eighteenth century. After the Napoleonic period it spread to Western Europe, and by the end of the nineteenth century it had touched most of Western civilization. The Industrial Revolution was characterized by unprecedented economic growth, the factory system of production, and the use of new, artificially powered machines for transportation and mechanical operations. The potential was tremendous; for the first time, human beings had the ability to produce far more than was needed to sustain a large percentage of the population. Whether that potential would be realized, and at what cost, remained to be seen.

In the wake of industrialization came great social changes. The middle and working classes were most affected by industrialization, and both grew in number and social influence as did the urban areas in which they worked and lived. But it was the middle class that benefited most, enjoying a rising standard of living, increased prestige, and growing political influence. Whether the working class benefited from industrialization during the early decades is a matter for debate among historians. Clearly it was this class that bore the burdens of urban social problems: overcrowded slums, poor sanitation, insufficient social services, and a host of related problems. The aristocracy, the peasantry, and the artisans—classes tied to the traditional agricultural economy and older means of production—slowly diminished in numbers and social importance as industrialization spread.

The selections in this chapter deal with the economic and social aspects of industrialization. Much-debated questions of economic history are addressed. Why did industrialization occur first in England? How did England differ from other areas that were relatively advanced economically? Most of the documents concern the human consequences of industrialization, questions of social history. The most popular area of interest, the effect of industrialization on the workers directly involved, is explored. What were the working conditions in the factories? How did industrialization affect the overall life style of these people? Did their standard of living improve or diminish as a result of industrialization? The middle class is also examined, especially middle-class attitudes and values. How did the middle class view industrialization? What were its attitudes toward money? How did the attitudes of and toward women change?

This chapter centers on industrialization in the first half of the nineteenth

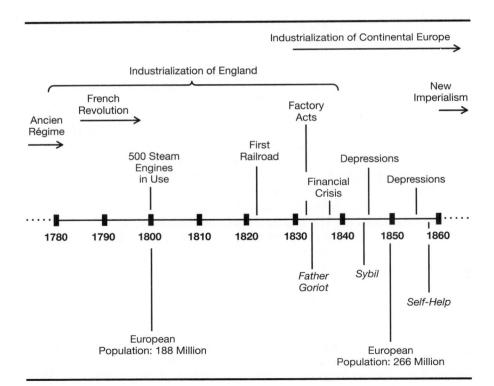

century. It should be recognized that industrialization spread unevenly, and it was not until the second half of the nineteenth century and even the beginning of the twentieth century that industrialization spread to many areas in Southern and Eastern Europe.

PRIMARY SOURCES

Testimony for the Factory Act of 1833: Working Conditions in England

Industrialization carried with it broad social and economic changes that were quickly felt by those involved. The most striking changes were in the working conditions in the new factories and mines. During the first decades of industrialization, there was little government control over working conditions and few effective labor organizations; laborers were thus at the mercy of factory owners who were pursuing profit in a competitive world. Investigations into conditions in factories and mines conducted by the British Parliament in the 1830s and 1840s led eventually to the enactment of legislation, such as the Factory Act of 1833. These parliamentary investigations provide us with extensive information about working conditions and attitudes toward them. The following selection contains three excerpts from a parliamentary commission's investigations into child labor in factories. The first is a summary by the commission of medical examiners from northeastern England. The second is the testimony of John Wright, a steward in a silk factory. The third is the testimony of William Harter, a silk manufacturer.

> **Consider:** *What these people perceived as the worst abuses of factory labor; the causes of the poor working conditions; how Harter might defend himself against the charges that he was abusing the working class; what biases the witnesses might hold.*

TESTIMONY OF THE COMMISSION OF MEDICAL EXAMINERS

The account of the physical condition of the manufacturing population in the large towns in the North-eastern District of England is less favourable. It is of this district that the Commissioners state, "We have found undoubted instances of children five years old sent to work thirteen hours a day; and frequently of children

SOURCE: Commission for Inquiry into the Employment of Children in Factories, *Second Report, with Minutes of Evidence and Reports by the Medical Commissioners*, vol. V, Session 29 January– 20 August, 1833 (London: His Majesty's Printing Office, 1833), pp. 5, 26–28.

nine, ten, and eleven consigned to labour for fourteen and fifteen hours." The effects ascertained by the Commissioners in many cases are, "deformity," and in still more "stunted growth, relaxed muscles, and slender conformation:" "twisting of the ends of the long bones, relaxation of the ligaments of the knees, ankles, and the like." "The representation that these effects are so common and universal as to enable some persons invariably to distinguish factory children from other children is, I have no hesitation in saying, an exaggerated and unfaithful picture of their general condition; at the same time it must be said, that the individual instances in which some one or other of those effects of severe labour are discernible are rather frequent than rare. . . .

"Upon the whole, there remains no doubt upon my mind, that under the system pursued in many of the factories, the children of the labouring classes stand in need of, and ought to have, legislative protection against the conspiracy insensibly formed between their masters and parents, to tax them to a degree of toil beyond their strength.

"In conclusion, I think it has been clearly proved that children have been worked a most unreasonable and cruel length of time daily, and that even adults have been expected to do a certain quantity of labour which scarcely any human being is able to endure. I am of opinion no child under fourteen years of age should work in a factory of any description for more than eight hours a day. From fourteen upwards I would recommend that no individual should, under any circumstances, work more than twelve hours a day; although if practicable, as a physician, I would prefer the limitation of ten hours, for all persons who earn their bread by their industry."

TESTIMONY OF JOHN WRIGHT

How long have you been employed in a silk-mill?—More than thirty years.

Did you enter it as a child?—Yes, betwixt five and six.

How many hours a day did you work then?—The same thirty years ago as now.

What are those hours?—Eleven hours per day and two over-hours: over-hours are working after six in the evening till eight. The regular hours are from six in the morning to six in the evening, and two others are two over-hours: about fifty years ago they began working over-hours. . . .

Why, then, are those employed in them said to be in such a wretched condition?—In the first place, the great number of hands congregated together, in some rooms forty, in some fifty, in some sixty, and I have known some as many as 100, which must be injurious to both health and growing. In the second place, the privy is in the factory, which frequently emits an unwholesome smell; and it would be worth while to notice in the future erection of mills, that there be betwixt the privy door and the factory wall a kind of a lobby of cage-work. 3dly, The tediousness and the everlasting sameness in the first process preys much on the spirits, and makes the hands spiritless. 4thly, the extravagant number of hours a child is compelled to labour and confinement, which for one week is seventy-six hours. . . . 5thly, About six months in the year we are obliged to use either gas, candles, or lamps, for the longest portion of that time, nearly six hours a day, being obliged to work amid the smoke and soot of the same; and also a large portion of oil and grease is used in the mills.

What are the effects of the present system of labour?—From my earliest recollections, I have found the effects to be awfully detrimental to the well-being of the operative; I have observed frequently children carried to factories, unable to walk, and that entirely owing to excessive labour and confinement. The degradation of the workpeople baffles all description: frequently have two of my sisters been obliged to be assisted to the factory and home again, until by-and-by they could go no longer, being totally crippled in their legs. And in the next place, I remember some ten or twelve years ago working in one of the largest firms in Macclesfield, (Messrs. Baker and Pearson,) with about twenty-five men, where they were scarce one half fit for His Majesty's service. Those that are straight in their limbs are stunted in their growth; much inferior to their fathers in point of strength. 3dly, Through excessive labour and confinement there is often a total loss of appetite; a kind of langour steals over the whole frame—enters to the very core—saps the foundation of the best constitution—and lays our strength prostrate in the dust. In the 4th place, by protracted labour there is an alarming increase of cripples in various parts of this town, which has come under my own observation and knowledge. . . .

Are all these cripples made in the silk factories?—Yes, they are, I believe. . . .

TESTIMONY OF WILLIAM HARTER

What effect would it have on your manufacture to reduce the hours of labour to ten?—It would instantly much reduce the value of my mill and machinery, and consequently of far prejudice my manufacture.

How so?—They are calculated to produce a certain quantity of work in a given time. Every machine is valuable in proportion to the quantity of work which it will turn off in a given time. It is impossible that the machinery could produce as much work in ten hours as in twelve. If the tending of the machines were a laborious occupation, the difference in the quantity of work might not always be in exact proportion to the difference of working time; but in my mill, and silk-mills in general, the work requires the least imaginable labour; therefore it is perfectly impossible that the machines could produce as much work in ten hours as in twelve. The produce would vary in about the same ratio as the working time.

Sybil, or the Two Nations: Mining Towns

Benjamin Disraeli

Nineteenth-century novels contain some of the most effective descriptions of industrial life. In addition to providing such description, Sybil, or the Two Nations *(1845), written by Benjamin Disraeli (1804–1881), a novelist and politician who also served as prime minister of England (1867–1868, 1874–1880), illustrates the thinking of a group of reforming Tory aristocrats, sometimes referred to as Young England. They hoped to gain working-class support against their political competitors, the liberal Whigs. In the following selection from this novel, Disraeli describes Marney, a rural mining town.*

> **Consider:** *The physical consequences of industrialization for the land and the town; the worst aspects of industrial labor, according to Disraeli; how this description compares with the testimony before the commission on child labor; who, if anyone, Disraeli would blame for all this.*

The last rays of the sun contending with clouds of smoke that drifted across the country, partially illumined a peculiar landscape. Far as the eye could reach, and the region was level, except where a range of limestone hills formed its distant limit, a wilderness of cottages, or tenements that were hardly entitled to a higher name, were scattered for many miles over the land; some detached, some connected in little rows, some clustering in groups, yet rarely forming continuous streets, but interspersed with blazing furnaces, heaps of burning coal, and piles of smouldering ironstone; while forges and engine chimneys roared and puffed in all directions, and indicated the frequent presence of the mouth of the mine, and the bank of the coal-pit. Notwithstanding the whole country might be compared to a vast rabbit warren, it was nevertheless intersected with canals, crossing each other at various levels; and though the subterranean operations were prosecuted with so much avidity that it was not uncommon to observe whole rows of houses awry, from the shifting and hollow nature of the land, still, intermingled with heaps of mineral refuse, or of metallic dross, patches of the surface might here and there be recognised, covered, as if in mockery, with grass and corn, looking very much like those gentlemen's sons that we used to read of in our youth, stolen by the chimneysweeps, and giving some intimations of their breeding beneath their grimy livery. But a tree or a shrub, such an existence was unknown in this dingy rather than dreary region.

It was the twilight hour; the hour at which in southern climes the peasant kneels before the sunset image of the blessed Hebrew maiden; when caravans halt in

---

SOURCE: Benjamin Disraeli, *Sybil, or the Two Nations* (New York: M. Walter Dunne, 1904), pp. 198–200.

their long course over vast deserts, and the turbaned traveller, bending in the sand, pays his homage to the sacred stone and the sacred city; the hour, not less holy, that announces the cessation of English toil, and sends forth the miner and the collier to breathe the air of earth, and gaze on the light of heaven.

They come forth: the mine delivers its gang and the pit its bondsmen; the forge is silent and the engine is still. The plain is covered with the swarming multitude: bands of stalwart men, broad-chested and muscular, wet with toil, and black as the children of the tropics; troops of youth, alas! of both sexes, though neither their raiment nor their language indicates the difference; all are clad in male attire; and oaths that men might shudder at issue from lips born to breathe words of sweetness. Yet these are to be, some are, the mothers of England! But can we wonder at the hideous coarseness of their language, when we remember the savage rudeness of their lives? Naked to the waist, an iron chain fastened to a belt of leather runs between their legs clad in canvas trousers, while on hands and feet an English girl, for twelve, sometimes for sixteen hours a day, hauls and hurries tubs of coals up subterranean roads, dark, precipitous, and plashy; circumstances that seem to have escaped the notice of the Society for the Abolition of Negro Slavery. Those worthy gentlemen, too, appear to have been singularly unconscious of the sufferings of the little trappers, which was remarkable, as many of them were in their own employ.

See, too, these emerge from the bowels of the earth! Infants of four and five years of age, many of them girls, pretty and still soft and timid; entrusted with the fulfilment of responsible duties, the very nature of which entails on them the necessity of being the earliest to enter the mine and the latest to leave it. Their labour indeed is not severe, for that would be impossible, but it is passed in darkness and in solitude. They endure that punishment which philosophical philanthropy has invented for the direst criminals, and which those criminals deem more terrible than the death for which it is substituted. Hour after hour elapses, and all that reminds the infant trappers of the world they have quitted, and that which they have joined, is the passage of the coal-waggons for which they open the air-doors of the galleries, and on keeping which doors constantly closed, except at this moment of passage, the safety of the mine and the lives of the persons employed in it entirely depend.

Self-Help: Middle-Class Attitudes
Samuel Smiles

Middle-class liberals were not totally unaware of the consequences of industrialization for society. Doctrines were developed that reflected and appealed to their attitudes. Such doctrines served to justify the position of the middle class, to support policies it usually

SOURCE: Samuel Smiles, *Self-Help* (Chicago: Belford, Clarke, 1881), pp. 21–23, 48–49.

favored, and to rationalize the poor state of the working class. Many of these doctrines appeared in Self-Help, *the popular book by Samuel Smiles, a physician, editor, secretary of two railroads, and author. First published in 1859,* Self-Help *became a best-seller in England and was translated into many languages. The following excerpt is a good example of the individualism and moral tone that appear throughout the book.*

> **Consider:** *How Smiles justifies his assertion that self-help is the only answer to problems; how Smiles would analyze the situation of the working class and how he would react to the testimony presented to the parliamentary commission on child labor.*

"Heaven helps those who help themselves" is a well tried maxim, embodying in a small compass the results of vast human experience. The spirit of self-help is the root of all genuine growth in the individual; and, exhibited in the lives of many, it constitutes the true source of national vigor and strength. Help from without is often enfeebling in its effects, but help from within invariably invigorates. Whatever is done *for* men or classes, to a certain extent takes away the stimulus and necessity of doing for themselves; and where men are subjected to over-guidance and over-government, the inevitable tendency is to render them comparatively helpless.

Even the best institutions can give a man no active help. Perhaps the most they can do is, to leave him free to develop himself and improve his individual condition. But in all times men have been prone to believe that their happiness and well-being were to be secured by means of institutions rather than by their own conduct. Hence the value of legislation as an agent in human advancement has usually been much overestimated. To constitute the millionth part of a Legislature, by voting for one or two men once in three or five years, however conscientiously this duty may be performed, can exercise but little active influence upon any man's life and character. Moreover, it is every day becoming more clearly understood, that the function of Government is negative and restrictive, rather than positive and active; being resolvable principally into protection—protection of life, liberty, and property. Laws, wisely administered, will secure men in the enjoyment of the fruits of their labor, whether of mind or body, at a comparatively small personal sacrifice; but no laws, however stringent, can make the idle industrious, the shiftless provident, or the drunken sober. Such reforms can only be effected by means of individual action, economy, and self-denial; by better habits, rather than by greater rights. . . .

Indeed, all experience serves to prove that the worth and strength of a State depend far less upon the form of its institutions than upon the character of its men. For the nation is only an aggregate of individual conditions, and civilization itself is but a question of the personal improvement of the men, women, and children of whom society is composed.

National progress is the sum of individual industry, energy, and uprightness, as national decay is of individual idleness, selfishness, and vice. What we are accustomed to decry as great social evils, will for the most part be found to be but the outgrowth of man's own perverted life; and though we may endeavor to cut them down and extirpate them by means of Law, they will only spring up again with fresh luxuriance in some other form, unless the conditions of personal life and character are radically improved. If this view be correct, then it follows that the highest patriotism and philanthropy consist, not so much in altering laws and modifying institutions, as in helping and stimulating men to elevate and improve themselves by their own free and independent individual action.

One of the most strongly marked features of the English people is their spirit of industry, standing out prominent and distinct in their past history, and as strikingly characteristic of them now as at any former period. It is this spirit, displayed by the commons of England, which has laid the foundations and built up the industrial greatness of the empire. This vigorous growth of the nation has been mainly the result of the free energy of individuals, and it has been contingent upon the number of hands and minds from time to time actively employed within it, whether as cultivators of the soil, producers of articles of utility, contrivers of tools and machines, writers of books, or creators of works of art. And while this spirit of active industry has been the vital principle of the nation, it has also been its saving and remedial one, counteracting from time to time the effects of errors in our laws and imperfections in our constitution.

The career of industry which the nation has pursued, has also proved its best education. As steady application to work is the healthiest training for every individual, so is it the best discipline of a state. Honorable industry travels the same road with duty; and Providence has closely linked both with happiness. The gods, says the poet, have placed labor and toil on the way leading to the Elysian fields. Certain it is that no bread eaten by man is so sweet as that earned by his own labor, whether bodily or mental. By labor the earth has been subdued, and man redeemed from barbarism; nor has a single step in civilization been made without it. Labor is not only a necessity and a duty, but a blessing: only the idler feels it to be a curse. The duty of work is written on the thews and muscles of the limbs, the mechanism of the hand, the nerves and lobes of the brain—the sum of whose healthy action is satisfaction and enjoyment. In the school of labor is taught the best practical wisdom; nor is a life of manual employment, as we shall hereafter find, incompatible with high mental culture.

Father Goriot: Money and the Middle Class
Honoré de Balzac

With industrialization the middle class rose in status and wealth. Increasingly, money became a common denominator in society, and the middle class was in a position to benefit from this. But the emphasis on money had its painful side even for the relatively

SOURCE: Honoré de Balzac, *Father Goriot* (New York: Century Co., 1904), pp. 264–265.

wealthy. Few have focused on this more profoundly and broadly than the French novelist Honoré de Balzac, who himself struggled with financial problems for much of his life. The following is an excerpt from his Father Goriot *(1834), in which Goriot, an old bourgeois, bemoans the way his daughters are treating him now that he is no longer so rich.*

Consider: *How Goriot sees money as both the cause for and the solution to his problems; the connections Balzac makes between money, social structure, and family life; how a worker might react to Goriot's problems.*

"Ah! if I were rich still, if I had kept my money, if I had not given all to them, they would be with me now; they would fawn on me and cover my cheeks with their kisses! I should be living in a great mansion; I should have grand apartments and servants and a fire in my room; and *they* would be about me all in tears, and their husbands and their children. I should have had all that; now—I have nothing. Money brings everything to you; even your daughters. My money. Oh! where is my money? If I had plenty of money to leave behind me, they would nurse me and tend me; I should hear their voices; I should see their faces. Ah, God! who knows? They both of them have hearts of stone. I love them too much; it was not likely that they should love me. A father ought always to be rich; he ought to keep his children well in hand, like unruly horses. I have gone down on my knees to them. Wretches! this is the crowning act that brings the last ten years to a proper close. If you but knew how much they made of me just after they were married. (Oh! this is cruel torture!) I had just given them each eight hundred thousand francs; they were bound to be civil to me after that, and their husbands too were civil. I used to go to their houses: it was, 'My kind father' here, 'My dear father' there. There was always a place for me at their tables. I used to dine with their husbands now and then, and they were very respectful to me. I was still worth something, they thought. How should they know? I had not said anything about my affairs. It is worth while to be civil to a man who has given his daughters eight hundred thousand francs apiece; and they showed me every attention then—but it was all for my money. Grand people are not great. I found that out by experience! I went to the theatre with them in their carriage; I might stay as long as I cared to stay at their evening parties. In fact, they acknowledged me their father; publicly they owned that they were my daughters. But I always was a shrewd one, you see, and nothing was lost upon me. Everything went straight to the mark and pierced my heart. I saw quite well that it was all sham and pretence, but there is no help for such things as these. I felt less at my ease at their dinner-table than I did downstairs here. I had nothing to say for myself. So these grand folks would ask in my son-in-law's ear, 'Who may that gentleman be?'—'The father-in-law with the dollars; he is very rich.'—'The devil, he is!' they would say, and look again at me with the respect due to my money.

Woman in Her Social and Domestic Character
Elizabeth Poole Sandford

Industrialization also had its effects on middle-class women. As the wealth and position of these women rose in a changing economic environment, previous models of behavior no longer applied. A variety of books and manuals appeared to counsel middle-class women on their proper role and behavior. The following is an excerpt from one of these, Woman in Her Social and Domestic Character *(1842), written by Mrs. John Sandford.*

> **Consider:** *Woman's ideal function in relation to her husband, according to this document; by implication, the role of the middle-class man in relation to his wife; possible explanations for this view of women.*

The changes wrought by Time are many. It influences the opinions of men as familiarity does their feelings; it has a tendency to do away with superstition, and to reduce every thing to its real worth.

It is thus that the sentiment for woman has undergone a change. The romantic passion which once almost deified her is on the decline; and it is by intrinsic qualities that she must now inspire respect. She is no longer the queen of song and the star of chivalry. But if there is less of enthusiasm entertained for her, the sentiment is more rational, and, perhaps, equally sincere; for it is in relation to happiness that she is chiefly appreciated.

And in this respect it is, we must confess, that she is most useful and most important. Domestic life is the chief source of her influence; and the greatest debt society can owe to her is domestic comfort: for happiness is almost an element of virtue; and nothing conduces more to improve the character of men than domestic peace. A woman may make a man's home delightful, and may thus increase his motives for virtuous exertion. She may refine and tranquillize his mind,—may turn away his anger or allay his grief. Her smile may be the happy influence to gladden his heart, and to disperse the cloud that gathers on his brow. And in proportion to her endeavors to make those around her happy, she will be esteemed and loved. She will secure by her excellence that interest and regard which she might formerly claim as the privilege of her sex, and will really merit the deference which was then conceded to her as a matter of course. . . .

Perhaps one of the first secrets of her influence is adaptation to the tastes, and sympathy in the feelings, of those around her. This holds true in lesser as well as in graver points. It is in the former, indeed, that the absence of interest in a companion is frequently most disappointing. Where want of congeniality impairs domestic comfort, the fault is generally chargeable on the female side. It is for

---

Source: Mrs. John Sandford (Elizabeth Poole Sandford), *Woman in Her Social and Domestic Character* (Boston: Otis, Broaders and Co., 1842), pp. 5–7, 15–16.

woman, not for man, to make the sacrifice, especially in indifferent matters. She must, in a certain degree, be plastic herself if she would mould others. . . .

To be useful, a woman must have feeling. It is this which suggests the thousand nameless amenities which fix her empire in the heart, and render her so agreeable, and almost so necessary, that she imperceptibly rises in the domestic circle, and becomes at once its cement and its charm.

✻

Nothing is so likely to conciliate the affections of the other sex as a feeling that woman looks to them for support and guidance. In proportion as men are themselves superior, they are accessible to this appeal. On the contrary, they never feel interested in one who seems disposed rather to offer than to ask assistance. There is, indeed, something unfeminine in independence. It is contrary to nature, and therefore it offends. We do not like to see a woman affecting tremors, but still less do we like to see her acting the amazon. A really sensible woman feels her dependence. She does what she can; but she is conscious of inferiority, and therefore grateful for support. She knows that she is the weaker vessel, and that as such she should receive honor. In this view, her weakness is an attraction, not a blemish.

In every thing, therefore, that women attempt, they should show their consciousness of dependence. If they are learners, let them evince a teachable spirit; if they give an opinion, let them do it in an unassuming manner. There is something so unpleasant in female self-sufficiency that it not unfrequently deters instead of persuading, and prevents the adoption of advice which the judgment even approves.

Women and the Working Class
Flora Tristan

As industrialization spread, working-class organizations developed. Opposed by governments and by the middle classes, these organizations faced great difficulties in creating a following and maintaining their existence. For the most part the new labor unions paid little attention to women and were dominated by men. However, there were women like Flora Tristan (1803–1844) who recognized the connections between the emancipation of women and forming working-class unions. In The Workers' Union *(1844), Tristan made the following appeal to French workers.*

> **Consider:** *The ways this might appeal to workers and particularly to working-class women; how this differs from the attitude of Elizabeth Poole Sandford or Samuel Smiles.*

SOURCE: Flora Tristan, *L'Union Ouvrière*, 2d ed. (Paris, 1844), p. 108, in Julia O'Faolain and Lauro Martines, eds., *Not in God's Image.* Copyright © 1973 by Julia O'Faolain and Lauro Martines. Reprinted by permission of Harper & Row, Publishers, Inc.

(1) To constitute the working class by setting up a compact, solid, and indissoluble union.

(2) The workers' union to choose and pay a defender who shall represent the working class before the nation [workers were without the voting franchise because of the 200-franc tax requirement], so as to establish universal acceptance of this class' right to exist [as an organization].

(3) To proclaim the legitimacy of hands (*bras*) as property, 25 million French workers having no property other than their hands.

(4) To secure the recognition of every man and woman's right to work.

(5) To secure the recognition of every man and woman's right to moral, intellectual, and vocational training.

(6) To examine the possibilities of organizing the labor force in present social conditions.

(7) To construct workers' union buildings in every department of France which shall provide intellectual and vocational training for working-class children and admit working men and women who have been disabled on the job or are sick or old.

(8) To proclaim the urgent necessity of giving working-class women moral, intellectual, and vocational training so that they may improve the morals of the men.

(9) To proclaim the fact that juridical equality between men and women is the only means of achieving the unity of humanity.

VISUAL SOURCES

Gare Saint Lazare
Claude Monet

From a visual standpoint, industrial civilization was strikingly different from its predecessor. The following 1877 painting of a railroad station in the heart of nineteenth-century Paris by the French Impressionist Claude Monet epitomizes the new industrial civilization. Steam, powerful engines, rapid transportation, and structures of iron and glass, all in an expanding urban environment, contrast sharply with the typical rural or urban images of previous eras.

> **Consider:** *The associations that a nineteenth-century viewer might have upon viewing this painting.*

Photo 8-1

Courtesy of the Fogg Art Museum, Harvard University.
Bequest, Collection of Maurice Wetheim, Class of 1906.

Illustration from *Life and Adventures of Michael Armstrong*

The following illustration is from a novel, Life and Adventures of Michael Armstrong *(1840), by the well-known British author, Mrs. Frances Trollope. The illustration depicts several of the main elements of the Industrial Revolution in England. It shows the inside of a textile factory—a factory in the most advanced of the new industries. Thanks to mechanization and artificial power, a few workers can now do the work of many. The workers—men, women, and children—are obviously poor. In the background stands the stern middle-class owner talking with others of his class while in the foreground a child worker embraces his middle-class counterpart for some kindness he has displayed. The scene is reflective of the typical middle-class view of the poor and poverty—as problems of morals,*

Photo 8-2

The Bettmann Archive/BBC Hulton

to be treated with pity and philanthropic concern but not yet requiring substantial social or economic change.

> **Consider:** *The ways in which this illustration reflects aspects of industrialization touched on by other documents in this chapter; the similarities and differences between this illustration and Photo 3-2 in Chapter 3.*

Industrialization and Demographic Change

A comparison of the first two maps, which show the population density of England in 1801 and 1851, reveals the relatively rapid increase in population and urbanization in certain areas of England during this period. The third map shows where industry (mainly textiles, metallurgy, and mining) was concentrated in 1851. A comparison of all three maps reveals the connections between shifting population density, urbanization, and industrialization during this period of early, rapid modernization of England's economy.

Map 8-1   Population Density: England, 1801

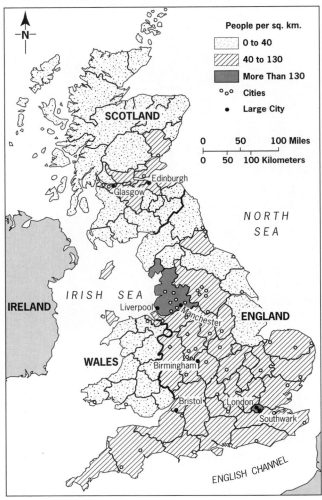

Consider: *What some of the geopolitical consequences of these connections between demographic and economic changes might be; what some of the social consequences of these same connections might be.*

Map 8-2   Population Density: England, 1851

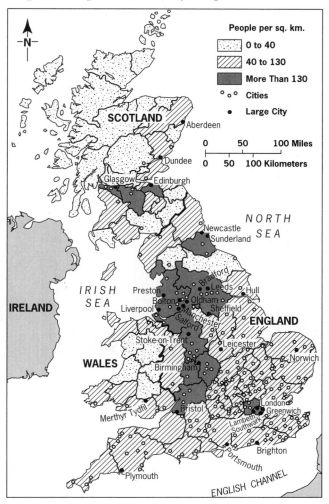

Map 8-3   Concentration of Industry in England, 1851

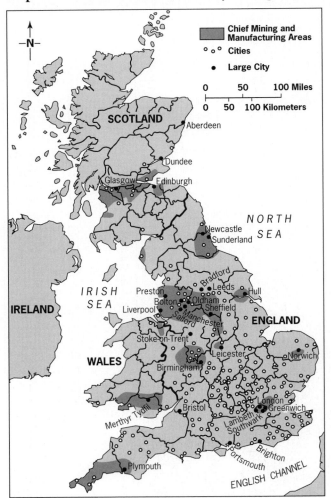

SECONDARY SOURCES

The Making of Economic Society: England, the First to Industrialize
Robert L. Heilbroner

Although it is clear that industrialization occurred first in England, it is not apparent why this should be so. During the eighteenth century France was prosperous and economically advanced. Other countries such as Belgium and the Netherlands possessed certain economic advantages over England and might have industrialized earlier but did not. In the following selection Robert Heilbroner, an economist and economic historian, addresses the question of why England was first and points out the differences between England and most other European nations in the eighteenth century.

> **Consider:** *Why Heilbroner stresses the role of the "New Men" over the other factors he lists; any disadvantages England had to overcome; whether it was simply the circumstances that gave rise to the "New Men" or whether it was the "New Men" who took advantage of the circumstances when most men in most other nations would not have.*

Why did the Industrial Revolution originally take place in England and not on the continent? To answer the question we must look at the background factors which distinguished England from most other European nations in the eighteenth century.

The first of these factors was simply that England was relatively wealthy. In fact, a century of successful exploration, slave-trading, piracy, war, and commerce had made her the richest nation in the world. Even more important, her riches had accrued not merely to a few nobles, but to a large upper-middle stratum of commercial bourgeoisie. England was thus one of the first nations to develop, albeit on a small scale, a prime requisite of an industrial economy: a "mass" consumer market. As a result, a rising pressure of demand inspired a search for new techniques.

Second, England was the scene of the most successful and thoroughgoing transformation of feudal society into commercial society. A succession of strong kings had effectively broken the power of the local nobility and had made England into a single unified state. As part of this process, we also find in England the strongest encouragement to the rising mercantile classes. Then too, as we have seen, the enclosure movement, which gained in tempo in the seventeenth and

SOURCE: Robert L. Heilbroner, *The Making of Economic Society*. Reprinted by permission of Prentice-Hall, Inc. (Englewood Cliffs, N.J., 1980), pp. 76–77, 80–81.

eighteenth centuries, expelled an army of laborers to man her new industrial establishments.

Third, England was the locus of a unique enthusiasm for science and engineering. The famous Royal Academy, of which Newton was an early president, was founded in 1660 and was the immediate source of much intellectual excitement. Indeed, a popular interest in gadgets, machines, and devices of all sorts soon became a mild national obsession: *Gentlemen's Magazine*, a kind of *New Yorker* of the period, announced in 1729 that it would henceforth keep its readers "abreast of every invention"—a task which the mounting flow of inventions soon rendered quite impossible. No less important was an enthusiasm of the British landed aristocracy for scientific farming: English landlords displayed an interest in matters of crop rotation and fertilizer which their French counterparts would have found quite beneath their dignity.

Then there were a host of other background causes, some as fortuitous as the immense resources of coal and iron ore on which the British sat; others as purposeful as the development of a national patent system which deliberately sought to stimulate and protect the act of invention itself. In many ways, England was "ready" for an Industrial Revolution. But perhaps what finally translated the potentiality into an actuality was the emergence of a group of new men who seized upon the latent opportunities of history as a vehicle for their own rise to fame and fortune. . . .

Pleasant or unpleasant, the personal characteristics fade beside one overriding quality. These were all men interested in expansion, in growth, in investment for investment's sake. All of them were identified with technological progress, and none of them disdained the productive process. An employee of Maudslay's once remarked, "It was a pleasure to see him handle a tool of any kind, but he was *quite splendid* with an 18-inch file." Watt was tireless in experimenting with his machines; Wedgwood stomped about his factory on his wooden leg scawling, "This won't do for Jos. Wedgwood," wherever he saw evidence of careless work. Richard Arkwright was a bundle of ceaseless energy in promoting his interests, jouncing about England over execrable roads in a post chaise driven by four horses, pursuing his correspondence as he traveled.

"With us," wrote a French visitor to a calico works in 1788, "a man rich enough to set up and run a factory like this would not care to remain in a position which he would deem unworthy of his wealth." This was an attitude entirely foreign to the rising English industrial capitalist. His work was its own dignity and reward; the wealth it brought was quite aside. Boswell, on being shown Watt and Boulton's great engine works at Soho, declared that he never forgot Boulton's expression as the latter declared, "I sell here, sir, what all the world desires to have—Power."

The new men were first and last *entrepreneurs*—enterprisers. They brought with them a new energy, as restless as it proved to be inexhaustible. In an economic, if not a political, sense, they deserve the epithet "revolutionaries," for the change they ushered in was nothing short of total, sweeping, and irreversible.

Early Industrial Society:
Progress or Decline?
Peter Stearns and Herrick Chapman

One of the most persistent debates over the early stages of the Industrial Revolution is whether a higher standard of living resulted for factory workers. A number of "optimistic" historians, relying primarily on statistical evidence such as wage rates, prices, and mortality rates, have argued that even during the early period factory workers experienced a rising standard of living. A group of more "pessimistic" historians, emphasizing qualitative data such as descriptions of the psychological, social, and cultural impact of the factory on workers' lives, argues that the standard of living declined for these workers during the first half of the nineteenth century. In the following selection Peter Stearns and Herrick Chapman focus on this debate, concluding that, at least for many workers, material conditions were modestly better.

> **Consider:** *The aspects of this selection that optimistic historians would emphasize and how pessimistic historians might respond; whether increased wage rates are a meaningful measure without a consideration of the psychological and social costs of that extra money.*

The question of whether conditions deteriorated or were improved by early factory employment has been hotly debated, particularly in the case of the British industrial revolution. There is evidence on both sides. Many have tried to prove that early industry was evil; others have asserted its beneficence. Even during the Industrial Revolution itself the question was argued with much partisan feeling. The issue is not merely an academic one. In order to understand the workers themselves, it is vital to know whether they experienced a deterioration in conditions as they entered industry. That the workers were in misery from a modern point of view cannot be denied; that they were severely limited in their conditions is obvious; but whether they felt themselves to be miserable, judging by the standards they knew, is far from clear. . . .

Furthermore, in England and elsewhere, rural conditions had usually been declining before the Industrial Revolution began. This was, after all, the main impulse for peasants to accept factory jobs. Peasant standards of living were low anyway; preindustrial society was simply poor. And the people entering industry were often drawn from the lowest categories of the peasantry. These were the people who suffered most from expanding population and declining domestic industry. There was deterioration of material conditions in the early industrial period, but it occurred primarily in the countryside among the landless and the domestic producers and among the unskilled in the slums of cities like London. When they found factory employment, workers seldom could note a significant

SOURCE: Reprinted with the permission of Macmillan College Publishing Company from *Society in Upheaval*, 3d ed., by Peter Stearns and Herrick Chapman. Copyright © 1992 by Macmillan College Publishing Company, Inc.

worsening of their situation: many factory workers actually gained some ground in standard of living.

The worst problem for factory workers, as for the poorer classes even in premodern times, was the instability of conditions. Sick workers were rarely paid and sometimes lost their jobs. With age workers' skill and strength declined, and so did their earnings. Old workers, lacking property to fall back on, suffered from falling wages and frequent unemployment. Machine breakdowns caused days and even weeks of unemployment. Most important, recurrent industrial slumps plunged many workers into profound misery. Wages fell, sometimes by as much as 50 percent; up to a quarter of the labor force lost their jobs. Some returned to the countryside to seek work or to roam in bands to find food. Some survived on charity; the charity rolls of manufacturing cities often embraced over half the working class, though only meager support was offered. Some sold or pawned their possessions. All reduced expenses by eating potatoes instead of bread and ignoring rent payments. Old age, finally, could bring disaster. Working-class life was thus punctuated by a number of personal and general crises, creating a sense of insecurity that haunted workers even in better times.

In prosperous years the worst feature of the average worker's material standard of living was housing. Rural cottages had often been flimsy and small, befouled by animals, but city housing was sometimes worse. . . .

With poor housing and urban crowding, along with the pressures of factory work itself, many workers were in poor health. Rates of infant mortality were high, and many workers had a life expectancy at birth only half as high as that of their employers. . . .

Unquestionably factory wages were better than those of the countryside. Highly skilled male workers, many of them former artisans, were paid three to six times as much as ordinary laborers. For early mechanization did not eliminate the need for skill, though it reduced the percentage of skilled workers and changed the skills required. Hence the men who built and installed machines or puddled iron or ran the more complex spinning machines required years to learn their trade fully. But even lesser-skilled workers could command a money wage that was higher than what was available in the countryside or to the transient workers of the cities. There was little left over for purchases beyond food, housing, and clothing. A bit of tobacco or a small contribution to a mutual aid group were all that the ordinary worker could afford. However, wages tended to go up with time. They definitely rose in England after 1840. The main factory centers in France saw an increase in real wages in the 1830s and 1840s, and there was improvement in Germany in the 1840s and 1850s, in Russia in the 1890s.

So it is safe to conclude that material conditions, though bad, provided modest gains and some solace for many workers during the early industrial period as a whole. On the average, conditions were better than the new workers' traditions had led them to expect.

The Family and Industrialization in Western Europe

Michael Anderson

The tremendous growth of interest in social history over the past twenty years has stimulated scholars from other disciplines to address historical questions. A number of sociologists have applied methods from their own discipline to social aspects of nineteenth-century industrialization. In the following selection Michael Anderson, a sociologist from the University of Edinburgh, discusses the effects of industrialization on the working-class family.

> **Consider:** *The specific ways in which the process of industrialization affected working-class families; how Anderson's interpretation might support the "optimists" or the "pessimists" in their debate over the effects of the Industrial Revolution on the working class; how the effects on middle-class families might differ.*

In industrial areas, then, the close interdependence of parents and children which was so important in peasant societies gave way, and this was reflected in changes in family relationships. The early stages of industrialization, however, probably changed relationships between husbands and wives much less, though freedom from such close supervision and a more private domestic situation may have allowed rather more affection to develop between them than had been the case in pre-industrial peasant families. Husband and wife were no longer cooperating in the same productive task, but this had never been universal anyway. There was, however, a continued need and possibility for both husbands and wives to work as producers to keep the family above the subsistence line. In a few areas wives actually left the house to work in the factories. More usually, as women had always done, the wives of factory workers worked at home producing small items of clothing, processing some kind of food or drink, taking in the middle class's washing, or running a small shop or lodging house. The manifold needs of an industrial community were thus met in a way which contributed to working class family solidarity while allowing mothers to supervise and care (perhaps rather better than before) for small children during the lengthening period before they were able to enter the labor force themselves.

Initially, then, it was only in a few areas, especially those specializing in mining, machine-making, metal manufacturing, shipbuilding and sawmilling, that a change occurred in the economic status of women and with it in their family situation. In these areas there were not enough openings for female wage employment and, in

SOURCE: Michael Anderson, "The Family and Industrialization in Western Europe," *The Forum Series.* Reprinted by permission of Forum Press (St. Louis, Mo., 1978), p. 14. Copyright © 1978 by Forum Press.

consequence, many women were forced into the almost totally new situation of full-time housewife. However, as more and more traditional tasks were taken over by the application of factory production methods to clothing and food preparation, the home increasingly became confined to consumption. Only then did the distinction between male productive work outside the home and female consumption-oriented work inside the home become common among the working class.

Though the evidence is patchy, it seems that, at least in some areas, this had an effect on relationships between husbands and wives. Since the husband became the only income producer, the rest of the family became more dependent on him than he was on them. Whatever the husband did, the wife had little power to resist. While the family as a whole relied materially on the father, he needed them only to the extent that he could obtain from them emotional or other rewards which he could not obtain elsewhere or to the extent to which public opinion in the neighborhood was effective in controlling his behavior (And with the weakened community control of large industrial cities, neighborhood control was often weak). Thus, in the working class, the idea that a woman's place was in the home and that her role was essentially an inferior domestic one is not of great antiquity. Rather it seems only to have developed as a response to a major shift in the power balance between husbands and wives which reflected the new employment situation of late nineteenth and early twentieth century industrial society.

Chapter Questions

1. Do you feel that industrialization should be considered a great boon, a mixed blessing, or a disaster for nineteenth-century Europeans? Why?

2. In retrospect, what policies might governments have adopted to minimize the pains of industrialization? What factors acted against the adoption of such policies?

3. In a debate over how industrialization should be evaluated, what would the arguments of middle-class liberals be? Of industrial workers? Of women?

CHAPTER NINE

The National State, Nationalism, and Imperialism: 1850–1914

Between 1850 and 1914 Europe was characterized politically by the development of the national state, the spread of nationalism, and the rise of the "new imperialism." The development of the national state took place after 1848. Governments, responding to economic and social pressures, increased their involvement in the economic and social life of their countries. This was apparent both in liberal England and in more conservative France under Louis Napoleon. There were similar trends during the national unification movements in Italy and particularly in Germany, where the state took on a wide range of new functions.

Nationalism had deep roots, notably in the experience of and reactions to the French Revolution and the Napoleonic invasions. Nationalism also played a central role in the revolutions of 1848. During the second half of the nineteenth century, nationalism continued to grow and to be capitalized upon by national governments. The most striking manifestations of nationalism came in the successful unification movements in Italy and Germany.

The rise of the new imperialism occurred in the latter decades of the nineteenth century. The European powers engaged in a sudden quest for control over new territories in Asia and Africa. Explorers, missionaries, traders, troops, and government officials quickly followed one another into these lands and established direct political control. In this process the West greatly increased its dominance over much of the rest of the world, bringing Western culture and institutions to the indigenous societies whether they wanted it or not.

The sources in this chapter explore each of these three developments. Some of the documents concentrate on the growth of the national state, particularly in Germany, where the authoritarian government expanded in an effort to adapt to the social and economic pressures of the times, and France, where forces for radical change were still strong. Some of the questions addressed are: How did the government in Germany react to demands for social legislation? What was the role of conservative forces in the German unification process, and how did their dominance affect the subsequent history of Germany? Other documents concern nationalism, particularly its meaning, its appeal, and its connections to liberalism and conservatism. How did nationalism change over the nineteenth century? What role did nationalism play in the unification movements in Germany and Italy? How was nationalism tied to the new imperialism of the period? Finally, most of the selections deal with imperialism, for not only was imperialism of far-reaching

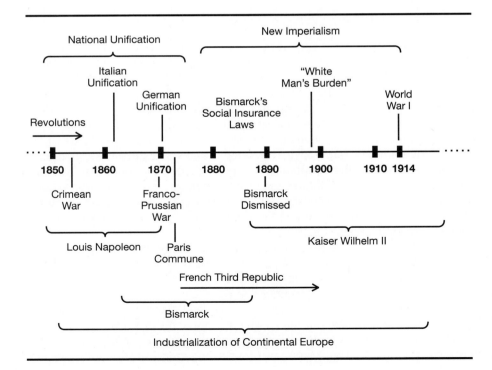

significance for much of the world, it has been a topic of considerable debate among historians. What were the nationalistic and economic motives for imperialism? What were some of the attitudes toward imperialism, particularly as reflected in materials glorifying it as a Christian and humanitarian movement? How is imperialism understood from a Marxist perspective? What were some of the consequences of imperialism?

Throughout these selections there is evidence for an increasing competitiveness among European states and political strains within those states. As will be seen in Chapter 11, these contributed to the outbreak of World War I and the revolutions that accompanied it.

PRIMARY SOURCES

Speeches on Pragmatism and State Socialism
Otto von Bismarck

The revolutions of 1848 were ultimately a blow to idealistic reform. Thereafter, governments pursued more limited goals. They tended to resort to more authoritarian measures, to avoid doctrinaire policies, and even to adopt certain programs of opposing groups in the hopes of weakening determined opposition to the government. Otto von Bismarck (1815–1898) did this in Germany. Born into a noble Prussian family, Bismarck rose to the position of chief minister under the king in 1862. The first selection below is from an 1862 speech to the Reichstag, in which he argues that the idealism of 1848 must be replaced by a conservative realism.

Bismarck remained in power until 1890. During this time he and his conservative supporters faced opposition from some liberals and from a growing number of socialists representing the working class. In the 1880s Bismarck supported some of the workers' demands for social insurance and pushed through such legislation as the German Workers' Insurance Laws. The remaining excerpts below Bismarck's speeches indicate the rationale behind these policies.

> **Consider:** *What Bismarck means when he says the great questions of the day will be decided by iron and blood; how Bismarck justifies his support of "socialist"*

SOURCES: Louis L. Snyder, ed., *Documents of German History* (New Brunswick, N.J.: Rutgers University Press, 1958), p. 202; William H. Dawson, *Bismarck and State Socialism* (London: Swan Sonnenschein and Co., 1890), pp. 29, 34–35, 63–64, 118–119.

policies; why Bismarck would support such policies; what conservatives have to gain and who stands to lose by enactment of these policies.

IRON AND BLOOD

. . . It is true that we can hardly escape complications in Germany, although we do not seek them. Germany does not look to Prussia's liberalism, but to her power. The south German States—Bavaria, Württemberg, and Baden—would like to indulge in liberalism, and because of that no one will assign Prussia's role to them! Prussia must collect her forces and hold them in reserve for an opportune moment, which has already come and gone several times. Since the Treaty of Vienna, our frontiers have not been favorably designed for a healthy body politic. Not by speeches and majorities will the great questions of the day be decided—that was the mistake of 1848 and 1849—but by iron and blood.

STATE SOCIALISM

Herr Richter has called attention to the responsibility of the State for what it does. But it is my opinion that the State can also be responsible for what it does not do. I do not think that doctrines like those of *'Laissez-faire, laissez-aller,'* 'Pure Manchesterdom in politics,' 'He who is not strong enough to stand must be knocked down and trodden to the ground,' 'To him that hath shall be given, and from him that hath not shall be taken away even that which he hath,'—that doctrines like these should be applied in the State, and especially in a monarchically, paternally governed State. On the other hand, I believe that those who profess horror at the intervention of the State for the protection of the weak lay themselves open to the suspicion that they are desirous of using their strength—be it that of capital, that of rhetoric, or whatever it be—for the benefit of a section, for the oppression of the rest, for the introduction of party domination, and that they will be chagrined as soon as this design is disturbed by any action of the Government.

°

Give the working-man the right to work as long as he is healthy; assure him care when he is sick; assure him maintenance when he is old. If you do that, and do not fear the sacrifice, or cry out at State Socialism directly the words 'provision for old age' are uttered,—if the State will show a little more Christian solicitude for the working-man, then I believe that the gentlemen of the Wyden (Social-Democratic) programme will sound their bird-call in vain, and that the thronging to them will cease as soon as working-men see that the Government and legislative bodies are earnestly concerned for their welfare.

Yes, I acknowledge unconditionally a right to work, and I will stand up for it as long as I am in this place. But here I do not stand upon the ground of Socialism, which is said to have only begun with the Bismarck Ministry, but on that of the Prussian common law.

°

Many measures which we have adopted to the great blessing of the country are Socialistic, and the State will have to accustom itself to a little more Socialism yet. We must meet our needs in the domain of Socialism by reformatory measures if we would display the wisdom shown in Prussia by the Stein-Hardenberg legislation respecting the emancipation of the peasantry. That was Socialism, to take land from one person and give it to another—a much stronger form of Socialism than a monopoly. But I am glad that this Socialism was adopted, for we have as a consequence secured a free and very well-to-do peasantry, and I hope that we shall in time do something of the sort for the labouring classes. Whether I, however, shall live to see it—with the general opposition which is, as a matter of principle, offered to me on all sides, and which is wearying me—I cannot say. But you will be compelled to put a few drops of social oil into the recipe which you give to the State—how much I do not know. . . . The establishment of the freedom of the peasantry was Socialistic; Socialistic, too, is every expropriation in favour of railways; Socialistic to the utmost extent is the aggregation of estates—the law exists in many provinces—taking from one and giving to another, simply because this other can cultivate the land more conveniently; Socialistic is expropriation under the Water Legislation, on account of irrigation, etc., where a man's land is taken away from him because another can farm it better; Socialistic is our entire poor relief, compulsory school attendance, compulsory construction of roads, so that I am bound to maintain a road upon my lands for travellers. That is all Socialistic, and I could extend the register further; but if you believe that you can frighten any one or call up specters with the word 'Socialism,' you take a standpoint which I abandoned long ago, and the abandonment of which is absolutely necessary for our entire imperial legislation.

✻

The whole matter centres in the question, Is it the duty of the State, or is it not, to provide for its helpless citizens? I maintain that it is its duty, that it is the duty not only of the *'Christian* State,' as I ventured once to call it when speaking of 'practical Christianity,' but of every State. It would be foolish for a corporation to undertake matters which the individual can attend to alone; and similarly the purposes which the parish can fulfill with justice and with advantage are left to the parish. But there are purposes which only the State as a whole can fulfill. To these belong national defence, the general system of communications, and, indeed, everything spoken of in article 4 of the constitution. To these, too, belong the help of the necessitous and the removal of those just complaints which provide Social Democracy with really effective material for agitation. This is a duty of the State, a duty which the State cannot permanently disregard. . . . As soon as the State takes this matter [of insurance] in hand—and I believe it is its duty to take it in hand—it must seek the cheapest form of insurance, and, not aiming at profit for itself, must keep primarily in view the benefit of the poor and needy. Otherwise we might leave the fulfillment of certain State duties—such as poor relief, in the widest sense of the words, is amongst others—like education and national defence with more right to share companies, only asking ourselves, Who will do it most cheaply? who will do it most effectively? If provision for the necessitous in a greater degree than is possible with the present poor relief legislation is a State duty, the State must take the matter in hand; it cannot rest content with the thought that a share company will undertake it.

If an establishment employing twenty thousand or more workpeople were to be ruined . . . we could not allow these men to hunger. We should have to resort to real State Socialism and find work for them, and this is what we do in every case of distress. If the objection were right that we should shun State Socialism as we would an infectious disease, how do we come to organise works in one province and another in case of distress—works which we should not undertake if the labourers had employment and wages? In such cases we build railways whose profitableness is questionable; we carry out improvements which otherwise would be left to private initiative. If that is Communism, I have no objection at all to it; though with such catchwords we really get no further.

The Duties of Man
Giuseppe Mazzini

Nationalism, a growing force since the French Revolution, tended to be associated with liberal and humanitarian ideals during the first half of the nineteenth century. After 1848 it became more pragmatic and conservative, as illustrated by the unification of Germany and Italy. Yet it was still based on some of the earlier ideals. These ideals are illustrated in both the life and writings of the Italian patriot Giuseppe Mazzini (1805–1872). Mazzini was a revolutionary for most of his life and strove continuously for an independent and united Italian Republic. His revolutionary efforts in the 1830s and 1840s failed; unification was ultimately accomplished under the more pragmatic leadership of Cavour in the 1860s. But his ideas represented a strong strain of mid-nineteenth-century nationalism both in Italy and in other countries. The following is an excerpt from Mazzini's most famous essay, The Duties of Man, *addressed to Italian workingmen.*

Consider: *The bases for Mazzini's nationalism; why these ideas might be appealing to the Italian working class; why Bismarck might approve of these ideas and whether there is anything he might reject.*

Your first duties—first as regards importance—are, as I have already told you, towards Humanity. You are *men* before you are either citizens or fathers. If you do not embrace the whole human family in your affection, if you do not bear witness to your belief in the Unity of that family, consequent upon the Unity of God, and in that fraternity among the peoples which is destined to reduce that unity to action; if, wheresoever a fellow-creature suffers, or the dignity of human nature is violated by falsehood or tyranny—you are not ready, if able, to aid the

SOURCE: Emilie Ashurst Venturi, *Joseph Mazzini: A Memoir* (London: Alexander & Shepheard, 1875), pp. 312–315.

unhappy, and do not feel called upon to combat, if able, for the redemption of the betrayed or oppressed—you violate your law of life, you comprehend not that Religion which will be the guide and blessing of the future.

But what can each of you, singly, *do* for the moral improvement and progress of Humanity? You can from time to time give sterile utterance to your belief; you may, on some rare occasions, perform some act of *charity* towards a brother man not belonging to your own land;—no more. But charity is not the watchword of the Faith of the Future. The watchword of the faith of the future is *Association*, and fraternal co-operation of all towards a common aim; and this is as far superior to all charity, as the edifice which all of you should unite to raise would be superior to the humble hut each one of you might build alone, or with the mere assistance of lending and borrowing stone, mortar, and tools.

But, you tell me, you cannot attempt united action, distinct and divided as you are in language, customs, tendencies, and capacity. The individual is too insignificant, and Humanity too vast. The mariner of Brittany prays to God as he puts to sea: *Help me, my God! my boat is so small and thy ocean so wide!* And this prayer is the true expression of the condition of each one of you, until you find the means of infinitely multiplying your forces and powers of action.

This means was provided for you by God when he gave you a country; when, even as a wise overseer of labour distributes the various branches of employment according to the different capacities of the workmen, he divided Humanity into distinct groups or nuclei upon the face of the earth, thus creating the germ of Nationalities. Evil governments have disfigured the divine design. Nevertheless you may still trace it, distinctly marked out—at least as far as Europe is concerned—by the course of the great rivers, the direction of the higher mountains, and other geographical conditions. They have disfigured it by their conquests, their greed, and their jealousy even of the righteous power of others; disfigured it so far that if we except England and France—there is not perhaps a single country whose present boundaries correspond to that design.

These governments did not, and do not, recognise any country save their own families or dynasty, the egotism of caste. But the Divine design will infallibly be realized. Natural divisions, and the spontaneous, innate tendencies of the peoples, will take the place of the arbitrary divisions sanctioned by evil governments. The map of Europe will be redrawn. The countries of the Peoples, defined by the vote of free men, will arise upon the ruins of the countries of kings and privileged castes, and between these countries harmony and fraternity will exist. And the common work of Humanity, of general amelioration and the gradual discovery and application of its Law of life, being distributed according to local and general capacities, will be wrought out in peaceful and progressive development and advance. Then may each one of you, fortified by the power and the affection of many millions, all speaking the same language, gifted with the same tendencies, and educated by the same historical tradition, hope, even by your own single effort, to be able to benefit all Humanity.

O my brothers, love your Country! Our country is our Home, the house that God has given us, placing therein a numerous family that loves us, and whom we love; a family with whom we sympathise more readily, and whom we understand more quickly than we do others; and which, from its being centred round a given spot, and from the homogeneous nature of its elements, is adapted to a special branch of activity. Our country is our common workshop, whence the products of our activity are sent forth for the benefit of the whole world; wherein the tools and implements of labour we can most usefully employ are gathered together: nor may we reject them without disobeying the plan of the Almighty, and diminishing our own strength.

Proclamation of the Paris Commune

While pragmatism and conservatism were strong in the decades after 1848, the forces for radical and even revolutionary reform did not remain dormant for long. This was demonstrated dramatically in 1871 by the establishment of the Paris Commune. The Paris Commune was formed after Paris was brought under siege by the Prussian army during the Franco-Prussian War. After being deserted by most of the wealthier Parisians, the remaining inhabitants refused to accept the authority of the provisional government in Versailles, which was willing to capitulate to the Prussian forces. The self-governing Commune set up by the Parisians was based on a mixture of relatively radical principles, many of which were stated in the following proclamation issued on April 19, 1871.

Consider: *The nature of the demands made by the Commune; how these demands contrast with pragmatism and conservatism; the role of nationalism in this proclamation.*

FRENCH REPUBLIC
LIBERTY EQUALITY FRATERNITY
PARIS COMMUNE
DECLARATION TO THE FRENCH PEOPLE

. . . [Once more] Paris labours and suffers for the whole of France, for whom she prepares by her battles and intellectual, moral, administrative, and economic regeneration, glory and prosperity.

What does she demand?

The recognition and consolidation of the Republic[, the only form of government compatible with the rights of the People and with the free, regular development of society].

The absolute independence of the Commune extended at all places in France,

---

SOURCE: Stewart Edwards, ed., *The Communards of Paris, 1871* (Ithaca, N.Y.: Cornell University Press), pp. 81–83.

thus assuring to each the integrity of its rights and to every Frenchman the full exercise of his faculties and aptitudes as a man, a citizen [and a worker].

The independence of the Commune has no other limits [than the right of all the other communes to an equal autonomy] who are adherents of the contract the association of which ought to secure the unity of France.

The inherent rights of the Commune are:

To vote the Communal budget of receipts and expenses; [to fix and assess] taxes; the direction of local services; the organisation of the magistracy, internal policy, and education; the administration of the property belonging to the Commune.

The choice by election or competition, with the responsibility and permanent right of control and revocation, of the Communal magistrates and officials of all classes.

The absolute guarantee of individual liberty, liberty of conscience [and liberty of work].

The permanent intervention of the citizens in Communal affairs by the free manifestation of their ideas and the free defence of their interests; guarantees given for those manifestations by the Commune, which alone is charged with [watching over and ensuring] the free and just exercise of the right of meeting and publicity.

The organisation of urban defence and of the National Guard, which must elect its chiefs and alone watch over the maintenance of order in the city.

Paris wishes nothing more under the head of local guarantees, on the well-understood condition of regaining, in a grand central administration and delegation from the federal communes, the realisation and practice of those same principles.

But [on the strength of] her independence, and profiting by her liberty of action, Paris reserves to herself liberty to bring about as may seem good to her administrative and economic reforms which the people demand, and to create such institutions as may serve to develop and further education, [production,] exchange, and credit; to universalise power and property according to the necessities of the moment, the wishes of those interested, and the data furnished by experience.

Our enemies deceive themselves [and the country] when they accuse Paris of seeking the destruction of French unity, established by the Revolution[, which our fathers acclaimed when they thronged from all corners of old France to the festival of the Federation].

Unity, such has been imposed upon us up to the present by the empire, the monarchy, and parliamentary government, is nothing but centralisation, despotic, unintelligent, arbitrary, and onerous.

Political unity, as desired by Paris, is a voluntary association of all local initiative, the free and spontaneous co-operation of all individual energies with the common object of wellbeing, liberty and security of all.

The Communal Revolution, [begun by popular initiative] on the 18th of March, inaugurated a new era of experimental, positive, and scientific politics.

It [marks the end of the old governmental] and clerical world, of militarism, of bureaucracy, [of exploitation,] of jobbing in monopolies, of privileges, to which the proletariat [owes] its slavery and the country its misfortune and disasters.

[Let this beloved and great country, therefore, deceived by lies and calumnies, be reassured!]

The strife between Paris and Versailles is one of those that cannot be decided by an illusory compromise; the issue should not be doubtful. The victory, fought for with such indomitable energy by the National Guard, will remain [on the side of intelligence (*Pidée*) and of] right. . . .

Speech at Hamburg, 1901: Imperialism
Kaiser Wilhelm II

Imperialism swept through Europe with extraordinary force in the late nineteenth century. For many the step between the increasingly assertive nationalism of the time and the new imperialism was a short one. This view is illustrated in the following speech given at Hamburg in 1901 by Kaiser Wilhelm II (1888–1919) of Germany. Addressing an audience with strong commercial interests, he refers to a recent intervention by European powers in China.

> **Consider:** *How Wilhelm II connects nationalism and imperialism; by what means he hopes to spread German influence throughout the world; the ways in which this speech might appeal to both liberals and conservatives.*

In spite of the fact that we have no such fleet as we should have, we have conquered for ourselves a place in the sun. It will now be my task to see to it that this place in the sun shall remain our undisputed possession, in order that the sun's rays may fall fruitfully upon our activity and trade in foreign parts, that our industry and agriculture may develop within the state and our sailing sports upon the water, for our future lies upon the water. The more Germans go out upon the waters, whether it be in the races of regattas, whether it be in journeys across the ocean, or in the service of the battle-flag, so much the better will it be for us. For when the German has once learned to direct his glance upon what is distant and great, the pettiness which surrounds him in daily life on all sides will disappear. Whoever wishes to have this larger and freer outlook can find no better place than one of the Hanseatic cities.[1] What we have learned out of the previous history of our development amounts really to what I already pointed out when I sent my brother to the East Asiatic station (Dec. 15, 1897). We have merely drawn the logical conclusions from the work which was left us by Emperor William the

---

SOURCE: C. Gauss, *The German Kaiser as Shown in His Public Utterances* (New York: Charles Scribner's Sons, 1915), pp. 181–183.

[1]The Hanseatic cities formed a league in the Late Middle Ages to facilitate trade.

Great, my memorable grandfather, and the great man whose monument we have recently unveiled. These consequences lie in the fact that we are now making our efforts to do what, in the old time, the Hanseatic cities could not accomplish, because they lacked the vivifying and protecting power of the empire. May it be the function of my Hansa during many years of peace to protect and advance commerce and trade!

In the events which have taken place in China I see the indication that European peace is assured for many years to come; for the achievements of the particular contingents have brought about a mutual respect and feeling of comradeship that can only serve the furtherance of peace. But in this period of peace I hope that our Hanseatic cities will flourish. Our new Hansa will open new paths and create and conquer new markets for them.

As head of the empire I therefore rejoice over every citizen, whether from Hamburg, Bremen, or Lübeck, who goes forth with this large outlook and seeks new points where we can drive in the nail on which to hang our armour. Therefore, I believe that I express the feeling of all your hearts when I recognize gratefully that the director of this company who has placed at our disposal the wonderful ship which bears my daughter's name has gone forth as a courageous servant of the Hansa, in order to make for us friendly conquests whose fruits will be gathered by our descendants.

In the joyful hope that this enterprising Hanseatic spirit may be spread even further, I raise my glass and ask all of those who are my comrades upon the water to join with me in a cheer for sailing and the Hanseatic spirit!

The Rise of Our East African Empire
Lord Lugard

Probably the most apparent motive for the new imperialism was economic. With new conquests made, people expected to develop new commerce and particularly new markets for manufactured goods. This attitude is reflected by Lord Lugard in his Rise of Our East African Empire *(1893), largely an account of his experiences in colonial service. Lugard, as a British soldier and administrator, helped bring large parts of Africa into the British Empire. Here he analyzes the "scramble" for Africa.*

Consider: *How Lugard connects nationalistic and economic motives for imperialism; some of the main arguments presented against imperialism and how Lugard responds to them; Lugard's perceptions of Africans and how such perceptions might facilitate the new imperialism.*

SOURCE: Captain F. D. Lugard, *The Rise of Our East African Empire*, vol. I (London: William Blackwood and Sons, 1893), pp. 379–382, 473.

The Chambers of Commerce of the United Kingdom have unanimously urged the retention of East Africa on the grounds of commercial advantage. The Presidents of the London and Liverpool chambers attended a deputation to her Majesty's Minister for Foreign Affairs to urge "the absolute necessity, for the prosperity of this country, that new avenues for commerce such as that in East Equatorial Africa should be opened up, in view of the hostile tariffs with which British manufacturers are being everywhere confronted." Manchester followed with a similar declaration; Glasgow, Birmingham, Edinburgh, and other commercial centres gave it as their opinion that "there is practically no middle course for this country, between a reversal of the free-trade policy to which it is pledged, on the one hand, and a prudent but continuous territorial extension for the creation of new markets, on the other hand." Such is the view of the Chambers of Commerce, and I might quote endless paragraphs from their resolutions and reports in the same sense.

This view has been strongly endorsed by some of our leading statesmen. Space forbids me to quote extracts from speeches by our greatest politicians, which I might else adduce as proof that they held the opinions of the Chambers of Commerce, which I have quoted, to be sound and weighty. . . .

The "Scramble for Africa" by the nations of Europe—an incident without parallel in the history of the world—was due to the growing commercial rivalry, which brought home to civilised nations the vital necessity of securing the only remaining fields for industrial enterprise and expansion. It is well, then, to realise that it is for our *advantage*—and not alone at the dictates of duty—that we have undertaken responsibilities in East Africa. It is in order to foster the growth of the trade of this country, and to find an outlet for our manufactures and our surplus energy, that our far-seeing statesmen and our commercial men advocate colonial expansion. . . .

There are some who say we have no *right* in Africa at all, that "it belongs to the natives." I hold that our right is the necessity that is upon us to provide for our ever-growing population—either by opening new fields for emigration, or by providing work and employment which the development of over-sea extension entails—and to stimulate trade by finding new markets, since we know what misery trade depression brings at home.

While thus serving our own interests as a nation, we may, by selecting men of the right stamp for the control of new territories, bring at the same time many advantages to Africa. Nor do we deprive the natives of their birthright of freedom, to place them under a foreign yoke. It has ever been the key-note of British colonial method to rule through and by the natives, and it is this method, in contrast to the arbitrary and uncompromising rule of Germany, France, Portugal, and Spain, which has been the secret of our success as a colonising nation, and has made us welcomed by tribes and peoples in Africa, who ever rose in revolt against the other nations named. In Africa, moreover, there is among the people a natural inclination to submit to a higher authority. That intense detestation of control which animates our Teutonic races does not exist among the tribes of

Africa, and if there is any authority that we replace, it is the authority of the Slavers and Arabs, or the intolerable tyranny of the "dominant tribe." . . .

So far, therefore, as my personal experience goes, I have formed the following estimate: (1) No kind of men I have ever met with—including British soldiers, Afghans, Burmese, and many tribes of India—are more amenable to discipline, more ready to fall into the prescribed groove willingly and quickly, more easy to handle, or require so little compulsion as the African. (2) To obtain satisfactory results a great deal of system, division of labour, supervision, etc., is required. (3) On the whole, the African is very quick at learning, and those who prove themselves good at the superior class of work take a pride in the results, and are very amenable to a word of praise, blame, or sarcasm.

The White Man's Burden
Rudyard Kipling

Imperialism was often glorified both by those actively involved in it and by the public at home. Part of this glorification involved perceiving imperialism as a Christian and nationalistic venture. More broadly it involved portraying imperialism as a heroic deed carried out by idealistic leaders of Western civilization in an effort to spread the "benefits" of "true civilization" to "less advanced" peoples of the world. One of the most popular expressions of this is found in the writings of Rudyard Kipling (1865–1936), particularly in his poem "The White Man's Burden," written in 1899 to celebrate the American annexation of the Philippines.

> **Consider:** *What Kipling means by "the White Man's burden"; how Kipling justifies imperialism; why such a justification might be so appealing.*

Take up the White Man's burden—
    Send forth the best ye breed—
Go, bind your sons to exile
    To serve your captives' need;
To wait, in heavy harness,
    On fluttered folk and wild—
Your new-caught sullen peoples,
    Half devil and half child.

Take up the White Man's burden—
    In patience to abide,

SOURCE: Rudyard Kipling, "The White Man's Burden," *McClure's Magazine*, vol. XII, no. 4 (February 1899), pp. 290–291.

To veil the threat of terror
    And check the show of pride;
By open speech and simple,
    An hundred times made plain,
To seek another's profit
    And work another's gain.

Take up the White Man's burden—
    The savage wars of peace—
Fill full the mouth of Famine,
    And bid the sickness cease;
And when your goal is nearest
    (The end for others sought)
Watch sloth and heathen folly
    Bring all your hope to nought.

Take up the White Man's burden—
    No iron rule of kings,
But toil of serf and sweeper—
    The tale of common things.
The ports ye shall not enter,
    The roads ye shall not tread,
Go, make them with your living
    And mark them with your dead.

Take up the White Man's burden,
    And reap his old reward—
The blame of those ye better
    The hate of those ye guard—
The cry of hosts ye humour
    (Ah, slowly!) toward the light:—
"Why brought ye us from bondage,
    Our loved Egyptian night?"

Take up the White Man's burden—
    Ye dare not stoop to less—
Nor call too loud on Freedom
    To cloke your weariness.
By all ye will or whisper,
    By all ye leave or do,
The silent sullen peoples
    Shall weigh your God and you.

Take up the White Man's burden!
    Have done with childish days—
The lightly-proffered laurel,
    The easy ungrudged praise:

Comes now, to search your manhood
    Through all the thankless years,
Cold, edged with dear-bought wisdom,
    The judgment of your peers.

VISUAL SOURCES

Imperialism Glorified
George Harcourt

The following 1900 painting by George Harcourt conveys some of the meaning of imperialism to Europeans. First displayed at the Royal Academy in 1900, it shows British soldiers leaving by train for the Boer War in South Africa. The soldiers are clearly cast in the role of masculine heroes, both in their own eyes as well as in the eyes of civilians, young and old. This is further evidenced by the couple in the center, representing the epitome of sentimentalized British masculinity and femininity. For many, imperialism enabled Europeans to have a sense of adventure and to prove their superiority to themselves and the rest of the world. Avoided in this picture is the reality of the bloodshed and exploitation to be experienced by these same soldiers and the populations of the colonized lands.

    Consider: *How this painting fits with Kipling's description of "the White Man's burden."*

Photo 9-1

The Bettmann Archive/BBC Hulton

Imperialism in Africa

The first map shows the approximate divisions among indigenous peoples in the centuries prior to European colonization. The second map highlights political and cultural divisions in nineteenth-century Africa prior to 1880. The third map shows the colonial partition of Africa between 1880 and 1914.

Together these maps indicate a number of things about imperialism in Africa. First, the manner and speed with which Africa was divided demonstrate the intense competition involved in this late-nineteenth-century imperial expansion. Second, the European parti-

Map 9-1   Divisions Among Indigenous Peoples

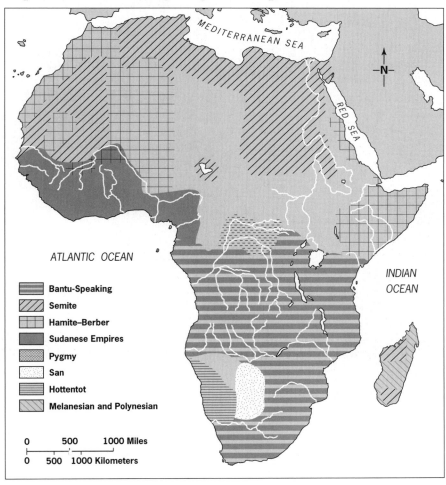

Map 9-2   Political and Cultural Divisions

tion of Africa did not take account of the already established social, political, cultural, and ethnic divisions among Africans. From this geopolitical perspective alone, one can imagine some of the disruption to native societies and cultures caused by imperialism. Third, these maps help explain problems experienced by Africans after decolonization occurred. The

Map 9-3   European Control of Africa

new African nations were generally formed on the basis of the arbitrary political lines established by European colonizers. Thus many African countries had to deal with persisting divisions and rivalries among their populations, stemming from the nineteenth-century partition of Africa.

Consider: How these maps help explain the effects of imperialism on Africans.

SECONDARY SOURCES

Nationalism: Myth and Reality
Boyd C. Shafer

Although growing nationalism was a general pattern during the nineteenth century, the forms that nationalism took and its actual meaning differed over time and in various areas. Indeed, "nationalism" is a term that historians have usually used quite loosely, adding to problems of understanding its meaning. In the following selection Boyd Shafer attempts to define nationalism by listing ten characteristics it embodies.

> **Consider:** *What it would mean to be a German or Italian "nationalist" during the second half of the nineteenth century, according to Shafer's definition of nationalism; what the political implications are of nationalism so defined; the elements of this definition that make nationalism such a historically powerful force.*

1. A certain defined (often vaguely) unit of territory (whether possessed or coveted).
2. Some common cultural characteristics such as language (or widely understood languages), customs, manners, and literature (folk tales and lore are a beginning). If an individual believes he shares these, and wishes to continue sharing them, he is usually said to be a member of the nationality.
3. Some common dominant social (as Christian) and economic (as capitalistic or recently communistic) institutions.
4. A common independent or sovereign government (type does not matter) or the desire for one. The "principle" that each nationality should be separate and independent is involved here.
5. A belief in a common history (it can be invented) and in a common origin (often mistakenly conceived to be racial in nature).
6. A love or esteem for fellow nationals (not necessarily as individuals).
7. A devotion to the entity (however little comprehended) called the nation, which embodies the common territory, culture, social and economic institutions, government, and the fellow nationals, and which is at the same time (whether organism or not) more than their sum.
8. A common pride in the achievements (often the military more than the cultural) of this nation and a common sorrow in its tragedies (particularly its defeats).

SOURCE: Excerpt from *Nationalism: Myth and Reality*, copyright 1955 and renewed 1983 by Boyd C. Shafer, reprinted by permission of Harcourt Brace & Company.

9. A disregard for or hostility to other (not necessarily all) like groups, especially if these prevent or seem to threaten the separate national existence.

10. A hope that the nation will have a great and glorious future (usually in territorial expansion) and become supreme in some way (in world power if the nation is already large).

A Sterner Plan for Italian Unity: Nationalism, Liberalism, and Conservatism

Raymond Grew

During the first half of the nineteenth century, nationalism was most often connected to liberalism. After the revolutions of 1848 there were increasing ties between nationalism and conservatism, particularly in the movements for national unification. In the following selection Raymond Grew, an advocate of comparative history from the University of Michigan, analyzes the relationships among nationalism, liberalism, and conservatism in a comparative context.

> **Consider:** *How nationalism could appeal to both liberals and conservatives; why, during the second half of the nineteenth century, liberal ideals were often sacrificed in the name of nationalism; using this and the preceding document, the bases on which nationalism might have been opposed.*

Insofar as politics was the public battle of ideas and interests, then nationalism was a denial of politics. For in stressing the values of unity, loyalty, and duty, nationalism saw political dispute as a source of weakness. It denied that there was conflict in the true interests of classes, groups or regions. The effect of nationalism was therefore inherently conservative in that it provided reason for supporting anyone thought to wield the power of the state effectively in behalf of national unity and strength, Disraeli or Gladstone, Napoleon III or Bismarck. Since order and unity, the cry of the political conservative, are essential to a strong state, and since, to the nationalist, most worthy ends required that strength, the nationalist was always tempted under pressure to move toward the political right, to sacrifice liberty to unity, discussion to authority, ends to means.

Yet the origins of nationalism were usually liberal and reformist; for everywhere it was a demand for change, the doctrine of the modernizers who, while they had

---

SOURCE: Raymond Grew, *A Sterner Plan for Italian Unity*. Reprinted by permission of Princeton University Press (Princeton, N.J., 1963), pp. 465–466. Copyright © 1963 by Princeton University Press.

too much to lose to want a social revolution, were self-consciously aware that theirs was an "underdeveloped" country. Nationalism could make its denial of politics effective because its ends were so clear, so easily defined in the model of the modern state. For the French that model had been England; for the Italians it was England and France. Italian nationalists were usually liberals, but their liberalism was primarily an admiration for the achievements of the liberal state. Because their model already existed, they looked directly to it, anxious to achieve an efficient bureaucracy, a responsible government, a progressive economic structure, all based on accepted and universally applied laws. Nationalism was a program to obtain these things quickly, not to evolve toward them but, if necessary, to superimpose them. The hurry to achieve these goals where nationalism itself was seriously opposed made a doctrinaire concern for means appear pedantic and unrealistic. Italian nationalists needed nothing so brutal as cynicism to justify "postponement" of controversy or the choice of practical means, though often this meant whittling away at the practices necessary to viable liberalism.

German Unification
Hajo Holborn

As in the case of Italy, nationalism in Germany during the first half of the nineteenth century was closely connected to liberalism. This was particularly so in the early stages of the revolutions of 1848. But with the failure of liberal nationalists to gain the concrete changes they strove for, steps toward unification over the next two decades followed a different path. In the following selection Hajo Holborn, a noted historian of Germany, analyzes the significance of that path for German history until the outbreak of World War I in 1914.

> **Consider:** *The ways in which liberalism was sacrificed during this period; how the relation between liberalism and nationalism was affected by the position of different social groups in Germany; how Bismarck's social policies support Holborn's interpretation.*

The achievement of German unity gave Bismarck the power to force the German liberals to decide whether they were more eager to see unity or liberty achieved in Germany. The majority of them proved willing to compromise with Bismarck. Since centralization went rather far under the new constitution he needed the liberal movement to some extent to counterbalance the particularistic German forces represented chiefly by the German princes. The constitution of the new German empire was, therefore, a bit more centralized and more liberal than Bismarck wished, but he maintained control of the crucial policy-making positions. No decisive power over military and foreign affairs by the constituted popular

SOURCE: Hajo Holborn, *The Political Collapse of Europe*. Reprinted by permission of Alfred A. Knopf, Inc. (New York, 1966), pp. 42–43. Copyright © 1966 by Alfred A. Knopf, Inc.

bodies was allowed in the second German empire. Bismarck made all sorts of concessions in the field of social and economic reform but was absolutely adamant with regard to the powers of the parliament. The direction of foreign and military matters remained a privilege of the Crown.

The pseudo-constitutional character of the new German empire was even more accentuated when in 1878 Bismarck decided to give up free trade and imposed a policy protecting the interests of the Prussian *Junker* agrarians against the importation of cheap Russian and American grain while at the same time introducing tariffs benefiting the growing German iron industries. Just as in 1866 and 1871 the German liberals had had to sacrifice the core of their political faith, so they were forced to jettison the major part of their economic program after 1878. The leading industrial groups of German society readily accepted a protectionist trade policy, and the unity of the liberal *bourgeoisie* crumbled. Thirty years after German liberalism had burst into existence in the Revolution of 1848, it ceased to be an independent political movement. Thereafter the majority of the German *bourgeoisie,* if they did not, like the higher *bourgeoisie,* become absolute supporters of the regime, were driven to further concession and compromise. The appearance of a powerful socialist workers' movement extinguished the last remaining fervor for reform among the liberal *bourgeoisie* and made them take cover under the wings of the established government. The second German empire was founded "by blood and iron" and socially stabilized by "iron and grain." For more than fifty years the German political scene was overshadowed by the alliance of the "barons of the halm"[1] and the "barons of the smokestack," who maintained the army and bureaucracy in power.

The Age of Empire
Eric J. Hobsbawn

Imperialism has been interpreted from a number of perspectives since the early twentieth century. The way that scholars view imperialism often reveals much about their own political and ideological views. Some of the earliest interpretations, such as those by J. H. Hobson and V. I. Lenin, were economic. They criticized imperialism as an outgrowth of capitalism, Hobson from the perspective of a liberal socialist, Lenin as a Marxist theorist and political leader. Economic interpretations of imperialism, often in newer versions, remain popular. This is illustrated in the following selection by the British historian E. J. Hobsbawn, who has written extensively on nineteenth-century Western civilization.

> **Consider:** *Why Hobsbawn considers economic results irrelevant to economic motives for imperialism; why Hobsbawn calls imperialism a natural by-product of the*

Source: From *The Age of Empire* by Eric Hobsbawn. Copyright © 1987 by E. J. Hobsbawn. Reprinted by permission of Pantheon Books, a division of Random House, Inc.

[1] Stems and stalks.

international economy; why political actions are secondary to the economic motives for imperialism.

A more convincing general motive for colonial expansion was the search for markets. The fact that this was often disappointed is irrelevant. The belief that the 'overproduction' of the Great Depression could be solved by a vast export drive was widespread. Businessmen, always inclined to fill the blank spaces on the map of world trade with vast numbers of potential customers, would naturally look for such unexploited areas: China was one which haunted the imagination of salesmen—what if every one of those 300 millions bought only one box of tin-tacks?—and Africa, the unknown continent, was another. The Chambers of Commerce of British cities in the depressed early 1880s were outraged by the thought that diplomatic negotiations might exclude their traders from access to the Congo basin, which was believed to offer untold sales prospects, all the more so as it was being developed as a paying proposition by that crowned businessman, King Leopold II of the Belgians. . . .

But the crux of the global economic situation was that a number of developed economies simultaneously felt the same need for new markets. If they were sufficiently strong their ideal was 'the open door' on the markets of the under-developed world; but if not strong enough, they hoped to carve out for themselves territories which, by virtue of ownership, would give national business a monopoly position or at least a substantial advantage. Partition of the unoccupied parts of the Third World was the logical consequence. In a sense, this was an extension of the protectionism which gained ground almost everywhere after 1879. . . . To this extent the 'new imperialism' was the natural by-product of an international economy based on the rivalry of several competing industrial economies, intensified by the economic pressures of the 1880s. It does not follow that any particular colony was expected to turn into Eldorado by itself, though this is what actually happened in South Africa, which became the world's greatest gold-producer. Colonies might simply provide suitable bases or jumping-off points for regional business penetration. . . .

At this point the economic motive for acquiring some colonial territory becomes difficult to disentangle from the political action required for the purpose, for protectionism of whatever kind is economy operating with the aid of politics. . . . Once rival powers began to carve up the map of Africa or Oceania, each naturally tried to safeguard against an excessive portion (or a particularly attractive morsel) going to the others. Once the status of a great power thus became associated with raising its flag over some palm-fringed beach (or, more likely, over stretches of dry scrub), the acquisition of colonies itself became a status symbol, irrespective of their value.

Imperialism as a Nationalistic Phenomenon
Carlton J. H. Hayes

Although the economic interpretation of imperialism has not lost its strength, other views have been offered recently as supplements and sometimes as direct alternatives to an economic interpretation. A direct alternative appears in the following selection by Carlton J. H. Hayes. One of the earliest historians to develop a sophisticated understanding of nationalism, Hayes argues that economic motives were at best secondary; on the whole, imperialism was a nationalistic phenomenon.

> **Consider:** *The evidence Hayes uses to reject economic interpretations of nationalism; how Hobsbawn might reply to this interpretation; the ways in which this view fits with the documents on nationalism in this chapter.*

The founding of new colonial empires and the fortifying of old ones antedated the establishment of neo-mercantilism, and that the economic arguments adduced in support of imperialism seem to have been a rationalization *ex post facto.* In the main, it was not Liberal parties, with their super abundance of industrials and bankers, who sponsored the outward imperialistic thrusts of the '70's and early '80's. Instead, it was Conservative parties, with a preponderantly agricultural clientele notoriously suspicious of moneylenders and big business, and, above all, it was patriotic professors and publicists regardless of political affiliation and unmindful of personal economic interest. These put forth the economic arguments which eventually drew bankers and traders and industrialists into the imperialist camp.

Basically the new imperialism was a nationalistic phenomenon. It followed hard upon the national wars which created an all-powerful Germany and a united Italy, which carried Russia within sight of Constantinople, and which left England fearful and France eclipsed. It expressed a resulting psychological reaction, an ardent desire to maintain or recover national prestige. France sought compensation for European loss in oversea gain. England would offset her European isolation by enlarging and glorifying the British Empire. Russia, halted in the Balkans, would turn anew to Asia, and before long Germany and Italy would show the world that the prestige they had won by might inside Europe they were entitled to enhance by imperial exploits outside. The lesser powers, with no great prestige at stake, managed to get on without any new imperialism, though Portugal and Holland displayed a revived pride in the empires they already possessed and the latter's was administered with renewed vigor. . . .

SOURCE: Excerpted from *A Generation of Materialism, 1871–1900,* pp. 223–224, by Carlton J. H. Hayes. Copyright 1941 by Harper & Row Publishers, Inc. Copyright renewed 1969 by Mary Evelyn Hayes. Reprinted by permission of HarperCollins Publishers, Inc.

Most simply, the sequence of imperialism after 1870 appears to have been, first, pleas for colonies on the ground of national prestige; second, getting them; third, disarming critics by economic argument; and fourth, carrying this into effect and relating the results to the neo-mercantilism of tariff protection and social legislation at home.

The Effects of Imperialism
David Landes

Earlier in the twentieth century, historians, even those quite critical of imperialism, saw its impact mainly in European terms. In recent decades the effects of imperialism have been viewed more from the perspective of native populations subject to imperial control. This has led to a subtler understanding of imperialism and helps explain some of the persisting problems between the West and many "underdeveloped" or "third world" countries. This perspective is illustrated in the following selection by David Landes, an economic historian from Harvard. Here he focuses on Egypt.

> **Consider:** *The nature of the double standard described by Landes; how this double standard affected people's and nations' attitudes; whether this view fits best with the nationalistic or the economic interpretation of imperialism.*

While most Europeans in Egypt lived according to principles, they had two sets of principles: the same rules did not apply in dealing with the in-group of Westerners and the out-group of natives. Some Europeans drew the line between the two societies more sharply than others. There were those for whom the Turk was of his nature treacherous, Moslem justice hopelessly corrupt, the native population mean and despicable. There were others who found the Turk not deliberately false, but lazy and neglectful; who recognized the validity of Moslem law within the framework of Egyptian society, but felt that it offered little protection to foreigners habituated to other codes and that the native tribunals were excessively submissive to government pressure; who had more sympathy than scorn for the Arab, and deplored his inadaptability to the discipline and precision implicit in modern industry and trade. Some saw in every Egyptian a potential enemy whose ill faith required constant vigilance and strong remedies; others looked upon the natives as children whose fumblings and misconduct were best handled by the paternal chastisement of their European friends and protectors. All, however, were agreed that Egyptian society was backward and Egyptian civilization inferior; that the European could not afford to submit to the customs of the country, but that the Egyptian would have to learn the ways and accept the justice of the

SOURCE: David S. Landes, *Bankers and Pashas.* Reprinted by permission of Harvard University Press (Cambridge, Mass., 1958), pp. 322–323. Copyright © 1958 by David S. Landes.

Europeans; that the standards of behaviour accepted in Europe, the values of honesty, fair play, reasonableness, and so on that shaped—at least in principle—the social and business relations of the West, had to be modified to fit the circumstances of a strange environment. . . .

More than anything, more even than the enormous material costs of imperialism, it was the imposition of inferior social and moral status that shaped the reaction of the Egyptian to the European. Actually, the one implies the other: material exploitation is difficult if not impossible without the sanction of a double set of values and a corresponding double code of behaviour; if they were not there to begin with, the exploiter would have to create them. The fact remains, however, that in the many-sided impact of imperialism, it is the injury to self-respect that hurts most. It is the resentment aroused by spiritual humiliation that gives rise to an irrational response to rational exploitation. The apparently unreasonable, and certainly unprofitable, resistance of many of the world's underdeveloped countries today to Western business enterprise makes sense only in this context.

Chapter Questions

1. What historical links are there between nationalism, the national state, and imperialism during the nineteenth century? How might all three be connected to industrialization, discussed in the previous chapter?

2. How would you explain the rise of imperialism in the late nineteenth century?

3. In what ways have some of our perceptions of imperialism changed since the late nineteenth century?

CHAPTER TEN

Culture, Thought, and Society: 1850–1914

From the mid-nineteenth century to 1914 the urban middle class dominated Europe socially and culturally. It was this class that was benefiting most from the continuing industrialization of the period. As the urban middle class grew in numbers and wealth, it asserted its own values and assumptions. Increasingly this class set the standards of life style, thought, and culture. At the same time, these standards were attacked from all sides, particularly by those sensitive to the problems of the working class. The contrast between the standards being established by the middle class and the challenges to those standards marks this period as one of great social, cultural, and intellectual ferment.

The selections in this chapter exemplify some of the main social, cultural, and intellectual developments of this period. Three broad questions are addressed. First, what were some of the main elements of the middle-class style of life? Some of the materials show how this life style was reflected in the physical setting of the middle class; others concentrate on the role women and the family played in this style of life. Second, what were some of the dominant intellectual currents favored by the middle class? Here liberalism as it was evolving toward the end of the century and ideas generally referred to as Social Darwinism are examined. Third, what were some of the main challenges to middle-class ideas and institutions? The most pervasive of these were Marxism and related social doctrines, but there were also conservative challenges, such as those from the Catholic Church and the challenges of racism.

What emerges from these sources is a picture of a dynamic society with a vast array of cultural and intellectual developments. In the decades following the outbreak of World War I, many would look back to this period as one of unusual progress. Some of the twentieth-century developments that in retrospect make the second half of the nineteenth century seem such a positive time will be examined in the next chapter.

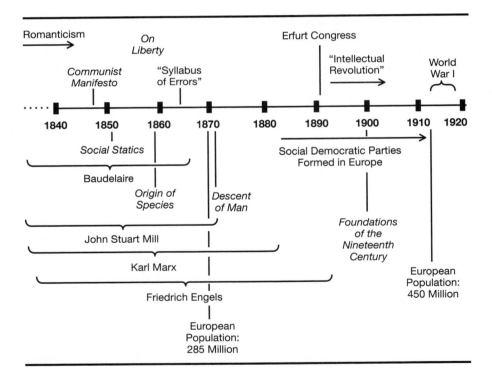

PRIMARY SOURCES

The Origin of Species

and

The Descent of Man
Charles Darwin

The nineteenth century was a period of great scientific ideas and discoveries. Perhaps the most important and certainly the most controversial was Darwin's theory of evolution. Charles Darwin (1809–1882), a British naturalist, gathered data while on voyages in the southern Pacific. He used those data to develop his theory of evolution by natural selection. This theory of evolution, particularly as applied to human beings, challenged Biblical accounts of creation. He argued that all life, including human life, evolved from lower forms. Evolution was slow and extended over a much longer period than had been assumed. Natural selection, or survival of the fittest, determined how species evolved. Darwin first formulated his findings and theory in an 1844 essay. However, it was only after 1859, when he published The Origin of Species by Means of Natural Selection, *that his ideas became well known and widely controversial. The first of two selections below is from that book. The second is from* The Descent of Man, *which he published in 1871.*

> **Consider:** *Why his ideas might be so welcome by some, so disturbing to others; the possible psychological impact of his ideas; how those favoring Biblical accounts might respond.*

. . . [C]an we doubt (remembering that many more individuals are born than can possibly survive) that individuals having any advantage, however slight, over others, would have the best chance of surviving and of procreating their kind? On the other hand, we may feel sure that any variation in the least degree injurious would be rigidly destroyed. This preservation of favourable individual differences and variations, and the destruction of those which are injurious, I have called Natural Selection, or the Survival of the Fittest. . . .

Natural selection acts solely through the preservation of variations in some way advantageous, which consequently endure. Owing to the high geometrical rate of increase of all organic beings, each area is already fully stocked with inhabitants; and it follows from this, that as the favoured forms increase in number, so,

SOURCE: Charles Darwin, *The Origin of Species by Means of Natural Selection*, 6th ed. (London: John Murray, 1872), pp. 63, 85. Charles Darwin, *The Descent of Man* (New York: D. Appleton and Co., 1883), pp. 606–607, 619.

generally, will the less favoured decrease and become rare. Rarity, as geology tells us, is the precursor to extinction.

°

The main conclusion here arrived at, and now held by many naturalists who are well competent to form a sound judgment, is that man is descended from some less highly organized form. The grounds upon which this conclusion rests will never be shaken, for the close similarity between man and the lower animals in embryonic development, as well as in innumerable points of structure and constitution, both of high and of the most trifling importance,—the rudiments which he retains, and the abnormal reversions to which he is occasionally liable,—are facts which cannot be disputed. They have long been known, but until recently they told us nothing with respect to the origin of man. Now when viewed by the light of our knowledge of the whole organic world, their meaning is unmistakable. The great principle of evolution stands up clear and firm, when these groups of facts are considered in connection with others, such as the mutual affinities of the members of the same group, their geographical distribution in past and present times, and their geological succession. It is incredible that all these facts should speak falsely. He who is not content to look, like a savage, at the phenomena of nature as disconnected, cannot any longer believe that man is the work of a separate act of creation. . . .

We have seen that man incessantly presents individual differences in all parts of his body and in his mental faculties. These differences or variations seem to be induced by the same general causes, and to obey the same laws as with the lower animals. In both cases similar laws of inheritance prevail. Man tends to increase at a greater rate than his means of subsistence; consequently he is occasionally subjected to a severe struggle for existence, and natural selection will have effected whatever lies within its scope. A succession of strongly-marked variations of a similar nature is by no means requisite; slight fluctuating differences in the individual suffice for the work of natural selection. . . .

[M]an with all his noble qualities, with sympathy which feels for the most debased, with benevolence which extends not only to other men but to the humblest living creature, with his god-like intellect which has penetrated into the movements and constitution of the solar system—with all these exalted powers—Man still bears in his bodily frame the indelible stamp of his lowly origin.

Social Statics: Liberalism and Social Darwinism

Herbert Spencer

The works of Herbert Spencer (1820–1903) epitomize the assertive liberal philosophy favored by successful mid-nineteenth-century industrialists. This was a period in which capitalism was relatively unrestrained and social legislation was only in its infancy. It was also the beginning of thinking from a biological and evolutionary perspective, as best evidenced by the publication of Charles Darwin's Origin of Species *in 1859. Spencer reflected all this in his massive writings. He rose from a railroad engineer to become editor of the London* Economist—*which espoused the views of industrial capitalism—and an independent author. Always a supporter of* laissez-faire, *he was best known for his advocacy of social evolution and acceptance of Darwinian ideas applied to society (Social Darwinism). Modern scholars consider him a founder of sociology. The following is an excerpt from* Social Statics, *first published in 1851.*

> **Consider:** *Why Spencer's views would be so appealing to the industrial middle class; on what grounds certain groups might oppose these views; the social policies that would flow from these ideas; ways these views reflect Darwin's ideas.*

Pervading all Nature we may see at work a stern discipline which is a little cruel that it may be very kind. . . . It seems hard that an unskillfulness which with all his efforts he cannot overcome, should entail hunger upon the artizan. It seems hard that a labourer incapacitated by sickness from competing with his stronger fellows, should have to bear the resulting privations. It seems hard that widows and orphans should be left to struggle for life or death. Nevertheless, when regarded not separately but in connexion with the interests of universal humanity, these harsh fatalities are seen to be full of beneficence—the same beneficence which brings to early graves the children of diseased parents, and singles out the intemperate and the debilitated as the victims of an epidemic.

There are many very amiable people who have not the nerve to look this matter fairly in the face. Disabled as they are by their sympathies with present suffering, from duly regarding ultimate consequences, they pursue a course which is injudicious, and in the end even cruel. We do not consider it true kindness in a mother to gratify her child with sweetmeats that are likely to make it ill. We should think it a very foolish sort of benevolence which led a surgeon to let his patient's disease progress to a fatal issue, rather than inflict pain by an operation. Similarly, we must call those spurious philanthropists who, to prevent present misery, would entail greater misery on future generations. That rigorous necessity which, when allowed to operate, becomes so sharp a spur to the lazy and so strong a bridle to the random, these paupers' friends would repeal, because of the wailings it here

---

SOURCE: Herbert Spencer, *Social Statics* (New York: D. Appleton and Co., 1896), pp. 149–151.

and there produces. Blind to the fact that under the natural order of things society is constantly excreting its unhealthy, imbecile, slow, vacillating, faithless members, these unthinking, though well-meaning, men advocate an interference which not only stops the purifying process, but even increases the vitiation—absolutely encourages the multiplication of the reckless and incompetent by offering them an unfailing provision, and *dis*courages the multiplication of the competent and provident by heightening the difficulty of maintaining a family. And thus, in their eagerness to prevent the salutary sufferings that surround us, these sigh-wise and groan-foolish people bequeath to posterity a continually increasing curse.

On Liberty
John Stuart Mill

During the second half of the nineteenth century, liberalism in theory and practice started to change. In general, it became less wedded to laissez-faire *policies and less optimistic than it was during the first half of the nineteenth century. This change is reflected in the thought of John Stuart Mill (1806–1873). He was the most influential British thinker of the mid-nineteenth century and probably the leading liberal theorist of the period. When he was young he favored the early liberalism of his father, James Mill, a well-known philosopher, and Jeremy Bentham, the author of utilitarianism. Over time he perceived difficulties with this early liberalism and new dangers. He modified his liberal ideas, a change that would later be reflected in liberal political policies of the late nineteenth and early twentieth centuries. In the following selection from* On Liberty *(1859), his most famous work, Mill analyzes this evolution of liberalism starting with the aims of liberals during the first half of the nineteenth century.*

> **Consider:** *What Mill feels was the essence of early liberalism; what crucial changes occurred to transform liberalism; what Mill means by tyranny of the majority.*

The aim, therefore, of patriots was to set limits to the power which the ruler should be suffered to exercise over the community; and this limitation was what they meant by liberty. It was attempted in two ways. First, by obtaining a recognition of certain immunities, called political liberties or rights, which it was to be regarded as a breach of duty in the ruler to infringe, and which if he did infringe, specific resistance, or general rebellion, was held to be justifiable. A second, and generally a later expedient, was the establishment of constitutional checks, by which the consent of the community, or of a body of some sort, supposed to represent its interests, was made a necessary condition to some of the more important acts of the governing power. To the first of these modes of limitation, the ruling power, in most European countries, was compelled, more or less, to submit. It was not so with the second; and, to attain this, or when already in some

---

Source: John Stuart Mill, *Utilitarianism, Liberty, and Representative Government* (London: J. M. Dent and Sons Ltd., Everyman Library, 1910), pp. 66–68.

degree possessed, to attain it more completely, became everywhere the principal object of the lovers of liberty. And so long as mankind were content to combat one enemy by another, and to be ruled by a master, on condition of being guaranteed more or less efficaciously against his tyranny, they did not carry their aspirations beyond this point.

A time, however, came, in the progress of human affairs, when men ceased to think it a necessity of nature that their governors should be an independent power, opposed in interest to themselves. It appeared to them much better that the various magistrates of the State should be their tenants or delegates, revocable at their pleasure. In that way alone, it seemed, could they have complete security that the powers of government would never be abused to their disadvantage. By degrees this new demand for elective and temporary rulers became the prominent object of the exertions of the popular party, wherever any such party existed; and superseded, to a considerable extent, the previous efforts to limit the power of rulers. As the struggle proceeded for making the ruling power emanate from the periodical choice of the ruled, some persons began to think that too much importance had been attached to the limitation of the power itself. *That* (it might seem) was a resource against rulers whose interests were habitually opposed to those of the people. What was now wanted was, that the rulers should be identified with the people; that their interest and will should be the interest and will of the nation. The nation did not need to be protected against its own will. There was no fear of its tyrannising over itself. Let the rulers be effectually responsible to it, promptly removable by it, and it could afford to trust them with power of which it could itself dictate the use to be made. Their power was but the nation's own power, concentrated, and in a form convenient for exercise. This mode of thought, or rather perhaps of feeling, was common among the last generation of European liberalism, in the Continental section of which it still apparently predominates. . . .

In time, however, a democratic republic came to occupy a large portion of the earth's surface, and made itself felt as one of the most powerful members of the community of nations; and elective and responsible government became subject to the observations and criticisms which wait upon a great existing fact. It was now perceived that such phrases as "self-government," and "the power of the people over themselves," do not express the true state of the case. The "people" who exercise the power are not always the same people with those over whom it is exercised; and the "self-government" spoken of is not the government of each by himself, but of each by all the rest. The will of the people, moreover, practically means the will of the most numerous or the most active *part* of the people; the majority, or those who succeed in making themselves accepted as the majority; the people, consequently, *may* desire to oppress a part of their number; and precautions are as much needed against this as against any other abuse of power. The limitation, therefore, of the power of government over individuals loses none of its importance when the holders of power are regularly accountable to the community, that is, to the strongest party therein. This view of things, recommending itself equally to the intelligence of thinkers and to the inclination of those important classes in European society to whose real or supposed interests democracy is adverse, has had no difficulty in establishing itself; and in political speculations "the tyranny of the majority" is now generally included among the evils against which society requires to be on its guard.

Like other tyrannies, the tyranny of the majority was at first, and is still vulgarly, held in dread, chiefly as operating through the acts of the public authorities. But reflecting persons perceived that when society is itself the tyrant—society collectively over the separate individuals who compose it—its means of tyrannising are not restricted to the acts which it may do by the hands of its political functionaries. Society can and does execute its own mandates: and if it issues wrong mandates instead of right, or any mandates at all in things with which it ought not to meddle, it practises a social tyranny more formidable than many kinds of political oppression, since, though not usually upheld by such extreme penalties, it leaves fewer means of escape, penetrating much more deeply into the details of life, and enslaving the soul itself. Protection, therefore, against the tyranny of the magistrate is not enough: there needs protection also against the tyranny of the prevailing opinion and feeling; against the tendency of society to impose, by other means than civil penalties, its own ideas and practices as rules of conduct on those who dissent from them; to fetter the development, and, if possible, prevent the formation, of any individuality not in harmony with its ways, and compel all characters to fashion themselves upon the model of its own. There is a limit to the legitimate interference of collective opinion with individual independence: and to find that limit, and maintain it against encroachment, is as indispensable to a good condition of human affairs, as protection against political despotism.

The Salon [Art Exhibit] of 1846: Art and the Bourgeoisie
Charles Baudelaire

The rising power of the middle class during the nineteenth century was recognized by observers in all fields. This power was not only economic, social, and political but cultural as well. Even artists, who early developed ambivalent and then hostile feelings toward the bourgeoisie, recognized this cultural power. This is illustrated in the following selection by Charles Baudelaire (1821–1867). Early in his career as an author, Baudelaire gained some popularity as an art critic. The following introduction to his critical account of the Salon of 1846 (art exhibit) held in Paris is addressed to the bourgeoisie.

> **Consider:** *How Baudelaire describes the bourgeoisie; Baudelaire's basis for his appeal to them to support art; how this document reveals the spreading cultural influence of the bourgeoisie.*

SOURCE: Charles Baudelaire, "The Salon of 1846," from *Art in Paris, 1845–1862*, Jonathan Mayne, trans. and ed. Published by Phaidon Press Ltd. (Oxford, England), pp. 41–43. Reprinted by permission of the publisher.

TO THE BOURGEOIS

You are the majority—in number and intelligence; therefore you are the force—which is justice.

Some are scholars, others are owners; a glorious day will come when the scholars shall be owners and the owners scholars. Then your power will be complete, and no man will protest against it.

Until that supreme harmony is achieved, it is just that those who are but owners should aspire to become scholars; for knowledge is no less of an enjoyment than ownership.

The government of the city is in your hands, and that is just, for you are the force. But you must also be capable of feeling beauty; for as not one of you today can do without power, so not one of you has the right to do without poetry.

You can live three days without bread—without poetry, never; and those of you who can say the contrary are mistaken; they are out of their minds.

The aristocrats of thought, the distributors of praise and blame, the monopolists of the things of the mind, have told you that you have no right to feel and to enjoy—they are Pharisees.

For you have in your hands the government of a city whose public is the public of the universe, and it is necessary that you should be worthy of that task.

Enjoyment is a science, and the exercise of the five senses calls for a particular initiation which only comes about through goodwill and need.

Very well, you need art.

Art is an infinitely precious good, a draught both refreshing and cheering which restores the stomach and the mind to the natural equilibrium of the ideal.

You understand its function, you gentlemen of the bourgeoisie—whether law-givers or businessmen—when the seventh or the eighth hour strikes and you bend your tired head towards the embers of your hearth or the cushions of your armchair.

That is the time when a keener desire and a more active reverie would refresh you after your daily labours.

But the monopolists have decided to keep the forbidden fruit of knowledge from you, because knowledge is their counter and their shop, and they are infinitely jealous of it. If they had merely denied you the power to create works of art or to understand the processes by which they are created, they would have asserted a truth at which you could not take offence, because public business and trade take up three quarters of your day. And as for your leisure hours, they should be used for enjoyment and pleasure.

But the monopolists have forbidden you even to enjoy, because you do not understand the technique of the arts, as you do those of the law and of business.

And yet it is just that if two-thirds of your time are devoted to knowledge, then the remaining third should be occupied by feeling—and it is by feeling alone that art is to be understood; and it is in this way that the equilibrium of your soul's forces will be established.

Truth, for all its multiplicity, is not two-faced; and just as in your politics you have increased both rights and benefits, so in the arts you have set up a greater and more abundant communion.

You, the bourgeois—be you king, law-giver, or businessman—have founded collections, museums and galleries. Some of those, which sixteen years ago were only open to the monopolists, have thrown wide their doors to the multitude.

You have combined together, you have formed companies and raised loans in order to realize the idea of the future in all its varied forms—political, industrial and artistic. In no noble enterprise have you ever left the initiative to the protesting and suffering minority, which anyway is the natural enemy of art.

For to allow oneself to be outstripped in art and in politics is to commit suicide; and for a majority to commit suicide is impossible.

And what you have done for France, you have done for other countries too. The Spanish Museum is there to increase the volume of general ideas that you ought to possess about art; for you know perfectly well that just as a national museum is a kind of communion by whose gentle influence men's hearts are softened and their wills unbent, so a foreign museum is an international communion where two peoples, observing and studying one another more at their ease, can penetrate one another's mind and fraternize without discussion.

You are the natural friends of the arts, because you are some of you rich men and the others scholars.

When you have given to society your knowledge, your industry, your labour and your money, you claim back your payment in enjoyments of the body, the reason and the imagination. If you recover the amount of enjoyments which is needed to establish the equilibrium of all parts of your being, then you are happy, satisfied and well-disposed, as society will be satisfied, happy and well-disposed when it has found its own general and absolute equilibrium.

And so it is to you, the bourgeois, that this book is naturally dedicated; for any book which is not addressed to the majority—in number and intelligence—is a stupid book.

1st May 1846

Women as Chemists [Pharmacists]
Our Sisters

Most occupations were defined as inappropriate for middle-class women. What few occupations were appropriate were often explained to middle-class women in "how to" guides that appeared in books and women's magazines, often written by women. The following is an excerpt from "What to Do with Our Daughters, or Remunerative Employment of

SOURCE: "What to Do with Our Daughters, or Remunerative Employment of Women—Women as Chemists," *Our Sisters*, February 1897, pp. 85–86, in Eleanor S. Riemer and John C. Fout, eds., *European Women: A Documentary History, 1789–1945* (New York: Schocken Books, 1980), p. 45.

Women—Women as Chemists [Pharmacists]," an 1897 article published in Our Sisters, *a popular magazine addressed to middle-class women.*

Consider: *What makes pharmacy appropriate for women; what kinds of activities are inappropriate for women as pharmacists and women in general.*

The Pharmaceutical Society, in opening up its ranks to women, has provided them with an eminently suitable calling. There is no lack of persons of both sexes who still loudly proclaim that a woman doctor is a thing unsexed. These persons could scarcely bring their arguments to bear against Pharmacy, and maintain that there is anything essentially unfeminine in the making up of drugs and pills. The calling of a chemist does not necessitate the possession on the part of a woman of all those faculties and qualities generally summed up as "strong-mindedness." In the peaceful seclusion of a drug shop, a woman chemist, unlike a doctor or a nurse, is not brought face to face with those stern realities: disease, pain, deformity, death. True, she works in with the doctor and the nurse, and her share in the healing of the sick is responsible enough; but for all that, her life work involves no such wear and tear, no such physical and mental strain, no such constant demands upon her endurance, patience, and staying power. Should her services be required for an operation to which some chemists devote attention, namely, tooth drawing, and should she not feel equal to the occasion, she need only refer the sufferer from toothache either to a dentist or a male colleague around the corner!

The Communist Manifesto
Karl Marx and Friedrich Engels

Although initially only one of many radical doctrines, Marxism proved to be the most dynamic and influential challenge to industrial capitalism and middle-class civilization in general. Its most succinct and popular statement is contained in the Communist Manifesto, *written by Karl Marx (1818–1883) and Friedrich Engels (1820–1895) and first published in 1848. Karl Marx was born in Germany, studied history and philosophy, and entered a career as a journalist, writer, and revolutionary. For most of his life he lived in exile in London. His collaborator, Friedrich Engels, was also born in Germany and lived in England, but there he helped manage his family's cotton business in Manchester. Their doctrines directly attacked the middle class and industrial capitalism, presenting communism as a philosophically, historically, and scientifically justified alternative that would inevitably replace capitalism. They saw themselves as revolutionary leaders of the growing proletariat (the working class). The following is a selection from the* Communist Manifesto.

SOURCE: Karl Marx and Friedrich Engels, *Manifesto of the Communist Party*, 2d ed. (New York: National Executive Committee of the Socialist Labor Party, 1898), pp. 30–32, 41–43, 60.

Consider: *The appeal of the ideas presented here; the concrete policies advocated by Marx and Engels; the historical and intellectual trends reflected in the Manifesto.*

A specter is haunting Europe—the specter of Communism. All the powers of old Europe have entered into a holy alliance to exorcise this specter; Pope and Czar, Metternich and Guizot, French radicals and German police spies.

Where is the party in opposition that has not been decried as Communistic by its opponents in power? Where the opposition that has not hurled back the branding reproach of Communism, against the more advanced opposition parties, as well as against its reactionary adversaries?

Two things result from this fact.

I. Communism is already acknowledged by all European powers to be in itself a power.

II. It is high time that Communists should openly, in the face of the whole world, publish their views, their aims, their tendencies, and meet this nursery tale of the Specter of Communism with a Manifesto of the party itself.

To this end the Communists of various nationalities have assembled in London, and sketched the following manifesto to be published in the English, French, German, Italian, Flemish and Danish languages.

○

In what relation do the Communists stand to the proletarians as a whole?

The Communists do not form a separate party opposed to other working class parties.

They have no interests separate and apart from those of the proletariat as a whole.

They do not set up any sectarian principles of their own by which to shape and mould the proletarian movement.

The Communists are distinguished from the other working class parties by this only: 1. In the national struggles of the proletarians of the different countries, they point out and bring to the front the common interests of the entire proletariat, independently of all nationality. 2. In the various stages of development which the struggle of the working class against the bourgeoisie has to pass through, they always and everywhere represent the interests of the movement as a whole.

The Communists, therefore, are on the one hand, practically, the most advanced and resolute section of the working class parties of every country, that section which pushes forward all others; on the other hand, theoretically, they have over the great mass of the proletariat the advantage of clearly understanding the line of march, the conditions, and the ultimate general results of the proletarian movement.

The immediate aim of the Communists is the same as that of all the other proletarian parties: formation of the proletariat into a class, overthrow of the bourgeois supremacy, conquest of political power by the proletariat.

The theoretical conclusions of the Communists are in no way based on ideas or principles that have been invented, or discovered, by this or that would-be universal reformer.

They merely express, in general terms, actual relations springing from an existing class struggle, from a historical movement going on under our very eyes. The abolition of existing property relations is not at all a distinctive feature of Communism.

All property relations in the past have continually been subject to historical change, consequent upon the change in historical conditions.

The French revolution, for example, abolished feudal property in favor of bourgeois property.

The distinguishing feature of Communism is not the abolition of property generally, but the abolition of bourgeois property. But modern bourgeois private property is the final and most complete expression of the system of producing and appropriating products, that is based on class antagonisms, on the exploitation of the many by the few.

In this sense the theory of the Communists may be summed up in the single sentence: Abolition of private property.

We have seen above that the first step in the revolution by the working class is to raise the proletariat to the position of the ruling class; to win the battle of democracy.

The proletariat will use its political supremacy to wrest, by degrees, all capital from the bourgeoisie; to centralize all instruments of production in the hands of the State, *i. e.*, of the proletariat organized as the ruling class; and to increase the total of productive forces as rapidly as possible.

Of course, in the beginning this cannot be effected except by means of despotic inroads on the rights of property and on the conditions of bourgeois production; by means of measures, therefore, which appear economically insufficient and untenable, but which, in the course of the movement, outstrip themselves, necessitate further inroads upon the old social order and are unavoidable as a means of entirely revolutionizing the mode of production.

These measures will, of course, be different in different countries.

Nevertheless in the most advanced countries the following will be pretty generally applicable:

1. Abolition of property in land and application of all rents of land to public purposes.
2. A heavy progressive or graduated income tax.
3. Abolition of all right of inheritance.
4. Confiscation of the property of all emigrants and rebels.
5. Centralization of credit in the hands of the State, by means of a national bank with State capital and an exclusive monopoly.
6. Centralization of the means of communication and transport in the hands of the State.
7. Extension of factories and instruments of production owned by the State;

the bringing into cultivation of waste lands, and the improvement of the soil generally in accordance with a common plan.

8.   Equal liability of all to labor. Establishment of industrial armies, especially for agriculture.

9.   Combination of agriculture with manufacturing industries: gradual abolition of the distinction between town and country, by a more equable distribution of the population over the country.

10.   Free education for all children in public schools. Abolition of children's factory labor in its present form. Combination of education with industrial production, etc., etc.

When, in the course of development, class distinctions have disappeared and all production has been concentrated in the hands of a vast association of the whole nation, the public power will lose its political character. Political power, properly so called, is merely the organized power of one class for oppressing another. If the proletariat during its contest with the bourgeoisie is compelled, by the force of circumstances, to organize itself as a class, if, by means of a revolution, it makes itself the ruling class, and, as such, sweeps away by force the old conditions of production, then it will, along with these conditions, have swept away the conditions for the existence of class antagonisms, and of classes generally, and will thereby have abolished its own supremacy as a class.

In place of the old bourgeois society with its classes and class antagonisms we shall have an association in which the free development of each is the condition for the free development of all.

Programme of the Social Democratic Party of Germany
The Erfurt Congress, 1891

Initially Marxism attracted few adherents, but within a few decades it had become extremely influential, particularly among left-wing working-class organizations and parties. This was particularly so in Germany, where the Social Democratic Party, founded in 1875, grew to the point at which after 1890 it gained more votes than any other party in Germany and became Europe's strongest socialist party. At the Erfurt Congress of 1891 the party defined its official program. The following excerpt from that program indicates the party's ideological basis.

> **Consider:** *How this relates to the ideas contained in the* Communist Manifesto; *the policies the party would support; what is appealing and what is threatening about this program.*

SOURCE: Bertrand Russell, *German Social Democracy* (London: Longmans, 1896), pp. 137–139.

PROGRAMME OF THE SOCIAL DEMOCRATIC PARTY OF GERMANY

The economic development of bourgeois society leads necessarily to the disappearance of production on a small scale (*Kleinbetrieb*), the principle of which consists in the worker's owning the means of production. This economic development separates the worker from his means of production, and transforms him into an unpropertied proletarian, while the means of production become the property of a comparatively small number of capitalists and great landlords.

Hand in hand with the monopolising of the means of production, goes the supplanting of scattered small businesses by colossal businesses, the development of the tool into the machine, and a gigantic growth of the productivity of human labour. But all the advantages of this change are monopolised by the capitalists and great landlords. For the proletariat and the sinking intermediate layers—small masters, peasants—it betokens growing increase of the insecurity of their existence, of misery, of oppression, of slavery, of humiliation and of exploration.

Ever greater grows the number of the proletariat, ever more extensive the army of superfluous workers, ever sharper the contrast between exploiters and exploited, and ever bitterer the class-warfare between bourgeoisie and proletariat, which divides modern society into two hostile camps, and is the common characteristic of all industrial countries.

The chasm between propertied and unpropertied is further widened by crises, rooted in the essence of the capitalistic method of production, which grow ever more far-reaching and more ravaging, which make general insecurity into the normal condition of society, and furnish the proof that the productive powers of modern society have outgrown its control, that private property in the means of production is irreconcilable with the due application and full development of those powers.

Private property in the means of production, which was formerly the means of securing to the producer the possession of his own product, has today become the means of expropriating peasants, handicraftsmen and small producers, and of putting the non-workers, capitalists and great landlords in possession of the product of the workers. Only the conversion of capitalistic private property in the means of production—land, quarries, and mines, raw material, tools, machines, means of communication—into common property, and the change of the production of goods into a socialistic production, worked for and through society, can bring it about that production on a large scale, and the ever-growing productiveness of human labour, shall develop, for the hitherto exploited classes, from a source of misery and oppression, into a source of the highest well-being and perfect universal harmony.

This social change betokens the emancipation, not only of the proletariat, but of the whole human race, which is suffering under the present conditions. But it can only be the work of the working classes, because all other classes, in spite of conflicts of interests among themselves, take their stand on the ground of private property in the means of production, and have, for their common aim, the maintenance of the foundations of existing society.

The struggle of the working class against capitalistic exploitation is of necessity a political struggle. The working class cannot carry on its economic contests, and cannot develop its economic organisation, without political rights. It cannot bring about the transference of the means of production into the possession of the community, without having obtained political power.

To give to this fight of the working class a conscious and unified form, and to show it its necessary goal—that is the task of the Social Democratic Party.

The interests of the working classes are the same in all countries with a capitalistic mode of production. With the extension of the world's commerce, and of production for the world-market, the position of the worker in every country grows ever more dependent on the position of the worker in other countries. The liberation of the working class, accordingly, is a work in which the workmen of all civilised countries are equally involved. In recognition of this, the Social Democratic Party of Germany feels and declares itself to be *one* with the class-conscious workmen of all other countries.

The Social Democratic Party of Germany does not fight, accordingly, for new class-privileges and class-rights, but for the abolition of class-rule and of classes themselves, for equal rights and equal duties of all, without distinction of sex or descent. Starting from these views, it combats, within existing society, not only the exploitation and oppression of wage-earners, but every kind of exploitation and oppression, whether directed against a class, a party, a sex, or a race.

Socialist Women: Becoming a Socialist
Anna Maier

Between 1850 and 1914 numerous working-class women joined unions and various working-class political organizations. As socialism became more popular in the last decades of the nineteenth century, more and more working-class women were attracted to socialist organizations. At first, most socialist leaders took little account of the specific needs of women workers, but over time more attention was paid to women's issues and women gained leadership roles within socialist organizations. In the following selection Anna Maier describes how she became a socialist by joining the Social Democrats in Austria during the 1890s.

> **Consider:** *What experiences led Anna Maier to become a socialist; the consequences of her becoming a socialist.*

When I turned thirteen my mother took me by the hand and we went to see the manager of a tobacco factory to get me a job. The manager refused to hire me

SOURCE: Adelheid Popp, ed., *A Commemorative Book: Twenty Years of the Austrian Women Workers' Movement* (Vienna, 1912), pp. 107–109, in Eleanor S. Riemer and John C. Fout, eds., *European Women: A Documentary History, 1789–1945* (New York: Schocken Books, 1980), pp. 94–95.

but my mother begged him to change his mind, since she explained, my father had died. I was hired. When I was getting ready to go to work the next day, my mother told me that I was to keep quiet and do what I was told. That was easier said than done. The treatment you received in this factory was really brutal. Young girls were often abused or even beaten by the older women. I rebelled strongly against that. I tried anything that might help improve things for me. As a child I was very pious and used to listen enthusiastically to the priests telling stories from the Bible. So, when things were going badly for me [at work], I would go to church on Sundays where I prayed so intently that I saw or heard nothing going on around me. When I went back to work on Monday, things were not any better and sometimes they were worse. I asked myself: Can there be a higher power that rewards good and punishes evil? I said to myself, no, that cannot be.

Several years went by. The *Women Workers' Newspaper [Arbeiterinnen-Zeitung]* began to appear and a few issues were smuggled into the factory by one of the older women. The more I was warned to stay away from this woman, the more I went to her to ask her if she would lend me a copy of the newspaper since I didn't have enough money to buy my own. At that time work hours were very long and the pay was very low. When my friend lent me a copy of the newspaper, I had to keep it hidden and I couldn't even let my mother see it if I took it home. I came to understand many things, my circle of acquaintances grew and when a political organization was founded in Sternberg, the workers were urged to join— only the men, the women were left out. A party representative came to us since I was already married by then. When he came by for the third time I asked him if I wasn't mature enough to become a member of the organization. He was embarrassed but replied: "When do you want to?" So I joined and I am a member of the party to this day.

I attended all the meetings, took part in all the demonstrations and it was not long before I was punished by the manager of the factory. I was taken off a good job and put in a poorer one just because I had become a Social Democrat. Nothing stopped me though; I said to myself, if this official is against it, out of fear to be sure, then it can't be all bad. When the tobacco workers' union was founded in November 1899, I joined and we had some big battles before we were able to make progress. Through these two organizations I have matured into a class-conscious fighter and I am now trying to win over mothers to the cause so that future children of the proletariat will have a happier youth than I had.

Syllabus of Errors
Pope Pius IX

Critics of middle-class liberalism were not limited to those demanding more rapid, radical changes such as the Marxists. From the time of the French Revolution, the conservative Cath-

SOURCE: From William E. Gladstone, *The Vatican Decrees in Their Bearing on Civil Allegiance: A Political Expostulation* (New York: Harper and Brothers, 1875), pp. 109–129.

olic Church was usually hostile to most of the changes favored by the middle class and by doctrines of liberalism. Indeed, in the decades just after mid-century, when it had become apparent that traditional society was on the wane, the Church became more intransigent than ever. In 1864 Pius IX, who served as pope from 1846 to 1878, issued the famous "Syllabus of Errors," in which most of the major forces of the nineteenth century were formally rejected. The following excerpts from that document should be read with care; they present views the Church specifically rejected as errors, not views accepted by the Church.

> **Consider:** *Why Pius IX took this stand; the dilemma faced by Catholics who were also middle class and liberal; the groups that might favor the Church's view as expressed here.*

15. Every man is free to embrace and profess the religion he shall believe true, guided by the light of reason.

16. Men may in any religion find the way of eternal salvation, and obtain eternal salvation.

✲

39. The commonwealth is the origin and source of all rights, and possesses rights which are not circumscribed by any limits.

✲

45. The entire direction of public schools, in which the youth of Christian states are educated, except (to a certain extent) in the case of episcopal seminaries, may and must appertain to the civil power, and belong to it so far that no other authority whatsoever shall be recognized as having any right to interfere in the discipline of the schools, the arrangement of the studies, the taking of degrees, or the choice and approval of the teachers.

✲

47. The best theory of civil society requires that popular schools open to the children of all classes, and, generally, all public institutes intended for instruction in letters and philosophy, and for conducting the education of the young, should be freed from all ecclesiastical authority, government, and interference, and should be fully subject to the civil and political power, in conformity with the will of rulers and the prevalent opinions of the age.

✲

56. Moral laws do not stand in need of the divine sanction, and there is no necessity that human laws should be conformable to the laws of nature, and receive their sanction from God.

57. Knowledge of philosophical things and morals, and also civil laws, may and must depart from divine and ecclesiastical authority.

✲

78. In the present day, it is no longer expedient that the Catholic religion shall be held as the only religion of the State, to the exclusion of all other modes of worship.

✿

80. The Roman Pontiff can and ought to reconcile himself to, and agree with, progress, liberalism, and civilization as lately introduced.

Foundations of the Nineteenth Century: Racism

Houston Stewart Chamberlain

During the second half of the nineteenth century, elements of nationalism, Darwinism, and Romanticism were combined by various writers to produce racist theories and provide justification for the growth of racist views. One of the most famous of these writers was Houston Stewart Chamberlain (1855–1927), an Englishman who moved to Germany and became a naturalized German. There he wrote Foundations of the Nineteenth Century *(1900), which soon became a popular success. In it he stressed the importance of racism for the development of civilization. The following selection from that book deals with the "German race."*

> **Consider:** *The characteristics of the "German race"; the ways in which this selection reflects racist thought; how this might relate to German nationalism.*

Let us attempt a glance into the depths of the soul. What are the specific intellectual and moral characteristics of this Germanic race? Certain anthropologists would fain teach us that all races are equally gifted; we point to history and answer: that is a lie! The races of mankind are markedly different in the nature and also in the extent of their gift, and the Germanic races belong to the most highly gifted group, the group usually termed Aryan. Is this human family united and uniform by bonds of blood? Do these stems really all spring from the same root? I do not know and I do not much care; no affinity binds more closely than elective affinity, and in this sense the Indo-European Aryans certainly form a family. . . .

Physically and mentally the Aryans are pre-eminent among all peoples; for that reason they are by right, as the Stagirite expresses it, the lords of the world. Aristotle puts the matter still more concisely when he says, "Some men are by nature free, others slaves"; this perfectly expresses the moral aspect. For freedom

---

SOURCE: Houston Stewart Chamberlain, *Foundations of the Nineteenth Century*, vol. I (New York: Howard Fertig, 1968), pp. 542–543.

is by no means an abstract thing, to which every human being has fundamentally a claim; a right to freedom must evidently depend upon capacity for it, and this again presupposes physical and intellectual power. One may make the assertion, that even the mere conception of freedom is quite unknown to most men. Do we not see the *homo syriacus* develop just as well and as happily in the position of slave as of master? Do the Chinese not show us another example of the same nature? Do not all historians tell us that the Semites and half-Semites, in spite of their great intelligence, never succeeded in founding a State that lasted, and that because every one always endeavoured to grasp all power for himself, thus showing that their capabilities were limited to despotism and anarchy, the two opposites of freedom?

Judaism in Music: Anti-Semitism
Richard Wagner

One of the darkest aspects of racist thought during the second half of the nineteenth century was its growing stress on anti-Semitism. Anti-Semitism has a long history, but it welled up with new strength after mid-century, particularly in Germany, where it became an important social and political force. An example of this bitter anti-Semitism comes from the pen of the great German composer, Richard Wagner (1813–1883). The following is an excerpt from "Judaism in Music," an article he published in a German journal in 1850.

> **Consider:** *The elements of Wagner's anti-Semitism; the support he uses for his arguments against the Jew; how this relates to the ideas of Houston Stewart Chamberlain.*

It is necessary for us to explain the *involuntary repugnance* we possess for the nature and personality of the Jews. . . . According to the present constitution of the world, the Jew in truth is already more than emancipate: He rules, and will rule, as long as Money remains the power before which all our doings and our dealings lose their force. . . . The public art taste has been brought between the busy fingers of the Jews, who reside over an art bazaar. . . . The Jew's outward appearance always has something disagreeably foreign about it. . . .

The Jew speaks the language of the nation in whose midst he dwells from generation to generation, but he always speaks it as an alien. Our whole European art and civilization have remained to the Jew a foreign tongue. In this speech, this art, the Jew can only after-speak and after-patch—cannot truly make a poem of

---

SOURCE: Louis L. Snyder, ed., *Documents of German History* (New Brunswick, N.J.: Rutgers University Press, 1958), pp. 192–193.

his words, an artwork of his doings. In the peculiarities of Semitic pronunciation the first thing that strikes our ear as quite outlandish and unpleasant, in the Jew's production of the voice sounds, is a creaking, squeaking, buzzing snuffle. . . . The Jew who is innately incapable of enouncing himself to us artistically through either his outward appearance or his speech, and least of all through his singing, has, nevertheless, been able in the widest-spread of modern art varieties, to wit, in Music, to reach the rulership of public taste. . . . Control of money through usury has led the Jews to power, for modern culture is accessible to none but the well-to-do. . . .

The Jews have never produced a true poet. [Heinrich Heine] reached the point where he duped himself into a poet, and was rewarded by his versified lies being set to music by our own composers. He was the conscience of Judaism, just as Judaism is the evil conscience of our modern civlization.

VISUAL SOURCES

The Hatch Family: The Upper Middle Class
Eastman Johnson

The following 1871 portrait of the Hatch family by the American artist Eastman Johnson shows a number of elements of the condition, style of life, and values of the upper middle class. Both the quality and quantity of the furnishings and the clothes indicate how materially well to do this family is. The clothes and demeanor convey the strong sense of propriety; yet the activities of the children and the position of their toys denote how child-centered this family is. The appropriate sexual roles are suggested: the father at center right in an authoritative pose, with pen in hand sitting at his desk, the grandfather on the left, keeping up on the news by reading a paper, the mother on the right, generally surveying her children, and the grandmother on the left, knitting. The large painting on the left as well as the sculptures on the right show this family to be properly supportive and appreciative of the arts. The large bookcase on the right indicates a respect for literature and learning. Heavy curtains largely block out the outside world; values of domesticity and privacy are evident.

Consider: *What lessons the nineteenth-century viewer might learn from this portrait.*

Photo 10-1

The Metropolitan Museum of Art, Gift of Frederick H. Hatch.

The Ages of Woman

This mid-nineteenth-century French engraving shows an idealized image of the ages of woman. In the center, three religious scenes represent the purity of woman's origins, place on earth, and final destination. Around this foundation is the woman at nine ages, from the happy playful child of ten years old to the solitary honorable grandmother of ninety years old. In between she is shown in her role as a middle-class wife, mother, and grandmother.

Consider: *What image of women's proper nature and role this conveys to nineteenth-century viewers; how this fits with the Eastman Johnson portrait and the analysis of European women by Riemer and Fout that follows; how an image of the ages of man might differ.*

Photo 10-2   The Ages of Woman

Cliché Musée des Arts et Traditions Populaire

Lunch Hour: The Working Class
Käthe Kollwitz

Accompanying the rise to prominence of the upper middle class was the growth of the urban working class, the two economically dependent on each other but in strikingly different conditions. This 1909 drawing by the German artist Käthe Kollwitz, entitled Lunch Hour, gives an impression of the condition and spirit of the German working

Photo 10-3

Private Collection. Photo courtesy Galerie St. Etienne, New York.

class. The workers seem to be part of an almost undifferentiated mass, dully and similarly clothed, eating low-quality meals in uncomfortable circumstances, and above all display- ing a physical and psychological fatigue and a pervasive sense of discouragement.

Consider: *How this drawing relates to the views of Marx and Engels.*

SECONDARY SOURCES

The Decline of Political Liberalism

F. H. Hinsley

Despite the apparent failures of 1848, political liberalism was at its zenith during the middle of the nineteenth century. By the last two decades of the century it was clearly on the decline or was at least evolving in striking new ways. This evolution is analyzed in the following selection from The New Cambridge Modern History *by F. H. Hinsley of Cam- bridge.*

> **Consider:** *The causes of the decline of political liberalism; the intellectual or ideo- logical developments that occurred in the second half of the nineteenth century, as reflected by the decline of political liberalism.*

The politics of the age was distinguished, even in the least authoritarian of states, as much by the growth of authority as by the extension of democracy; and less by the extension of democracy and the democratisation of government than by an advance towards the democratisation of government policies and of the political context in which governments operated. It is these facts which account for the collapse of liberalism—for its exhaustion in more democratic countries as well as for its frustration in less democratic circumstances and its distortion in situations that were in between.

In the advanced countries of western Europe during the 1870's, when liberalism was at its zenith in its European home, liberal governments, abandoning the liberal opposition to the power of the state and seeing the state as the most effective means of securing the liberal conception of freedom in changed circumstances, accepted the early steps towards the inevitable extension of the functions of government and the use of unprecedented state compulsion on individuals for

SOURCE: F. H. Hinsley, "Introduction," in *The New Cambridge Modern History*, vol. XI, F. H. Hinsley, ed. (Cambridge, England: Cambridge University Press, 1962), pp. 32–34. Reprinted by permission of the publisher.

social ends—embracing the notion of state education, legalising trade unions, justifying public health measures, adopting even insurance and factory legislation. No governments in such countries, whatever their political complexion, could, indeed, have opposed such developments. From the end of the 1870's, however, they were overrun and overturned in those countries by the further progress of those twin forces, the masses and the modern state. Every advance in the role of the state, every new aspect of the social problem, every recognition of the emergence of the masses, every new turn of policy—whether towards protectionism and imperialism or towards social regulation and the extension of the franchise—conflicted with the liberal belief in freedom of contract and of enterprise, in free trade, in individual liberty, in public economy, in the minimum of government interference. Liberalism's great contribution, the constitutional state, and its guiding principles, the freedom of the individual, legal equality and conflict with the Church, were—to the varying extents that they had been already established in these states—taken over by more empirical and conservative politicians. Liberalism became more doctrinaire and more narrowly associated with urban and big business interests—even while industrial organisation itself, with the movement from personal to corporate control, was deserting it. The liberal parties split into moderate (national, social or imperialist) and radical wings on these current issues and lost office. Liberal rule or its equivalent ended in Great Britain in 1885, in Germany in 1878, in Austria and the Netherlands in 1879, in Sweden in 1880, in Belgium in 1884, in France in 1885. In Italy under Depretis and Crispi and in some states beyond western Europe liberal parties remained in power. But, liberal only in name, they embraced protectionism and imperialism, undertook social regulation and retained of the old liberal creed only opposition to the extension of the franchise and to the pretensions of the Church. In these states, as in even more authoritarian countries, authentic liberalism remained a relevant if a weakened basis for opposition to established authority. But even in that role, and even when it was not proscribed by the increased possibilities of repression, it was doomed to frustration by the growth of the need for social regulation and strong government and by the demand for those things by the mass of the population.

The Unfinished Revolution: Marxism Interpreted
Adam B. Ulam

Critical analyses of Marx and Marxism abound and from almost all points of view. From the historian's perspective, one of the most useful ways to approach Marx and Marxism is to place both in their historical context. This is done in the following excerpt from The

SOURCE: Adam B. Ulam, *The Unfinished Revolution* (New York: Random House, Inc., 1960), pp. 42–44. Reprinted by permission of the author.

Unfinished Revolution *by Adam Ulam, a professor of government at Harvard who has written extensively on the history of Marxism and the Soviet Union. Here he attempts to explain aspects of both the content and the appeal of Marxism by pointing to intellectual traditions affecting Marx and social realities conditioning those who accepted it.*

> **Consider:** *Why Marxism is most appealing during the early period of industrialization; how Ulam would explain the apparent failure of Marxism to take hold in twentieth-century nations such as the United States; what Ulam means when he calls Marx a child of rationalistic optimism; how a more pro-Marxist scholar might respond to this interpretation.*

Here, then, is a theory attuned even more closely than other parts of Marxism to the facts and feelings of an early period of industrialization. The class struggle is the salt of Marxism, its most operative revolutionary part. As a historical and psychological concept, it expresses a gross oversimplification, but it is the oversimplification of a genius. The formula of the class struggle seizes the essence of the mood of a great historical moment—a revolution in basic economy—and generalizes it into a historical law. It extracts the grievances of groups of politically conscious workers in Western Europe, then a very small part of the whole proletariat, and sees in it the portent and meaning of the awakening of the whole working class everywhere. The *first* reaction of the worker to industrialization, his feelings of grievance and impotence before the machine, his employer, and the state which stands behind the employer, are assumed by Marx to be typical of the general reactions of the worker to industrialization. What does change in the process of the development of industry is that the worker's feeling of impotence gives way to class consciousness, which in turn leads him to class struggle and socialism. Marx's worker is the historical worker, but he is the historical worker of a specific period of industrial and political development.

Even in interpreting the psychology of the worker of the transitional period, Marx exhibited a rationalistic bias. The worker's opposition to the capitalist order is a total opposition to its laws, its factories, and its government. But this revolutionary consciousness of the worker is to take him next to Marxist socialism, where he will accept the factory system and the state, the *only* difference being the abolition of capitalism. Why shouldn't the revolutionary protest of the worker flow into other channels: into rejection of industrialism as well as capitalism, into rejection of the socialist as well as the capitalist state? It is here that Marx is most definitely the child of his age, the child of rationalistic optimism: the workers will undoubtedly translate their anarchistic protests and grievances into a sophisticated philosophy of history. They will undoubtedly realize that the forces of industrialism and modern life, which strip them of property, status, and economic security, are in themselves benevolent in their ultimate effects and that it is only capitalism and the capitalists which make them into instruments of oppression. The chains felt by the proletariat are the chains of the industrial system. The chains Marx urges them to throw off are those of capitalism. Will the workers understand the difference? And if they do, will they still feel that in destroying capitalism they have a "world to win"?

European Women

Eleanor S. Riemer and John C. Fout

In recent years many historians have pointed out the limitations facing middle-class women between 1850 and 1914. As investigations into women's history have multiplied and deepened, new interpretations have been made. In the following selection the historians Eleanor S. Riemer and John C. Fout argue that middle-class women during this period increasingly questioned their roles and often expanded their activities into new, important areas.

> **Consider:** *How middle-class women's maternal and housewifely roles were justified; ways in which middle-class women expanded their roles; how middle-class women's new roles affected their attitudes.*

Middle-class women, too, faced new situations and challenges in the nineteenth and twentieth centuries. Although some lower-middle-class women continued to work alongside their shopkeeper husbands as they had in the past, most married middle-class women did not, and never expected to have to work for wages. Their lives were centered on caring for their children and homes. But most middle-class women did not lead leisured existences. Indeed, they found that the demands on their time and energy increased as modernization progressed, and middle-class families' standards for cleanliness, food preparation, and physical comfort were upgraded.

Middle-class women's maternal and housewifely roles were justified in the nineteenth century by a twofold conception of women's nature and capabilities. On the one hand, women were considered passive creatures who were physically and intellectually inferior to men. Thus, women needed protection and direction from their fathers and husbands. On the other hand, women, because they were nonaggressive and sexually passive and were removed from the contamination of the competitive workaday world, were deemed morally superior to men and were to be respected for that. A woman's unique capability and greatest responsibility in life was caring for the moral and spiritual needs of her family.

The contradictions within this ideal and women's attempts to reconcile or dispel them are recurring and major themes in the documents. From the middle of the nineteenth century large numbers of middle-class women consciously and methodically expanded their maternal and moral roles—and thus their sphere of competence—outside their homes to society at large. One way they accomplished this was by transforming middle- and upper-class women's traditional, and often haphazard, charitable work into organized movements for social reform. These women became increasingly interested in the problems of poor women and chil-

SOURCE: From *European Women: A Documentary History, 1789–1945*, edited by Eleanor S. Riemer and John C. Fout. Copyright © 1980 by Schocken Books, Inc. Reprinted by permission of Schocken Books, published by Pantheon Books, a division of Random House, Inc.

dren. They believed they understood and shared many of the concerns of working-class mothers and considered these women and their children the primary victims of the economic and social dislocations caused by urbanization and the new industrial order.

Through their social welfare and reform work, middle-class women gained a sense of both their own competence and their limitations in a world controlled by men. Many also realized that although women of their class expected to be dependent wives, economic and social realities were such that there was no guarantee women would be supported by men throughout their lives. Many came to believe that their own limited educations and the restrictions placed on them by the law and the ideals of ladylike conduct left women ill-equipped for the roles they might have to—or want to—play in life. Thus, the reform of society and reforms for women became closely identified and often were confronted simultaneously by organized women all over Europe.

Chapter Questions

1. Give support for the argument that the nineteenth century was above all a middle-class century.
2. What common elements are there among the various criticisms of the middle class, its ideas, and its life style?
3. How would you explain the rise of Marxist and socialist ideas and movements during the second half of the nineteenth century?
4. Contrast the ways in which the social, cultural, and economic changes of the period affected men and women.

III

THE TWENTIETH CENTURY: 1914 TO THE PRESENT

CHAPTER ELEVEN

War and Revolution: 1914–1920

Historians usually mark the end of the nineteenth century not at the turn of the century but with the outbreak of World War I in 1914. Although a number of wars took place after 1815, none covered all of Europe, none was long, and none was very costly. Indeed, many Europeans optimistically believed that the Western nations had become too economically interdependent and culturally mature to become involved in massive wars ever again. At the outbreak of World War I no one expected it to be so widespread or long-lasting. In fact, the fighting continued for four years before the war was finally concluded. The destruction was so unprecedented and the fighting so brutal that one had to question whether Western civilization had progressed at all. The war was such a strain that the most modernized nations, England, France, and Germany, for example, mobilized the total resources of their societies, while less modernized nations like Russia were unable to support the effort.

Revolutions occurred in a number of areas, most notably in Germany, the Austro-Hungarian Empire, and Russia. The revolutions in Russia were the most significant. In March 1917 the tsarist government was swept from power by relatively moderate, liberal groups. In November of that year the new Provisional Government was toppled by the Bolsheviks, who initiated a Communist regime that proved surprisingly resilient. Under this government, the Soviet Union was to become a significant force in world politics.

In some ways the Paris Peace Conference in 1919 brought the period to a close, but the problems facing diplomats and heads of state meeting in Versailles were overwhelming. The Soviet Union was not invited to the conference, and the Germans were virtually ignored. Few left the conference satisfied and many harbored resentments that would color domestic and international politics during the 1920s and 1930s.

This chapter focuses on World War I and the Russian Revolution. With World War I, the two major issues for historians are the cause and the settlement. What caused this apparently unwanted war to break out and who, if anyone, was most to blame? Was the Peace of Paris a success or a failure? Some of the selections also explore tactics used to fight the war, people's experiences during the war, and the results of the war. Other documents deal with the ways the war affected women. With the Russian Revolution, the question is not only why it occurred but moreover how and why the Bolsheviks—through most of 1917 only a small party—were ultimately able to gain and maintain power against extremely long odds. A number of documents

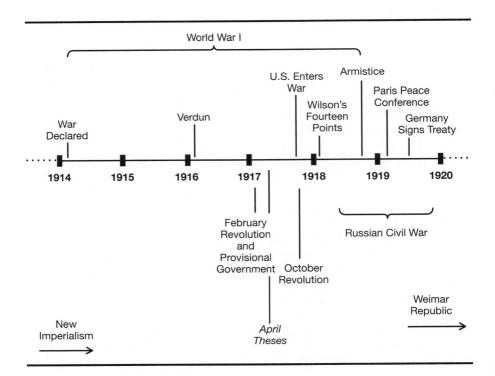

illustrate Lenin's strategy and Bolshevik policy as well as the variety of scholarly efforts to answer these questions.

Many feel that the events during this period of war constituted a fundamental break with the past. The significance of World War I and the Russian Revolution are shown in the developments in the two decades that followed. These will be covered in Chapters 12 and 13.

PRIMARY SOURCES

Letter to the Editor of the London Times: War and Political Ideology
V. Bourtzeff

At the beginning of World War I, there was tremendous popular enthusiasm and unity behind governments for the war effort. What is most surprising was that even socialist and other leftist political parties joined in this support. Socialists had long argued that working-class interests transcended national boundaries and that they would not support a nationalistic war entered into by a government dominated by capitalists. The following letter from V. Bourtzeff, a Russian Socialist, appeared in the London Times *about six weeks after the outbreak of the war in 1914.*

> **Consider:** *Why Bourtzeff supported the government's war effort; how Bourtzeff connects his opposition to the government's policies and his support for the government in the war; assuming these to be typical expectations at the beginning of the war, the ways World War I was a psychologically shattering experience for Europeans.*

TO THE EDITOR OF "THE TIMES":

Sir—May I be allowed to say a few words in connection with the excellent letter by my compatriot, Professor Vinogradov, which appeared in your paper today (September 14)? Professor Vinogradov is absolutely right when he says that not

SOURCE: Frank A. Golder, ed., *Documents of Russian History, 1914–1917*, Emanuel Aronsberg, trans. Reprinted by permission of Prentice-Hall, Inc., pp. 38–39. Copyright © 1927 by Prentice-Hall, Inc.

only is it desirable that complete unity of feeling should exist in Russian political circles, but that this unity is already an accomplished fact.

The representatives of all political parties and of all nationalities in Russia are now at one with the Government, and this war with Germany and Austria, both guided by the Kaiser, has already become a national war for Russia.

Even we, the adherents of the parties of the Extreme Left, and hitherto ardent anti-militarists and pacifists, even we believe in the necessity of *this* war. *This* war is a war to protect justice and civilization. It will, we hope, be a decisive factor in our united *war against war*, and we hope that after it, it will at last be possible to consider seriously the question of disarmament and universal peace. There can be no doubt that victory at that (personally I await this in the immediate future), will be on the side of the Allied nations—England, France, Belgium, Servia, and Russia.

The German peril, the curse which has hung over the whole world for so many decades, will be crushed, and crushed so that it will never again become a danger to the peace of the world. The peoples of the world desire peace.

To Russia this war will bring regeneration.

We are convinced that after this war there will no longer be any room for political reaction, and Russia will be associated with the existing group of cultured and civilized countries.

Professor Vinogradov is right when he says that in Russia not one of the political Left parties has at the present time modified its program in any way in view of the war. The word on all lips in Russia now is "Freedom." All are hungrily awaiting a general amnesty, freedom of the Press and of national life.

All the parties without any exceptions have supported the Government without even waiting for it to make any definite announcement about these crying needs. This is the measure of the belief of the people in the inevitableness of liberal reforms. The Government unfortunately still seems irresolute, and has up till now only done the minimum to justify the popular belief in it, but we are convinced that circumstances will develop in such a way that the Government will not be able to delay for long that which has become for Russia a *historical necessity*. And the sooner this happens the better.

To ensure the complete success of Russia in this war against Germany and Austria, and also for the time when the terms of peace will be discussed, the strongest and most firm national unity is necessary. And this unity of all nationalities and all parties will be possible only when the Russian Government will frankly and resolutely inaugurate a new and free era in the political life of the country.

We are convinced that we have supporting us both the public opinion of England and that of her Allies—France and Belgium.

Yours truly,
V. Bourtzeff

Reports from the Front: The Battle for Verdun, 1916

The widely anticipated short war typified by heroic offensive thrusts failed to materialize. Instead, it turned into a long, extraordinarily brutal struggle. On the Western front, opposing armies slaughtered each other from their trenches. There are numerous reports of life at the front, such as the following account by a French Army officer of the battle for Verdun in 1916.

Consider: *Why the defense was at such an advantage; why there was a willingness to sacrifice so much for such small advances.*

The Germans attacked in massed formation, by big columns of five or six hundred men, preceded by two waves of sharpshooters. We had only our rifles and our machine guns, because the 75's could not get to work.

Fortunately the flank batteries succeeded in catching the Boches on the right. It is absolutely impossible to convey what losses the Germans must suffer in these attacks. Nothing can give the idea of it. Whole ranks are mowed down, and those that follow them suffered the same fate. Under the storm of machine gun, rifle and 75 fire, the German columns were plowed into furrows of death. Imagine if you can what it would be like to rake water. Those gaps filled up again at once. That is enough to show with what disdain of human life the German attacks are planned and carried out.

In these circumstances German advances are sure. They startle the public, but at the front nobody attaches any importance to them. As a matter of fact, our trenches are so near those of the Germans that once the barbed wire is destroyed the distance between them can be covered in a few minutes. Thus, if one is willing to suffer a loss of life corresponding to the number of men necessary to cover the space between the lines, the other trench can always be reached. By sacrificing thousands of men, after a formidable bombardment, an enemy trench can always be taken.

There are slopes on Hill 304 where the level of the ground is raised several meters by mounds of German corpses. Sometimes it happens that the third German wave uses the dead of the second wave as ramparts and shelters. It was behind ramparts of the dead left by the first five attacks, on May 24th, that we saw the Boches take shelter while they organized their next rush.

We make prisoners among these dead during our counterattacks. They are men who have received no hurt, but have been knocked down by the falling of the human wall of their killed and wounded neighbors. They say very little. They are

SOURCE: From *Source Records of the Great War*, vol. IV, ed. Charles F. Horne (New York: National Alumni, 1923), pp. 222–223.

for the most part dazed with fear and alcohol, and it is several days before they recover.

Dulce et Decorum Est: Disillusionment
Wilfred Owen

The experience of World War I was profoundly disillusioning to those who believed in nineteenth-century ideals. After World War I, Europe was no longer characterized by the sense of optimism, progress, and glory that had typified Europe for most of the period between the eighteenth century and 1914. This is evidenced in war poems that no longer glorified the struggle but instead conveyed a sense of the horror and futility about it. One of the best of these antiwar poets was Wilfred Owen, born in England in 1893 and killed in action in 1918, one week before the armistice. The following poem has the ironic ending, "It is sweet and proper to die for one's country."

Consider: *The psychological consequences of war for the soldiers; other ways this same disillusionment might be shown in novels, plays, paintings, or even historical analyses of the time.*

DULCE ET DECORUM EST

Bent double, like old beggars under sacks,
Knock-kneed, coughing like hags, we cursed through sludge,
Till on the haunting flares we turned our backs
And towards our distant rest began to trudge.
Men marched asleep. Many had lost their boots
But limped on, blood-shod. All went lame; all blind;
Drunk with fatigue; deaf even to the hoots
Of tired, outstripped Five-Nines that dropped behind.

Gas! Gas! Quick, boys!—An Ecstasy of fumbling,
Fitting the clumsy helmets just in time;
But someone still was yelling out and stumbling
And flound'ring like a man in fire or lime . . .
Dim, through the misty panes and thick green light,
As under a green sea, I saw him drowning.
In all my dreams, before my helpless sight,
He plunges at me, guttering, choking, drowning.

SOURCE: C. Day Lewis, *Collected Poems of Wilfred Owen.* Reprinted by permission of New Directions and Chatto & Windus, p. 55. Copyright © Chatto & Windus, Ltd., 1946, 1963, and The Owen Estate.

If in some smothering dreams you too could pace
Behind the wagon that we flung him in,
And watch the white eyes writhing in his face,
His hanging face, like a devil's sick of sin;
If you could hear, at every jolt, the blood
Come gargling from the froth-corrupted lungs,
Obscene as cancer, bitter as the cud
Of vile, incurable sores on innocent tongues,—
My friend, you would not tell with such high zest
To children ardent for some desperate glory,
The old Lie: Dulce et decorum est
Pro patria mori.

Minutes of the Tsar's Council of Ministers, 1915: Breakdown in Russia

When the war did not come to an end after the first few months of fighting, the strains of supporting a long-term military struggle began to appear in those countries that were least modernized politically and economically. This was clearest in the case of Russia, which had been struggling to modernize under the leadership of an inefficient autocratic government. As early as 1915 the government found itself increasingly unable to establish control over a country experiencing tremendous needs. Some of this sense of things out of control and the problems caused by the strains of war are revealed in the minutes of a meeting of the Council of Ministers on August 24, 1915.

> **Consider:** *Why the Russian government was experiencing such difficulty in establishing control; how the war fueled already existing problems within Russia.*

AUGUST 24, 1915

Scherbatov: The Council of Ministers knows that there were disturbances in Moscow which ended in bloodshed. . . . There were even more serious disorders at Ivanovo-Voznesensk when it was necessary to fire on the crowd with the result that sixteen were killed and thirty wounded. There was a critical moment when it was uncertain what the garrison would do. . . .

Shakhovskoi: I have information . . . that the workmen are quite aroused. Any kind of spark may start a fire. . . .

Goremykin: . . . I should like to ask the Minister of the Interior what measures

---

SOURCE: Frank A. Golder, ed., *Documents of Russian History, 1914–1917*, Emanuel Aronsberg, trans. Reprinted by permission of Prentice-Hall, Inc., pp. 184–185. Copyright © 1927 by Prentice-Hall, Inc.

he is taking to put an end to the lawlessness . . . going on everywhere. His principal function is to protect the State from disorder and danger.

Scherbatov: The Minister of the Interior is taking all the measures which his duty and present circumstances permit. I have more than once called your attention to the abnormal position of the Minister. Half of European Russia is out of his jurisdiction. Elsewhere in the rear the real government is in the hands of lieutenants who have despotic inclinations and little understanding. I have brought to your notice the fact that even in Petrograd, which gives tone to the whole of Russia, the Minister of the Interior is a mere resident. He has only as much power as the war lords will grant him. . . . How can you expect me to fight the growing revolutionary movement when I am refused the support of the troops on the ground that they are unreliable, that one can not be certain that they will fire on the mob? You can not quiet the whole of Russia by the police alone, especially now when the ranks of the police are being thinned out . . . hourly and the population is growing daily more excited by the speeches in the Duma, by newspaper stories, by continuous defeats, and rumors of disorders in the rear. The demonstrations and disorders come about from most unforeseen causes. At Moscow patriotic reasons were responsible. Newspapers gave out that the Dardanelles had been taken and that our troops had recaptured Kovno. One silver-tongued orator was arrested and trouble started. . . . I agree that something ought to be done. But how can you do anything when you have no support, when those in responsible places [ministers] can not get a hearing [Emperor] on questions on which the fate of the State may depend? . . . I have in my portfolio several telegrams from governors. They inform me that the flow of refugees, German-colonists and Jews driven out by the military authorities is ever rising and that the local population is so aroused against the newcomers that they receive them with clubs. . . . The governors ask for instructions and help. What can the Minister of the Interior reply. . . . Among the workmen, as among the population in general, there are terrible reports of graft in connection with war orders. . . .

Program of the Provisional Government in Russia

In the spring of 1917 a revolution finally toppled the disintegrating tsarist government in Russia. A relatively moderate, liberal Provisional Government was formed under the leadership of men like Prince Lvov and Paul Miliukov. While the Provisional Government had to share and even compete for power with the more radical workers' political organizations—the soviets—it initially acted with speed to make important changes. The following is the early program of the Provisional Government, issued on March 16, 1917.

SOURCE: Frank A. Golder, ed., *Documents of Russian History, 1914–1917,* trans. Emanuel Aronsberg (New York: Prentice-Hall, Inc., 1927).

Consider: *The attitudes revealed by this document; the nature of the reforms initiated; what this implies about the problems under the tsarist government and the discontents that supported the revolution.*

Citizens, the Provisional Executive Committee of the members of the Duma, with the aid and support of the garrison of the capital and its inhabitants, has triumphed over the dark forces of the Old Régime to such an extent as to enable it to organize a more stable executive power. . . .

The Cabinet will be guided in its actions by the following principles:

1. An immediate general amnesty for all political and religious offenses, including terrorist acts, military revolts, agrarian offenses, etc.
2. Freedom of speech and press; freedom to form labor unions and to strike. These political liberties should be extended to the army in so far as war conditions permit.
3. The abolition of all social, religious and national restrictions.
4. Immediate preparation for the calling of a Constituent Assembly, elected by universal and secret vote, which shall determine the form of government and draw up the Constitution for the country.
5. In place of the police, to organize a national militia with elective officers, and subject to the local self-government body.
6. Elections to be carried out on the basis of universal, direct, equal, and secret suffrage.
7. The troops that have taken part in the revolutionary movement shall not be disarmed or removed from Petrograd.
8. On duty and in war service, strict military discipline should be maintained, but when off duty, soldiers should have the same public rights as are enjoyed by other citizens.

The Provisional Government wishes to add that it has no intention of taking advantage of the existence of war conditions to delay the realization of the above-mentioned measures of reform.

April Theses: The Bolshevik Opposition
V. I. Lenin

Faced with a continuing war and deep discontent, the Provisional Government soon came under attack by people like Vladimir Ilyich Lenin (1870–1924), who called for more radi-

SOURCE: From V. I. Lenin, *Collected Works*, vol. XXIV (Moscow: Progress Publishers, 1964), pp. 21–24. Reprinted by permission of the Copyright Agency of the U.S.S.R.

cal changes. Lenin, who spent much of his life as a revolutionary—often in exile—had risen to the leadership of the Bolshevik faction of the Russian Marxists. He combined the skills of a superb Marxist theoretician and a revolutionary organizer. In April 1917 the Germans aided his return to Russia in an effort to weaken the new government there. On his arrival, Lenin presented his April Theses, *at first criticized by Russian Marxists but eventually accepted by the Bolshevik Central Committee.*

> **Consider:** *Why Lenin rejects support for the Provisional Government; to whom this program might be appealing and why; the ways in which this program is particularly Marxist.*

1. In our attitude towards the war, which under the new government of Lvov and Co. unquestionably remains on Russia's part a predatory imperialist war owing to the capitalist nature of that government, not the slightest concession to a "revolutionary defencism" is permissible. . . .

2. The specific feature of the present situation in Russia is that the country is *passing* from the first stage of the revolution—which, owing to the insufficient class-consciousness and organisation of the proletariat, placed power in the hands of the bourgeoisie—to its *second* stage, which must place power in the hands of the proletariat and the poorest sections of the peasants. . . .

3. No support for the Provisional Government; . . .

5. Not a parliamentary republic—to return to a parliamentary republic from the Soviets of Workers' Deputies would be a retrograde step—but a republic of Soviets of Workers', Agricultural Labourers' and Peasants' Deputies throughout the country, from top to bottom. Abolition of the police, the army and the bureaucracy.
   The salaries of all officials, all of whom are elective and displaceable at any time, not to exceed the average wage of a competent worker.

6. The weight of emphasis in the agrarian programme to be shifted to the Soviets of Agricultural Labourers' Deputies.
   Confiscation of all landed estates.
   Nationalisation of *all* lands in the country, the land to be disposed of by the local Soviets of Agricultural Labourers' and Peasants' Deputies. The organisation of separate Soviets of Deputies of Poor Peasants. The setting up of a model farm on each of the large estates (ranging in size from 100 to 300 dessiatines, according to local and other conditions, and to the decisions of the local bodies) under the control of the Soviets of Agricultural Labourers' Deputies and for the public account.

7. The immediate amalgamation of all banks in the country into a single national bank, and the institution of control over it by the Soviet of Workers' Deputies.

8. It is not our *immediate* task to "introduce" socialism, but only to bring social production and the distribution of products at once under the *control* of the Soviets of Workers' Deputies.

Speech to the Petrograd Soviet—November 8, 1917: The Bolsheviks in Power

V. I. Lenin

The Provisional Government fell in a revolution in November 1917. Under the leadership of Lenin and Leon Trotsky (1877–1940), the tightly organized Bolsheviks quickly took control. On November 8, 1917, Lenin made the following speech to a meeting of the Petrograd Soviet.

> **Consider:** *The policies Lenin supported and how they compare with the program in his* April Theses; *the ways in which Lenin was relying on forces outside of Russia to sustain the initial success of this revolution.*

Comrades, the workmen's and peasants' revolution, the need of which the Bolsheviks have emphasized many times, has come to pass.

What is the significance of this revolution? Its significance is, in the first place, that we shall have a soviet government, without the participation of bourgeoisie of any kind. The oppressed masses will of themselves form a government. The old state machinery will be smashed into bits and in its place will be created a new machinery of government by the soviet organizations. From now on there is a new page in the history of Russia, and the present, third Russian revolution shall in its final result lead to the victory of Socialism.

One of our immediate tasks is to put an end to the war at once. But in order to end the war, which is closely bound up with the present capitalistic system, it is necessary to overthrow capitalism itself. In this work we shall have the aid of the world labor movement, which has already begun to develop in Italy, England, and Germany.

A just and immediate offer of peace by us to the international democracy will find everywhere a warm response among the international proletariat masses. In order to secure the confidence of the proletariat, it is necessary to publish at once all secret treaties.

In the interior of Russia a very large part of the peasantry has said: Enough playing with the capitalists; we will go with the workers. We shall secure the confidence of the peasants by one decree, which will wipe out the private property of the landowners. The peasants will understand that their only salvation is in union with the workers.

We will establish a real labor control on production.

SOURCE: Frank A. Golder, ed., *Documents of Russian History, 1914–1917*, Emanuel Aronsberg, trans. Reprinted by permission of Prentice-Hall, Inc., pp. 618–619. Copyright © 1927 by Prentice-Hall, Inc.

We have now learned to work together in a friendly manner, as is evident from this revolution. We have the force of mass organization which has conquered all and which will lead the proletariat to world revolution.

We should now occupy ourselves in Russia in building up a proletarian socialist state.

Long live the world-wide socialistic revolution.

The Fourteen Points
Woodrow Wilson

Each nation entered World War I for its own mixture of pragmatic and idealistic reasons. In considering their war aims and a possible peace settlement, governments did not antic-ipate the changes that would occur in this unexpectedly long and costly war. By 1918 various governments had fallen and the United States had entered the conflict. On Janu-ary 8, 1918, in an address to a joint session of the U.S. Congress, President Woodrow Wilson (1856–1924) presented his Fourteen Points, a delineation of American war aims and proposals for a peace settlement. The Fourteen Points served as a basis for debate at the Paris Peace Conference in 1919 and represented the most idealistic statement of what might be gained in a final peace settlement.

> **Consider:** *The ideals that hold these points together; the grievances recognized and unrecognized in these points; the assumptions about what measures would pre-serve peace in the postwar world.*

We entered this war because violations of right had occurred which touched us to the quick and made the life of our own people impossible unless they were corrected and the world secured once for all against their recurrence. What we demand in this war, therefore, is nothing peculiar to ourselves. It is that the world be made fit and safe to live in; and particularly that it be made safe for every peace-loving nation which, like our own, wishes to live its own life, determine its own institutions, be assured of justice and fair dealing by the other peoples of the world as against force and selfish aggression. All the peoples of the world are in effect partners in this interest, and for our own part we see very clearly that unless justice be done to others it will not be done to us. The program of the world's peace, therefore, is our program; and that program, the only possible program, as we see it, is this:

I. Open covenants of peace, openly arrived at, after which there shall be no private international understandings of any kind but diplomacy shall proceed always frankly and in the public view.

II. Absolute freedom of navigation upon the seas, outside territorial waters,

SOURCE: Woodrow Wilson, "Fourteen Points," *Congressional Record*, vol. LVI, part I (1918), Washington, D.C.: U.S. Government Printing Office, pp. 680–681.

alike in peace and in war, except as the seas may be closed in whole or in part by international action. . . .

III. The removal, so far as possible, of all economic barriers and the establishment of an equality of trade conditions among all the nations consenting to the peace and associating themselves for its maintenance.

IV. Adequate guarantees given and taken that national armaments will be reduced to the lowest point consistent with domestic safety.

V. A free, open-minded, and absolutely impartial adjustment of all colonial claims, based upon a strict observance of the principle that in determining all such questions of sovereignty the interests of the populations concerned must have equal weight with the equitable claims of the government whose title is to be determined.

VI. The evacuation of all Russian territory and such a settlement of all questions affecting Russia as will secure the best and freest cooperation of the other nations of the world in obtaining for her an unhampered and unembarrassed opportunity for the independent determination of her own political development and national policy and assure her of a sincere welcome into the society of free nations under institutions of her own choosing; and, more than a welcome, assistance also of every kind that she may need and may herself desire. . . .

VII. Belgium, the whole world will agree, must be evacuated and restored, without any attempt to limit the sovereignty which she enjoys in common with all other free nations. . . .

VIII. All French territory should be freed and the invaded portions restored, and the wrong done to France by Prussia in 1871 in the matter of Alsace-Lorraine, which has unsettled the peace of the world for nearly fifty years, should be righted, in order that peace may once more be made secure in the interest of all.

IX. A readjustment of the frontiers of Italy should be effected along clearly recognizable lines of nationality.

X. The peoples of Austria-Hungary, whose place among the nations we wish to see safeguarded and assured, should be accorded the freest opportunity of autonomous development.

XI. Rumania, Serbia, and Montenegro should be evacuated; occupied territories restored; Serbia accorded free and secure access to the sea; and the relations of the several Balkan states to one another determined by friendly counsel along historically established lines of allegiance and nationality; and international guarantees of the political and economic independence and territorial integrity of the several Balkan states should be entered into.

XII. The Turkish portions of the present Ottoman Empire should be assured a secure sovereignty, but the other nationalities which are now under Turkish rule should be assured an undoubted security of life and an absolutely unmolested opportunity of autonomous development. . . .

XIII. An independent Polish state should be erected which should include the territories inhabited by indisputably Polish populations. . . .

XIV. A general association of nations must be formed under specific covenants for the purpose of affording mutual guarantees of political independence and territorial integrity to great and small states alike.

In regard to these essential rectifications of wrong and assertions of right we feel ourselves to be intimate partners of all the governments and peoples associated together against the Imperialists. We cannot be separated in interest or divided in purpose. We stand together until the end. . . .

We have no jealousy of German greatness, and there is nothing in this program that impairs it. We grudge her no achievement or distinction of learning or of pacific enterprise such as have made her record very bright and very enviable. We do not wish to injure her or to block in any way her legitimate influence or power. . . .

Neither do we presume to suggest to her any alteration or modification of her institutions. But it is necessary . . . that we should know whom her spokesmen speak for when they speak to us, whether for the Reichstag majority or for the military party and the men whose creed is imperial domination. . . .

An evident principle runs through the whole program I have outlined. It is the principle of justice to all peoples and nationalities, and their right to live on equal terms of liberty and safety with one another, whether they be strong or weak. . . . The people of the United States could act upon no other principle; and to the vindication of this principle they are ready to devote their lives, their honor, and everything that they possess. The moral climax of this the culminating and final war for human liberty has come, and they are ready to put their own strength, their own highest purpose, their own integrity and devotion to the test.

VISUAL SOURCES

World War I: The Front Lines

The following photo displays the physical and psychological realities of life on the Western front during World War I. The war is being fought from trenches with soldiers at machine guns guarding land made barren by artillery barrages, throwing hand grenades at the often unseen enemy, and using poison gas (note the gas mask). It is difficult to find in such a scene a sense of a progressive civilization, of the dignity of the individual, or of reasoned interaction among nations—the ideals held by nineteenth-century Western civilization. Considering the use of such weapons, we can easily imagine the carnage and the sense of futility that resulted from the "heroic" offensive charges of the foot soldiers that were so common for most of the war.

Consider: *How this supports the description of life on the front lines during the Verdun battle.*

Photo 11-1

World War I: The Home Front and Women

The following picture of a British war plant gives an idea of how industrialization and technology have helped turn any extended war into a massive strain. Large factories had to be built or converted to the production of war munitions, here heavy artillery shells. A new labor force had to be trained, often involving a change of values: Here women and older men predominate to make up for the drain on manpower caused by the armed services. Finally, this picture suggests the enormous logistical organization and government cooperation with capitalist enterprises necessary to keep a modern war effort going.

The need for labor on the home front resulted in large numbers of women entering the labor force or changing jobs. The following two charts (pp. 248–249) indicate the changing employment of women in Great Britain between 1914 and 1918, the first chart for all employment, the second chart for industrial employment.

> **Consider:** *The ways in which a modern war effort affects a nation's people and economy, even though the war is being fought on foreign soil; the potential significance for women of these changes in employment.*

Photo 11-2

Chart 11-1   Women in the Labor Force, Great Britain, 1914–1918

Numbers of women working	In July 1914	In July 1918	In July 1918, over (+) or under (−) numbers in July 1914
On their own account or as employers	430,000	470,000	+40,000
In industry	2,178,600	2,970,000	+792,000
In domestic service	1,658,000	1,258,000	−400,000
In commerce, etc.	505,500	934,500	+429,000
In national and local government, including education	262,200	460,200	+198,000
In agriculture	190,000	228,000	+38,000
In employment of hotels, public houses, theatres, etc.	181,000	220,000	+39,000
In transport	18,200	117,200	+99,000
In other, including professional employment and as home workers	542,500	652,500	+110,000
Altogether in occupations	5,966,000	7,311,000	+1,345,000
Not in occupations but over 10	12,946,000	12,496,000	−450,000
Under 10	4,809,000	4,731,000	−78,000
Total females	23,721,000	24,538,000	+817,000

Chart 11-2   Women in Industry, Great Britain, 1914–1918

Trades	Estimated number of females employed in July 1914	Estimated number of females employed in July 1918	Difference between numbers of females employed in July 1914, and July 1918	Percentage of females to total number of workpeople employed		Estimated number of females directly replacing males in Jan. 1918
				July 1914	July 1918	
Metal	170,000	594,000	+ 424,000	9	25	195,000
Chemical	40,000	104,000	+ 64,000	20	39	35,000
Textile	863,000	827,000	− 36,000	58	67	64,000
Clothing	612,000	568,000	− 44,000	68	76	43,000
Food, drink, and tobacco	196,000	235,000	+ 39,000	35	49	60,000
Paper and printing	147,500	141,500	− 6,000	36	48	21,000
Wood	44,000	79,000	+ 35,000	15	32	23,000
China and earthenware	32,000					
Leather	23,100	197,100	+ 93,000	4	10	62,000
Other	49,000					
Government establishments	2,000	225,000	+ 223,000	3	47	197,000
Total	2,178,600	2,970,600	+ 792,000	26	37	704,000

SOURCE: *Women in Industry: Report of the War Cabinet Committee on Women in Industry.* London: His Majesty's Stationery Office, 1919.

Revolutionary Propaganda

The following Russian poster of 1919 illustrates some of the message and appeal of the Communists. It shows capitalist, Church, and monarch in league in a ruthlessly commanding position over exploited workers and peasants: Death trails in their wake.

Consider: *How this poster reflects the ideas contained in the documents by Lenin.*

Photo 11-3

SECONDARY SOURCES

The Origins of World War I: Militant Patriotism
Roland N. Stromberg

Almost before World War I was over, scholars were debating its causes. With the depth of emotional involvement characterizing this war, objective evaluation was difficult. Scholars often had difficulty distinguishing analysis of causes from placement of blame. In recent years many scholars have been struck by the almost universal enthusiasm with which people greeted the news that war had been declared in August 1914. This has led some scholars to reevaluate traditional interpretations of the causes for World War I and emphasize the underlying social forces that led people to welcome its outbreak. In the following selection Roland Stromberg, a historian of modern Europe at the University of Wisconsin, examines various attempts to explain the outbreak of war and suggests that the willingness of European peoples to go to war may have been more important than "the system of sovereign states" or any other cause for World War I.

> **Consider:** *The explanations that Stromberg rejects and why he rejects them; how militant patriotism played a role in the outbreak of the war.*

No wonder the sudden outbreak of a major international war at the beginning of August caught everyone by surprise. The sobering lesson was that war could happen without anybody seeming to want it or to will it. All kinds of myths grew up later, as bewildered people attempted to explain the outbreak of war. As usual, conspiracy theories flourished. In particular it was alleged that the Germans plotted war; Wilhelm II, the unhappy German monarch, was depicted in the Allied countries as a monster with tentacles reaching out to ensnare small countries. That "Prussian militarism" was the canker in the olive branch became an article of faith in France and England and later, after she had joined the war, in the United States. For their part, the Germans believed that jealous neighbors plotted to encircle and destroy a country whose only crime was her economic success.

Then, too, the theory arose that the capitalistic economic system, far from being a force for peace, had engineered the war because war was profitable or because there was competition for markets and raw materials. Although they may contain germs of truth, all such simple-minded "devil theories" must be dismissed as inadequate to the serious study of events, more interesting as folklore than as history.

Source: Roland N. Stromberg, *Europe in the Twentieth Century* (Englewood Cliffs, N.J.: Prentice-Hall, Inc., 1980), pp. 43–44, 74.

Though it is tempting to look for it, no single all-embracing cause can success-fully explain the war or any other major historical event. . . .

The states of Europe were like individuals living in a primeval state of nature marked by incessant strife between one and another. They acknowledged no higher authority that might have forced them to keep the peace. What was called "international law" was not in fact binding on them, being backed by no more than a moral or customary sanction. . . .

More and more people had acquired a larger stake in defending the state. This was the natural result of democratization and increase in wealth. However imper-fectly or inequitably these had come about, the large majority of citizens had some interest in defending the political community of which they were a part. All over Europe, 1914 was to prove that the masses as well as the classes were militantly patriotic when they thought their country was being attacked. . . .

Virtually no one had expected war; it came with dramatic suddenness. When it did come, . . . a sense of joy rather than of gloom prevailed. Huge cheering crowds surrounded the kaiser, stood outside Buckingham Palace, saluted departing French troops at the railroad stations, made love publicly in St. Petersburg. A Parisian observer on August 2 described a "human torrent, swelling at every corner" screaming, shouting, singing the "Marseillaise." In Berlin, crowds passed through the streets incessantly for two days singing "Deutschland über alles" and "Wacht am Rhein." A mob attacked the German embassy in St. Petersburg. An "indescribable crowd" blocked the streets around government offices in London a few minutes after midnight August 4–5, and continued to fill the streets for days. It was with exultation, not sorrow, that the peoples of Europe greeted the war, a fact that in the last analysis may go farther to explain its coming than all the details of diplomacy. . . .

Germany and the Coming of War
Hartmut Pogge von Strandmann

In an attempt to understand the origins of World War I and why it lasted so long, many scholars focus on the role of Germany, but differ greatly on what the underpinnings of German involvement were. In the following selection Hartmut Pogge von Strandmann analyzes what made war acceptable to the German population and what sustained the war efforts for four years.

> **Consider:** *Ways in which forces for war within Germany were part of European-wide developments; why, according to the author, there was support for the war*

SOURCE: From Hartmut Pogge von Strandmann, "Germany and the Coming of War," in *The Coming of the First World War*, p. 123, ed. R. J. W. Evans and Hartmut Pogge von Strandmann. © 1988 Oxford University Press. Reprinted by permission of Oxford University Press.

effort in Germany; how this analysis of Germany compares to Stromberg's analysis for the origins of the war.

However strongly the political and military leadership was influenced by the public and its political debates, the war was not started for domestic reasons nor to defend a social status quo. The concept of expansion based on a military victory found enough support to command a consensus among the military, political, and business leaders of Wilhelmine Germany. The drive to the east and to the west was underpinned by an imperialist culture which spread the virtues of Social Darwinism, the conquest of markets, the penetration of spheres of influence, competition between capitalist partners, the winning of living-space, and the rising power of the state. Buoyed up by an assumed military superiority, general economic strength and particular industrial vigour, widespread optimism and a mood of belligerence, the military and political leaders found, when they made the decision to push for war, that this was an acceptable option to many Germans, possibly even to the majority. The notion of 'cultural despair' is of limited value. There were no signs of panic and no indications that Wilhelmine Germany could not continue to muddle through politically for years to come. Confidence, determination, and the belief in victory were the ingredients of a willingness to fight an expansionist war, disguised as a defensive or preventive action, which was widely shared by political and military leaders, political groupings, as well as large sectors of the population. This consensus enabled Germany to sustain the war effort until the military defeats of August and September 1918.

The Revolution in War and Diplomacy
Gordon A. Craig

The technology and tactics used in World War I were strikingly different from those used in previous wars. This, combined with the war's length and the waning distinction between civilian and military targets, made it difficult for people to perceive the enemy in terms other than extreme hatred. This was reflected in the demands for retribution made both during and at the end of the war, inevitably affecting the peace settlements that followed. In the following selection Gordon Craig of Princeton and Stanford, a noted military and diplomatic historian who has done extensive work on German history, analyzes these attitudes and their causes while comparing World War I with previous wars.

Consider: *How the primary documents on the experience of World War I relate to this interpretation; why it was difficult for governments of belligerent nations to*

Source: Gordon A. Craig, "The Revolution in War and Diplomacy," Jack J. Roth, ed., *World War I: A Turning Point in Modern History*. Reprinted by permission of Alfred A. Knopf, Inc., pp. 12–14. Copyright © 1967 by Alfred A. Knopf, Inc.

compromise; whether this description of what happened in World War I is likely to be true for almost any extended twentieth-century war.

The war of 1914 was the first total war in history, in the sense that very few people living in the belligerent countries were permitted to remain unaffected by it during its course. This had not been true in the past. Even during the great wars against Napoleon many people could go on living as if the world were at peace. . . .

This kind of detachment, which was true also of the wars in Central Europe in the 1860s, was wholly impossible during World War I. This was, for one thing, the first war in which the distinction between soldier and civilian broke down, a development that was partly due to the expansion of warfare made possible by . . . technological innovations. . . . When dirigibles began to drop bombs over London and submarines began to sink merchant ships, war had invaded the civilian sphere and the battle line was everywhere. . . .

Moreover . . . precisely because war became so total and was so prolonged, it also became ideological, taking on a religious cast that had not characterized warfare in the West since the Thirty Years' War. . . .

The civilian . . . could not look the enemy in the face and recognize him as another man; he knew only that it was "the enemy," an impersonal, generalized concept, that was depriving him of the pleasures of peace. As his own discomfort grew, his irritation hardened into a hatred that was often encouraged by government propagandists who believed that this was the best way of maintaining civilian morale. Before long, therefore, the enemy was considered to be capable of any enormity and, since this was true, any idea of compromise with him became intolerable. The foe must be beaten to his knees, no matter what this might cost in effort and blood; he must be made to surrender unconditionally; he must be punished with peace terms that would keep him in permanent subjection.

The result of this was . . . that rational calculation of risk versus gain, of compromise through negotiation . . . became virtually impossible for the belligerent governments.

Women, Work, and World War I

Bonnie S. Anderson and Judith P. Zinsser

As men were drawn into the armed forces during World War I and there were new demands for arms and other goods to support the war effort, the demand for women workers grew. Women entered the work force in great numbers, often taking jobs previ-

---

SOURCE: Excerpts from *A History of Their Own*, vol. II, by Bonnie Anderson and Judith Zinsser. Copyright © 1988 by Harper & Row, Publishers, Inc., pp. 112–114. Reprinted by permission of Harper & Row, Publishers, Inc.

ously only offered to men. Historians have pointed to this as a crucial change for women, but recently other historians question how much women, in the long run, benefited from their experiences as workers during World War I. In the following excerpt from A History of Their Own, *Bonnie S. Anderson and Judith P. Zinsser argue that the changes for women were fewer and less long-lasting than generally assumed.*

> **Consider:** *Why, according to Anderson and Zinsser, changes for women were more apparent than real, more short-term than long-lasting; how employers, governments, and the mass media undermined changes for women; how this document relates to the visual sources on the home front and women.*

The improved standard of living, smaller family size, maternity benefits, protective legislation, unions, and new jobs comprised the most important changes in the lives of urban working-class women between the 1870s and the 1920s. Compared to these changes, the impact of World War I (1914–1918) on these women's lives was relatively minor. While middle- and upper-class women often reported that the war freed them from nineteenth-century attitudes limiting both work and personal life, working-class women's lives changed relatively little. Unlike more privileged women, working-class women were used to earning income outside the home, and their entry into war work was more likely to be exploitative than liberating. Unlike more privileged women, working-class women and girls had rarely been shielded by a "double standard" of sexual behavior for women and men; rather, working-class women made the maintenance of the double standard possible for men of property. For working-class women in the cities, the growth of the new white-collar job was the one new trend fostered by the war which was not reversed afterward. Otherwise, World War I brought only a temporary suspension of the normal conditions of work outside the home, and traditional patterns returned in the postwar era.

As soon as the war broke out, European governments moved to suspend protective legislation for women for the duration. Just as nations expected working-class men to serve in the military, so they exhorted working-class women to serve in the factories, taking the places of the men who had joined the armed forces. Drawn by high wages as well as patriotism, women thronged into these new, previously male jobs. . . .

Governments initially insisted that women receive equal pay for doing a job formerly done by a man, but this policy was largely ineffective: factories tended to divide up jobs into smaller operations and pay women at a lesser rate. Women's industrial wages rose during the war, both relative to men's and absolutely, but they still remained measurable as a percentage of male earnings. In Paris, women in metallurgy earned only 45 percent of what men earned before the war; by 1918, the women earned 84 percent of what men earned. In Germany, women's industrial earnings relative to men's rose by about 5 percent. Both women and men seemed to view the changes brought by the war as temporary. After the war, the men would return to their jobs, the women would leave men's work, and all would return to normal. . . .

As soon as the war was over, all belligerent governments acted quickly to remove women from "men's" jobs. In England, these women were made "redundant" and let go; in France, they were offered a bonus payment if they left factory work; and in Germany, the government issued regulations calling for women to be dismissed before men if necessary. These policies were effective: by 1921, fewer French and English women worked in industry than had before the war. Women's earnings decreased to return to lower percentages of men's, and the promise of "equal remunerations for work of equal value" made in the Versailles Treaty of 1919 remained a dead letter. Mass media concentrated on the relatively superficial changes in women's clothing, hair styles, and use of cosmetics and ignored the deeper continuities which structured most women's lives.

Peace and Diplomacy
Arthur Walworth

Historians have traditionally condemned the settlement of World War I worked out at Versailles. They usually argue that it compared poorly with the previous Vienna settlement ending the Napoleonic Wars. Yet some historians have challenged this view, arguing that the circumstances of peacemaking were extraordinarily difficult at the end of World War I. In the following selection Arthur Walworth analyzes the pressures and obstacles facing the peacemakers.

> **Consider:** *The choices and compromises the diplomats would have to make; in these circumstances, what the diplomats might have done; how Walworth's interpretation compares to that of Craig.*

A belligerent spirit of nationalism, fortified by the patriotic sacrifices that war had called forth, ran strong and limited the freedom of the peacemakers to pursue the distant goals of idealists. The prevailing hatred toward the defeated enemy made it difficult for diplomats to make a rational peace without being denounced as "pro-German." The wisest of the statesmen realized, after the cessation of the fighting, that unless they were able to reverse the baneful psychology of wartime quickly, no enduring peace could be signed, much less dictated.

Furthermore, the European democracies during the war had set up obstacles that would embarrass the diplomats in the making of peace. Under the necessity of survival the governments of the Allied powers had made secret commitments to the satisfaction of national aspirations. The 1915 Treaty of London, concluded in order to bring Italy into the conflict on the side of the Allies, had promised that nation a frontier that would place hundreds of thousands of Austrians and Slavs under Italian rule. To persuade the Japanese to step up their naval activity, Japan had been offered concessions in China and a share of Germany's islands in the Pacific. Although agreements to which Russia was a party became invalid when

SOURCE: From Arthur Walworth, *Wilson and His Peacemakers*, pp. xii–xiii. Copyright 1986 W. W. Norton. Reprinted by permission of W. W. Norton & Company, Inc.

the Soviet government made peace with Germany, nevertheless the interests of France, Great Britain, and Italy in the lands of the Ottoman Empire remained as they had been defined in understandings reached in 1916 and 1917. These secret understandings gained force from popular indignation against the violations of treaty obligations at the time of the outbreak of war in 1914.

The settlement at the war's end could not disregard the commitments and the national aspirations that existed in 1919 and that no one could expect to alter quickly. Compromises were inevitable. For one thing, there had to be an accommodation among various prescriptions for dealing with the German enemy. At the end of the war the European diplomats were of two minds about a policy to preserve the peace. One, the more appealing to the English-speaking authorities, would avoid peace terms that might incite violent reactions among the vanquished and also would provide for a continuing process of adjustment. The other, advocated by the French, would create alliances with a preponderance of military power that could put down any opposition. During the long war of attrition France's deficiency in manpower had worsened; it was clear that the French nation, fighting alone, could not hope to withstand another onset of German might.

The February Revolution in Russia
Michael T. Florinsky

Historians often respond to the challenge of explaining the occurrence of a major revolution by constructing a complex set or theory of causes. For Marxist historians, the February Revolution in Russia, which brought down the tsar in 1917, was of extraordinary importance. These historians and others point to long-term economic and social factors as crucial in causing this revolution. Many historians, however, argue that the causes were more immediate and less complex. Michael T. Florinsky, a highly respected author of several works on Russian history, represents the latter group of historians, focusing on World War I as the key cause for the revolution. In the following excerpt Florinsky refers to the Rasputin episode, in which the reactionary tsarina—who held considerable power—came under the influence of the corrupt mystic, Grigori Rasputin.

> **Consider:** *The explanations for the revolution that Florinsky rejects; Florinsky's explanation and whether he provides support for his explanation; how a Marxist historian might react to this explanation.*

The Reason Why. The Rasputin episode—for in the context of Russian history it was no more than an episode—did much harm to the prestige of the monarchy with the educated classes, as did the hostility of the government towards any manifestation of liberalism, however modest, including the program of the Pro-

SOURCE: Reprinted with the permission of Macmillan College Publishing Company from *Russia: A Short History* by Michael T. Florinsky. Copyright © 1969 by Macmillan College Publishing Company, Inc.

gressive Bloc. Nevertheless these developments cannot be regarded as the true or a major cause of the revolution. The empress was unpopular with the masses, not because of Rasputin or of her meddling in the affairs of state, but because she was of German birth (she was, indeed, frequently referred to as "the German") and was suspected of pro-German sympathies, which is contrary to all available evidence. Nor is it reasonable to ascribe the revolution to the skillful propaganda of subversive groups, to say nothing of a carefully-thought-out master plan devised by Lenin or someone else. During the war the organized revolutionary movement was at low ebb. The strikes of July 1914, staged on the occasion of the visit of the French president to St. Petersburg, were followed by massive police retaliation that all but wiped out the revolutionary organizations. Their leaders, who were soon to acquire world-wide fame, were scattered, and many of them behind bars. Lenin was in Switzerland, Trotsky in New York, Stalin in Siberia. The revolution took many of them by surprise. Revolutionary policies had numerous adherents in wartime organizations and in the armed forces, but if their preachments proved successful it was because they fell on fertile ground. The true and basic causes of the revolution were military defeats, staggering losses, demoralization of the army, plight of the refugees, economic hardships, lack of understanding of the objects of the war, and general longing for peace at any price.

An unsuccessful war is never popular, and the war of 1914–1917 on the Russian front was unsuccessful. Russian casualties were officially estimated at over 7 million, half of them missing and prisoners-of-war. According to confidential official reports, refusals to fight and mass surrender to the enemy began in 1914 and became widespread during the retreat in 1915. The Russian steamroller, in which the Western allies put their hope in the dark hours of the war, did not come up to expectation. Food shortages, the patent inability of the government to cope with mounting emergencies, frustration, and near chaos bred weariness, disaffection, and disillusionment. It is the sum total of these conditions that spelled the end of the monarchy and made the revolution inevitable.

Red October: The Bolshevik Revolution of 1917
Robert V. Daniels

How one interprets the Russian Revolution has much to do with how one views Marxism in general and the Russian application of Marxism during the twentieth century in particular. As with the French Revolution, a body of highly ideological historiography has grown up that is difficult to separate from the times in which it was written. In the following selection Robert Daniels, a professor of Russian history, describes different schools of interpretation and emphasizes the difficulty of the task facing the Bolsheviks.

SOURCE: Robert V. Daniels, *Red October: The Boshevik Revolution of 1917* (New York: Charles Scribner's Sons, 1967), p. 215.

Consider: *The relative strengths and weaknesses of both the official Communist and anti-Communist interpretations; how historians from each side might utilize the primary documents in this chapter to support their own views.*

The official Communist history of the revolution has held rigidly to an orthodox Marxist interpretation of the event: it was an uprising of thousands upon thousands of workers and peasants, the inevitable consequence of the international class struggle of proletariat against bourgeoisie, brought to a head first in Russia because it was "the weakest link in the chain of capitalism." At the same time it is asserted, though the contradiction is patent, that the revolution could not have succeeded without the ever-present genius leadership of Lenin. This attempt to have it both ways has been ingrained in Communist thinking ever since Lenin himself campaigned in the name of Marx for the "art of insurrection."

Anti-Communist interpretations, however they may deplore the October Revolution, are almost as heavily inclined to view it as the inescapable outcome of overwhelming circumstances or of long and diabolical planning. The impasse of the war was to blame, or Russia's inexperience in democracy, or the feverish laws of revolution. If not these factors, it was Lenin's genius and trickery in propaganda, or the party organization as his trusty and invincible instrument. Of course, all of these considerations played a part, but when they are weighed against the day by day record of the revolution, it is hard to argue that any combination of them made Bolshevik power inevitable or even likely.

The stark truth about the Bolshevik Revolution is that it succeeded against incredible odds in defiance of any rational calculation that could have been made in the fall of 1917. The shrewdest politicians of every political coloration knew that while the Bolsheviks were an undeniable force in Petrograd and Moscow, they had against them the overwhelming majority of the peasants, the army in the field, and the trained personnel without which no government could function. Everyone from the right-wing military to the Zinoviev-Kamenev Bolsheviks judged a military dictatorship to be the most likely alternative if peaceful evolution failed. They all thought—whether they hoped or feared—that a Bolshevik attempt to seize power would only hasten or assure the rightist alternative.

Chapter Questions

1. In what ways was World War I an outgrowth of the major trends of the late nineteenth century? Why is World War I nevertheless often considered a dividing line between the nineteenth and twentieth centuries?

2. What role did World War I play in explaining the Russian Revolution and the Bolsheviks' rise to power?

3. What was there about the causes and process of World War I that made the peace settlement at the end of the war so difficult?

CHAPTER TWELVE

Democracy, Depression, and Instability: The 1920s and 1930s

The two decades following World War I were marked by instability and uncertainty. Except in Russia, where the Bolsheviks had taken power, it appeared that liberal democracy had been established throughout Europe as a result of World War I. But soon a trend toward authoritarianism appeared, with many nations suffering from political fluctuations. The economic problems left from World War I and the immediate postwar period did not disappear despite a brief period of fragile prosperity in the mid-1920s. In 1929 the stock market crash in New York initiated the Great Depression in the United States, which quickly spread to Europe. Huge numbers of people suffered economically, and governments were pressured to effect radical solutions to the problems. Not surprisingly, there were great social strains through all of this. The difficulty of recovering from World War I was exacerbated by this political and economic instability. Swept by uncertainty about the present and the future, society seemed to polarize into opposing classes and around opposing ideologies.

A similar uncertainty characterized intellectual trends. The optimism and faith in rationality typical of the eighteenth and nineteenth centuries gave way

to movements such as relativism in the physical and social sciences, Freudianism in psychology, and seeming anarchy in the arts. The West was no
longer so confident, and events of the 1920s and 1930s added to that lack
of confidence.

The selections in this chapter exemplify these trends. Historians usually
focus on Germany during the 1920s in describing the general unrest and the
efforts made to respond to it. What was the nature of the political and economic disorder in Germany during the 1920s? In what ways was there a
sense that things were out of hand and that the population was composed of
many opposing factions? The Great Depression dealt the worst blow to the
industrial economy. How did the Depression make the future of capitalism
uncertain? What policies were pursued by governments to deal with the
Depression? How was the Depression related to political disorder during the
1930s? What was the long-term significance of the Depression? Finally, a
general sense of disillusionment and uncertainty characterized intellectual
life. In what ways was disillusionment particularly strong for the generation
that came of age in 1914? How did Freudian psychoanalysis reflect this? In
what ways was there a feeling that nineteenth-century ideals were gone and
that twentieth-century people might be worse off than their predecessors?

A gloomy picture of life during the 1920s and 1930s emerges from these
materials. The growth of totalitarianism during this period, to be examined in
the next chapter, will add to this negative image.

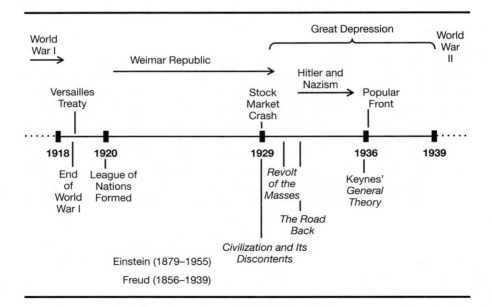

PRIMARY SOURCES

The Road Back
Erich Maria Remarque

and

Restless Days
Lilo Linke

With the establishment of the Weimar Republic at the end of World War I, Germany had a government system much like those of the other Western democracies. But the German government was burdened with tremendous economic problems, continued social turmoil, and inexperienced politicians laboring with the legacy of World War I. This society and its mood are particularly well reflected in the cultural productions of the period, for example, in the following selections from Erich Maria Remarque and Lilo Linke. Remarque, whose All Quiet on the Western Front *(1929) and* The Road Back *(1931) were two of the most popular books of the period, was a German soldier during World War I. The first selection is from* The Road Back, *which focuses on the life in Germany faced by the returning soldier. The second selection is from Linke's autobiography,* Restless Days.

> **Consider:** *Any connections between World War I and subsequent economic problems; the political problems facing the Weimar Republic; how such an environment might prove fertile for the rise of a political figure like Hitler.*

Demonstrations in the streets have been called for this afternoon. Prices have been soaring everywhere for months past, and the poverty is greater even than it was during the war. Wages are insufficient to buy the bare necessities of life, and even though one may have the money it is often impossible to buy anything with it. But ever more and more gin palaces and dance halls go up, and ever more and more blatant is the profiteering and swindling.

Scattered groups of workers on strike march through the streets. Now and again there is a disturbance. A rumour is going about that troops have been concentrated at the barracks. But there is no sign of it as yet.

Here and there one hears cries and counter-cries. Somebody is haranguing at a street corner. Then suddenly everywhere is silence.

A procession of men in the faded uniforms of the front-line trenches is moving slowly toward us.

It is formed up by sections, marching in fours. Big white placards are carried before: *Where is the Fatherland's gratitude?—The War Cripples are starving.*

The men with one arm are carrying the placards, and they look around continually to see if the procession is still coming along properly behind them, for they are the fastest.

These are followed by men with sheep dogs on short, leather leads. The animals have the red cross of the blind at their collars. . . .

Behind the blind come the men with one eye, the tattered faces of men with head wounds: wry, bulbous mouths, faces without noses and without lower jaws, entire faces one great red scar with a couple of holes where formerly were a mouth and a nose. But above this desolation, quiet, questioning, sad human eyes.

On these follow the long lines of men with legs amputated. Some already have artificial limbs that spring forward obliquely as they walk and strike clanking on the pavement, as if the whole man were artificial, made up of iron and hinges. Others have their trouser legs looped up and made fast with safety pins. These go on crutches or sticks with black rubber pads.

Then come the shakers, the shell-shocked. Their hands, their heads, their clothes, their bodies quake as though they still shudder with horror. They no longer have control of themselves; the will has been extinguished, the muscles and nerves have revolted against the brain, the eyes become void and impotent.

✦

It was no good to go on assuming that a common basis for all the different groups and classes in Germany could be found. The break between them became daily wider and more irreparable. The plebiscite of the Right "against the Young Plan and the war-guilt lie" proved just as unsuccessful as those arranged in former years by the Left, but the poison of the defamatory agitation remained in the body of the community, and we watched its effects with anxiety.

In my own family the political antagonism was growing past endurance. In October Fritz had finished his apprenticeship in an old-established export house, at the precise moment when the firm went bankrupt—a minor incident compared with such events as the breakdown of the Frankfurt General Insurance Company and the Civil Servants' Bank or the enforced reorganization and amalgamation of the Deutsche Bank and the Disconto-Gesellschaft, which all happened in the course of the year and dangerously damaged the whole economic life of Germany. Yet for my brother the bankruptcy of his firm overshadowed all other happenings, since it meant that he lost his job. His three years' training was in vain—there was not a single export firm which was not forced to dismiss as many of its employees as possible. . . .

"Yes, that's just it—millions! If it isn't my fault, whose fault is it? I tell you— your friends, the French, the English, the Americans, all those damnable nations who inflict on us one dishonorable penalty after the other—they are to blame for all this. Before the war the whole world bought German goods. My firm exported to Africa, to the German colonies. Hundreds of thousands we turned over every year. But they have robbed us of our colonies, of all our foreign markets. They have stolen the coal-mines in the Saar and in Upper Silesia, they squeeze millions of marks out of our bleeding country. We'll never rise again unless we free ourselves by another war."

"Don't be foolish, Fritz. Things are bad in the whole world."

"I don't care about the world, I care only about Germany, which you and your pacifists have delivered into the hands of our enemies. I despise you, you are not worthy to call yourself a German."

Program of the Popular Front— January 11, 1936

The Great Depression of the 1930s was a major blow to Western stability. In many areas it led to the fall of established governments and the rise of right-wing groups. In France in 1934, Socialists and Communists, in part fearing the rise of fascism, drew together into the Popular Front. In 1936, under the leadership of Léon Blum (1872–1950), the Popular Front came to power, but only for about two years. The following is an excerpt from the program of the Popular Front, January 11, 1936.

> **Consider:** *The ways in which this document reflects the turmoil of public life during the 1930s; how the Popular Front proposes to deal with the Depression; to what groups such a program would most appeal and why.*

I. *Defence of Freedom.*
   1. A general amnesty.
   2. Measures against the Fascist Leagues:
      (*a*) The effective disarmament and dissolution of all semi-military formations, in accordance with the law.
      (*b*) The enforcement of legal measures in cases of incitement to murder or any attempt against the safety of the State.
   4. The Press:
      (*a*) The repeal of the laws and decrees restricting freedom of opinion. . . .
         (iii) Measures ending the private monopoly of commercial advertising and the scandals of financial advertising, and preventing the formation of newspaper trusts.
      (*c*) Organization by the State of wireless broadcasts with a view to assuring the accuracy of wireless news and the equality of political and social organizations in relation to radio.

SOURCE: From David Thomson, *Democracy in France.* Reprinted by permission of Oxford University Press (Oxford, England, 5th ed., 1969), pp. 310–314.

    5. Trade Union Liberties:

       (a) Application and observance of trade union freedom for all.

       (b) Recognition of women's labour rights. . . .

II. *Defence of Peace.*

    1. Appeal to the people, and especially the working classes, for collaboration in the maintenance and organization of peace.

    2. International collaboration within the framework of the League of Nations for collective security, by defining the aggressor and by joint application of sanctions in cases of aggression.

    3. Ceaseless endeavour to pass from armed peace to disarmed peace, first by a convention of limitation, and then by the general, simultaneous and effectively controlled reduction of armaments.

    4. Nationalization of war industries and suppression of private trade in armaments.

    5. Repudiation of secret diplomacy; international action and public negotiation to bring back to Geneva the states which have left it, without weakening the essential principles of the League of Nations, which are the principles of collective security and indivisible peace. . . .

III. *Economic Demands.*

    1. Restoration of purchasing power destroyed or reduced by the crisis.

       (a) Against unemployment and the crisis in industry.

         (i) Establishment of a national unemployment fund.

         (ii) Reduction of the working week without reduction of the weekly wage.

         (iii) Bringing your workers into employment by establishing a system of adequate pensions for aged workers.

         (iv) Rapid execution of a public works programme, both urban and rural, linking local investments with schemes financed by the State and local authorities. . . .

    2. Against the robbery of investors and for the better organization of credit:

       (a) Regulation of banking business. . . .

       (c) In order to remove credit and investment from the control of the economic oligarchy, the Bank of France must cease to be a private concern, and 'The Bank of France' must become 'France's Bank.' . . .

IV. *Financial Purification.* . . .

    3. Democratic reform of the system of taxation so as to relax the fiscal burden blocking economic recovery, and raising revenue by measures against large fortunes. Rapid steepening of income tax on incomes above 75,000 francs a year; reorganization of death duties; special taxes on monopoly profits, but in such a way as to have no effects on retail prices. Measures against tax evasions, in connexion with transferable ('bearer') securities.

The Revolt of the Masses
José Ortega y Gasset

The disillusionment of the 1920s and 1930s, often associated with the effects of World War I, is reflected in many of the more profound attempts to understand Western civilization and the human condition. But this intellectual trend should not be seen only as a reaction to World War I. In The Revolt of the Masses *(1930), one of the most influential works of the period, José Ortega y Gasset (1883–1955) laments the population increase, the rise of the "masses," and the decline of the elite, cultured, liberal civilization of the nineteenth century. Ortega, a strong liberal and antimonarchist, became professor of metaphysics at the University of Madrid in 1910 and Spain's leading intellectual. Anticipating the defeat of the Republicans, he fled Spain in 1936. In the following excerpt from* The Revolt of the Masses, *he introduces the themes he will deal with in the rest of the book.*

> **Consider:** *Why the rise to power of the masses is so serious; how Ortega distinguishes the "masses" from the "qualified minorities"; whether he presents a valid criticism of modern democracy.*

There is one fact which, whether for good or ill, is of utmost importance in the public life of Europe at the present moment. This fact is the accession of the masses to complete social power. As the masses, by definition, neither should nor can direct their own personal existence, and still less rule society in general, this fact means that actually Europe is suffering from the greatest crisis that can afflict peoples, nations, and civilisation. Such a crisis has occurred more than once in history. Its characteristics and its consequences are well known. So also is its name. It is called the rebellion of the masses. . . .

There exist, then, in society, operations, activities, and functions of the most diverse order, which are of their very nature special, and which consequently cannot be properly carried out without special gifts. For example: certain pleasures of an artistic and refined character, or again the functions of government and of political judgment in public affairs. Previously these special activities were exercised by qualified minorities, or at least by those who claimed such qualification. The mass asserted no right to intervene in them; they realised that if they wished to intervene they would necessarily have to acquire those special qualities and cease being mere mass. They recognised their place in a healthy dynamic social system. . . .

The characteristic of the hour is that the commonplace mind, knowing itself to be commonplace, has the assurance to proclaim the rights of the commonplace and to impose them wherever it will. As they say in the United States: "to be different is to be indecent." The mass crushes beneath it everything that is different, everything that is excellent, individual, qualified and select. Anybody who is not like everybody, who does not think like everybody, runs the risk of being

---

SOURCE: José Ortega y Gasset, *The Revolt of the Masses*. Reprinted by permission of W. W. Norton & Co., Inc. (New York, 1932), pp. 11, 16, 18.

eliminated. And it is clear, of course, that this "everybody" is not "everybody." "Everybody" was normally the complex unity of the mass and the divergent, specialised minorities. Nowadays, "everybody" is the mass alone. Here we have the formidable fact of our times, described without any concealment of the brutality of its features.

Civilization and Its Discontents
Sigmund Freud

Psychoanalysis became one of the most powerful intellectual influences in the twentieth century. In part, it was based on the older eighteenth- and nineteenth-century optimism about the power of human rationality and scientific investigation: It assumed that human behavior could be even more deeply understood than before through scientific observation and that rational understanding could alleviate pain and problems. In other ways, however, it reflected the late-nineteenth- and early-twentieth-century attack on rationality: It argued that much of human behavior is irrational, unconscious, and instinctual. Finally, it echoed some of the pessimism fostered by the experience of World War I: Civilization was increasingly threatened by deep, antisocial drives such as for sex or aggression. Sigmund Freud (1856–1939), the person most responsible for developing psychoanalysis, was a Viennese neurologist who became increasingly interested in psychoanalysis as a theory of human behavior, as a method of investigation, and as a treatment for certain illnesses. The following is a selection from Civilization and Its Discontents *(1929), written in the aftermath of World War I and toward the end of Freud's life. In it Freud speaks of the fragility of civilization.*

> **Consider:** *How this selection reflects the experience of World War I; the ways in which this document reflects and contributes to the sense of uncertainty common in this period; similarities between Ortega and Freud.*

The element of truth behind all this, which people are so ready to disavow, is that men are not gentle creatures who want to be loved, and who at the most can defend themselves if they are attacked; they are, on the contrary, creatures among whose instinctual endowments is to be reckoned a powerful share of aggressiveness. As a result, their neighbour is for them not only a potential helper or sexual object, but also someone who tempts them to satisfy their aggressiveness on him, to exploit his capacity for work without compensation, to use him sexually without his consent, to seize his possessions, to humiliate him, to cause him pain, to torture and to kill him. *Homo homini lupus.*[1] Who, in the face of all his experience of life

---

SOURCE: Sigmund Freud, *Civilization and Its Discontents*, in *The Standard Edition of the Complete Psychological Works of Sigmund Freud,* James Strachey, trans. and ed. Reprinted by permission of W. W. Norton & Co., Inc. (New York, 1961), pp. 58–59, 92, The Hogarth Press, Ltd., Sigmund Freud Copyrights Ltd., and The Institute of Psycho-Analysis.

[1]['Man is a wolf to man'. Derived from Plautus, *Asinaria* II, iv, 88.]

and of history, will have the courage to dispute this assertion? As a rule this cruel aggressiveness waits for some provocation or puts itself at the service of some other purpose, whose goal might also have been reached by milder measures. In circumstances that are favourable to it, when the mental counter-forces which ordinarily inhibit it are out of action, it also manifests itself spontaneously and reveals man as a savage beast to whom consideration towards his own kind is something alien. Anyone who calls to mind the atrocities committed during racial migrations or the invasions of the Huns, or by the people known as Mongols under Jenghiz Khan and Tamerlane, or at the capture of Jerusalem by the pious Crusaders, or even, indeed, the horrors of the recent World War—anyone who calls these things to mind will have to bow humbly before the truth of this view.

The existence of this inclination to aggression, which we can detect in ourselves and justly assume to be present in others, is the factor which disturbs our relations with our neighbour and which forces civilization into such a high expenditure [of energy]. In consequence of this primary mutual hostility of human beings, civilized society is perpetually threatened with disintegration. The interest of work in common would not hold it together; instinctual passions are stronger than reasonable interests. Civilization has to use its utmost efforts in order to set limits to man's aggressive instincts and to hold the manifestations of them in check by psychical reaction-formations. Hence, therefore, the use of methods intended to incite people into identifications, and aim-inhibited relationships of love, hence the restriction upon sexual life, and hence too the ideal's commandment to love one's neighbour as oneself—a commandment which is really justified by the fact that nothing else runs so strongly counter to the original nature of man. In spite of every effort, these endeavours of civilization have not so far achieved very much. It hopes to prevent the crudest excesses of brutal violence by itself assuming the right to use violence against criminals, but the law is not able to lay hold of the more cautious and refined manifestations of human aggressiveness.

⁂

The fateful question for the human species seems to me to be whether and to what extent their cultural development will succeed in mastering the disturbance of their communal life by the human instinct of aggression and self-destruction. It may be that in this respect precisely the present time deserves a special interest. Men have gained control over the forces of nature to such an extent that with their help they would have no difficulty in exterminating one another to the last man. They know this, and hence comes a large part of their current unrest, their unhappiness and their mood of anxiety. And now it is to be expected that the other of the two 'Heavenly Powers,' eternal Eros, will make an effort to assert himself in the struggle with his equally immortal adversary. But who can foresee with what success and with what result?[2]

---

[2][The final sentence was added in 1931—when the menace of Hitler was already becoming apparent.]

VISUAL SOURCES

Decadence in the Weimar Republic
George Grosz

The following 1921 drawing by the German artist George Grosz shows some of the problems facing Western societies, particularly Germany, shortly after World War I. The wealthy few indulge in leisure activities while guards protect their factories. The rest of the people are crippled veterans, bankrupt businessmen, old women, young children, and the poor. They appear to feel isolated, distrustful, and out of place. The subject matter of this drawing is typical of art and literature that attacked capitalism and militarism between the wars.

   Consider: *How this drawing relates to the selection by Linke or the one by Remarque.*

Photo 12-1

The Granger Collection

Unemployment, Politics, and Women in the Weimar Republic

Economic and political developments often go hand in hand. Many historians argue that this was particularly the case in Germany during the 1920s and early 1930s. The following two charts deal with the Weimar Republic in Germany between 1924 and 1932. The first shows election results by political parties to the Reichstag; the second shows unemployment figures.

Chart 12-1   Elections to the German Reichstag, 1924–1932

	May 4, 1924	December 7, 1924	May 20, 1928	September 14, 1930	July 31, 1932	November 6, 1932
Number of Eligible Voters (in millions)	38.4	39.0	41.2	43.0	44.2	44.2
Votes Cast (in millions)	29.7	30.7	31.2	35.2	37.2	35.7
National Socialist German Workers Party	1,918,000 6.6%	908,000 3%	810,000 2.6%	6,407,000 18.3%	13,779,000 37.3%	11,737,000 33.1%
German Nationalist People's Party (Conservative)	5,696,000 19.5%	6,209,000 20.5%	4,382,000 14.2%	2,458,000 7%	2,187,000 5.9%	3,131,000 8.8%
Center Party (Catholic)	3,914,000 13.4%	4,121,000 13.6%	3,712,000 12.1%	4,127,000 11.8%	4,589,000 12.4%	4,230,000 11.9%
Democratic Party (The German State Party)	1,655,000 5.7%	1,921,000 6.3%	1,506,000 4.9%	1,322,000 3.8%	373,000 1%	339,000 1%
Social Democratic Party	6,009,000 20.5%	7,886,000 26%	9,153,000 29.8%	8,576,000 24.5%	7,960,000 21.6%	7,251,000 20.4%
Communist Party	3,693,000 12.6%	2,712,000 9%	3,265,000 10.6%	4,590,000 13.1%	5,370,000 14.3%	5,980,000 16.9%

Chart 12-2   Unemployment in Germany, 1924–1932

1924	1928	1930	July 31, 1932	October 31, 1932
978,000	1,368,000	3,076,000	5,392,000	5,109,000

SOURCE: Joachim Remak, ed., *The Nazi Years: A Documentary History* (Englewood Cliffs, N.J.: Simon & Schuster, Inc., 1969), p. 44.

The Nazi party used unemployment as part of its political appeal to women, as revealed in the following 1921 poster. It states: "Women! Millions of Men Are Without Work. Millions of Children Are Without a Future. Save the German Family! Vote for Adolf Hitler!"

Consider: *Why certain political parties gained and others lost as unemployment grew during the Depression years; how these charts relate to the drawing by Grosz, the selections by Linke and Remarque, and the Nazi poster; ways this poster was designed to appeal to particular to German women.*

Photo 12-2

Katherine Young, from Merry Wiesner, Julius Ruff, and William Wheeler, *Discovering the Western Past*, vol. II (Boston: Houghton Mifflin Co., 1989), p. 324.

SECONDARY SOURCES

The Generation of 1914: Disillusionment
Robert Wohl

The end of World War I raised hopes and expectations among large numbers of people. In a few years those hopes and expectations turned into disappointment and disillusionment, coloring the two decades between World Wars I and II. In the following selection Robert Wohl analyzes the origins and meaning of this disillusionment, focusing on the shared experiences of the generation of Europeans who were born during the 1890s and who had to shoulder much of the burden of the war.

> **Consider:** *Why the first few years of peace were so crucial for the creation of cynicism and disillusionment among survivors of the war; the forms disillusionment took; possible consequences of the developments of 1917–1920 according to Wohl.*

When we think of the army of returning veterans during the 1920s, we see them through the eyes of Remarque and Hemingway as a generation of men crippled, both physically and morally, by their service in the war. Many no doubt were. Yet it is a fact that the famed cynicism and disillusionment of the survivors were, to a great extent, a product of the first few years of peace. To understand this mood of disillusionment we must recall the attitudes and expectations that soldiers brought home with them, attitudes and expectations that were also widespread among the younger population as a whole.

Many soldiers had, like Omodeo, come to think that the war must have a secret meaning that only the future would reveal; they found it necessary to believe that their sacrifice and suffering would not be in vain; and they clung to the hope that the war would turn out to have been a rite of purification with positive results. Sensing this feeling and realizing its importance, political leaders in all countries encouraged the fighting and civilian sectors of the population to expect from peace not merely an end to bloodshed but a real alteration and improvement in the tenor and quality of life. It was said, and widely believed, that class barriers would fall; that selfishness would give way to cooperation; that harmony would reign; that conflict among nations would cease; and that everyone's sacrifice and suffering would somehow be compensated.

These expectations were often encapsulated in the word "revolution," but people of different social backgrounds assigned very different meanings to the term. Governments encouraged these hopes with their propaganda, and in 1918 Wilson came to incarnate the dream of renovation. The Wilsonian vision of a world safe for democracy merged with the equally vague idea of a revolution carried out by returning soldiers in the name of the values of manhood and self-sacrifice they had discovered on the battlefield. . . .

Disillusionment comes in many forms. The special form it took in Europe in the 1920s had to do with the development of the political situation and the frustration of apocalyptic hopes. Between 1917 and 1920 a revolutionary wave broke over every European country. Armies grew restive and mutinied; urban populations staged riots and insurrections over dwindling food supplies and rising prices; unions swelled in membership far beyond their prewar size; and workers began to challenge factory owners for the control of production. . . .

This disillusionment was felt by men and women of all age-groups in all parts of Europe; but the feeling of betrayal and defeat was especially strong among returning veterans born in the 1890s. They suffered from a tremendous sense of anticlimax, and the younger they were the more disoriented they felt. . . .

The developments of 1917–1920 engendered disappointment and frustration; they gave rise to bitterness and cynicism; but among young war veterans, the dream of cultural and political renewal did not die. Brought up in a crepuscular atmosphere of cultural crisis, subjected while still young to the ordeal of the war, witnesses during the immediate postwar years to a wave of revolution that swept away century-old empires and shook to its foundations every European institution, intellectuals born in the last two decades of the nineteenth century could not divest themselves of the feeling that the apocalypse had only been postponed and that any restoration of the postwar era would be temporary. The survival of the revolutionary regime in Russia, the creation of Communist parties throughout Europe, the victory of the Fascist movement in Italy, the collapse of parliamentary government in Spain, the difficulties that Great Britain and France experienced in regaining their prewar dynamism, and the onset of the worldwide economic crisis in 1929 confirmed these intellectuals in their belief that the world of their childhood was dead and that a new postwar world was being born.

Government and the Governed:
The Interwar Years
R. H. S. Crossman

Many scholars saw the 1920s as a period of failure and missed opportunities. This was particularly true of liberal or left-wing scholars from Western democracies, for they looked for the origins of the disastrous rise of dictatorships and the Great Depression in those years. The following selection by R. H. S. Crossman exemplifies this perspective. Educated at Oxford, Crossman became a leading figure in the Labour Party's left wing

SOURCE: R. H. S. Crossman, *Government and the Governed.* Reprinted by permission of G. P. Putnam's Sons (New York, 1940), pp. 255–257. Copyright © 1940 by G. P. Putnam's Sons.

and wrote numerous works on philosophy and politics. Here, in a work published in 1940, Crossman analyzes the period between 1918 and 1933.

> **Consider:** *Opportunities that were missed in 1918 and 1919; policies that the Western democracies might have initiated during this period that could have changed the course of events.*

Seen in retrospect, the period from 1918–1933 is marked by a growing lethargy in the victor nations. Neither at home nor abroad did democracy undertake a single great constructive enterprise. Victory seemed to have deprived France and Britain of their dynamic: their Conservatives ceased to be ardent imperialists, and their Socialists lost their revolutionary fervour. A spirit of collective pacifism possessed them, and made the people content with the lazy approval of high ideals, the verbal condemnation of injustice, chicanery and oppression. Holding all the power, the Western democracies disdained to use it, so long as the status quo was in any way tolerable. The attitude of America was not dissimilar, except that here the League idea was rejected and the Monroe doctrine was still regarded as America's contribution to world peace.

A myth is only justifiable if it stimulates to action. But "Collective Pacifism" was a sedative, not a stimulant. It intoxicated the democracies with a feeling of moral superiority and well-being, while it sapped their sense of responsibility. Gradually statesmen and peoples alike began to believe that the League of Nations was a force able to do the work which previously fell to the various nations. Instead of relying on themselves and on co-operation with their allies, they began to rely on the League to preserve peace. Since the League had no coercive power at its disposal, this trust was wholly unjustified.

No one Party or section of the population can be blamed for this collapse of democratic morale. The great opportunity had been missed in 1918–19: and it was difficult for the Western democracies to recover from that failure. They had encouraged nationalism as the basis of government; they had retained economic imperialism and permitted international finance to function independently of government policy. In brief, they had as far as possible returned to pre-war conditions. Having done so, they sought to humanize them. That they failed is an indication that good intentions and kindness, unbacked by resolution and knowledge, may disguise injustices but never eradicate them. Kindness and good-will no doubt console the patient suffering from cancer, but they will not cure the cancer; and the patient whose practitioner only displays these qualities, may, in his intolerable agonies, turn to a quack and curse the Christian humanity which his practitioner displays.

The Great Depression in Europe

James M. Laux

Most scholars agree that the Great Depression was very important, but they disagree over its precise significance. For Marxists, it was the greatest in a series of periodic economic crises inevitably flowing from the capitalist system and an indication that this system would soon collapse. For liberal economic historians, it was an indictment of conservative, nationalistic economic policies that would be forced to give way to modern Keynesian policies characterized by greater government activity and planning. For others, it was a crucial cause of the rise of Nazism and World War II itself. In the following selection James Laux analyzes the impact of the Great Depression, emphasizing various changes in attitude that stemmed from it.

> **Consider:** *Whether, as some scholars argue, the Great Depression forced governments to modify* laissez-faire *just enough to save capitalism as a whole; why economic planning appeared more attractive after the experience of the Depression.*

The Depression, perhaps, had the most serious impact in Europe on people's thinking about economic matters. Looking back on the experience, most Europeans agreed that the orthodoxy of laissez-faire no longer held. They would not again accept the view that a government must interfere as little as possible in the operation of the economic system. Governments must accept wider responsibilities than balancing their own budgets. The value of the currency in terms of gold must give way to economic expansion if the two appear to conflict. Laissez-faire already was wheezing and laboring in the 1920s; after the decade of the 1930s it was nearly prostrate. As so often happens, a philosophy came along to justify this changed attitude, a new approach to theoretical economics worked out by the Englishman John Maynard Keynes. The most influential economist of the twentieth century, Keynes published his classic work in 1936, *The General Theory of Employment, Interest and Money*. He argued that governments can and should manipulate capitalist economies, by running surpluses or deficits, by investing heavily in public works, by changing the size of the money and credit supply, and by altering rates of interest. In his analysis he emphasized the total economy, the relations among savings, investment, production, and consumption, what is called macroeconomics, rather than an investigation of a single firm or sector. A critic of socialism, Keynes scorned the significance of government ownership of production facilities, but promoted government intervention in an economy to make capitalism work better.

Bolstering this view were the remarkable production achievements of many

SOURCE: James M. Laux, from "The Great Depression in Europe" (*The Forum Series*). Reprinted by permission of Forum Press (St. Louis, Mo., 1974), pp. 13–14. Copyright © 1974 by Forum Press.

European industrial states during the two world wars. In these crises national economies expanded military production enormously under government direction. Many asked why such techniques could not be applied in peacetime also, but to make consumer products rather than tools of destruction.

The upshot was that by 1945 if not 1939 most Europeans abandoned the idea that they lived at the mercy of an impersonal economic system whose rules could not be changed and accepted the proposition that the economy could operate the way people wanted it to. From this it was a short step to the concept of planning the future development of the economy—both the whole and particular segments of it. Economic planning became an acceptable posture for capitalist societies and enjoyed a considerable reputation. Some of those who supported it perhaps underestimated the possible merits of free markets as guiding production decisions and did seem to assume that planners somehow possess more wisdom than ordinary human beings.

Economic nationalism was a more immediate result of the Depression—the policy that short-run national economic interests have highest priority and that international economic cooperation and trade must give way before narrowly conceived national interests. Economic nationalism showed its sharpest teeth in those European states where political nationalism reached a peak—Germany, Italy, and the Soviet Union. Its strength declined in western Europe after the Second World War as people saw once again that economic prosperity among one's neighbors could bring great benefits to oneself. In an expanding continental or world economy everyone can get richer. But one wonders if economic nationalism may not revive in western Europe, especially if it seems a popular policy in a crisis.

The Great Depression had important political repercussions too. In Germany, the Depression's tragic gloom made the dynamism of the Nazi movement seem more attractive. It is difficult to imagine the Nazis achieving power without the Depression and its pervasive unemployment in the background. In France, the Depression convinced many that the regime of the Third Republic had lost its élan and relevance to twentieth-century problems, but the lack of a widely popular alternative meant that the Republic could limp along until a disastrous military defeat brought it down. In Britain, the Depression was less serious and no fundamental challenge to the political regime developed. The Conservatives held power for most of the interwar period and their failure to work actively to absorb the large unemployment that continued there until late in the 1930s brought widespread rancor and bitterness against them. Doubts as to the Conservatives' ability to manage a peacetime economy led to the first majority Labour government in the 1945 election. More profoundly, the years of heavy unemployment bred a very strong anticapitalist sentiment in much of British labor, a sentiment that led them after the war to demand moves toward socialism, such as nationalization of major industries.

The Depression helped convince Europeans that their governments must try to manage their economies. Most agreed that full employment and expanding output should be the goals. They did not agree on the means to achieve these ends.

The Freudian Model of Human Nature

Erich Fromm

Sigmund Freud had many followers and many critics. The German psychoanalyst Erich Fromm (1900–1980) falls into both categories: He was a neo-Freudian who nevertheless differed with Freud on a number of important points. In the following selection from The Crisis of Psychoanalysis, *Fromm examines the social and historical bases of Freud's thoughts and presents a brief analysis of the Freudian model of human nature.*

> **Consider:** *The ways in which this interpretation is supported by the selections from Freud's* Civilization and Its Discontents; *how Freud's views reflect his times.*

To appreciate the social basis of Freud's views, it is useful to recognize from the outset that he was a liberal critic of bourgeois society, in the sense in which liberal reformers in general were critical. He saw that society imposes unnecessary hardships on man, which are conducive to worse results rather than the expected better ones. He saw that this unnecessary harshness, as it operated in the field of sexual morality, led to the formation of neuroses that, in many cases, could have been avoided by a more tolerant attitude. (Political and educational reform are parallel phenomena.) But Freud was never a radical critic of capitalistic society. He never questioned its socio-economic bases, nor did he criticize its ideologies—with the exception of those concerning sexuality.

As for his concept of man, it is important to point out first that Freud, rooted in the philosophy of humanism and enlightenment, starts out with the assumption of the existence of *man* as such—a universal man, not only man as he manifests himself in various cultures, but someone about whose structure generally valid and empirical statements can be made. Freud, like Spinoza before him, constructed a "model of human nature" on the basis of which not only neuroses, but all fundamental aspects, possibilities, and necessities of man, can be explained and understood.

What is this Freudian model?

Freud saw man as a closed system driven by two forces: the self-preservative and the sexual drives. The latter are rooted in chemophysiological processes moving in a phased pattern. The first phase increases tension and unpleasure; the second reduces the built-up tension and in so doing creates that which subjectively is felt as "pleasure." Man is primarily an isolated being, whose primary interest is the optimal satisfaction of both his ego and his libidinous interest. Freud's man is the physiologically driven and motivated *homme machine*. But, secondarily, man is also a social being, because he needs other people for the satisfaction of his

---

SOURCE: From *The Crisis of Psychoanalysis: Essays on Freud, Marx, and Social Psychology.* Copyright © 1970 by Erich Fromm. Reprinted by permission of Henry Holt and Company, Inc.

libidinous drives as well as those of self-preservation. The child is in need of mother (and here, according to Freud, libidinous desires follow the path of the physiological needs); the adult needs a sexual partner. Feelings like tenderness or love are looked upon as phenomena that accompany, and result from, libidinous interests. Individuals need each other as means for the satisfaction of their physiologically rooted drives. Man is primary unrelated to others, and is only secondarily forced—or seduced—into relationships with others.

Freud's *homo sexualis* is a variant of the classic *homo economicus*. It is the isolated, self-sufficient man who has to enter into relations with others in order that they may mutually fulfill their needs. *Homo economicus* has simple economic needs that find their mutual satisfaction in the exchange of goods on the commodity market. The needs of *homo sexualis* are physiological and libidinous, and normally are mutually satisfied by the relations between the sexes. In both variants the persons essentially remain strangers to each other, being related only by the common aim of drive satisfaction. This social determination of Freud's theory by the spirit of the market economy does not mean that the theory is wrong, except in its claim of describing the situation of *man as such;* as a description of interpersonal relations in bourgeois society, it is valid for the majority of people.

More important, however, is Freud's new appreciation of the role of human destructiveness. Not that he had omitted aggression in his first theoretical model. He had considered aggression to be an important factor, but it was subordinated to the libidinous drives and those for self-preservation. In the new theory destructiveness becomes the rival of, and eventually the victor over the libido and the ego drives. Man cannot help wanting to destroy, for the destructive tendency is rooted in his biological constitution. Although he can mitigate this tendency to a certain point, he can never deprive it of its strength. His alternatives are to direct his destructiveness either against himself or against the world outside, but he has no chance of liberating himself from this tragic dilemma.

There are good reasons for the hypothesis that Freud's new appreciation of destructiveness has its roots in the experience of the first World War. This war shook the foundations of the liberal optimism that had filled the first period of Freud's life. Until 1914 the members of the middle class had believed that the world was rapidly approaching a state of greater security, harmony and peace. The "darkness" of the middle ages seemed to lift from generation to generation; in a few more steps, so it seemed, the world—or at least Europe—would resemble the streets of a well-lighted, protected capital. In the bourgeois euphoria of the *belle époque* it was easily forgotten that this picture was not true for the majority of the workers and peasants of Europe, and even less so for the populations of Asia and Africa. The war of 1914 destroyed this illusion; not so much the beginning of the war, as its duration and the inhumanity of its practices. Freud, who during the war still believed in the justice and victory of the German cause, was hit at a deeper psychic level than the average, less sensitive person. He probably sensed that the optimistic hopes of enlightenment thought were illusions, and concluded that man, by nature, was destined to be destructive. Precisely because he was a reformer, the war must have hit him all the more forcefully. Since he was no radical critic of society and no revolutionary, it was impossible for him to hope for essential social changes, and he was forced to look for the causes of the tragedy in the nature of man.

Chapter Questions

1. Which developments focused on in this chapter are most closely related to the experience and results of World War I?
2. In what ways do the trends of the 1920s and 1930s support the argument that Western civilization reached its apogee between 1789 and 1914 and that starting with World War I it was clearly on the decline? What factors might be pointed out to mitigate or counter this interpretation?

CHAPTER THIRTEEN

Totalitarianism

The end of World War I and the arrangements made at the Paris Peace Conference in 1919 seemed to represent success for parliamentary democracy. But during the 1920s and 1930s, that success proved to be more apparent than real. The 1917 revolution had already brought a Communist regime to power in Russia. During the following two decades, Communist parties spread throughout Europe and were perceived as a great threat, but they did not come to power outside of the Soviet Union. Authoritarian movements of the right became the most immediate danger to parliamentary democracy. The first of these movements was Mussolini's fascism, which became dominant in Italy in 1922. By the end of the decade regimes in Eastern and Southern Europe were becoming more authoritarian. This trend became stronger during the Depression of the 1930s. There was a retreat toward nationalistic economic policies and greater central control by governments attempting to deal with the despair, destruction, and dislocation accompanying the Depression. In Central, Eastern, and Southern Europe, the Depression fueled already strong tendencies toward dictatorships and fascism. The most extreme of rightist ideology was Hitler's Nazism, which became

dominant in Germany in 1933. By the end of that decade, Europe was embroiled in a new World War even greater than World War I.

Historians and social scientists looking at this period often focus on the
rise of totalitarianism. This is a controversial term that is hard to evaluate
objectively. Generally, it refers to a form of government that shares certain
traits. It rejects individualism, a single party is in power, and the state controls
almost all aspects of life (economic activities, social organizations, cultural
institutions, the military, and politics). It has one official, revolutionary ideology, and terror, propaganda, and mass communications are used as tools of
power. Yet there have been important differences among totalitarian states.
Communism in Russia under Stalin and its professed opposite, Nazism in
Germany, sprang from different sources and ideologies. Even though
German Nazism and Italian fascism resembled each other, some scholars
question whether Italian fascism was thorough and effective enough to be
considered totalitarian. Other nationalistic authoritarian regimes of the right,
from Eastern Europe to Spain and Portugal, shared only certain elements of
totalitarian fascism. Nevertheless, the concept of totalitarianism does provide
us with a tool to use in interpreting important developments between the two
world wars.

This chapter addresses a number of broad questions. What were the main
features of the totalitarian regimes? How were they similar to and different
from one another? How can their appeal and the power they commanded
over people be explained? In what ways were they related to nineteenth- and
early-twentieth-century trends?

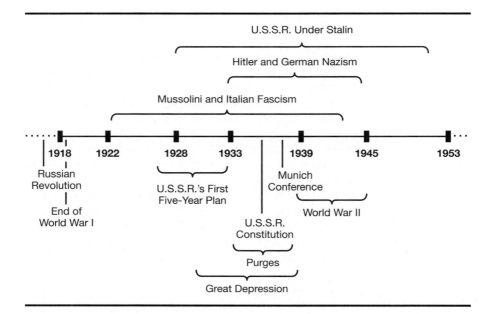

The selections in this chapter survey totalitarianism from a variety of perspectives. The concept itself is questioned. How useful is it? Is it historically bound to a few regimes of the 1920s, 1930s, and 1940s, or is it more broadly applicable? What characteristics do totalitarian regimes share and how do these regimes differ from nontotalitarian systems? The three regimes most commonly identified with totalitarianism—fascism, Nazism, and communism—are examined. The selections on Mussolini and Italian fascism focus on the ideology of fascism and its historical place. An effort is made to distinguish German Nazism from Italian fascism, to analyze Nazism's appeal, to understand the extremes possible under such a system, and to evaluate the role of Hitler in shaping Nazism. Three of the most controversial aspects of Stalin and Russian communism are examined: Stalin's justification for the policy against the *kulaks* in 1929, his analysis of democracy as part of his defense of the 1936 Soviet Constitution, and his massive purges of the 1930s.

In addition to offering broad insights into totalitarianism during the 1920s and 1930s, the selections in this chapter provide some of the background of World War II, which will be covered in the next chapter.

PRIMARY SOURCES

The Doctrine of Fascism
Benito Mussolini

Italy was the first European power to turn to fascism. She was one of the victors in World War I, but the war was costly and Italy did not gain much. After the war the country was marked by instability, weak governments, and an apparent threat from the left. Benito Mussolini (1883–1945), a former leader of the Socialist party and a veteran of the war, organized the Italian Fascist party in 1919. Strongly nationalistic, the party stood against the Versailles Treaty, left-wing radicalism, and the established government. After leading his Blackshirts in a march on Rome in 1922, Mussolini was invited by King Victor Emmanuel III to form a government. Over the next few years Mussolini effectively eliminated any opposition and installed his fascist state system, which would last some twenty years. The following document contains excerpts from "The Political and Social Doctrine of Fascism," an article signed by Mussolini and written with the philosopher Giovanni Gentile that originally appeared in the Enciclopedia Italiana *in 1932. It de-*

SOURCE: Benito Mussolini, "The Political and Social Doctrine of Fascism," *International Conciliation*, No. 306 (January 1935), pp. 7–17. Originally published by the Carnegie Endowment for International Peace, as part of the *International Conciliation Series*.

scribes the ideological foundations of Italian fascism. These excerpts emphasize the rejection of traditional democracy, liberalism, and socialism as well as faith in the authoritarian, fascist state.

> **Consider:** *The greatest sources of appeal in the doctrine according to Mussolini; the ways in which this doctrine can be considered a rejection of major historical trends that had been developing over the previous century; the government policies that would logically flow from such a doctrine.*

Fascism, the more it considers and observes the future and the development of humanity quite apart from political considerations of the moment, believes neither in the possibility nor the utility of perpetual peace. It thus repudiates the doctrine of Pacifism—born of a renunciation of the struggle and an act of cowardice in the face of sacrifice. War alone brings up to its highest tension all human energy and puts the stamp of nobility upon the peoples who have the courage to meet it. . . .

The Fascist accepts life and loves it, knowing nothing of and despising suicide; he rather conceives of life as duty and struggle and conquest, life which should be high and full, lived for oneself, but above all for others—those who are at hand and those who are far distant, contemporaries, and those who will come after. . . .

Such a conception of life makes Fascism the complete opposite of that doctrine, the base of so-called scientific and Marxian Socialism, the materialist conception of history. . . . Fascism, now and always, believes in holiness and in heroism; that is to say, in actions influenced by no economic motive, direct or indirect. . . .

Fascism repudiates the conception of "economic" happiness, to be realized by Socialism and, as it were, at a given moment in economic evolution to assure to everyone the maximum of well-being. Fascism denies the materialist conception of happiness as a possibility, and abandons it to its inventors, the economists of the first half of the nineteenth century. . . .

After Socialism, Fascism combats the whole complex system of democratic ideology, and repudiates it, whether in its theoretical premises or in its practical application. Fascism denies that the majority, by the simple fact that it is a majority, can direct human society; it denies that numbers alone can govern by means of a periodical consultation, and it affirms the immutable, beneficial, and fruitful inequality of mankind, which can never be permanently leveled through the mere operation of a mechanical process such as universal suffrage. . . .

Fascism denies, in democracy, the absurd conventional untruth of political equality dressed out in the garb of collective irresponsibility, and the myth of "happiness" and indefinite progress. But if democracy may be conceived in diverse forms—that is to say, taking democracy to mean a state of society in which the populace are not reduced to impotence in the State—Fascism may write itself down as "an organized, centralized, and authoritative democracy."

Fascism has taken up an attitude of complete opposition to the doctrines of Liberalism, both in the political field and the field of economics. . . . Fascism uses in its construction whatever elements in the Liberal, Social, or Democratic doctrines still have a living value; it maintains what may be called the certainties which we owe to history, but it rejects all the rest—that is to say, the conception that there can be any doctrine of unquestioned efficacy for all times and all peoples. Given that the nineteenth century was the century of Socialism, of Liberalism, and of Democracy, it does not necessarily follow that the twentieth century must also be a century of Socialism, Liberalism, and Democracy: political doctrines pass, but humanity remains; and it may rather be expected that this will be a century of authority, a century of the Left, a century of Fascism. For if the nineteenth century was a century of individualism (Liberalism always signifying individualism) it may be expected that this will be the century of collectivism, and hence the century of the State. It is a perfectly logical deduction that a new doctrine can utilize all the still vital elements of previous doctrines. . . .

The foundation of Fascism is the conception of the State, its character, its duty, and its aim. Fascism conceives of the State as an absolute, in comparison with which all individuals or groups are relative, only to be conceived of in their relation to the State. The conception of the Liberal State is not that of a directing force, guiding the play and development, both material and spiritual, of a collective body, but merely a force limited to the function of recording results: on the other hand, the Fascist State is itself conscious, and has itself a will and a personality—thus it may be called the "ethic" State. . . .

If every age has its own characteristic doctrine, there are a thousand signs which point to Fascism as the characteristic doctrine of our time. For if a doctrine must be a living thing, this is proved by the fact that Fascism has created a living faith; and that this faith is very powerful in the minds of men, is demonstrated by those who have suffered and died for it.

Fascism has henceforth in the world the universality of all those doctrines which, in realizing themselves, have represented a stage in the history of the human spirit.

Mein Kampf
Adolf Hitler

The most extreme and racist form of fascism arose in Germany under the Nazis, led by Adolf Hitler (1889–1945). After serving in World War I, Hitler joined and soon took control of the small National Socialist German Workers party. In the early 1930s, after years of relative obscurity, the Nazi party gained popularity with a nationalistic program attacking the Versailles Treaty, the Weimar Republic, the Communists, and above all the Jews. In 1933 Hitler was appointed chancellor and Germany was soon transformed into a Nazi state. Hitler's ideology, his mental processes, and some of the ideas behind Nazism

SOURCE: Adolf Hitler, *Mein Kampf*, R. Manheim, trans. Reprinted by permission of Houghton Mifflin Company (New York, 1943), pp. 290–296, 300–302, 305–308, 312–320, 323–327, 580–583, 649–655, and the Hutchinson Publishing Group Ltd. (London, 1943). Copyright © 1943 and © renewed 1971 by Houghton Mifflin Co. (U.S. Rights), and by the Hutchinson Publishing Group Ltd. (Canadian Rights).

are illustrated in his rather formless book Mein Kampf *("My Struggle"). It was written in 1924 while he was in jail for his efforts to overthrow the government of Bavaria in southern Germany. With the growing popularity of the Nazi party in the early 1930s, the book became a best-seller. In these selections from* Mein Kampf, *Hitler displays his anti-Semitism, argues that a racial analysis is central to an understanding of history, and indicates his vision of German expansion eastward at the expense of Russia.*

> **Consider:** *How Hitler connects the Jews, the Marxists, and German expansion eastward; on what points Mussolini might agree with Hitler here; the ways in which these ideas might be appealing, popular, or acceptable in the historical circumstances of Germany in the early 1930s.*

If we were to divide mankind into three groups, the founders of culture, the bearers of culture, the destroyers of culture, only the Aryan could be considered as the representative of the first group. From him originate the foundations and walls of all human creation, and only the outward form and color are determined by the changing traits of character of the various peoples. He provides the mightiest building stones and plans for all human progress and only the execution corresponds to the nature of the varying men and races. . . .

Blood mixture and the resultant drop in the racial level is the sole cause of the dying out of old cultures; for men do not perish as a result of lost wars, but by the loss of that force of resistance which is contained only in pure blood.

All who are not of good race in this world are chaff. . . .

With satanic joy in his face, the black-haired Jewish youth lurks in wait for the unsuspecting girl whom he defiles with his blood, thus stealing her from her people. With every means he tries to destroy the racial foundations of the people he has set out to subjugate. Just as he himself systematically ruins women and girls, he does not shrink back from pulling down the blood barriers for others, even on a large scale. It was and it is Jews who bring the Negroes into the Rhineland, always with the same secret thought and clear aim of ruining the hated white race by the necessarily resulting bastardization, throwing it down from its cultural and political height, and himself rising to be its master.

For a racially pure people which is conscious of its blood can never be enslaved by the Jew. In this world he will forever be master over bastards and bastards alone.

And so he tries systematically to lower the racial level by a continuous poisoning of individuals.

And in politics he begins to replace the idea of democracy by the dictatorship of the proletariat.

In the organized mass of Marxism he has found the weapon which lets him dispense with democracy and in its stead allows him to subjugate and govern the peoples with a dictatorial and brutal fist.

He works systematically for revolutionization in a twofold sense: economic and political.

Around peoples who offer too violent a resistance to attack from within he weaves a net of enemies, thanks to his international influence, incites them to war, and finally, if necessary, plants the flag of revolution on the very battlefields.

In economics he undermines the states until the social enterprises which have become unprofitable are taken from the state and subjected to his financial control.

In the political field he refuses the state the means for its self-preservation, destroys the foundations of all national self-maintenance and defense, destroys faith in the leadership, scoffs at its history and past, and drags everything that is truly great into the gutter.

Culturally he contaminates art, literature, the theater, makes a mockery of natural feeling, overthrows all concepts of beauty and sublimity, of the noble and the good, and instead drags men down into the sphere of his own base nature.

Religion is ridiculed, ethics and morality represented as outmoded, until the last props of a nation in its struggle for existence in this world have fallen.

Now begins the great last revolution. In gaining political power the Jew casts off the few cloaks that he still wears. The democratic people's Jew becomes the blood-Jew and tyrant over peoples. In a few years he tries to exterminate the national intelligentsia and by robbing the peoples of their natural intellectual leadership makes them ripe for the slave's lot of permanent subjugation.

The most frightful example of this kind is offered by Russia, where he killed or starved about thirty million people with positively fanatical savagery, in part amid inhuman tortures, in order to give a gang of Jewish journalists and stock exchange bandits domination over a great people.

The end is not only the end of the freedom of the peoples oppressed by the Jew, but also the end of this parasite upon the nations. After the death of his victim, the vampire sooner or later dies too. . . .

✧

And so we National Socialists consciously draw a line beneath the foreign policy tendency of our pre-War period. We take up where we broke off six hundred years ago. We stop the endless German movement to the south and west, and turn our gaze toward the land in the east. At long last we break off the colonial and commercial policy of the pre-War period and shift to the soil policy of the future.

If we speak of soil in Europe today, we can primarily have in mind only *Russia* and her vassal border states.

Here Fate itself seems desirous of giving us a sign. By handing Russia to Bolshevism, it robbed the Russian nation of that intelligentsia which previously brought about and guaranteed its existence as a state. For the organization of a Russian state formation was not the result of the political abilities of the Slavs in Russia, but only a wonderful example of the state-forming efficacity of the German element in an inferior race. Numerous mighty empires on earth have been created in this way. Lower nations led by Germanic organizers and overlords have more than once grown to be mighty state formations and have endured as long as the racial nucleus of the creative state race maintained itself. For centuries Russia drew nourishment from this Germanic nucleus of its upper leading strata. Today it can be regarded as almost totally exterminated and extinguished. It has been replaced by the Jew. Impossible as it is for the Russian by himself to shake off the yoke of the Jew by his own resources, it is equally impossible for the Jew to maintain the mighty empire forever. He himself is no element of organization, but a ferment of decomposition. The Persian empire in the east is ripe for collapse. And the end of Jewish rule in Russia will also be the end of Russia as a state. We have been chosen by Fate as witnesses of a catastrophe which will be the mightiest confirmation of the soundness of the folkish theory.

Nazi Propaganda Pamphlet
Joseph Goebbels

Propaganda was strongly emphasized by the Nazis as a method of acquiring and maintaining power. Joseph Goebbels (1897–1945), an early leader in the Nazi party, was made chief of propaganda in 1929, minister for propaganda and national enlightenment in 1933, and a member of Hitler's cabinet council in 1938. The following is an excerpt from a 1930 pamphlet, written by Goebbels, describing why the Nazis are nationalists, "socialists," and against Jews and Marxists.

> **Consider:** *How this document reflects the character of life in Germany during the 1920s; to whom this document was designed to appeal and in what ways it might be a convincing piece of propaganda; in tone, quality, and ideas, how this compares with Mussolini's "Doctrine of Fascism"; how Nazi "socialism" differs from more traditional or Marxist conceptions of socialism.*

WHY ARE WE NATIONALISTS?

We are NATIONALISTS because we see in the NATION the only possibility for the protection and the furtherance of our existence.

The NATION is the organic bond of a people for the protection and defense of their lives. He is nationally minded who understands this IN WORD AND IN DEED.

Today, in GERMANY, NATIONALISM has degenerated into BOURGEOIS PATRIOTISM, and its power exhausts itself in tilting at windmills. It says GERMANY and means MONARCHY. It proclaims FREEDOM and means BLACK-WHITE-RED.

WE ARE NATIONALISTS BECAUSE WE, AS GERMANS, LOVE GERMANY. And because we love Germany, we demand the protection of its national spirit and we battle against its destroyers.

WHY ARE WE SOCIALISTS?

We are SOCIALISTS because we see in SOCIALISM the only possibility for maintaining our racial existence and through it the reconquest of our political freedom and the rebirth of the German state. SOCIALISM has its peculiar form first of all through its comradeship in arms with the forward-driving energy of a newly awakened nationalism. Without nationalism it is nothing, a phantom, a

SOURCE: From Louis L. Snyder, *The Weimar Republic.* Reprinted by permission of D. Van Nostrand Co. (New York, 1966), pp. 201–203. Copyright © 1966 by Litton Educational Publishing, Inc.

theory, a vision of air, a book. With it, it is everything, THE FUTURE, FREE-DOM, FATHERLAND!

It was a sin of the liberal bourgeoisie to overlook THE STATE-BUILDING POWER OF SOCIALISM. It was the sin of MARXISM to degrade SOCIALISM to a system of MONEY AND STOMACH.

SOCIALISM IS POSSIBLE ONLY IN A STATE WHICH IS FREE INSIDE AND OUTSIDE.

DOWN WITH POLITICAL BOURGEOIS SENTIMENT: FOR REAL NATIONALISM!

DOWN WITH MARXISM: FOR TRUE SOCIALISM!

UP WITH THE STAMP OF THE FIRST GERMAN NATIONAL SOCIALIST STATE!

AT THE FRONT THE NATIONAL SOCIALIST GERMAN WORKERS PARTY!

WHY DO WE OPPOSE THE JEWS?

We are ENEMIES OF THE JEWS, because we are fighters for the freedom of the German people. THE JEW IS THE CAUSE AND THE BENEFICIARY OF OUR MISERY. He has used the social difficulties of the broad masses of our people to deepen the unholy split between Right and Left among our people. He has made two halves of Germany. He is the real cause for our loss of the Great War.

The Jew has no interest in the solution of Germany's fateful problems. He CANNOT have any. FOR HE LIVES ON THE FACT THAT THERE HAS BEEN NO SOLUTION. If we would make the German people a unified community and give them freedom before the world, then the Jew can have no place among us. He has the best trumps in his hands when a people lives in inner and outer slavery. THE JEW IS RESPONSIBLE FOR OUR MISERY AND HE LIVES ON IT.

That is the reason why we, AS NATIONALISTS and AS SOCIALISTS, oppose the Jew. HE HAS CORRUPTED OUR RACE, FOULED OUR MORALS, UNDERMINED OUR CUSTOMS, AND BROKEN OUR POWER.

THE JEW IS THE PLASTIC DEMON OF THE DECLINE OF MANKIND.

WE ARE ENEMIES OF THE JEWS BECAUSE WE BELONG TO THE GERMAN PEOPLE. THE JEW IS OUR GREATEST MISFORTUNE.

It is not true that we eat a Jew every morning at breakfast.

It is true, however, that he SLOWLY BUT SURELY ROBS US OF EVERYTHING WE OWN.

THAT WILL STOP, AS SURELY AS WE ARE GERMANS.

The German Woman and National Socialism [Nazism]

Guida Diehl

From the beginning, the Nazi party stood against any expansion of women's political or economic roles. Indeed, the Nazi policy was to keep women in their own separate sphere as mothers and wives and remove them from jobs and politics—the man's sphere. Nevertheless, many women supported the Nazi party and joined Nazi women's organizations. The following selection is from a book published in 1933 by Guida Diehl, a leader of pro-Nazi women's organizations.

Consider: *The ways this might appeal to German women; how this fits with other ideals of Nazism.*

This tumultuous age with all its difficulties and challenges must create a new type of woman capable of partaking in the achievements of the Third Reich and of fulfilling the womanly task that awaits her.

Let us not forget that this new woman holds her honor high above all else. A man's honor rests on fulfilling the tasks of public life entrusted to him. He safeguards his honor by doing his work honorably and with firmness of character and pride. A woman's honor rests on the province specifically entrusted to her, for which she is responsible, the province where new life is to grow: love, marriage, family, motherhood. A woman who does not accept this responsibility, who misuses this province for mere enjoyment, who will not let herself be proudly wooed before she surrenders—which is nature's way—who does not in marriage provide a new generation with the basis of a family—such a woman desecrates her honor. For we live in a time when womanly worth and dignity, womanly honor and pride, are of the utmost importance for the future of the nation, for the next generation. Therefore, the proud safeguarding of her honor must be an essential characteristic of this new type of woman. The German man wants to look up again to the German maid, the German woman. He wants to admire in her this dignity, this pride, this safeguarding of her honor and her heroic fighting spirit along with her native, cheerful simplicity. He wants to know again that German women and German fidelity go hand in hand, and that it is worthwhile to live and die for such German womanhood.

SOURCE: Guida Diehl, *The German Woman and National Socialism* (Eisenach, 1933), pp. 111–113, in Eleanor S. Riemer and John C. Fout, eds., *European Women: A Documentary History, 1789–1945* (New York: Schocken Books, 1980), pp. 108–109.

The Theory and Practice of Hell: The Nazi Elite

Eugene Kogon

The SS was Hitler's special corps, serving as his bodyguard and elite police force. Members of the SS usually became extremely dedicated to the ideas and practices of Nazism and carried out its precepts with extraordinary ruthlessness. The following is a statement from an SS officer recorded in a 1937 interview conducted by Eugene Kogon, less than one year before Kogon was arrested and taken to the concentration camp at Buchenwald. The officer was being trained as one of the elite of the Nazi state. Here he reveals his assumptions as a committed follower of Hitler and Nazism.

> **Consider:** *The role this officer assumes the SS will play in the Nazi state and the ways this role was particularly appropriate to a fascist system; how this document helps account for the appeal of the SS to those deciding to join it; how the ideas revealed here might serve as psychological justification for some of the atrocities committed by the SS.*

"What we trainers of the younger generation of Führers aspire to is a modern governmental structure on the model of the ancient Greek city states. It is to these aristocratically run democracies with their broad economic basis of serfdom that we owe the great cultural achievements of antiquity. From five to ten per cent of the people, their finest flower, shall rule; the rest must work and obey. In this way alone can we attain that peak performance we must demand of ourselves and of the German people.

"The new Führer class is selected by the SS—in a positive sense by means of the National Political Education Institutes (*Napola*) as a preparatory stage, of the *Ordensburgen* as the academies proper of the coming Nazi aristocracy, and of a subsequent active internship in public affairs; in a negative sense by the extermination of all racially and biologically inferior elements and by the radical removal of all incorrigible political opposition that refuses on principle to acknowledge the philosophical basis of the Nazi State and its essential institutions.

"Within ten years at the latest it will be possible for us in this way to dictate the law of Adolf Hitler to Europe, put a halt to the otherwise inevitable decay of the continent, and build up a true community of nations, with Germany as the leading power keeping order."

SOURCE: Excerpt from *The Theory and Practice of Hell* by Eugene Kogon. Copyright © 1950 by Farrar, Straus & Giroux, Inc. Reprinted by permission of Farrar, Straus & Giroux, Inc.

The Informed Heart: Nazi Concentration Camps

Bruno Bettelheim

Organized, official racial persecution, particularly of the Jews, was a direct consequence of Nazi theories, attitudes, and practices. During the 1920s and early 1930s, however, the extent of the persecution was unanticipated. The most extreme form of this occurred in the late 1930s, with the introduction of forced labor and concentration camps, later to be followed by camps in which a policy of literal extermination was pursued resulting in the killing of millions of Jews and others. In the following selection Bruno Bettelheim, a psychoanalyst in Austria at the time and later a leading psychoanalyst in the United States, describes his experiences in the concentration camps at Dachau and Buchenwald. He focuses on the dehumanizing processes involved and some of the ways prisoners adapted in an effort to survive.

> **Consider:** *The methods used to gain control over the prisoners; the psychological means developed by Bettelheim and other prisoners to cope with and survive this experience; how the existence, nature, and functioning of these camps reflect the theory and practice of Nazi totalitarianism.*

Usually the standard initiation of prisoners took place during transit from the local prison to the camp. If the distance was short, the transport was often slowed down to allow enough time to break the prisoners. During their initial transport to the camp, prisoners were exposed to nearly constant torture. The nature of the abuse depended on the fantasy of the particular SS man in charge of a group of prisoners. Still, they all had a definite pattern. Physical punishment consisted of whipping, frequent kicking (abdomen or groin), slaps in the face, shooting, or wounding with the bayonet. These alternated with attempts to produce extreme exhaustion. For instance, prisoners were forced to stare for hours into glaring lights, to kneel for hours, and so on.

From time to time a prisoner got killed, but no prisoner was allowed to care for his or another's wounds. The guards also forced prisoners to hit one another and to defile what the SS considered the prisoners' most cherished values. They were forced to curse their God, to accuse themselves and one another of vile actions, and their wives of adultery and prostitution. . . .

The purpose of this massive initial abuse was to traumatize the prisoners and break their resistance; to change at least their behavior if not yet their personalities. This could be seen from the fact that tortures became less and less violent to the degree that prisoners stopped resisting and complied immediately with any SS order, even the most outrageous. . . .

It is hard to say just how much the process of personality change was speeded up by what prisoners experienced during the initiation. Most of them were soon

---

totally exhausted; physically from abuse, loss of blood, thirst, etc.; psychologically from the need to control their anger and desperation before it could lead to a suicidal resistance. . . .

If I should try to sum up in one sentence what my main problem was during the whole time I spent in the camps, it would be: to protect my inner self in such a way that if, by any good fortune, I should regain liberty, I would be approximately the same person I was when deprived of liberty. So it seems that a split was soon forced upon me, the split between the inner self that might be able to retain its integrity, and the rest of the personality that would have to submit and adjust for survival. . . .

I have no doubt that I was able to endure the horrors of the transport and all that followed, because right from the beginning I became convinced that these dreadful and degrading experiences were somehow not happening to "me" as a subject, but only "me" as an object. . . .

All thoughts and feelings I had during the transport were extremely detached. It was as if I watched things happening in which I took part only vaguely. . . .

This was taught me by a German political prisoner, a communist worker who by then had been at Dachau for four years. I arrived there in a sorry condition because of experiences on the transport. I think that this man, by then an "old" prisoner, decided that, given my condition, the chances of my surviving without help were slim. So when he noticed that I could not swallow food because of physical pain and psychological revulsion, he spoke to me out of his rich experience: "Listen you, make up your mind: do you want to live or do you want to die? If you don't care, don't eat the stuff. But if you want to live, there's only one way: make up your mind to eat whenever and whatever you can, never mind how disgusting. Whenever you have a chance, defecate, so you'll be sure your body works. And whenever you have a minute, don't blabber, read by yourself, or flop down and sleep."

Problems of Agrarian Policy in the U.S.S.R.: Soviet Collectivization
Joseph Stalin

Joseph Stalin (1879–1953) rose from his working-class origins to become a leading member of the Bolsheviks before the 1917 revolution, the general secretary of the Russian Communist party in 1922, and the unchallenged dictator of the U.S.S.R. by 1929. In 1927 Stalin and the leadership of the Russian Communist party decided on a policy for the

---

SOURCE: J. V. Stalin, "Problems of Agrarian Policy in the U.S.S.R.," in *Problems of Leninism*, ed. J. V. Stalin (Moscow: Foreign Languages, 1940), pp. 303–305, 318–321. Reprinted by permission of the Copyright Agency of the U.S.S.R.

planned industrialization of the U.S.S.R.—the First Five-Year Plan. At the same time they decided on a policy favoring the collectivization of agriculture. By 1929 Stalin made that policy more drastic, using massive coercion against the kulaks *(relatively rich independent peasants). Kulaks resisted this enforced collectivization and widespread death and destruction resulted. Nevertheless, by 1932 much of Russian agriculture was collectivized. The following is an excerpt from a 1929 speech delivered by Stalin at the Conference of Marxist Students of the Agrarian Question. In it he explains and justifies the policy of collectivization and the need to eliminate the kulaks as a class.*

> **Consider:** *The relations of this policy toward the kulaks to the policy for the planned industrialization of the U.S.S.R.; how Stalin justifies this policy as "socialist" as opposed to "capitalist"; the differences between Stalin's attitudes and ideas toward the kulaks and Hitler's toward the Jews.*

Can we advance our socialized industry at an accelerated rate while having to rely on an agricultural base, such as is provided by small peasant farming, which is incapable of expanded reproduction, and which, in addition, is the predominant force in our national economy? No, we cannot. Can the Soviet government and the work of Socialist construction be, for any length of time, based on two *different* foundations; on the foundation of the most large-scale and concentrated Socialist industry and on the foundation of the most scattered and backward, small-commodity peasant farming? No, they cannot. Sooner or later this would be bound to end in the complete collapse of the whole national economy. What, then, is the solution? The solution lies in enlarging the agricultural units, in making agriculture capable of accumulation, of expanded reproduction, and in thus changing the agricultural base of our national economy. But how are the agricultural units to be enlarged? There are two ways of doing this. There is the *capitalist* way, which is to enlarge the agricultural units by introducing capitalism in agriculture—a way which leads to the impoverishment of the peasantry and to the development of capitalist enterprises in agriculture. We reject this way as incompatible with the Soviet economic system. There is a second way: the *Socialist* way, which is to set up collective farms and state farms, the way which leads to the amalgamation of the small peasant farms into large collective farms, technically and scientifically equipped, and to the squeezing out of the capitalist elements from agriculture. We are in favour of this second way.

And so, the question stands as follows: either one way or the other, either *back*—to capitalism or *forward*—to Socialism. There is no third way, nor can there be. The "equilibrium" theory makes an attempt to indicate a third way. And precisely because it is based on a third (non-existent) way, it is Utopian and anti-Marxian. . . .

Now, as you see, we have the material base which enables us to *substitute* for kulak output the output of the collective farms and state farms. That is why our offensive against the kulaks is now meeting with undeniable success. That is how the offensive against the kulaks must be carried on, if we mean a real offensive and not futile declamations against the kulaks.

That is why we have recently passed from the policy of *restricting* the exploiting proclivities of the kulaks to the policy of *eliminating the kulaks as a class.*

Well, what about the policy of expropriating the kulaks? Can we permit the expropriation of kulaks in the regions of solid collectivization? This question is asked in various quarters. A ridiculous question! We could not permit the expropriation of the kulaks as long as we were pursuing the policy of restricting the exploiting proclivities of the kulaks, as long as we were unable to launch a determined offensive against the kulaks, as long as we were unable to substitute for kulak output the output of the collective farms and state farms. At that time the policy of not permitting the expropriation of the kulaks was necessary and correct. But now? Now the situation is different. Now we are able to carry on a determined offensive against the kulaks, to break their resistance, to eliminate them as a class and substitute for their output the output of the collective farms and state farms. Now, the kulaks are being expropriated by the masses of poor and middle peasants themselves, by the masses who are putting solid collectivization into practice. Now, the expropriation of the kulaks in the regions of solid collectivization is no longer just an administrative measure. Now, the expropriation of the kulaks is an integral part of the formation and development of the collective farms. That is why it is ridiculous and fatuous to expatiate today on the expropriation of the kulaks. You do not lament the loss of the hair of one who has been beheaded.

There is another question which seems no less ridiculous: whether the kulak should be permitted to join the collective farms. Of course not, for he is a sworn enemy of the collective-farm movement. Clear, one would think.

Report to the Congress of Soviets, 1936: Soviet Democracy
Joseph Stalin

In 1936 a new constitution for the U.S.S.R. was established. Although in form it was democratic and apparently rather liberal, in fact it did nothing to challenge Stalin's power or the Communist party as the only legitimate political organization. Part of the problem has to do with differing conceptions of the word "democracy." In the following selection from his report to the Extraordinary Eighth Congress of Soviets of the U.S.S.R. in 1936, Stalin defends the constitution, comparing the meanings of "democracy" and "political freedom" in the U.S.S.R. with their significance in other societies.

Consider: *The concerns revealed by this document; why Stalin goes to such pains to justify the new constitution; the legitimacy of the distinction made between democracy in capitalist countries and democracy in the U.S.S.R.*

SOURCE: James H. Meisel and Edward S. Kozera, eds., *Materials for the Study of the Soviet System* (Ann Arbor, Mich.: The George Wahr Publishing Co., 1950), pp. 236–237. Reprinted by permission of the publisher.

I must admit that the draft of the new Constitution does preserve the regime of the dictatorship of the working class, just as it also preserves unchanged the present leading position of the Communist Party of the U.S.S.R. [Loud applause.] If the esteemed critics regard this as a flaw in the Draft Constitution, that is only to be regretted. We Bolsheviks regard it as a merit of the Draft Constitution. [Loud applause.]

As to freedom for various political parties, we adhere to somewhat different views. A party is a part of a class, its most advanced part. Several parties, and, consequently, freedom for parties, can exist only in a society in which there are antagonistic classes whose interests are mutually hostile and irreconcilable—in which there are, say, capitalists and workers, landlords and peasants, kulaks and poor peasants, etc. But in the U.S.S.R. there are no longer such classes as the capitalists, the landlords, the kulaks, etc. In the U.S.S.R. there are only two classes, workers and peasants, whose interests—far from being mutually hostile—are, on the contrary, friendly. Hence there is no ground in the U.S.S.R. for the existence of several parties, and, consequently, for freedom for these parties. In the U.S.S.R. there is ground only for one party, the Communist Party. In the U.S.S.R. only one party can exist, the Communist Party, which courageously defends the interests of the workers and peasants to the very end. . . .

They talk of democracy. But what is democracy? Democracy in capitalist countries, where there are antagonistic classes, is, in the last analysis, democracy for the strong, democracy for the propertied minority. In the U.S.S.R., on the contrary, democracy is democracy for the working people, i.e., democracy for all. But from this it follows that the principles of democratism are violated, not by the draft of the new Constitution of the U.S.S.R., but by the bourgeois constitutions. That is why I think that the Constitution of the U.S.S.R. is the only thoroughly democratic Constitution in the world.

VISUAL SOURCES

Nazi Mythology
Richard Spitz

The following is an example of Nazi propaganda art, with its characteristic blend of realistic style and romantic vision. It shows Nazi soldiers and civilian folk marching in brotherly comradeship toward Valhalla, the final resting place of Aryan heroes. Above them, Nazi flags and wounded soldiers are being lifted together toward the same heavens. Stereotypes, rather than distinct individuals, are shown: The soldiers all look almost the same, and on the right there are representatives of civilian youth, middle-aged and elderly people,

Photo 13-1

U.S. Army Photo by Garner

farmers, and workers. Those being glorified are all males and almost all soldiers. Viewers of this picture are supposed to feel proud, to feel that sacrifices for the state will be rewarded and that the greatest glory comes from military service. In subject and style, this picture represents a rejection of the major twentieth-century artistic trends.

Consider: *How this picture fits the image and ideals of Nazism as reflected in the documents by Hitler and Goebbels and the statements of the SS officer.*

Socialist Realism

K. I. Finogenov

The following example of socialist realism has great similarities to Nazi art: its realistic style, its romantic vision, its propagandistic purpose. In this case, however, the emphasis on economic themes is greater than that on military themes. Painted in 1935 by K. I. Finogenov, it shows Communist party and government leaders, led by Stalin, on a modern Soviet farm. On the right an expert checks the soil. In the background a new tractor is displayed. All the figures are relatively well dressed; no one looks like a peasant farmer.

Photo 13-2

Tass from Sovfoto

Consider: *How this picture relates to the role of the government in the Soviet Union and to Stalin's place in it; what insight into the agricultural policy during the 1930s the picture is supposed to convey; how the image presented here fits with Stalin's explanation of collectivization; how this picture compares with that of Joseph II in Chapter 4 (Photo 4-2).*

Authoritarianism and Totalitarianism, 1919–1937

The following map shows the spread of authoritarian and totalitarian governments in Europe between 1919 and 1937. Although no firm rules apply here, those countries retaining parliamentary democratic forms of government generally had a longer tradition of democratic institutions, were more satisfied winners in World War I, and were located in more advanced industrialized areas in northwestern Europe.

Consider: *Taking account of the relevant geography, historical background, and experience of World War I, the commonalities of two or more countries that became dictatorships or changed to right-wing authoritarian regimes.*

Map 13-1   The Spread of Authoritarian Governments

Parliamentary Democracies

Communist Governments, 1917

Parliamentary Governments that became, at least temporarily, totalitarian or right-wing authoritarian regimes (with dates of change).

0   100   200 Miles

0   200   400 Kilometers

SECONDARY SOURCES

Fascism in Western Europe
H. R. Kedward

Both fascism and communism, as they were practiced during the first half of the twenti-
eth century, are traditionally categorized as totalitarian systems. Yet fascism is typically
placed on the extreme right of the political spectrum, communism on the extreme left.
Indeed, the two usually consider each other archenemies. In the following selection H. R.
Kedward, a British historian at the University of Sussex, takes account of these facts in
developing and diagraming a working political definition of fascism.

> **Consider:** *Why the extreme left should be placed next to the extreme right on the*
> *political spectrum, even though they consider each other enemies; the historical*
> *developments that justify using the second diagram for the twentieth century and*
> *the first for the nineteenth century; the characteristics of fascism according to*
> *Kedward.*

It could be argued that the best way to define fascism is not in a positive but in a
negative way, by references to its opposites, but this too presents difficulties. At
one time its opposite was naturally assumed to be communism, since fascism was
said to be on the extreme Right of politics and communism on the extreme Left.
This appeared self-evident when the traditional semicircle of political parties was
drawn, i.e.:

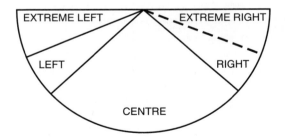

Such a diagram served the political scene of the 19th century when socialism
was on the extreme Left and autocratic conservatism on the extreme Right, but
in the 20th century a new diagram is needed in the form of a circle, i.e.:

SOURCE: H. R. Kedward, *Fascism in Western Europe: 1900–1945.* Reproduced by kind permission of Blackie and Son Ltd. (Bishopbriggs, Glasgow, 1971), pp. 240–241.

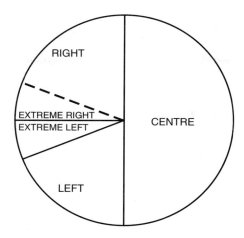

This circular image does greater justice to the realities of 20th-century politics by recognizing that extreme Left and extreme Right, communism and fascism, converge at many points and are in some cases indistinguishable. Doriot, for example, moved with ease from French communism to his Fascist P.P.F. without changing his attitudes or methods, and most of the conclusions on Nazi culture . . . could be applied to Stalinism. The circle, however, does not minimize the differences which kept the two systems apart. Travelling the longest route round the circle, it is a very long way indeed from extreme Left to extreme Right. Thus communism and fascism are as distinct in some respects as they are similar in others.

This was most clearly apparent in the Spanish Civil War. If one looked at methods, the Communists were as violent, as authoritarian and as tightly organized as the Fascists; they were both supported by dictators, Stalin on the one hand and Hitler and Mussolini on the other, and they were both as intolerant of any deviation from the party line. They were next to each other on the circle. But if one looked at this history and their ideology the two had little in common: the Communists stood in the Marxist tradition and aimed at proletarian revolution, while the Fascists had their national values and a vision of an organic society. They were quite distinct.

Fascism therefore will only be partly defined by its opposition to communism. It is perhaps more profitable to look for its political opposites across the circle in the centre, where one finds progressive conservatism, liberalism and radical individualism. It is at least historically true that in the countries where these political attitudes were most entrenched—Britain, France and Belgium—neither fascism nor communism came to power.

Retreat from Totalitarianism
Michael Curtis

*In recent years the traditional view of totalitarianism has been called into question. Crit-
ics argue that there are such important differences between fascism and communism and
between the ideals and policies of various fascist and Communist states that it is no longer
useful to group all under the single category of "totalitarian." Michael Curtis, a professor
of political science, exemplifies this critical approach, emphasizing that while the term
totalitarianism may have been useful for some purposes, it now creates more confusion
than clarity.*

> **Consider:** *How the primary sources support or undermine Curtis' argument; the
> main distinctions between fascism and communism and whether these distinctions
> go to the heart of the concept of totalitarianism, making that concept inapplicable
> to both; whether totalitarianism should be considered only a temporary European
> development of the 1920s, 1930s, and 1940s.*

Useful as the concept of totalitarianism has been as an explanatory tool for distinguishing political systems, reservations of two kinds are in order. The first is that
the concept is only partly applicable to the three countries—Germany, the Soviet
Union, and, especially, Italy—out of whose experience the theory was erected,
and this has great importance in properly evaluating these countries. The second
is that political behavior in the Soviet Union has changed sufficiently to render
the concept inadequate. Moreover, the polycentrism of the Communist countries
makes a monolithic explanation incorrect. . . .

The totalitarian concept does not sufficiently allow for the enormously different
purposes sought by the three ideologies or beliefs, for the different intellectual
levels of those beliefs, for the different styles of behavior and symbolic references
of the regimes, and for the different groups who supported and benefited by them.
Totalitarianism of the left, as Talmon has argued, begins with man, his rationality,
and salvation; totalitarianism of the right begins with the collective entity—the
state, the nation, or the race.

To offer brief lists of the major characteristics of the belief systems is to illustrate
their different purposes. Nazism was characterized by nationalism, racism, emphasis on the *Volk*, anti-Semitism, stress on violence and force, appeal to national
unity that would supersede the interests and differences of rank and class. With
its rejection of democracy, secularization, rationalism, and positivism, its belief in
domestic virtues, its vision of an attractive mythical past and rural harmony, its
distaste for industrial civilization and urbanism, nazism was the counterrevolution
in action and ultimately nihilistic in nature. The precapitalist, feudal aspects of

---

SOURCE: Michael Curtis, "Retreat from Totalitarianism," in Carl J. Friedrich, ed., *Totalitarianism
in Perspective*. Reprinted by permission of Holt, Rinehart and Winston (New York, 1969),
pp. 63, 109–111, 113. Copyright © 1969 by Holt, Rinehart and Winston.

nazism are illustrated by the Teutonic imagery, elitist decision-making through the Führer and the Gauleiter appointed by him, the oath of personal loyalty to Hitler, the stress on honor, blood, and soil, the end to the dependence of the German peasant on the market economy. Ernst Nolte has commented that, while Italian fascism recalled a remote but tangible historical era, the Nazis appealed to the prehistoric and the archaic.

The Nazis drew their main strength from the lower-middle class, marginal groups, military desperados, and those who had suffered by greater industrialization. But, uninterested in changing the nature of the social order, the Nazis were prepared to cooperate with those traditional groups such as the military and the bureaucracy that were not regarded as opponents. Though some 40 per cent of the full professors in economics and the social sciences vacated their chairs between 1932 and 1938, many academics, jurists, and even Nobel Prize winners capitulated before the regime. Hitler, in March, 1933, spoke of his regime as "the union between the symbols of the old greatness and the new strength." And the new strength was based on the manipulation of crowds, the display of strength through demonstrations, parades, and mass meetings, the welding of what Hitler, in *Mein Kampf,* called "the enormous human dragon" into a potent political force.

Contrasted with these characteristics are the ends of Marxism: that it seeks a society based on equality and humanitarianism, that it envisages the elimination of political coercion, that it seeks to build a rational social order, an industrialized economy, a higher form of democracy than that existing in the capitalist countries, and that it seeks to create a new type of civilization, internationalist rather than insular and parochial in nature. The traditional social and economic elite groups have no place in such a civilization or new type of society, and a wholly new political instrument is necessary. That the Communist regime distorted these high expectations and ended political liberty is not to deny the loftiness of the ideas.

The differentiation between a counterrevolutionary and a revolutionary purpose is crucial in the evaluation of the Nazi and Communist regimes. The objective of the first remains negative—the downfall of the existing regime—or nebulous, depending on the will of the dictator. The regime is essentially a destructive one in which positive achievement is gratuitous or related only to some destructive function. It is the product of a real dilemma of liberal democracy, a sort of suicidal reaction against a civilization that had failed to provide sufficient emotional satisfaction or material benefits for the mass of the people. In no real way can nazism or fascism be regarded as the continuation or inheritance of the French Revolution. The Nazi movement, as Rauschning wrote, had no fixed aims, either economic or political, either in domestic or foreign affairs. Its strength lay in incessant activity, its Valhalla the lust for power and the quest for adventure.

For Communist countries, the creation of an egalitarian and humane society, while not necessarily observed in practice, is its informing spirit, and action can be related to that fundamental objective. The Russian Revolution began, Deutscher noted, "with the dazzling blaze of a great vision." There is no inherent insistence on violence in the Communist, as in the Nazi or Fascist, system. In the post-Stalin Communist systems, violence is an incidental factor, a means by which to achieve a desired end. But violence was an intrinsic facet of Nazi or Fascist behavior, unrelated to rational purpose. In Italy, the aggressive defenders of "law and order in the streets" and the strikebreakers became the *squadrista*. For Hitler, "force was the first law" and war, the normal condition of mankind. The means as well as the ends of the regimes were different in theory. The Nazi and Fascist regimes saw themselves as perpetual dictatorships from the beginning. The Bolsheviks took power on behalf of the Soviet of Workers' and Soldiers' Deputies, and the dictatorship of the proletariat has always been regarded as a transitional stage toward a free society. . . .

The Rise of Fascism
F. L. Carsten

Historians have employed a variety of perspectives in an effort to understand the rise of fascism during the two decades following World War I. Focusing on the appeal of fascism, several historians have analyzed what social classes and groups of people supported fascist movements. In the following selection F. L. Carsten argues that while fascism appealed to all social groups, certain groups responded more strongly to it than others.

> **Consider:** *Why fascism might have been particularly appealing to the lower middle classes; what other groups it appealed to and why.*

Unlike many middle-class or working-class parties, the Fascists appealed to all social groups, from the top to the bottom of the social scale. Excluded were only those who were their favourite objects of attack: the profiteers, the parasites, the financial gangsters, the ruling cliques, the rapacious capitalists, the reactionary landowners. But even there exceptions were made if it suited the Leader's book. There is no doubt, however, that certain social groups responded much more strongly to the Fascist appeal than others. This is particularly true of those who were uprooted and threatened by social and economic change, whose position in society was being undermined, who had lost their traditional place, and were frightened of the future. These were, above all, the lower middle classes—or rather certain groups within them: the artisans and independent tradesmen, the small farmers, the lower grade government employees and white-collar workers. Perhaps even more important in the early stages were the former officers and non-commissioned officers of the first world war for whom no jobs were waiting, who had got accustomed to the use of violence, and felt themselves deprived of their 'legitimate' rewards. In Italy, in Germany, and elsewhere the 'front' gener-

Source: From F. L. Carsten, *The Rise of Fascism*, pp. 232–234. Copyright 1980. Reprinted by permission of the Regents of the University of California Press and the University of California.

ation played a leading part in the rise of Fascism. For its members fighting was a way of life which they transferred to the domestic scene. They loved battles for their own sake. It is no accident that the most important Fascist movements had their origin in the year 1919, the year of the Hungarian and Munich Soviet republics, of civil war which aroused fear and hatred in many hearts. Those who had been badly frightened did not easily forget. The occupation of the factories in northern Italy in the following year had the same effect. . . .

Apart from the groups already mentioned, there were the youngsters at school and university who became ardent believers in Fascism at an early stage. They were fed up with the existing society, bored with their daily duties, and strongly attracted by a movement which promised a radical change, which they could invest with a romantic halo. These youths came from middle-class or lower middle-class families. They could not easily find the way into the Communist camp. But they found the weak and changing governments of the post-war period utterly unattractive. In the Weimar Republic, in the post-war Italian kingdom, in the corrupt governments of Rumania, in the powerless governments of Spain, there was nothing to fire the enthusiasm of youth: they were dreary and pedestrian, the offices filled with mediocrities and time-servers. It was this, rather than any economic threat, that led so many idealist students into the Fascist camp. Similarly, many young officers and soldiers of the post-war generation were attracted by visions of national greatness and the promise of a revision of the peace treaties. A perusal of the autobiographical notes compiled by men who joined the National Socialist Party in its early years shows that pride of place belongs to a strong nationalism, the desire to see Germany strong and united again, freed from the 'chains of Versailles', and also from the faction fights and the 'horse-trading' of the political parties. This often went together with hatred of the Communists and Socialists, and with anti-Semitism. Those who joined the Party were usually very young; they loved the frequent fights and battles in which they got involved together with their comrades, as well as the uniforms and the propaganda marches.

Hitler: A Study in Tyranny
Alan Bullock

It is difficult to analyze Nazism without focusing on its leader, Adolf Hitler. The close connection between Nazism and Hitler raises two questions of particular importance for historians. First, what was the role of the individual in shaping history, here of Hitler in shaping German Nazism? Second, to what extent were Hitler and Nazism uniquely German developments related to particular characteristics of Germany's past? Alan Bullock, a British historian and author of what has long been considered the most authoritative biography of Hitler, addresses these issues in the following selection from his Hitler: A Study in Tyranny.

SOURCE: Excerpt from *Hitler: A Study in Tyranny* by Alan Bullock. Copyright © 1962 by Alan Bullock. Reprinted by permission of HarperCollins Publishers, Inc.

Consider: *Whether Hitler should be viewed as an extreme of a broader historical trend affecting not only Germany but Europe as a whole during the 1920s and 1930s; how someone taking a more psychological approach might argue with Bullock's interpretation of Hitler and Nazism; how this approach fits with that of Kedward.*

Many attempts have been made to explain away the importance of Hitler, from Chaplin's brilliant caricature in *The Great Dictator* to the much less convincing picture of Hitler the pawn, a front man for German capitalism. Others have argued that Hitler was nothing in himself, only a symbol of the restless ambition of the German nation to dominate Europe; a creature flung to the top by the tides of revolutionary change, or the embodiment of the collective unconscious of a people obsessed with violence and death.

These arguments seem to me to be based upon a confusion of two different questions. Obviously, Nazism was a complex phenomenon to which many factors—social, economic, historical, psychological—contributed. But whatever the explanation of this episode in European history—and it can be no simple one—that does not answer the question with which this book has been concerned, what was the part played by Hitler. It may be true that a mass movement, strongly nationalist, anti-Semitic, and radical, would have sprung up in Germany without Hitler. But so far as what actually happened is concerned—not what might have happened—the evidence seems to me to leave no doubt that no other man played a role in the Nazi revolution or in the history of the Third Reich remotely comparable with that of Adolf Hitler.

The conception of the Nazi Party, the propaganda with which it must appeal to the German people, and the tactics by which it would come to power—these were unquestionably Hitler's. After 1934 there were no rivals left and by 1938 he had removed the last checks on his freedom of action. Thereafter, he exercised an arbitrary rule in Germany to a degree rarely, if ever, equalled in a modern industrialized state.

At the same time, from the re-militarization of the Rhineland to the invasion of Russia, he won a series of successes in diplomacy and war which established an hegemony over the continent of Europe comparable with that of Napoleon at the height of his fame. While these could not have been won without a people and an Army willing to serve him, it was Hitler who provided the indispensable leadership, the flair for grasping opportunities, the boldness in using them. . . .

The view has often been expressed that Hitler could only have come to power in Germany, and it is true—without falling into the same error of racialism as the Nazi—that there were certain features of German historical development, quite apart from the effects of the Defeat and the Depression, which favoured the rise of such a movement.

This is not to accuse the Germans of Original Sin, or to ignore the other sides of German life which were only grossly caricatured by the Nazis. But Nazism was not some terrible accident which fell upon the German people out of a blue sky.

It was rooted in their history, and while it is true that a majority of the German people never voted for Hitler, it is also true that thirteen million did. Both facts need to be remembered.

From this point of view Hitler's career may be described as a *reductio ad absurdum* of the most powerful political tradition in Germany since the Unification. This is what nationalism, militarism, authoritarianism, the worship of success and force, the exaltation of the State, and *Realpolitik* lead to, if they are projected to their logical conclusion. . . .

Hitler, indeed, was a European, no less than a German phenomenon. The conditions and the state of mind which he exploited, the *malaise* of which he was the symptom, were not confined to one country, although they were more strongly marked in Germany than anywhere else. Hitler's idiom was German, but the thoughts and emotions to which he gave expression have a more universal currency.

Hitler recognized this relationship with Europe perfectly clearly. He was in revolt against 'the System' not just in Germany but in Europe, against the liberal bourgeois order, symbolized for him in the Vienna which had once rejected him. To destroy this was his mission, the mission in which he never ceased to believe; and in this, the most deeply felt of purposes, he did not fail.

Dictatorship in Russia: Stalin's Purges
Stephen J. Lee

In 1934 a colleague of Stalin was assassinated by a member of the Communist party. Shortly afterward, Stalin initiated mass purges of the Communist party. By 1939, when the purges had ended, vast numbers of people had been executed or imprisoned. Analysts have tried to explain these purges in a variety of ways. In the following selection Stephen Lee describes this historical controversy.

> **Consider:** *How the interpretations differ; which interpretation makes the most sense to you; whether purges, or their like, are an inherent or predictable characteristic of any totalitarian regime.*

The most spectacular and notorious of all Stalin's policies was his deliberate creation of a state of total terror. His direct responsibility for this has never been questioned and plenty of evidence was provided by Khrushchev in 1956. . . .

Although the enormity of Stalin's purges defy a completely logical explanation, a number of motives have been suggested. One is that Stalin had a disastrously

SOURCE: From Stephen J. Lee, *The European Dictatorships, 1918–1945*, pp. 53–55. Copyright 1987. Reprinted by permission of the authors and Methuen & Co. as publishers.

flawed personality. Khrushchev, for example, later emphasized his brutality, vindictiveness, pathological distrust and 'sickly' suspicion. More recently, Tucker has maintained that, in addition to serving a political function, the trials also rationalized 'Stalin's own paranoid tendency'. A second reason for the purges is that Stalin was never one to resort to half measures. He aimed to wipe out the entire generation of Bolsheviks who had assisted Lenin between 1917 and 1924. This alone would guarantee Stalin as the sole heir to Lenin and would secure his position for a lifetime. Most of the threats to his power were latent and would possibly not reveal themselves for several years. They should, nevertheless, be dealt with as soon as possible. Since these latent threats were impossible to identify, a large number of people who would ultimately prove innocent of any form of opposition to Stalin, would also have to go. It was only by having such a clean sweep that Stalin could make sure of eradicating those who would be a threat. . . .

A third explanation of the purges is that they were ideologically necessary. Stalin argued that he was merely continuing the tactics of Lenin in 1918 and that he was accelerating the move towards a 'classless society'. If this desirable aim of Communism were to be achieved, class conflict would have to be intensified so that it could be ended the more quickly. The state would achieve its objectives 'not through the weakening of its power but through it becoming as strong as possible so as to defeat the remnants of the dying classes and to defend itself against capitalist encirclement'.

This brings us to the most frequently discussed aspect of Stalin's purges: how were they affected by the external situation? Two very different answers have been provided.

The first is that Stalin was obsessed with the fear that the west would smash the Soviet regime before his industrialization programme was complete. It therefore made sense to adopt a pragmatic approach to foreign policy; Germany, the main threat, could be won over by a temporary policy of cooperation. Stalin found it no more difficult to collaborate with Fascism than with any other European system, for he regarded it merely as a variant of western capitalism. The old-style Bolsheviks, by contrast, were profoundly anti-Fascist and saw Hitler as a far more deadly enemy than either France or Britain. According to R. Tucker and R. Conquest, Stalin therefore considered it essential to remove the anti-Hitler element to make possible the accommodation with Germany which eventually materialized in August 1939, in the Nazi-Soviet Non-Aggression Pact.

I. Deutscher puts a different cast. Stalin's main worry was that his regime would be destroyed from *within*—by internal revolt. There seemed little chance of this happening in 1936. Unless, of course, some major external catastrophe occurred, which could lead to a revival of the scenario of the First World War; military crisis could well bring about a revolution. Stalin's solution was therefore to destroy any elements within Russia which could possibly take advantage of such a situation. The show trials dealt with these potential threats by magnifying the charge against them.

Chapter Questions

1. In light of the evidence and interpretations presented in this chapter about the nature of totalitarianism, how would you explain its appeal or relative success in the twentieth century? In what ways should Italian fascism, German Nazism, and Russian communism be distinguished here?

2. Considering some of the theories and practices of totalitarian governments during the 1920s, 1930s, and 1940s, would you conclude that totalitarianism almost inevitably leads to violence and war, or rather that it happens to involve violence and war because of particular historical circumstances of the times? In this respect, should fascism be distinguished from communism? Why or why not?

3. In what ways do Italian fascism and German Nazism differ in theory and practice from liberal democracy? In what ways does Russian communism differ from both?

CHAPTER FOURTEEN

World War II and the Postwar World

World War II broke out in 1939 and was even more destructive than World War I. In 1945 Europe emerged from the war facing an overwhelming task of recovery. She had lost her position of dominance in the world, reflected in the successful independence movement among her colonies and the rise of the two new superpowers: the United States and the Soviet Union. Nevertheless, by the early 1960s, Europe had greatly recovered from the war and was enjoying considerable prosperity.

This chapter deals with five developments between 1939 and the early 1960s. First, almost all of Western civilization became embroiled in the war that broke out in 1939 and that did not end until two atomic bombs were dropped on Japan in 1945. What were the origins of World War II? What connections between Hitler, Nazism, and appeasement might have led to the outbreak of the war in 1939? How can some of the destruction of the war be explained?

Second, by 1947 the growing hostility between the United States and the Soviet Union became formalized in speeches, policies, and alliances, resulting in a division between Eastern and Western Europe and more broadly between Communist and non-Communist countries throughout the world: The Cold War had broken out. The Cold War remains a controversial issue among American historians as well as between Western and Soviet scholars. Why did it occur? What policies characterized the Cold War?

Third, Europe recovered from World War II more rapidly than expected. By the 1950s most countries were back on their feet, thanks in part to aid from the superpowers. By the early 1960s Western Europe was enjoying unprecedented prosperity and relative political and social stability. What were some of the political and social changes that occurred in this process of recovery? How are they exemplified by the establishment of a Labour government in Britain in 1945?

Fourth, nuclear weapons spread with unexpected rapidity. The potential of nuclear weapons was demonstrated in the final days of the war with Japan. The proliferation of nuclear arms in the 1950s and 1960s seemed to threaten civilization. How have nuclear weapons affected people? What has the nature of the debate over nuclear weapons been? What role could the United Nations play in international disputes that might lead to nuclear war?

Fifth, European powers were unable to hold on to all their colonies in the

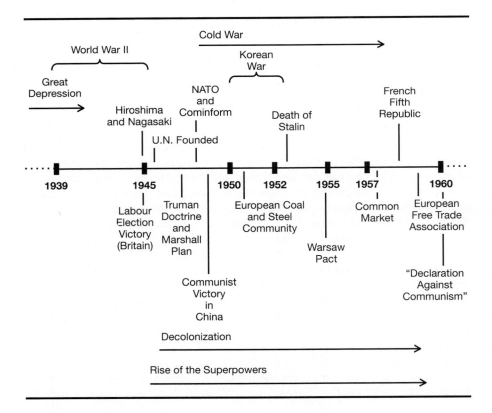

two decades following the war. What were some of the arguments made and the strategies used in the struggle over decolonization? What role did the United Nations play in this struggle?

While these developments have undergone some modification in the last thirty years, they remain part of the present along with other trends that will be examined in the final chapter.

PRIMARY SOURCES

The Truman Doctrine and The Marshall Plan

During World War II the Soviet Union and the United States were allied against their common enemies, the Axis powers. Shortly after the end of the war, animosity began to reappear between the former allies. By 1947 that animosity had risen to the point where it was formalized in government programs and international policies; the Cold War had broken out. In the United States this was most clearly announced in two policy decisions excerpted here. The first is a speech delivered by President Truman on March 12, 1947, to Congress, concerning proposed aid to Greece and Turkey, which appeared in danger of falling under the influence of the Soviet Union. The principles contained in this speech became known as the Truman Doctrine. The second is a statement made by Secretary of State George C. Marshall on November 10, 1947, to Senate and House Committees on Foreign Relations, proposing massive aid to Europe. This proposal became known as the Marshall Plan.

> **Consider:** *The American perception of the Soviet Union and its allies; the purposes of this foreign policy; how the Soviet Union would probably perceive and react to this foreign policy.*

The peoples of a number of countries of the world have recently had totalitarian regimes forced upon them against their will. The Government of the United States had made frequent protests against coercion and intimidation, in violation of the Yalta agreement, in Poland, Rumania, and Bulgaria. I must also state that in a number of other countries there have been similar developments.

SOURCE: U.S. Congress, *Congressional Record*, 80th Congress, 1st Session (Washington, D.C.: U.S. Government Printing Office, 1947), vol. 93, p. 1981.

SOURCE: U.S. Congress, Senate Committee on Foreign Relations, *A Decade of American Foreign Policy: Basic Documents, 1941–1949* (Washington, D.C.: U.S. Government Printing Office, 1950), pp. 1270–1271.

At the present moment in world history nearly every nation must choose between alternative ways of life. The choice is too often not a free one.

One way of life is based upon the will of the majority, and is distinguished by free institutions, representative government, free elections, guaranties of individual liberty, freedom of speech and religion, and freedom from political oppression.

The second way of life is based upon the will of a minority forcibly imposed upon the majority. It relies upon terror and oppression, a controlled press and radio, fixed elections, and the suppression of personal freedoms.

I believe that it must be the policy of the United States to support free peoples who are resisting attempted subjugation by armed minorities or by outside pressures.

I believe that we must assist free peoples to work out their own destinies in their own way.

I believe that our help should be primarily through economic and financial aid, which is essential to economic stability and orderly political processes.

*

As a result of the war, the European community which for centuries had been one of the most productive and indeed creative portions of the inhabited world was left prostrate. This area, despite its diversity of national cultures and its series of internecine conflicts and wars, nonetheless enjoys a common heritage and a common civilization.

The war ended with the armies of the major Allies meeting in the heart of this community. The policies of three of them have been directed to the restoration of that European community. It is now clear that only one power, the Soviet Union, does not for its own reasons share this aim.

We have become involved in two wars which have had their origins in the European continent. The free peoples of Europe have fought two wars to prevent the forcible domination of their community by a single great power. Such domination would have inevitably menaced the stability and security of the world. To deny today our interest in their ability to defend their own heritage would be to disclaim the efforts and sacrifices of two generations of Americans. We wish to see this community restored as one of the pillars of world security; in a position to renew its contribution to the advancement of mankind and to the development of a world order based on law and respect for the individual.

The record of the endeavors of the United States Government to bring about a restoration of the whole of that European community is clear for all who wish to see. We must face the fact, however, that despite our efforts, not all of the European nations have been left free to take their place in the community of which they form a natural part.

Thus the geographic scope of our recovery program is limited to those nations which are free to act in accordance with their national traditions and their own estimates of their national interests. If there is any doubt as to this situation, a glance at the present map of the European continent will provide the answer.

The present line of division in Europe is roughly the line upon which the Anglo-

American armies coming from the west met those of the Soviet Union coming from the east. To the west of that line the nations of the continental European community have been grappling with the vast and difficult problems resulting from the war in conformity with their own national traditions without pressure or menace from the United States or Great Britain. Developments in the European countries to the east of that line bear the unmistakable imprint of an alien hand.

British Labor's Rise to Power
Harry W. Laidler

During World War II governments became involved in social and economic activities to an unprecedented degree. Although with the end of the war this changed to some degree, there was still significant acceptance of government involvement in society. In Great Britain this was combined with an increasing acceptance of the Labour party, whose strength had been growing since the end of World War I. In the elections of 1945, this party, made up of a combination of Socialist and trade-union groups, gained a majority and took office, replacing the Conservatives led by Winston Churchill. The new government initiated policies that substantially changed the relationship between the government and the people during the period following World War II. Excerpts from the Labour party platform set forth shortly before the 1945 elections are presented here.

> **Consider:** *The ways in which this platform constituted a major assault on capitalism and* laissez-faire; *how this platform might reflect the experience of the Great Depression and the world wars; how a Conservative might argue against this platform.*

The Labor party is a socialist party, and proud of it. Its ultimate purpose at home is the establishment of the socialist commonwealth of Great Britain—free, democratic, efficient, progressive, public-spirited, its material resources organized in the service of the British people.

But socialism cannot come overnight, as the product of a week-end revolution. The members of the Labor party, like the British people, are practical-minded men and women.

There are basic industries ripe and over-ripe for public ownership and management in the direct service of the nation. There are many smaller businesses rendering good service which can be left to go on with their useful work.

There are big industries not yet ripe for public ownership which must nevertheless be required by constructive supervision to further the nation's needs and not to prejudice national interests by restrictive antisocial monopoly or cartel

SOURCE: Harry W. Laidler, "British Labor's Rise to Power," in *League for Industrial Democracy Pamphlet Series* (New York: League for Industrial Democracy, 1945), pp. 24–25. Reprinted by permission of the publisher.

agreements—caring for their own capital structures and profits at the cost of a lower standard of living for all.

In the light of these considerations, the Labor party submits to the nation the following industrial program:

1. *Public Ownership of the Fuel and Power Industries.* For a quarter of a century the coal industry, producing Britain's most precious national raw material, has been floundering chaotically under the ownership of many hundreds of independent companies. Amalgamation under public ownership will bring great economies in operation and make it possible to modernize production methods and to raise safety standards in every colliery in the country. Public ownership of gas and electricity undertakings will lower charges, prevent competitive waste, open the way for co-ordinated research and development, and lead to the reforming of uneconomic areas of distribution. Other industries will benefit.

2. *Public Ownership of Inland Transport.* Co-ordination of transport services by rail, road, air and canal cannot be achieved without unification. And unification without public ownership means a steady struggle with sectional interests or the entrenchment of a private monopoly, which would be a menace to the rest of industry.

3. *Public Ownership of Iron and Steel.* Private monopoly has maintained high prices and kept inefficient high-cost plants in existence. Only if public ownership replaced private monopoly can the industry become efficient.

   These socialized industries, taken over on a basis of fair compensation, to be conducted efficiently in the interests of consumers, coupled with proper status and conditions for the workers employed in them.

4. *Public Supervision of Monopolies and Cartels* with the aim of advancing industrial efficiency in the service of the nation. Anti-social restrictive practices will be prohibited.

5. A *First and Clear-cut Program for the Export Trade.* We would give State help in any necessary form to get our export trade on its feet and enable it to pay for the food and raw materials without which Britain must decay and die. But State help on conditions—conditions that industry is efficient and go-ahead. Laggards and obstructionists must be led or directed into a better way. Here we dare not fail.

6. *The Shaping of Suitable Economic and Price Controls* to secure that first things shall come first in the transition from war to peace and that every citizen (including the demobilized Service men and women) shall get fair play. There must be priorities in the use of raw materials, food prices must be held, homes for the people must come before mansions, necessities for all before luxuries for the few. We do not want a short boom followed by collapse as after the last war; we do not want a wild rise in prices and inflation, followed by a smash and widespread unemployment. It is either sound economic controls—or smash.

The Fearful Choice:
Nuclear Weapons
Philip Toynbee

The intensity of the Cold War and the existence of nuclear weapons on both sides created a tense atmosphere in the West during the 1950s and early 1960s. This atmosphere was reflected in the construction of public and private survival shelters against nuclear attack. It was also reflected in debates over the effectiveness of nuclear weapons to deter the opposing side from attack, the possibility of bilateral disarmament, and the necessity for unilateral destruction of nuclear weapons. In the following selection from a 1956 debate, Philip Toynbee of Great Britain argued for the last position.

> **Consider:** *How Toynbee justifies a policy of unilateral nuclear disarmament; how one might respond to this argument; how the attitude expressed here relates to attitudes expressed by Truman and Marshall.*

It is obvious, surely, that this is an issue which has nothing whatever to do with party politics and nothing whatever to do with our estimations of American and Russian society. In the terrible context of nuclear war even the vital differences between Communism and Western freedom become almost unimportant. We would infinitely prefer our Western system of freedom and privacy to prevail in the world; and if we are spared we shall have an opportunity of trying to ensure that it does so. But even if it didn't prevail *mankind* would still be given the opportunity of prevailing. Mr. Kennan has said that anything would be better than a policy which led inevitably to nuclear war. But surely anything is better than a policy which allows for the *possibility* of nuclear war.

The issue has nothing to do with politics. It has little to do with causes and highmindedness. Those who have had at least a partial vision of our destruction are like people who have leant out of the window of an express train and seen that a bridge is down a little further along the line. They are urging the driver and their fellow-passengers that the train should be stopped. But the others reply, many of them from behind their newspapers, that the train can't possibly be stopped because they have important engagements in the city. As for the bridge, it may not be down after all, and even if it is the train will probably manage to jump across it somehow. Besides, it does no good to the reputation of our railways if express trains are to be halted in this way. And finally, we ought surely to be aware that there is another express train coming in the opposite direction which will certainly fall down into the river just as soon as we do.

SOURCE: Philip Toynbee, *The Fearful Choice* (London: Victor Gollancz, Ltd., 1956), pp. 21–22. Reprinted by permission of the publisher.

At the very least, then, let those who wish to continue with the arms-race be prepared with competent methods of killing off their mutilated families before killing their mutilated selves. Only when we see that they have made these preparations shall we be able to believe that they have faced the implications of their policy.

Declaration Against Colonialism
The General Assembly of the United Nations

Most colonized peoples gained their independence from Western powers during the twenty years that followed World War II. This reflected both the weakness of Europe after the war and the strength of anti-imperialist sentiments around the world. Yet the process of decolonization was difficult in itself and was complicated by the ideological differences that divided nations. In 1960, after a bitter debate, the United Nations adopted the following "Declaration Against Colonialism." Although no nation voted against the resolution, Australia, Belgium, the Dominican Republic, France, Great Britain, Portugal, South Africa, Spain, and the United States abstained.

> **Consider:** *Possible reasons these nations abstained; justifications used by nations for not giving up their colonial possessions; what this declaration reveals about the strengths and weaknesses of the United Nations.*

The General Assembly.

Mindful of the determination proclaimed by the peoples of the world in the Charter of the United Nations to reaffirm faith in fundamental human rights, in the dignity and worth of the human person, in the equal rights of men and women and of nations large and small and to promote social progress and better standards of life in larger freedom,

Conscious of the need for the creation of conditions of stability and well-being and peaceful and friendly relations based on respect for the principles of equal rights and self-determination of all peoples, and of universal respect for, and observance of, human rights and fundamental freedoms for all without distinction as to race, sex, language or religion,

Recognizing the passionate yearning for freedom in all dependent peoples and the decisive role of such peoples in the attainment of their independence,

Aware of the increasing conflicts resulting from the denial of or impediments

---

SOURCE: General Assembly of the United Nations, "Declaration Against Colonialism," *Official Records of the General Assembly*, Fifteenth Session, Resolution 1514, December 14, 1960.

in the way of the freedom of such peoples, which constitute a serious threat to world peace,

Considering the important role of the United Nations in assisting the movement for independence in Trust and Non-Self-Governing Territories,

Recognizing that the people of the world ardently desire the end of colonialism in all its manifestations,

Convinced that the continued existence of colonialism prevents the development of international economic co-operation, impedes the social, cultural and economic development of dependent peoples and militates against the United Nations ideal of universal peace,

Affirming that peoples may, for their own ends, freely dispose of their natural wealth and resources without prejudice to any obligations arising out of international economic co-operation, based upon the principle of mutual benefit, and the international law,

Believing that the process of liberation is irresistible and irreversible and that, in order to avoid serious crises, an end must be put to colonialism and all practices of segregation and discrimination associated therewith,

Welcoming the emergence in recent years of a large number of dependent territories into freedom and independence, and recognizing the increasingly powerful trends towards freedom in such territories which have not yet attained independence,

Convinced that all peoples have an inalienable right to complete freedom, the exercise of their sovereignty and the integrity of their national territory,

Solemnly proclaims the necessity of bringing to a speedy and unconditional end colonialism in all its forms and manifestations;

And to this end

Declares that:

1. The subjection of peoples to alien subjugation, domination and exploitation constitutes a denial of fundamental human rights, is contrary to the Charter of the United Nations and is an impediment to the promotion of world peace and co-operation.

2. All peoples have the right to self-determination; by virtue of that right they freely determine their political status and freely pursue their economic, social and cultural development.

3. Inadequacy of political, economic, social or educational preparedness should never serve as a pretext for delaying independence.

4. All armed action or repressive measures of all kinds directed against dependent peoples shall cease in order to enable them to exercise peacefully and freely their right to complete independence, and the integrity of their national territory shall be respected.

5. Immediate steps shall be taken, in Trust and Non-Self-Governing Territories or all other territories which have not yet attained independence, to transfer all powers to the peoples of those territories, without any conditions

or reservations, in accordance with their freely expressed will and desire, without any distinction as to race, creed or color, in order to enable them to enjoy complete independence and freedom.

6. Any attempt aimed at the partial or total disruption of the national unity and the territorial integrity of a country is incompatible with the purposes and principles of the Charter of the United Nations.

7. All States shall observe faithfully and strictly the provisions of the Charter of the United Nations, the Universal Declaration of Human Rights and the present Declaration on the basis of equality, noninterference in the internal affairs of all States, and respect for the sovereign rights of all peoples and their territorial integrity.

VISUAL SOURCES

The Atomic Bomb
Henry L. Stimson

World War II was a turning point in many ways, perhaps most obviously in the nature of weaponry available to human beings engaged in war. In the final stages of World War II efforts to develop atomic weapons came to fruition with the creation of the atomic bomb. The following United States Air Force photo shows the atomic bomb exploding over Nagasaki, Japan, on August 9, 1945. This was three days after the first atomic bomb was dropped on Hiroshima. Within a few days Japan surrendered, ending the war. Shortly thereafter, controversy developed over whether it was necessary or just to drop the bomb. In the following excerpt Henry L. Stimson, United States Secretary of War during World War II, reflects on the decision to drop the bomb.

In the decades since 1945 the mushroom-shaped cloud has come to symbolize several things besides the end of World War II: deterrence by nuclear terror; World War III; inhumanity; power out of control; the death of the earth.

> **Consider:** *How Stimson justifies use of the bomb; how someone might argue against the use of the bomb; your associations with this photo; what other associations people might have; how these associations relate to developments since World War II.*

SOURCE: Excerpts from *On Active Service in Peace and War* by Henry L. Stimson and McGeorge Bundy. Copyright 1948 by Henry Stimson and McGeorge Bundy. Reprinted by permission of HarperCollins Publishers, Inc.

. . . [T]he atomic bomb was more than a weapon of terrible destruction; it was a psychological weapon. In March, 1945, our Air Forces had launched the first great incendiary raid on the Tokyo area. In this raid more damage was done and more casualties were inflicted than was the case at Hiroshima. . . .

As Dr. Karl Compton has said, "it was not one atomic bomb, or two, which brought surrender; it was the experience of what an atomic bomb will actually do to a community, *plus the dread of many more*, that was effective."

The bomb thus served exactly the purpose we intended. The peace party was able to take the path of surrender, and the whole weight of the Emperor's prestige

Photo 14-1

National Archives, U.S. Office of War Information

was exerted in favor of peace. When the Emperor ordered surrender, and the small but dangerous group of fanatics who opposed him were brought under control, the Japanese became so subdued that the great undertaking of occupation and disarmament was completed with unprecedented ease. . . .

The decision to use the atomic bomb was a decision that brought death to over a hundred thousand Japanese. No explanation can change that fact and I do not wish to gloss it over. But this deliberate, premeditated destruction was our least abhorrent choice. The destruction of Hiroshima and Nagasaki put an end to the Japanese war. It stopped the fire raids, and the strangling blockage; it ended the ghastly specter of a clash of great land armies.

The Destruction of Europe

The following map shows the destruction inflicted on Dresden in the Anglo-American bombing raid of February 13–14, 1945, during the last stages of World War II. As in other "area bombings" made by Allied forces during the war, thousands of civilians were killed in this raid. This shows the blurring of civilian and military targets and the growing use of terror in modern warfare. Military targets such as factories, railway bridges, railway marshaling yards, main railway lines, troop bunkers and barracks, arsenals, and command headquarters were for the most part not significantly damaged. Instead, the destruction was concentrated on the heavily populated inner city, which was almost completely leveled by fires from incendiary bombing.

Map 14-1   Dresden, 1945

Consider: *The possible explanations for this raid and its effects; how warfare conducted in this manner seems to contradict the classic ideals of Western civilization concerning the value of the individual and individual rights.*

The Cold War and European Integration

The following map gives some idea of the movements toward the Cold War and toward European integration in the two decades following World War II. Militarily, West and East divided into NATO, led by the United States, and the Warsaw Pact Organization, led by the U.S.S.R. Economically, Western European nations became increasingly tied together through organizations such as the Benelux Customs Union, the European Coal and Steel Community, the European Economic Community (Common Market), and the European Free Trade Association; the East joined in the Council for Mutual Economic Assistance (Comecon). Although military cooperation and economic cooperation were not always linked together, such linkage often did take place.

> **Consider:** *The geographic logic, if any, of the political and economic decisions that were made by the various countries; how maps of the world indicating regional economic cooperation, military alliances, political upheavals, and international "hotspots" might show the extent and intensity of the Cold War and regional cooperation even more fully than this map of Europe.*

Map 14-2   The Economic and Military Division of Europe

ICELAND

ATLANTIC OCEAN

SWEDEN

FINLAND

NORWAY

NORTH SEA

BALTIC SEA

SOVIET UNION

UNITED KINGDOM

DENMARK

IRELAND

NETHER-LANDS

POLAND

EAST GERMANY

BELGIUM

WEST GERMANY

CZECHOSLOVAKIA

LUXEMBOURG

FRANCE

SWITZ.

AUSTRIA

HUNGARY

RUMANIA

YUGOSLAVIA

BLACK SEA

PORTUGAL

SPAIN

ITALY

BULGARIA

ALBANIA

GREECE

TURKEY

ALGERIA

MEDITERRANEAN SEA

	Common Market
	European Free Trade Association
	Council for Mutual Economic Assistance
■	NATO
▲	Warsaw Pact

0   400 Miles

0   400 Kilometers

SECONDARY SOURCES

Appeasement at Munich Attacked

George F. Kennan

The traditional view in the debate over who was responsible for the outbreak of World War II is that Hitler was emboldened by the unnecessarily weak policy of appeasement pursued by the Western democracies during the 1930s. One element of this appeasement was the Munich Conference of 1938 at which England and France agreed to the dismemberment of Czechoslovakia in return for Hitler's promise to demand no further territories. In the following selection George F. Kennan, former U.S. ambassador to the Soviet Union and Pulitzer Prize winner for a two-volume work on Soviet-American relations, presents the traditional view of appeasement.

> **Consider:** *From the point of view of the French and British statesmen actually participating in the Munich Conference of 1938 whether Kennan's criticism is justified; the implications of the argument about the causes of or blame for World War II.*

The Munich agreement was a tragically misconceived and desperate act of appeasement at the cost of the Czechoslovak state, performed by Chamberlain and the French premier, Daladier, in the vain hope that it would satisfy Hitler's stormy ambition, and thus secure for Europe a peaceful future. We know today that it was unnecessary—unnecessary because the Czech defenses were very strong, and had the Czechs decided to fight they could have put up considerable resistance; even more unnecessary because the German generals, conscious of Germany's relative weakness at that moment, were actually prepared to attempt the removal of Hitler then and there, had he persisted in driving things to the point of war. It was the fact that the Western powers and the Czechoslovak government did yield at the last moment, and that Hitler once again achieved a bloodless triumph, which deprived the generals of any excuse for such a move. One sees again, as so often in the record of history, that it sometimes pays to stand up manfully to one's problems, even when no certain victory is in sight.

SOURCE: George F. Kennan, *Russia and the West Under Lenin and Stalin* (Boston: Atlantic–Little, Brown, 1961), p. 322. Reprinted by permission of Little, Brown and Company.

The Origins of the Second World War: Appeasement Defended

A. J. P. Taylor

The traditional view attacking appeasement as unjustified and a major cause of World War II has been questioned from different perspectives. Perhaps the most controversial perspective comes from A. J. P. Taylor, a popular, outspoken British historian who has written extensively on modern European history. In the following selection from The Origins of the Second World War, *Taylor argues that the appeasers have been unfairly faulted for their policies.*

> **Consider:** *The ways that Taylor and Kennan would disagree about the legitimacy of appeasement rather than the facts of appeasement; the implications of Taylor's argument about the causes of or blame for World War II; the advantages and dangers of looking at appeasement in the 1930s as a historical lesson to be learned for dealing with more recent circumstances.*

He got as far as he did because others did not know what to do with him. Here again I want to understand the "appeasers", not to vindicate or to condemn them. Historians do a bad day's work when they write the appeasers off as stupid or as cowards. They were men confronted with real problems, doing their best in the circumstances of their time. They recognised that an independent and powerful Germany had somehow to be fitted into Europe. Later experience suggests that they were right. At any rate, we are still going round and round the German problem. Can any sane man suppose, for instance, that other countries could have intervened by armed force in 1933 to overthrow Hitler when he had come to power by constitutional means and was apparently supported by a large majority of the German people? Could anything have been designed to make him more popular in Germany, unless perhaps it was intervening to turn him out of the Rhineland in 1936? The Germans put Hitler into power; they were the only ones who could turn him out. Again the "appeasers" feared that the defeat of Germany would be followed by a Russian domination over much of Europe. Later experience suggests that they were right here also. Only those who wanted Soviet Russia to take the place of Germany are entitled to condemn the "appeasers"; and I cannot understand how most of those who condemn them are now equally indignant at the inevitable result of their failure.

Nor is it true that the "appeasers" were a narrow circle, widely opposed at the time. To judge by what is said now, one would suppose that practically all Conservatives were for strenuous resistance to Germany in alliance with Soviet Russia

SOURCE: A. J. P. Taylor, *The Origins of the Second World War*, 2d ed. (New York: Atheneum Publishers, 1965), pp. 291–292. Reprinted by permission of the publisher.

and that all the Labour party were clamouring for great armaments. On the contrary, few causes have been more popular. Every newspaper in the country applauded the Munich settlement with the exception of *Reynolds' News*. Yet so powerful are the legends that even when I write this sentence down I can hardly believe it. Of course the "appeasers" thought firstly of their own countries as most statesmen do and are usually praised for doing. But they thought of others also. They doubted whether the peoples of eastern Europe would be best served by war. The British stand in September 1939 was no doubt heroic; but it was heroism mainly at the expense of others. The British people suffered comparatively little during six years of war. The Poles suffered catastrophe during the war, and did not regain their independence after it. In 1938 Czechoslovakia was betrayed. In 1939 Poland was saved. Less than one hundred thousand Czechs died during the war. Six and a half million Poles were killed. Which was better—to be a betrayed Czech or a saved Pole? I am glad Germany was defeated and Hitler destroyed. I also appreciate that others paid the price for this, and I recognise the honesty of those who thought the price too high.

The Origins of World War II
Keith Eubank

The issues involved with appeasement, which have so often been a focus for analysis, lead to the broader questions of why war broke out in 1939 and whether it could have been prevented. Keith Eubank, a diplomatic historian, takes a balanced approach in attempting to answer these questions.

> **Consider:** *Whether anything might have prevented war; how Kennan would react to Eubank's interpretation; the extent to which World War II was a direct consequence of the ideas and doctrines of Nazism rather than of political and diplomatic developments of the 1930s.*

The war that came to Europe in 1939 came because the only alternative for Hitler—when faced with a country that would not succumb to threats—was war. Hitler had promised to restore Germany to its rightful place in the world. Poland had received German territory through the Treaty of Versailles. Therefore, Hitler could not back down from Poland; he had to proceed with his objectives, and the only thing that would be able to alter his course would be war.

Many political commentators since 1939 have claimed that, if nations had acted earlier, there would have been no war. If the League had fought Japan over Manchuria, they claim, or if the League had defended Ethiopia, in 1935, or if France and Britain had invaded the Rhineland in 1936, then Hitler could not have

---

SOURCE: Keith Eubank, *The Origins of World War II* (New York: Thomas Y. Crowell, 1969), pp. 166–167. Reprinted by permission of Harper & Row, Publishers, Inc. Copyright © 1969 by Keith Eubank.

attacked Poland. But it would have been impossible for Britain and France to have entered any kind of war—offensive or defensive, small-scale or large-scale—before 1939, because neither the people nor the governments of the two countries were conditioned to the idea of war. The only way they could accept war after 1918 was for it to be thrust upon them by a series of crises, such as those that finally culminated in the German invasion of Poland. Arguments over when and where Hitler should have been halted, then, are purely academic, because before September 1, 1939 Hitler had done nothing that any major power considered dangerous enough to warrant precipitating a major European war.

Nor was there any existing coalition that could have opposed Hitler's massive forces. For Britain sought to appease Hitler, the French feared a repetition of the bloody sacrifices of 1914–1918, Stalin wanted an agreement with Hitler on partitioning Europe, and the United States rejected all responsibility for Europe. Peace would have been possible in 1939 only if there had existed a great military alliance, including both France and Britain, but headed by the United States and the Soviet Union, that was prepared to defend the governments of eastern Europe. But, until Hitler would force them into an alliance, capitalism and communism were prevented from cooperating to oppose nazism by their ideological differences, jealousies, suspicions, and power politics.

Origins of the Cold War
James L. Gormly

The period between the end of World War II and the mid-1960s was marked by the Cold War between the two superpowers emerging from World War II, the United States and the U.S.S.R. Initially American historians analyzed the Cold War with assumptions not too different from policymakers': The United States was only responding defensively to an aggressive Soviet Union intent on spreading its control and Communist ideology over the world. But by the 1960s other interpretations were being offered, most notably a revisionist position holding the Cold War to be at least in part a result of an aggressive, provocative American foreign policy. In the following selection James Gormly describes the competing interpretations and suggests how the controversy might be analyzed.

Consider: *Whether the Cold War was inevitable or could have been avoided; how the speeches by Truman and Marshall support one side or the other; which view makes the most sense to you.*

Those who place the major responsibility for the Cold War on the Soviet Union argue that Stalin, as dictator and leader of a totalitarian system, easily could have moderated the nation's interests to meet U.S. objections and ensure peace. Ac-

SOURCE: From James L. Gormly, *From Potsdam to the Cold War*, pp. 220–223. Copyright 1990 by Scholarly Resources, Inc. Reprinted by permission of Scholarly Resources, Inc.

cording to this view, if the generalissimo was not an expansionist wanting to overrun central and Western Europe, he should have articulated the defensive and limited nature of his goals to the Truman administration and the American public. Instead, the Russians would not accept the U.S. vision for a stable and prosperous world or trust that Washington accepted the legitimacy of the Soviet Union and recognized its need for some degree of influence over regions along its borders. Moscow needed "a hostile international environment" to maintain control and the integrity of the Soviet state. Thus, Stalin was either an expansionist or unwilling to communicate his aims, and the United States, supported by Britain, had no other option than to react aggressively. . . .

Other analysts place a large amount of the blame on the United States and its unwillingness to accept expressed Soviet needs and to articulate to the Russians and Stalin that Washington trusted them and recognized the legitimacy of their system and state. Some explain U.S. behavior as an outgrowth of the American Open Door ideology, which sought to ensure for the nation's businesses access to world markets. Still others credit U.S. actions to a general arrogance of power that translated the country's tremendous economic and military strength and accomplishments into a moral, ideological superiority. According to this theory, many Soviets feared that the West still hoped to destroy their state. To convince them that America intended to be a friend and thereby avoid the Cold War, the United States should have shelved its presumptuousness and global goals and demonstrated an affirmation of the Soviet Union's right to rule and enjoy the fruits of its victory. To ease fears and mistrust, Washington needed to recognize Russia's new borders, its diplomatic equality, and its spheres of influence in Eastern Europe. Instead, the U.S. government continued to follow the path suggested by Ambassador Harriman, who stated that the administration should supply assistance to the Soviets only if they "played the international game with us in accordance with our standards." . . .

Given the situation, the belief that U.S. actions divided the world into two camps and necessitated a rapid Sovietization of Eastern Europe seems as logical as the view that Russian expansionism forced the United States to institute its containment policy. To evaluate and assess either theory fully and to determine if the Cold War international system could have been avoided requires an examination of Soviet records, but, even without such information, and using existing American and British documents, one can conclude that U.S. policymakers made few efforts after the Potsdam Conference to reassure Moscow that mutual cooperation was possible and that Washington had no intention of seeking the destruction of the Soviet state.

The Positive Role of the United Nations in a Split World
Dag Hammarskjöld

One of the most idealistic institutions stemming from World War II was the United Nations, formed by agreement of the major powers in 1945 and eventually including most nations of the world. Its primary purpose is to preserve peace, which has become even more pressing with the proliferation of nuclear weapons. But despite some successes, the United Nations has come under attack for favoring policies in opposition to a perceived national interest and for being unable to take effective action when armed conflicts broke out. In the following selection Dag Hammarskjöld, secretary-general of the United Nations from 1953 to 1961, analyzes and defends the position and actions of the UN.

> **Consider:** *Why, according to Hammarskjöld, the UN has been unable to resolve many major international problems; how one might respond to this argument; whether policies such as those enunciated by Truman and Marshall support or conflict with the goals and efforts of the UN.*

With its constitution and structure, it is extremely difficult for the United Nations to exercise an influence on problems which are clearly and definitely within the orbit of present-day conflicts between power blocs. If a specific conflict is within that orbit, it can be assumed that the Security Council is rendered inactive, and it may be feared that even positions taken by the General Assembly would follow lines strongly influenced by considerations only indirectly related to the concrete difficulty under consideration. Whatever the attitude of the General Assembly and the Security Council, it is in such cases also practically impossible for the Secretary-General to operate effectively with the means put at his disposal, short of risking seriously to impair the usefulness of his office for the Organization in all the other cases for which the services of the United Nations Secretariat are needed.

This clearly defines the main field of useful activity of the United Nations in its efforts to prevent conflicts or to solve conflicts. Those efforts must aim at keeping newly arising conflicts outside the sphere of bloc differences. Further, in the case of conflicts on the margin of, or inside, the sphere of bloc differences, the United Nations should seek to bring such conflicts out of this sphere through solutions aiming, in the first instance, at their strict localization. In doing so, the Organization and its agents have to lay down a policy line, but this will then not be for one party against another, but for the general purpose of avoiding an extension or achieving a reduction of the area into which the bloc conflicts penetrate. . . .

SOURCE: Dag Hammarskjöld, "The Positive Role of the United Nations in a Split World," *United Nations Review*, vol. VII, no. 4 (October 1960), pp. 24–25. Reprinted by permission of the *UN Chronicle*.

Those who look with impatience at present-day efforts by the United Nations to resolve major international problems are inclined to neglect, or to misread, the significance of the efforts which can be made by the United Nations in the field of practical politics in order to guide the international community in a direction of growing stability. They see the incapacity of the United Nations to resolve the major bloc conflicts as an argument against the very form of international cooperation which the Organization represents. In doing so, they forget what the Organization has achieved and can achieve, through its activities regarding conflicts which are initially only on the margin of, or outside, the bloc conflicts, but which, unless solved or localized, might widen the bloc conflicts and seriously aggravate them. Thus the Organization in fact also exercises a most important, though indirect, influence on the conflicts between the power blocs by preventing the widening of the geographical and political area covered by these conflicts and by providing for solutions whenever the interests of all parties in a localization of conflict can be mobilized in favor of its efforts.

The Wretched of the Earth

Frantz Fanon

When discussing colonialism in the decades following World War II, most historians focus on its political and economic consequences. Some observers, however, point to the deeper psychological consequences of colonialism. The best known of these observers was Frantz Fanon (1925–1961), a French psychiatrist from the French West Indies whose writings supported the Algerian rebels in their struggle for independence from France after World War II. In his book The Wretched of the Earth *(1961), Fanon argues that colonialism had its greatest impact on the people physically involved in it: the foreign occupiers (settlers) and the colonized (natives). In the following excerpt from that book, Fanon emphasizes the great physical and psychological gap between these two groups.*

> **Consider:** *What connections there are between the physical and the psychological gaps separating settlers and natives; the attitudes of the settlers toward the natives; the attitudes of the natives toward the settlers and their institutions.*

The colonial world is a world cut in two. The dividing line, the frontiers are shown by barracks and police stations. In the colonies it is the policemen and the soldier who are the official, instituted go-betweens, the spokesmen of the settler and his rule of oppression. . . .

It is obvious here that the agents of government speak the language of pure force. The intermediary does not lighten the oppression, nor seek to hide the

---

SOURCE: Frantz Fanon, *The Wretched of the Earth*, trans. Constance Farrington. Copyright © 1963 by Presence Africaine. Used by permission of Grove Weidenfeld.

domination; he shows them up and puts them into practice with the clear conscience of an upholder of the peace; yet he is the bringer of violence into the home and into the mind of the native. . . .

The settlers' town is a strongly-built town, all made of stone and steel. It is a brightly-lit town; the streets are covered with asphalt, and the garbage-cans swallow all the leavings, unseen, unknown and hardly thought about. The settler's feet are never visible, except perhaps in the sea; but there you're never close enough to see them. His feet are protected by strong shoes although the streets of his town are clean and even, with no holes or stones. The settler's town is a well-fed town, an easygoing town; its belly is always full of good things. The settler's town is a town of white people, of foreigners.

The town belonging to the colonised people, or at least the native town, the negro village, the medina, the reservation, is a place of ill fame, peopled by men of evil repute. They are born there, it matters little where or how; they die there, it matters not where, nor how. It is a world without spaciousness; men live there on top of each other, and their huts are built one on top of the other. The native town is a hungry town, starved of bread, of meat, of shoes, of coal, of light. The native town is a crouching village, a town on its knees, a town wallowing in the mire. It is a town of niggers and dirty arabs. The look that the native turns on the settler's town is a look of lust, a look of envy; it expresses his dreams of possession—all manner of possession: to sit at the settler's table, to sleep in the settler's bed, with his wife if possible. The colonised man is an envious man. And this the settler knows very well; when their glances meet he ascertains bitterly, always on the defensive "They want to take our place". It is true, for there is no native who does not dream at least once a day of setting himself up in the settler's place.

This world divided into compartments, this world cut in two is inhabited by two different species. The originality of the colonial context is that economic reality, inequality and the immense difference of ways of life never come to mask the human realities. When you examine at close quarters the colonial context, it is evident that what parcels out the world is to begin with the fact of belonging to or not belonging to a given race, a given species. . . .

It is not enough for the settler to delimit physically, that is to say with the help of the army and the police force, the place of the native. As if to show the totalitarian character of colonial exploitation the settler paints the native as a sort of quintessence of evil. Native society is not simply described as a society lacking in values. It is not enough for the colonist to affirm that those values have disappeared from, or still better never existed in, the colonial world. The native is declared insensible to ethics; he represents not only the absence of values, but also the negation of values. . . .

The Church in the colonies is the white people's Church, the foreigner's Church. She does not call the native to God's ways but to the ways of the white man, of the master, of the oppressor. And as we know, in this matter many are called but few chosen.

Chapter Questions

1. To what extent do the trends described in this chapter give further support to the argument that Western civilization has been on the decline since World War I in comparison to the heights it reached in the nineteenth century? What developments might be cited to refute this argument?

2. How might one make an argument that the fundamental historical shift in the last two hundred years did not come with World War I but rather with World War II, as indicated by the consequences of that war and the developments of the postwar period?

3. Do you think the Cold War was caused primarily by developments related to World War II or by the ideological differences between Communist and non-Communist countries? Were there any ways in which the Cold War might have been averted?

CHAPTER FIFTEEN

The Present in Perspective

The most recent years in Western history are particularly difficult to evaluate. They are so much a part of the present that it is almost impossible to gain a historical perspective on them.

While many of the basic trends of the postwar era examined in the previous chapter have continued, some important changes have become apparent—particularly in the last few years. The Cold War between the United States and the Soviet Union waned during the late 1980s and ended with the collapse of communism after 1989. Revolutionary changes have been taking place in what was the Soviet Union and in Eastern Europe. For the West, these changes may be so far-reaching as to constitute a historical watershed—a marking of the end of the twentieth century and the beginning of the twenty-first century. The rest of Europe, and indeed much of the world, had already been pursuing increasingly independent courses from the two superpowers. The strife-ridden, oil-rich Middle East has become an area of great concern and importance to the world community. Certain areas in Asia—like Japan, South Korea, Taiwan, and Singapore—have developed strong economies, helping to shift the economic balance of power in the world. New technological accomplishments, ranging from space exploration to the production of computers, affect our civilization in many ways. Numerous other recent trends and events could be added to this necessarily brief list.

This chapter is not organized in the usual way, for the sources are so much a part of the present that the usual distinctions between primary and secondary sources are no longer useful. The selections deal with three kinds of developments. The first concerns changes in the Communist world, particularly the former Soviet Union, and related political changes. The second has to do with social, cultural, and ecological trends that have been of particular significance and still affect us today. The third involves interpreting the present era as a whole and the future.

There is much ambivalence about recent developments. Our own involvement makes evaluation of the present particularly difficult. At best, the selections in this chapter can throw elements of the present into perspective.

The Short Century—It's Over
John Lukacs

Historians have traditionally been interested in dividing their study and analysis of civilizations into eras or periods that make some sense—ideally that begin and end with some watershed developments and have some unifying characteristics. This is particularly difficult to do for our own time, for we lack some historical perspective. In the following selection John Lukacs, writing in 1991 before the dissolution of the Soviet Union, argues that in 1989 watershed events occurred in the West, bringing the twentieth century to an end and initiating the twenty-first century.

> **Consider:** *How Lukacs supports his argument; whether his argument works as well for the non-Western world; what this might mean for the future.*

The 20th century is now over, and there are two extraordinary matters about this.

First, this was a short century. It lasted 75 years, from 1914 to 1989. Its two principal events were the two world wars. They were the two enormous mountain ranges that dominated its landscape. The Russian Revolution, the atom bomb, the end of the colonial empires, the establishment of the Communist states, the emergence of the two superpowers, the division of Europe and of Germany—all of these were the consequences of the two world wars, in the shadow of which we were living, until now.

The 19th century lasted exactly 99 years, from 1815 to 1914, from the end of Napoleon's wars to the start of the—so called—First World War. The 18th century lasted 126 years, from 1689 to 1815, from the beginning of the world wars between

England and France (of which the American War of Independence was but part) until their end at Waterloo.

Second, we know that the 20th century is over. In 1815, no one knew that this was the end of the Atlantic world wars and the beginning of the Hundred Years' Peace. At that time, everyone, friends as well as enemies of the French Revolution, were concerned with the prospect of great revolutions surfacing again. There were revolutions after 1815, but the entire history of the 19th century was marked by the absence of world wars during 99 years. Its exceptional prosperity and progress were due to that.

In 1689, the very word "century" was hardly known. The "Oxford English Dictionary" notes its first present usage, in English, in 1626. Before that the word meant a Roman military unit of 100 men; then it began to have another meaning, that of 100 years. It marked the beginning of our modern historical consciousness.

We know that the 20th century is over—not merely because of our historical consciousness (which is something different from a widespread knowledge of history) but mainly because the confrontation of the two superpowers, the outcome of the Second World War, has died down. The Russians have retreated from Eastern Europe and Germany has been reunited. Outside Europe, even the Korean and the Vietnam wars, the missile crisis in Cuba and other political crises such as Nicaragua were, directly or indirectly, involved with that confrontation.

In 1991, we live in a very different world, in which both the U.S. and the Soviet Union face grave problems with peoples and dictators in the so-called third world. Keep in mind that the ugly events in Lithuania are no exception to this: They involve the political structure of the Soviet Union itself. Even its name, the Union of Soviet Socialist Republics, is becoming an anachronism, as once happened with the Holy Roman Empire.

Keep in mind, too, that no matter when and how the gulf war ends, the so-called Middle East will remain a serious problem both for the U.S. and the Soviet Union. Even in the case of a smashing American political or military victory, its beneficial results will be ephemeral. To think—let alone speak—of a Pax Americana in the Middle East is puerile nonsense.

Not only the configuration of great powers and their alliances but the very structure of political history has changed. Both superpowers have plenty of domestic problems. In the Soviet Union, this has now become frighteningly actual; in the U.S., the internal problems are different but not superficial. The very sovereignty and cohesion of states, the authority and efficacy of the governments are not what they were.

Are we going to see ever larger and larger political units? "Europe" will, at best, become a free-trade economic zone, but a Union of Europe is a mirage. Or are we more likely going to see the break-up of several states into small national ones? Are we going to see a large-scale migration of millions of peoples, something that has not happened since the last centuries of the Roman Empire? This is at least possible. The very texture of history is changing before our very eyes.

Are we on the threshold of a new Dark Ages? We must hope not. The main task before us is the rethinking of the word "progress." Like that of "century," the meaning of that word, too, is more recent than we have been accustomed to think. Before the 16th century, that is, before the opening of the so-called modern age (another misnomer, suggesting that this age would last forever) progress simply meant an advance in distance, not in time, without the sense of evolutionary improvement.

Thereafter, the word "progress" began to carry the unquestionable optimistic meaning of endless material and scientific promise, until, during the 20th century, it began to lose some of its shine, because of the increasingly questionable benefits of technology. At the beginning of the 20th century, technology and barbarism seemed to be antitheses. They no longer are. But technology and its threat to the natural environment are only part of the larger problem of progress, a word and an ideal whose more proper and true application is the task of the 21st century that has already begun.

After Communism:
Causes for the Collapse
Robert Heilbroner

The rapid collapse of communism in the Soviet Union and Eastern Europe has stunned most observers. Only in retrospect have reasons for this collapse been presented with any conviction. Scholars are now struggling to interpret what has happened. One of these is Robert Heilbroner, who has written extensively on economics, economic history, and current affairs. In the following selection he focuses on the Soviet economic system, particularly the Soviet's central planning system, as the key to the collapse.

> **Consider:** *Why the Soviet's central planning system might have worked well enough in the early stages of industrialization or for specific projects, but not well enough for a mature industrialized economy; why the collapse of communism in the Soviet Union has such widespread significance.*

Socialism has been a great tragedy this century, its calamitous finale the collapse of Communism in the Soviet Union and Eastern Europe. I doubt very much whether socialism has now disappeared from history, but there is no doubt that the collapse marks its end as a model of economic clarity. Moreover, I suspect that its economic failure may haunt socialism longer than the pathologies of Communism. Early on, one could see that the Soviets were headed toward political disaster, but much of that disaster seemed attributable to the hopeless political heritage of Russian history, not to socialism per se. It was the economic side of the Russian collapse that came as a shock. The prodigies of Russian prewar industrialization appeared to be an incontrovertible argument for the capacity of a planned economic system to achieve growth, and the argument appeared to be confirmed by the spectacular performance of the Soviets during the years of reconstruction immediately following the Second World War. Thus, there may have been discomfiture but there was not much surprise when the Soviet economy during the nineteen-fifties grew twice as fast as the American economy. Surprise did not appear until the nineteen-seventies, when the Soviet growth rate slipped to only half of ours, and consternation was not evident until the middle to late nineteen-eighties, when C.I.A. and academic specialists alike began to report something very close to zero growth. But collapse! No one expected collapse.

There is still no definitive account as to exactly why the Soviet economic system collapsed—one can never find the nail for whose want the shoe was lost. There were undoubtedly elements of this economic disaster with their roots in history: the bureaucrat is well known to Russian literature. Perhaps the final blow was delivered by *glasnost*, which released long-pent-up anger against economic conditions; or perhaps by the Soviet attempt to meet the Star Wars initiative—one hears many such guesses. All we know for certain is that the system deteriorated to a point far beyond the worst economic crisis ever experienced by capitalism, and that the villain in this deterioration was the central planning system itself. The conclusion one inevitably comes to is that to whatever extent socialism depends on such a system it will not work. . . .

The great problem of central planning lies buried in the procedures by which the economy is given its marching orders. As in a military campaign, which central planning resembles in many ways, production is brought about by a series of commands from the top, not by the independent decisions of regimental commanders, company captains, and platoon sergeants. This means that the economy "works" because—and only to the extent that—the quantity, quality, size, weight, and selling price of every nut, bolt, hinge, beam, tractor, and hydroelectric turbine have been previously determined. At the supreme headquarters, the numbers for gross national product are announced. In considerably lower and dingier offices, the numbers for nuts, bolts, and turbines are calculated, but it is apparent that if the plans for the latter are off, the plans for the former may be impossible to attain.

Planning thus requires that the immense map of desired national output be carved up into millions of individual pieces, like a jigsaw puzzle—the pieces produced by hundreds of thousands of enterprises, and the whole thing finally reassembled in such a way as to fit. That would be an extraordinarily difficult task even if the map of desired output were unchanged from year to year, but, of course, it is not: the chief planners change their objectives, and new technologies or labor shortages or bad weather or simply mistakes get in the way. In 1986, before *perestroika* was officially formulated, Gosplan, the highest planning commission in the Soviet Union, issued two thousand sets of instructions for major "product groups," such as construction materials, metals, and automotive vehicles. Gossnab, the State Material and Technical Supply Commission, then divided these product groups into fifteen thousand categories—lumber, copper, and trucks, for instance—and the various ministries in charge of the categories in turn subdivided them into fifty thousand more finely detailed products (shingles, beams, laths, boards) and then into specific products in each category (large, medium, and small shingles). These plans then percolated down through the hierarchy of production, receiving emendations or protests as they reached the level of plant managers and engineers, and thereafter travelled back up to the ministerial level. In this Byzantine process, perhaps the most difficult single step was to establish "success indicators"—desired performance targets—for enterprises. For many years, targets were given in physical terms—so many yards of cloth or tons of nails—but that led to obvious difficulties. If cloth was rewarded by the yard, it was woven loosely to make the yarn yield more yards. If the output of nails was determined by their number, factories produced huge numbers of pinlike nails; if by weight, smaller numbers of very heavy nails. The satiric magazine *Krokodil* once ran a cartoon of a factory manager proudly displaying his record output, a single gigantic nail suspended from a crane.

The difficulty, of course, was that the inevitable mismatches and mistakes could not be set to rights by the decisions of platoon sergeants or regimental commanders who were able to see that the campaign was not going as expected.

✲

I am not very sanguine about the prospect that socialism will continue as an important form of economic organization now that Communism is finished. This statement will come as a wry commentary to those who remember that Marx defined socialism as the stage that precedes Communism. But the collapse of the planned economies has forced us to rethink the meaning of socialism. As a semireligious vision of a transformed humanity, it has been dealt devastating blows in the twentieth century. As a blueprint for a rationally planned society, it is in tatters.

The Perils of the New Nationalism
Eric J. Hobsbawn

In recent years many commentators have noted a growth of nationalism and movements for political separatism. While some of this is part of older nationalistic trends common in the West since the nineteenth century, there seems to be something different about this new impulse. In the following selection Eric Hobsbawn, who deplores the drive to create new states for each "nation" of ethnically and linguistically distinct people, analyzes this new nationalism, emphasizing four reasons for its strength.

Consider: *How recent events have encouraged political separatism; what the possible consequences of these movements might be.*

SOURCE: From Eric Hobsbawn, "The Perils of the New Nationalism," *The Nation* 255:537 +, September 4, 1992. Copyright © 1995 E. J. Hobsbawn. Reprinted by permission of the author.

There are today four rather different reasons such sentiments, and their political expression in separatism, are widely supported. The first is that the collapse of the Communist system, which imposed political stability over a large part of Europe, has reopened the wounds of World War I, or, more precisely, of the misconceived and unrealistic peace settlements after it. The explosive nationalist issues in Central and Eastern Europe today are not ancient ethnic conflicts but those created during the formation of the successor states to the collapsing multi-ethnic Habsburg, Ottoman and Czarist Russian empires. Baltic and Caucasian separatism, and conflicts between Serbs and Croats, and Czechs and Slovaks, were not serious problems in 1917, or could not have existed before the establishment of Yugoslavia and Czechoslovakia. What has made those problems acute is not the strength of national feeling, which was no greater than in countries like Britain and Spain, but the disintegration of central power, for this forced even Soviet or Yugoslav republics that did not dream of separation, like Kazakhstan and Macedonia, to assert independence as a means of self-preservation.

The breakdown of Communist systems has given separatist agitations elsewhere enormous encouragement, but it has no direct bearing on them. Such as they are, the prospects of independence for, say, Scotland, Quebec, Euskadi (the Basque country) or Corsica remain the same as before. They do not depend on what happens in the East.

The second reason is more general, though probably more important in the West than in the East. The massive population movements of the past forty years—within and between countries and continents—have made xenophobia into a major political phenomenon, as the earlier mass migrations of 1880–1920 did to a smaller extent. Xenophobia encourages ethnic nationalism, since the essence of both is hostility to other groups (the "not-we"). United States nationalism is by origin entirely nonlinguistic. It is only because of mass Hispanic immigration that today demands are made, for the first time, that English should be the *official* language of the United States. However, mutual ethnic hatred does not necessarily produce separatism, as the United States also proves.

The third reason is that the politics of group identity are easier to understand than any others, especially for peoples who, after several decades of dictatorship, lack both political education and experience. In Central Europe, argues Miroslav Hroch, a leading Czech historian, language is once again replacing complicated concepts like constitutions and civil rights. Nationalism is among the simple, intuitively comprehensible beliefs that substitute for less understandable political programs. It is not the only one.

The fourth reason is perhaps the most fundamental. To quote the Czech historian: "Where an old regime disintegrates, where old social relations have become unstable, amid the rise of general insecurity, belonging to a common language and culture may become the only certainty in society, the only value beyond ambiguity and doubt." In the former Communist countries this insecurity and disorientation may derive from the collapse of the predictable planned economy and the social security that went with it. In the West there are other forms of disorientation and insecurity that have built up during the past decades, when the world and human life changed more rapidly and profoundly than ever before in human history.

Modernization: The Western and Non-Western Worlds

Although almost all areas of the world that were once colonies of the Western powers gained independence during the quarter-century following World War II, the penetration of the rest of the world by Western ideas, values, institutions, and products has been extremely widespread. This is illustrated in the following photograph showing a citizen of Kuwait, an oil-rich sheikdom of the Persian Gulf, carrying a Western television set across a road. He is wearing Western-style tennis shoes that were probably manufactured in the Far East. In the background are a bilingual store sign and Western automobiles. Reflected in the glass of the television set is a modern building probably designed by a Western architect and built under the direction of an international construction firm using both foreign and domestic labor and materials. This photograph suggests that some of the formerly

Photo 15-1

Bruno Barbey/Magnum

colonized areas are taking economic, political, and social steps in the same direction as Western industrialized states.

> **Consider:** *The effects of Westernization on non-Western culture as illustrated by this photo.*

The Second Sex
Simone de Beauvoir

and

A Feminist Manifesto
Redstockings

It is increasingly recognized that women, both individually and in organizations, have been struggling for changes for a long time. The effort to gain consciousness and under-standing of what it means to be a woman—politically, socially, economically, and sexu-ally—has become central to women's struggles for change in the mid-twentieth century. The most important book in Europe and probably all of the West to explore this effort is The Second Sex, *by Simone de Beauvoir, first published in France in 1949. In this book de Beauvoir, a well-known French novelist, social critic, and existential philosopher, ar-gues that women have been forced into a position subordinate to men in numerous obvi-ous and subtle ways. During the 1960s and 1970s women's struggle for change spread and took on a new militancy. Throughout the West, women were arguing for change in what came to be known, especially in the United States, as the women's liberation move-ment. Numerous women's organizations formed, and many issued publications stating their views.*

The first of the following two selections on the liberation of women is from The Second Sex. *De Beauvoir stresses the status and role of woman as the "Other" in comparison to man. The second selection is an example of one of the more radical statements of femi-nism. It was issued in July 1969 by Redstockings, an organization of New York feminists.*

> **Consider:** *How de Beauvoir relates women to "Negroes" and proletarians; the handicaps facing women according to de Beauvoir; the primary demands of the Redstockings; how this group justifies its demands; how men might react to this selection.*

The parallel drawn . . . between women and the proletariat is valid in that neither ever formed a minority or a separate collective unit of mankind. And instead of a single historical event it is in both cases a historical development that explains

---

SOURCE: Simone de Beauvoir, *The Second Sex,* H. M. Parshley, trans. Reprinted by permission of Alfred A. Knopf, Inc., pp. xvii–xxii, xxvii. Copyright © 1952 by Alfred A. Knopf, Inc.
SOURCE: Redstockings, July 7, 1969, mimeograph.

their status as a class and accounts for the membership of *particular individuals* in that class. But proletarians have not always existed, whereas there have always been women. They are women in virtue of their anatomy and physiology. Throughout history they have always been subordinated to men, and hence their dependency is not the result of a historical event or a social change—it was not something that *occurred*. The reason why otherness in this case seems to be an absolute is in part that it lacks the contingent or incidental nature of historical facts. A condition brought about at a certain time can be abolished at some other time, as the Negroes of Haiti and others have proved; but it might seem that a natural condition is beyond the possibility of change. In truth, however, the nature of things is no more immutably given, once for all, than is historical reality. If woman seems to be the inessential which never becomes the essential, it is because she herself fails to bring about this change. Proletarians say "We"; Negroes also. Regarding themselves as subjects, they transform the bourgeois, the whites, into "others." But women do not say "We," except at some congress of feminists or similar formal demonstration; men say "women," and women use the same word in referring to themselves. They do not authentically assume a subjective attitude. The proletarians have accomplished the revolution in Russia, the Negroes in Haiti, the Indo-Chinese are battling for it in Indo-China; but the women's effort has never been anything more than a symbolic agitation. They have gained only what men have been willing to grant; they have taken nothing, they have only received.

The reason for this is that women lack concrete means for organizing themselves into a unit which can stand face to face with the correlative unit. They have no past, no history, no religion of their own; and they have no such solidarity of work and interest as that of the proletariat. They are not even promiscuously herded together in the way that creates community feeling among the American Negroes, the ghetto Jews, the workers of Saint-Denis, or the factory hands of Renault. They live dispersed among the males, attached through residence, housework, economic condition, and social standing to certain men—fathers or husbands—more firmly than they are to other women. If they belong to the bourgeoisie, they feel solidarity with men of that class, not with proletarian women; if they are white, their allegiance is to white men, not to Negro women. The proletariat can propose to massacre the ruling class, and a sufficiently fanatical Jew or Negro might dream of getting sole possession of the atomic bomb and making humanity wholly Jewish or black; but women cannot even dream of exterminating the males. The bond that unites her to her oppressors is not comparable to any other. The division of the sexes is a biological fact, not an event in human history. Male and female stand opposed within a primordial *Mitsein*, and woman has not broken it. The couple is a fundamental unity with its two halves riveted together, and the cleavage of society along the line of sex is impossible. Here is to be found the basic trait of woman: she is the Other in a totality of which the two components are necessary to one another. . . .

Now, woman has always been man's dependent, if not his slave; the two sexes have never shared the world in equality. And even today woman is heavily handicapped, though her situation is beginning to change. Almost nowhere is her legal status the same as man's, and frequently it is much to her disadvantage. Even when her rights are legally recognized in the abstract, long-standing custom prevents their full expression in the mores. In the economic sphere men and women can almost be said to make up two castes; other things being equal, the former hold the better jobs, get higher wages, and have more opportunity for success than their new competitors. In industry and politics men have a great many more positions and they monopolize the most important posts. In addition to all this, they enjoy a traditional prestige that the education of children tends in every way to support, for the present enshrines the past—and in the past all history has been made by men. At the present time, when women are beginning to take part in the affairs of the world, it is still a world that belongs to men—they have no doubt of it at all and women have scarcely any. To decline to be the Other, to refuse to be a party to a deal—this would be for women to renounce all the advantages conferred upon them by their alliance with the superior caste. Man-the-sovereign will provide woman-the-liege with material protection and will undertake the moral justification of her existence; thus she can evade at once both economic risk and the metaphysical risk of a liberty in which ends and aims must be contrived without assistance. Indeed, along with the ethical urge of each individual to affirm his subjective existence, there is also the temptation to forgo liberty and become a thing. This is an inauspicious road, for he who takes it—passive, lost, ruined— becomes henceforth the creature of another's will, frustrated in his transcendence and deprived of every value. But it is an easy road; on it one avoids the strain involved in undertaking an authentic existence. When man makes of woman the *Other*, he may, then, expect her to manifest deep-seated tendencies toward complicity. Thus, woman may fail to lay claim to the status of subject because she lacks definite resources, because she feels the necessary bond that ties her to man regardless of reciprocity, and because she is often very well pleased with her role as the *Other*.

Now, what peculiarly signalizes the situation of woman is that she—a free and autonomous being like all human creatures—nevertheless finds herself living in a world where men compel her to assume the status of the Other. They propose to stabilize her as object and to doom her to immanence since her transcendence is to be overshadowed and forever transcended by another ego (*conscience*) which is essential and sovereign. The drama of woman lies in this conflict between the fundamental aspirations of every subject (ego)—who always regards the self as the essential—and the compulsions of a situation in which she is the inessential.

°

I. After centuries of individual and preliminary political struggle, women are uniting to achieve their final liberation from male supremacy. Redstockings is dedicated to building their unity and winning our freedom.

II. Women are an oppressed class. Our oppression is total, affecting every facet of our lives. We are exploited as sex objects, breeders, domestic servants, and cheap labor. We are considered inferior beings, whose only purpose is to enhance men's lives. Our humanity is denied. Our prescribed behavior is enforced by the threat of physical violence.

Because we have lived so intimately with our oppressors, in isolation from each other, we have been kept from seeing our personal suffering as a political condition. This creates the illusion that a woman's relationship with her man is a matter of interplay between two unique personalities, and can be worked out individually. In reality, every such relationship is a *class* relationship, and the conflicts between individual men and women are *political* conflicts that can only be solved collectively.

III. We identify the agents of our oppression as men. Male supremacy is the oldest, most basic form of domination. All other forms of exploitation and oppression (racism, capitalism, imperialism, and the like) are extensions of male supremacy: men dominate women, a few men dominate the rest. All power structures throughout history have been male-dominated and male-oriented. Men have controlled all political, economic, and cultural institutions and backed up this control with physical force. They have used their power to keep women in an inferior position. *All men* receive economic, sexual, and psychological benefits from male supremacy. *All men* have oppressed women.

IV. Attempts have been made to shift the burden of responsibility from men to institutions or to women themselves. We condemn these arguments as evasions. Institutions alone do not oppress; they are merely tools of the oppressor. To blame institutions implies that men and women are equally victimized, obscures the fact that men benefit from the subordination of women, and gives men the excuse that they are forced to be oppressors. On the contrary, any man is free to renounce his superior position provided that he is willing to be treated like a woman by other men.

We also reject the idea that women consent to or are to blame for their own oppression. Women's submission is not the result of brainwashing, stupidity, or mental illness but of continual, daily pressure from men. We do not need to change ourselves, but to change men.

The most slanderous evasion of all is that women can oppress men. The basis for this illusion is the isolation of individual relationships from their political context and the tendency of men to see any legitimate challenge to their privileges as persecution.

V. We regard our personal experience, and our feelings about that experience, as the basis for an analysis of our common situation. We cannot rely on existing ideologies as they are all products of male supremacist culture. We question every generalization and accept none that are not confirmed by our experience.

Our chief task at present is to develop female class consciousness through sharing experience and publicly exposing the sexist foundation of all our institutions. Consciousness-raising is not "therapy," which implies the existence of individual solutions and falsely assumes that the male-female relationship is purely personal, but the only method by which we can ensure that our program for liberation is based on the concrete realities of our lives.

The first requirement for raising class consciousness is honesty, in private and in public, with ourselves and other women.

VI. We identify with all women. We define our best interest as that of the poorest, most brutally exploited woman.

We repudiate all economic, racial, educational, or status privileges that divide us from other women. We are determined to recognize and eliminate any prejudices we may hold against other women.

We are committed to achieving internal democracy. We will do whatever is necessary to ensure that every woman in our movement has an equal chance to participate, assume responsibility, and develop her political potential.

VII. We call on all our sisters to unite with us in struggle.

We call on all men to give up their male privileges and support women's liberation in the interests of our humanity and their own.

In fighting for our liberation we will always take the side of women against their oppressors. We will not ask what is "revolutionary" or "reformist," only what is good for women.

The time for individual skirmishes has passed. This time we are going all the way.

Televised Violence

Most observers agree that television has had a great impact on the lives of people within Western civilization and throughout the world, but exactly what that impact has been is open to debate. The following picture illustrates one of the most controversial issues that have been raised. It shows a television camera crew filming the live action in Vietnam. The images filmed by such crews were displayed on daily newscasts in America and elsewhere, giving civilians a virtual firsthand, up-to-the-minute, perhaps overly realistic impression of what the war was like. However, critics argue that because such images became so common, because they were displayed just before and just after the most mundane of other television shows (typically, situation comedies), and because they were viewed so often from the

Photo 15-2

comfort of a living room, the image of a very real war may have come to seem unreal. Indeed, one must wonder whether this picture itself is not part of a staged scene for a movie (as was the case with a scene the audience sees being filmed in Apocalypse Now, *a major movie of 1979–1980).*

> **Consider:** *Other ways in which the media in the twentieth century have affected people's perception and understanding of war.*

Number 1
Jackson Pollock

Twentieth-century artistic styles have tended to become increasingly removed from popular tastes and from what the general public has been used to expecting from art. This was particularly the case with the style of action painting or abstract expressionism, which came to the fore shortly after World War II. The leading painter in this school of art was

Photo 15-3

Collection, The Museum of Modern Art, New York. Purchase. Photography by Soichi Sunami.

SOURCE: Francis V. O'Connor, *Jackson Pollock*. Reprinted by permission of The Museum of Modern Art (New York, 1967), and Mrs. Lee Krasner Pollock, pp. 79–80. Copyright © 1967 by The Museum of Modern Art.

Jackson Pollock (1912–1956), who executed the work shown above, entitled Number 1, in 1948. *In 1950 Pollock was interviewed by Francis V. O'Connor, a well-known art critic; a selection from that interview follows.*

Consider: *How Pollock's statements and this painting reflect some of the trends of twentieth-century history.*

Mr. Pollock, in your opinion, what is the meaning of modern art?

Modern art to me is nothing more than the expression of contemporary aims of the age that we're living in.

Did the classical artists have any means of expressing their age?

Yes, they did it very well. All cultures have had means and techniques of expressing their immediate aims—the Chinese, the Renaissance, all cultures. The thing that interests me is that today painters do not have to go to a subject matter outside of themselves. Most modern painters work from a different source. They work from within.

Would you say that the modern artist has more or less isolated the quality which made the classical works of art valuable, that he's isolated it and uses it in a purer form?

Ah—the good ones have, yes.

Mr. Pollock, there's been a good deal of controversy and a great many comments have been made regarding your method of painting. Is there something you'd like to tell us about that?

My opinion is that new needs need new techniques. And the modern artists have found new ways and new means of making their statements. It seems to me that the modern painter cannot express this age, the airplane, the atom bomb, the radio, in the old forms of the Renaissance or of any other past culture. Each age finds its own technique.

Which would also mean that the layman and the critic would have to develop their ability to interpret the new techniques.

Yes—that always somehow follows. I mean, the strangeness will wear off and I think we will discover the deeper meanings in modern art.

I suppose every time you are approached by a layman they ask you how they should look at a Pollock painting, or any other modern painting—what they look for—how do they learn to appreciate modern art?

I think they should not look for, but look passively—and try to receive what the painting has to offer and not bring a subject matter or preconceived idea of what they are to be looking for.

Would it be true to say that the artist is painting from the unconscious, and the—canvas must act as the unconscious of the person who views it?

The unconscious is a very important side of modern art and I think the unconscious drives do mean a lot in looking at paintings.

Then deliberately looking for any known meaning or object in an abstract painting would distract you immediately from ever appreciating it as you should?

I think it should be enjoyed just as music is enjoyed—after a while you may like it or you may not. But—it doesn't seem to be too serious. I like some flowers and others, other flowers I don't like. I think at least it gives—I think at least give it a chance.

Well, I think you have to give anything that sort of chance. A person isn't born to like good music, they have to listen to it and gradually develop an understanding of it or liking for it. If modern painting works the same way—a person would have to subject himself to it over a period of time in order to be able to appreciate it.

I think that might help, certainly.

Mr. Pollock, the classical artists had a world to express and they did so by representing the objects in that world. Why doesn't the modern artist do the same thing?

H'm—the modern artist is living in a mechanical age and we have a mechanical means of representing objects in nature such as the camera and photograph. The modern artist, it seems to me, is working and expressing an inner world—in other words—expressing the energy, the motion, and other inner forces.

Would it be possible to say that the classical artist expressed his world by representing the objects, whereas the modern artist expresses his world by representing the effects the objects have upon him?

Yes, the modern artist is working with space and time, and expressing his feelings rather than illustrating.

The Philosophy of Existentialism
Jean-Paul Sartre

One of the most popular and provocative philosophies to emerge in the mid-twentieth century was existentialism. Although the origins of existentialism can be found in nineteenth-century writers such as Søren Kierkegaard and Friedrich Nietzsche, its most popular exponent was the French novelist, playwright, philosopher, and political activist Jean-Paul Sartre (1905–1980). Sartre's interpretation of existentialism reflects the dilemma of a twentieth-century atheist who can no longer accept traditional ways for determining standards of conduct. The following excerpt is from a lecture given by Sartre in Paris in 1945. In it he is describing the nature of existentialism and responding to critics.

Consider: *What Sartre means when he says that man [or woman] chooses himself [or herself]; the ethical implications of this philosophy.*

Man is nothing else but what he makes of himself. Such is the first principle of existentialism. It is also what is called subjectivity. The name we are labeled with

SOURCE: Jean-Paul Sartre, *The Philosophy of Existentialism*, Wade Baskin, ed. Reprinted by permission of Philosophical Library, Inc. (New York, 1965), pp. 35–36.

when charges are brought against us. But what do we mean by this, if not that man has a greater dignity than a stone or table? For we mean that man first exists, that is, that man first of all is the being who hurls himself toward a future and who is conscious of imagining himself as being in the future. Man is at the start a plan which is aware of itself, rather than a patch of moss, a piece of garbage, or a cauliflower; nothing exists prior to this plan; there is nothing in heaven; man will be what he will have planned to be. Not what he will want to be. Because by the word "will" we generally mean a conscious decision, which is subsequent to what we have already made of ourselves. I may want to belong to a political party, write a book, get married; but all that is only a manifestation of an earlier, more spontaneous choice that is called "will." But if existence really does precede essence, man is responsible for what he is. Thus, existentialism's first move is to make every man aware of what he is and to make the full responsibility of his existence rest on him. And when we say that man is responsible for himself, we do not only mean that he is responsible for his own individuality, but that he is responsible for all men.

The word subjectivism has two meanings, and our opponents play on the two. Subjectivism means, on the one hand, that an individual chooses and makes himself; and, on the other, that it is impossible for man to transcend human subjectivity. The second of these is the essential meaning of existentialism. When we say that man chooses his own self, we mean that every one of us does likewise; but we also mean by that that in making this choice he also chooses all men. In fact, in creating the man that we want to be, there is not a single one of our acts which does not at the same time create an image of man as we think he ought to be. To choose to be this or that is to affirm at the same time the value of what we choose, because we can never choose evil. We always choose the good, and nothing can be good for us without being good for all.

If, on the other hand, existence precedes essence, and if we grant that we exist and fashion our image at one and the same time, the image is valid for everybody and for our whole age. Thus, our responsibility is much greater than we might have supposed, because it involves all mankind. If I am a workingman and choose to join a Christian trade-union rather than be a communist, and if by being a member I want to show that the best thing for man is resignation, that the kingdom of man is not of this world, I am not only involving my own case—I want to be resigned for everyone. As a result, my action has involved all humanity. To take a more individual matter, if I want to marry, to have children; even if this marriage depends solely on my own circumstances or passion or wish, I am involving all humanity in monogamy and not merely myself. Therefore, I am responsible for myself and for everyone else. I am creating a certain image of man of my own choosing. In choosing myself, I choose man.

Our Psychological Age
Philip Rieff

*One of the greatest changes occurring in recent decades may lie not in the external eco-
nomic, social, or political developments usually pointed to by historians but in the internal life and cultural ideals of Western people. An extremely bold and provocative interpretation along these lines is that of the American sociologist Philip Rieff. An admirer of
Freud, Rieff has written an extraordinarily perceptive critical analysis of Freud's work in
Freud, the Mind of the Moralist. In the following excerpt from that work, Rieff argues
that the present age is one of "psychological man [or woman]," as distinct from the preceding ages of "economic," "religious," and "political man [woman]."*

> **Consider:** *The characteristics of "psychological man [woman]"; how "psychologi-
> cal man [woman]" differs from earlier character types or ideals; how Rieff's inter-
> pretation reflects other intellectual developments of the twentieth century.*

In this age, in which technics is invading and conquering the last enemy—man's
inner life, the psyche itself—a suitable new character type has arrived on the
scene: the psychological man. Three character ideals have successively dominated
Western civilization: first, the ideal of the political man, formed and handed down
to us from classical antiquity; second, the ideal of the religious man, formed and
handed down to us from Judaism through Christianity, and dominant in the
civilization of authority that preceded the Enlightenment; third, the ideal of the
economic man, the very model of our liberal civilization, formed and handed down
to us in the Enlightenment. This last has turned out to be a transitional type, with
the shortest life-expectancy of all; out of his tenure has emerged the psychological
man of the twentieth century, a child not of nature but of technology. He is not
the pagan ideal, political man, for he is not committed to the public life. He is
most unlike the religious man. We will recognize in the case history of psychological man the nervous habits of his father, economic man: he is anti-heroic, shrewd,
carefully counting his satisfactions and dissatisfactions, studying unprofitable commitments as the sins most to be avoided. From this immediate ancestor, psychological man has constituted his own careful economy of the inner life.

The psychological man lives neither by the ideal of might nor by the ideal of
right which confused his ancestors, political man and religious man. Psychological
man lives by the ideal of insight—practical, experimental insight leading to the
mastery of his own personality. The psychological man has withdrawn into a world
always at war, where the ego is an armed force capable of achieving armistices
but not peace. The prophetic egoist of Western politics and Protestant Christianity
who, through the model with which he provided us, also laid down the lines along

which the world was to be transformed, has been replaced by the sage, intent upon the conquest of his inner life, and, at most, like Freud, laying down the lines along which those that follow him can salvage something of their own. Turning away from the Occidental ideal of action leading toward the salvation of others besides ourselves, the psychological man has espoused the Oriental ideal of salvation through self-contemplative manipulation. Ironically, this is happening just at the historic moment when the Orient, whose westernmost outpost is Russia, has adopted the Occidental ideal of saving activity in the world. The West has attempted many successive transformations of the enemy, the world. It now chooses to move against its last enemy, the self, in an attempt to conquer it and assimilate it to the world as it is. For it is from the self that the troublesome, world-rejecting ideal of the religious man came forth.

Freudianism closes off the long-established quarrel of Western man with his own spirit. It marks the archaism of the classical legacy of political man, for the new man must live beyond reason—reason having proved no adequate guide to his safe conduct through the meaningless experience of life. It marks the repudiation of the Christian legacy of the religious man, for the new man is taught to live a little beyond conscience—conscience having proved no adequate guide to his safe conduct through life, and furthermore to have added absurd burdens of meaning to the experience of life. Finally, psychoanalysis marks the exhaustion of the liberal legacy represented historically in economic man, for now men must live with the knowledge that their dreams are by function optimistic and cannot be fulfilled. Aware at last that he is chronically ill, psychological man may nevertheless end the ancient quest of his predecessors for a healing doctrine. His experience with the latest one, Freud's, may finally teach him that every cure must expose him to new illness.

The Earth in Deficit
Thomas Berry

Over the past two decades it has become increasingly apparent that modern civilization is exacting a price from nature. Scholars point out that the world's air and water are becoming polluted, the world's species are being diminished or destroyed, and the world's resources are being threatened. In the following selection Thomas Berry, a Christian theologian, analyzes how serious these problems are, arguing that the earth is being put into deficit.

Consider: *What Berry means by the earth deficit; the causes for these ecological problems; possible solutions to these problems.*

SOURCE: Thomas Berry, "Wonderworld as Wasteland: The Earth in Deficit," *Cross Currents*, Winter 1985–1986, pp. 408–410, 412.

The reality of our present economy is such that we must have certain forebodings not simply as regards the well-being of the human community but even of the planet itself in its most basic life systems. . . .

In the natural world there exists an amazing richness of life expression in the ever-renewing cycle of the seasons. There is a minimum of entropy. The inflow of energy and the outflow are such that the process is sustainable over an indefinite period of time—so long as the human process is integral with these processes of nature, so long is the human economy sustainable into the future. The difficulty comes when the industrial mode of our economy disrupts the natural processes, when human technologies are destructive of earth technologies. In such a situation the productivity of the natural world and its life systems is diminished. When nature goes into deficit, then we go into deficit. . . .

. . . the earth deficit is the real deficit, the ultimate deficit, the deficit so absolute in some of its major consequences as to be beyond adjustment from any source in heaven or earth. Since the earth system is the ultimate guarantor of all deficits, a failure here is a failure of last resort. Neither economic viability nor improvement in life conditions for the poor can be realized in such circumstances. They can only worsen, especially when we consider rising population levels throughout the developing world.

This deficit in its extreme expression is not only a resource deficit but the death of a living process, not simply the death of *a* living process but of *the* living process—a living process which exists, so far as we know, only on the planet earth. This is what makes our problems definitively different from those of any other generation of whatever ethnic, cultural, political or religious tradition or of any other historical period. For the first time we are determining the destinies of the earth in a comprehensive and irreversible manner. The immediate danger is not *possible* nuclear war but *actual* industrial plundering.

Economics on this scale is not simply economics of the human community; it is economics of the earth community in its comprehensive dimensions. Nor is this a question of profit or loss in terms of personal or community well-being in a functioning earth system. Economics has invaded the earth system itself. Our industrial economy is closing down the planet in the most basic modes of its functioning. The air, the water, the soil are already in a degraded condition. Forests are dying on every continent. The seas are endangered. Aquatic life forms in lakes and streams and in the seas are contaminated. The rain is acid.

While it is unlikely that we could ever extinguish life in an absolute manner, we are eliminating species at a rate never before known in historic time and in a manner never known in biological time. Destruction of the tropical rain forests of the planet will involve destroying the habitat of perhaps half the living species of earth.

Thus the mythic drive to control our world continues, even though so much is known about the earth, its limited resources, the interdependence of life systems, the delicate balance of its ecosystems, the consequences of disturbing the atmospheric conditions, of contaminating the air, the soil, the waterways and the seas, the limited quantity of fossil fuels in the earth, the inherent danger of chemicals discharged into natural surroundings. Although much of this has been known for generations, neither the study nor the commercial-industrial practise of economics has shown any capacity to break free from the mythic commitment to progress, or any awareness that we are in reality creating wasteworld rather than wonder-world. This mythic commitment to continuing economic growth is such that none of our major newspapers or newsweeklies considers having a regular ecological section, equivalent to sports or business or arts or entertainment, although the ecological issues are more important than any of these, more important than the daily national and international political news. The real history that is being made is interspecies and human-earth history, not inter-nation history. Our real threat is from the retaliatory powers of the abused earth, not from other nations.

Chapter Questions

1. The closeness of the last twenty-five years makes it difficult to know what trends and developments will be the most significant historically. Those selected for this chapter are just a few of the possibilities. What others might have been selected? What evidence would demonstrate their importance?

2. It is possible to argue that most of what is claimed to be new about the last twenty-five years is not really so new, that it is just our impression that it is new because we have been living through it. How might this argument be supported? How might it be refuted?